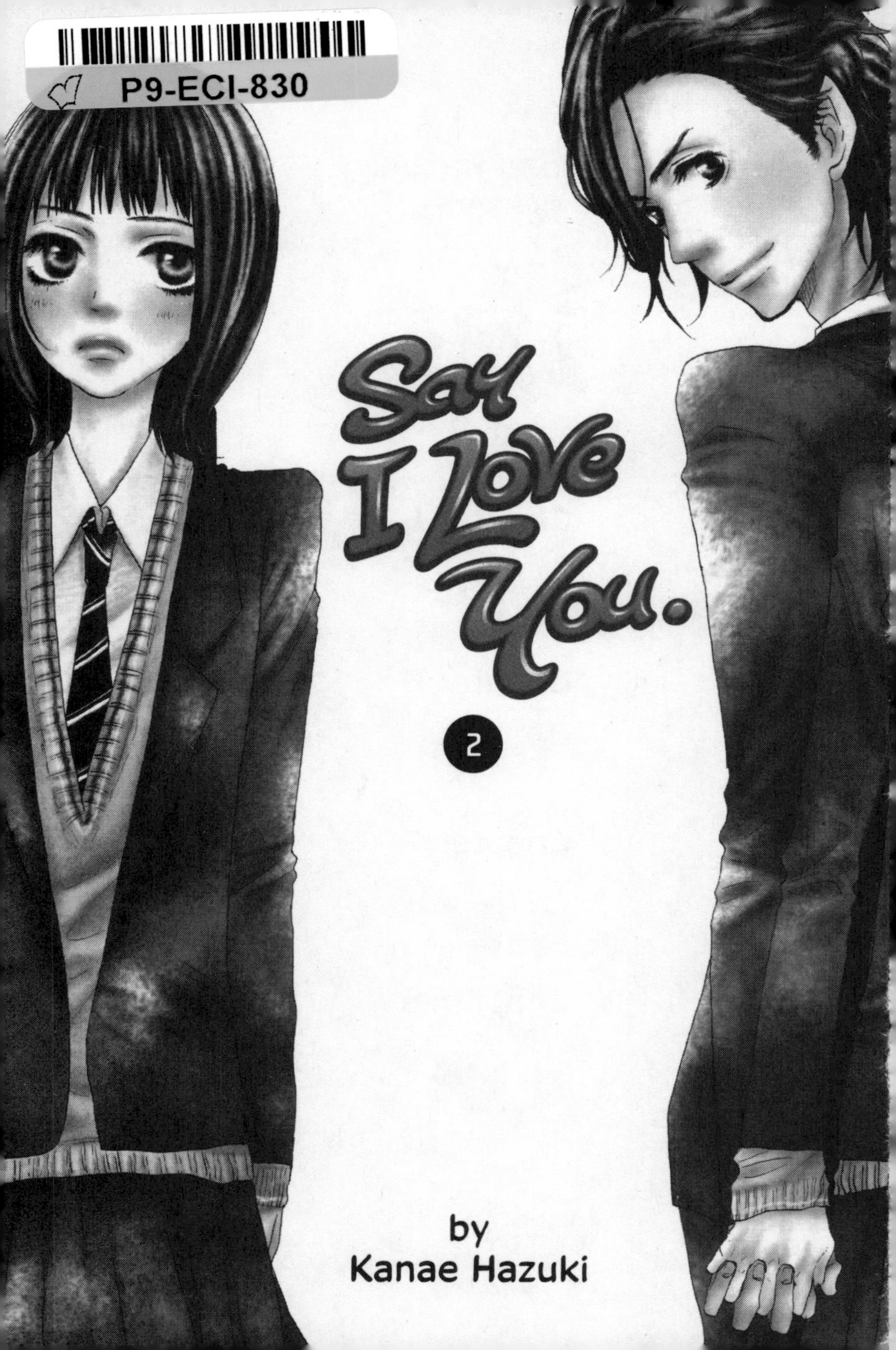

Say I Love You.

2

by
Kanae Hazuki

Kanae Hazuki
presents

Chapter 5

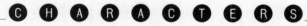

CHARACTERS

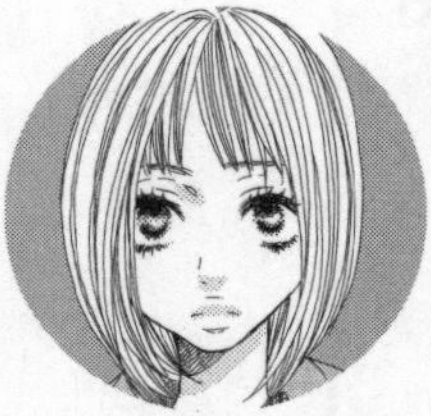

Mei Tachibana

A girl who hasn't had a single friend, let alone a boyfriend, in sixteen years, and has lived her life trusting no one. She finds herself attracted to Yamato, who, for some reason, just won't leave her alone.

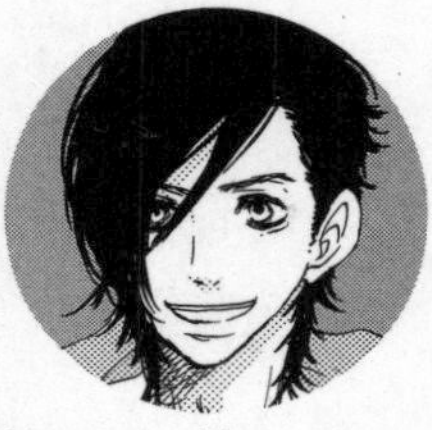

Yamato Kurosawa

The most popular boy at Mei's school. He has the love of many girls, yet for some reason, he is obsessed with Mei, the brooding weirdo girl from another class.

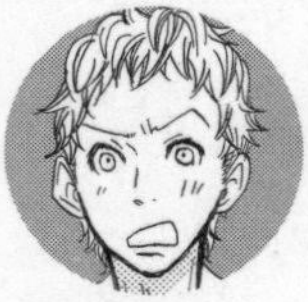

Nakanishi

Yamato's friend and Mei's classmate. He used to harass Mei, which is how Mei and Yamato met.

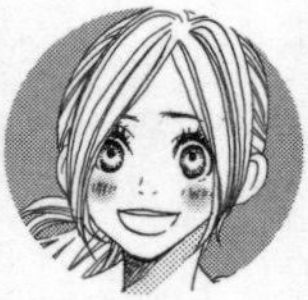

Asami

A girl in Mei's class who admires Yamato. Unlike her other classmates, she interacts with Mei just as she interacts with everyone else. She has started dating Yamato's friend Nakanishi.

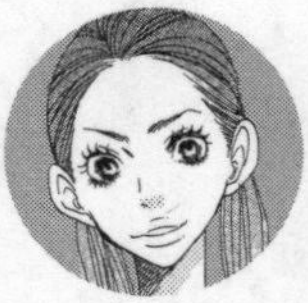

Aiko

A girl who is jealous of Mei. Apparently she is the only person Yamato has slept with, and she still likes him, but she has a few FWBs.

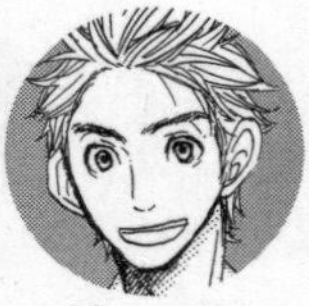

Masashi

Yamato's friend. He has a crush on Aiko and can often be seen following her around, but Aiko only has eyes for Yamato.

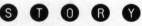

STORY

Mei Tachibana spent sixteen years without a single friend or boyfriend. One day, she accidentally injured Yamato Kurosawa, the most popular boy in her school—ironically, that made him like her, and he unilaterally decided that they were friends. He even kissed her to protect her from a stalker. And he kissed her like he meant it. Mei has a very difficult time opening her heart, but she is gradually drawn in by Yamato's kindness and sincerity, and starts to realize that she is in love with him. But she is troubled when Aiko tells her, "I've slept with him"!

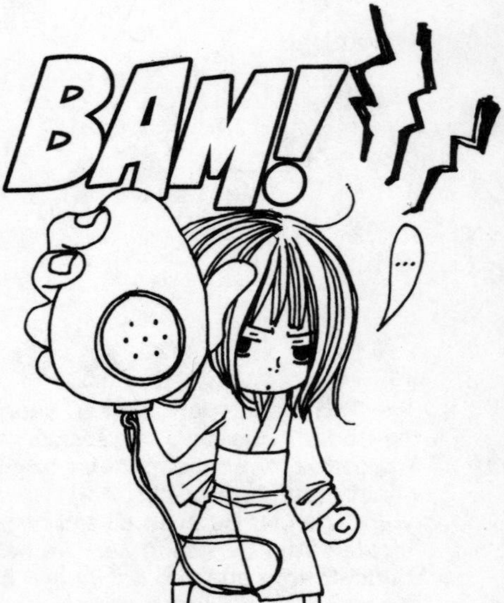
BAM!
...
•Wearing toe socks

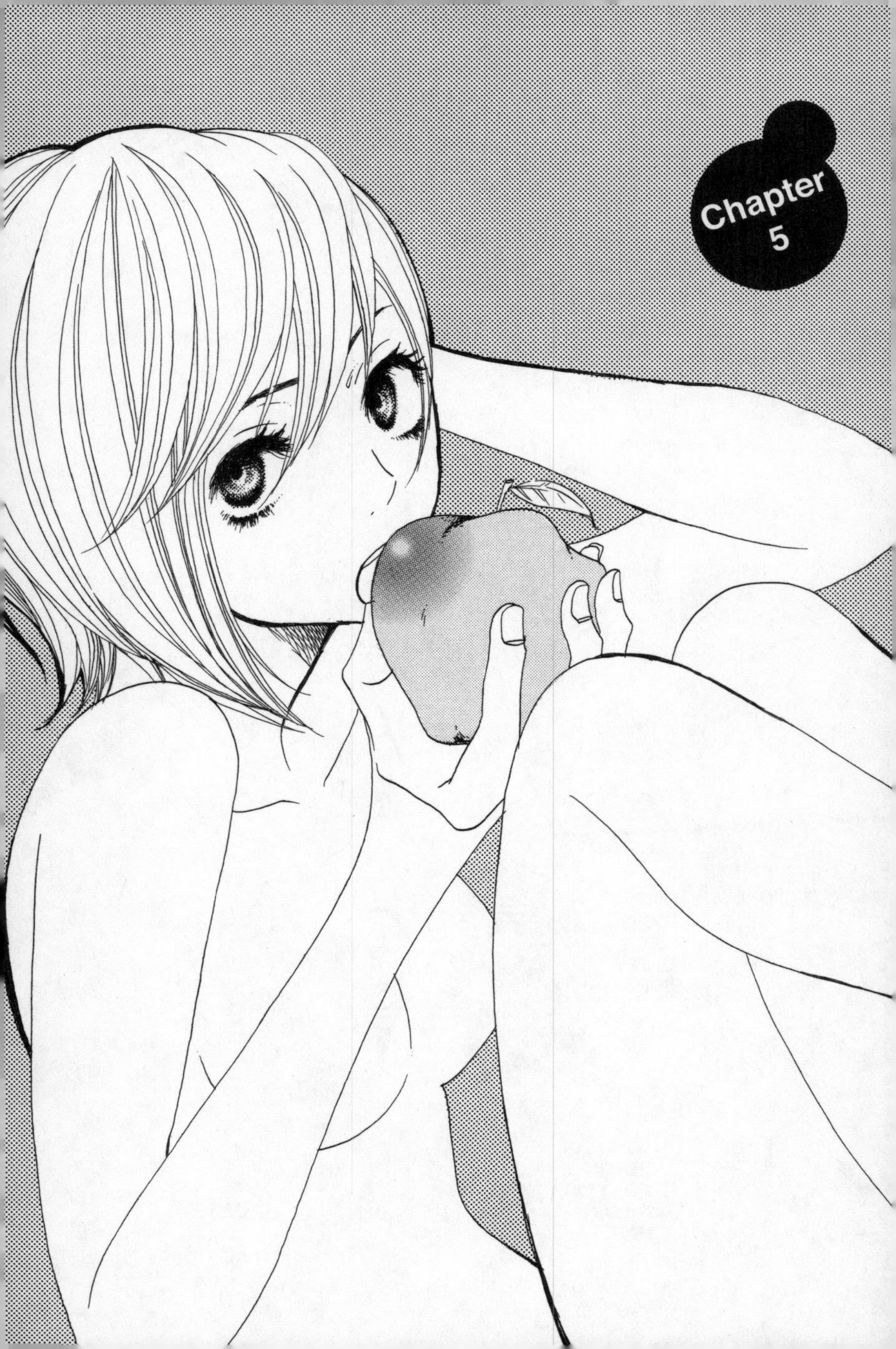
Chapter
5

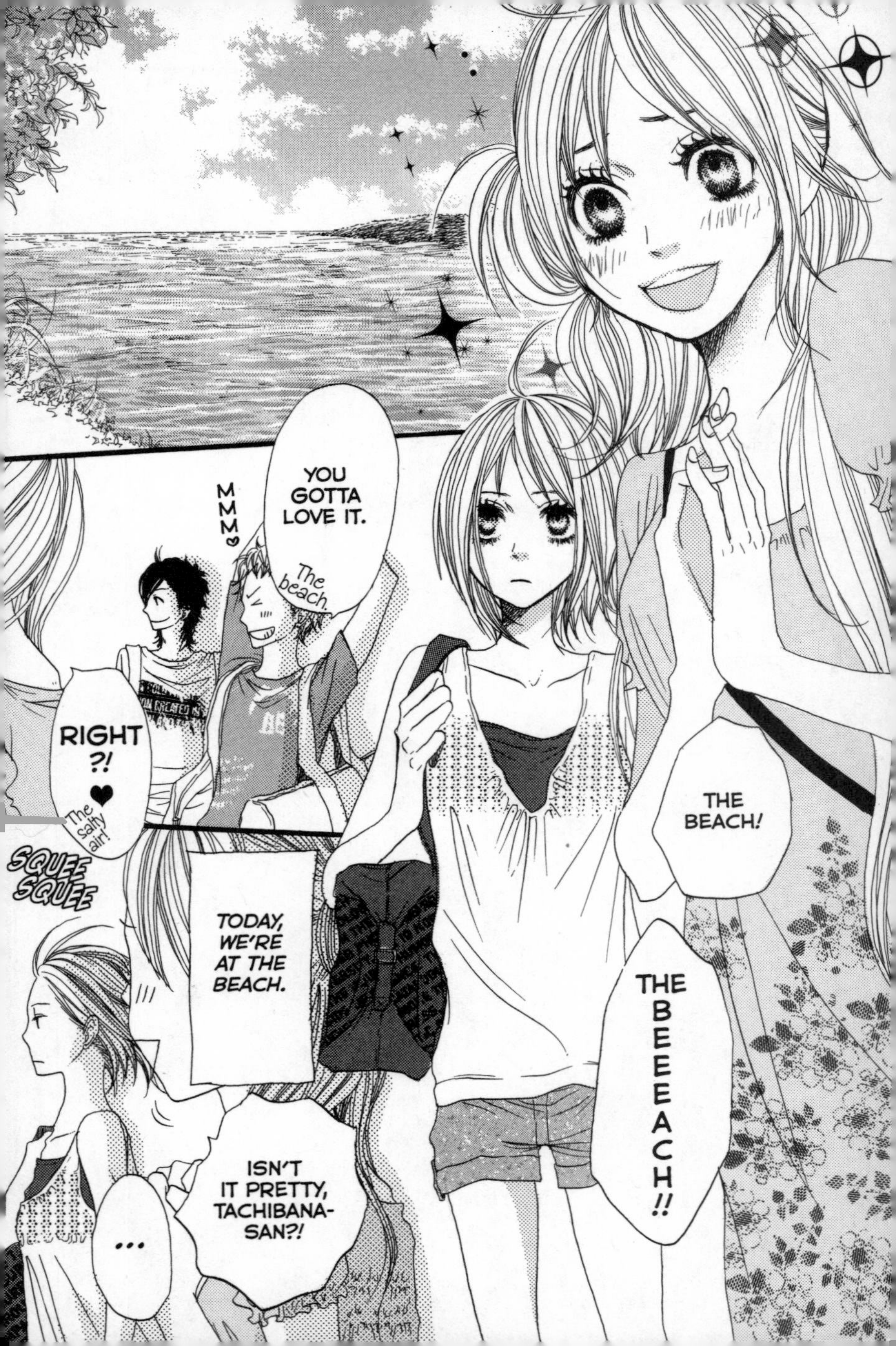
THE BEACH!
THE BEEEACH!!
YOU GOTTA LOVE IT.
The beach.
MMM♥
RIGHT?! ♥
The salty air!
TODAY, WE'RE AT THE BEACH.
SQUEE SQUEE
ISN'T IT PRETTY, TACHIBANA-SAN?!
...

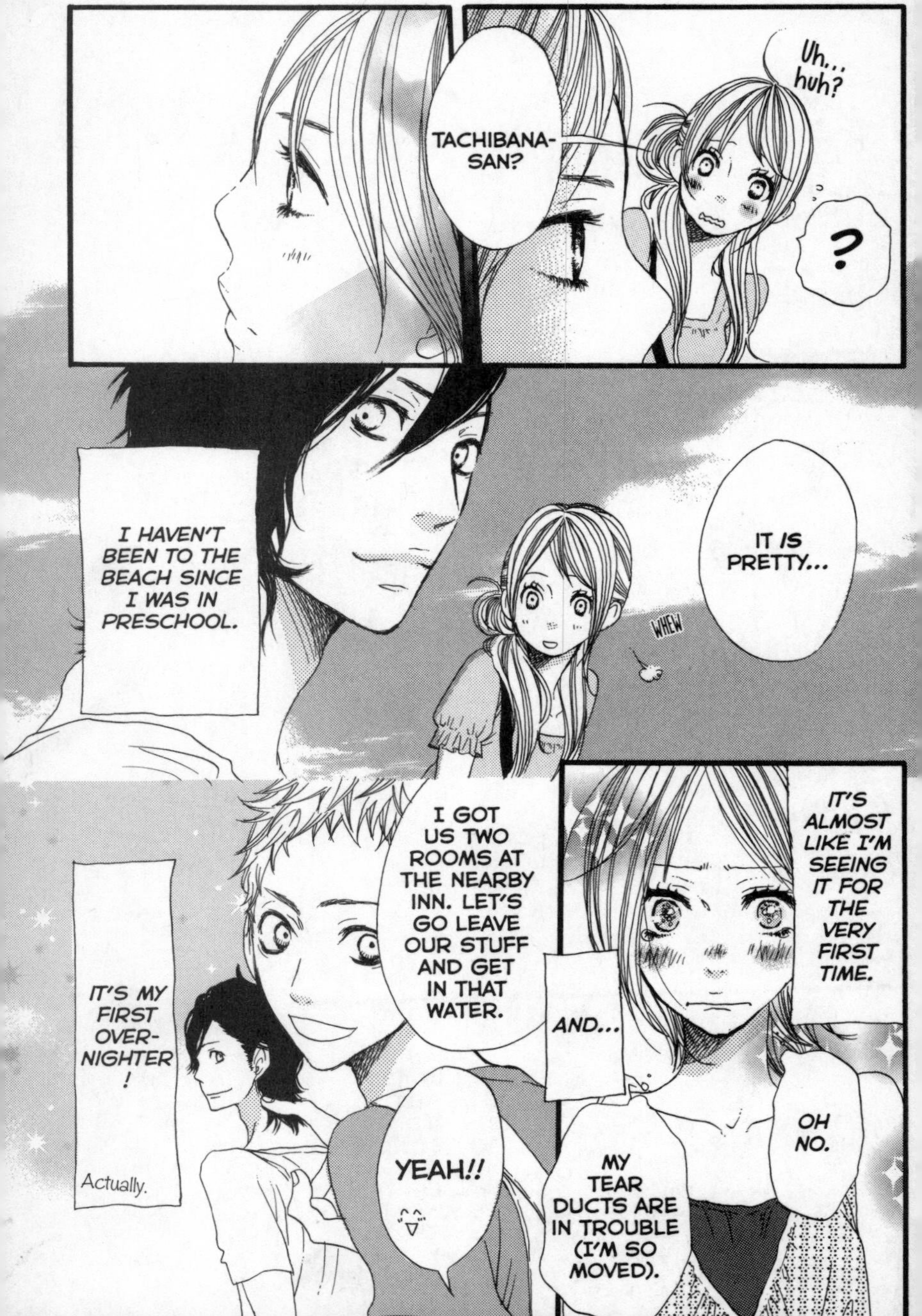
Uh... huh?
?
TACHIBANA-SAN?
IT IS PRETTY...
WHEW
I HAVEN'T BEEN TO THE BEACH SINCE I WAS IN PRESCHOOL.
IT'S ALMOST LIKE I'M SEEING IT FOR THE VERY FIRST TIME.
OH NO.
AND...
MY TEAR DUCTS ARE IN TROUBLE (I'M SO MOVED).
I GOT US TWO ROOMS AT THE NEARBY INN. LET'S GO LEAVE OUR STUFF AND GET IN THAT WATER.
YEAH!!
IT'S MY FIRST OVER-NIGHTER!
Actually.

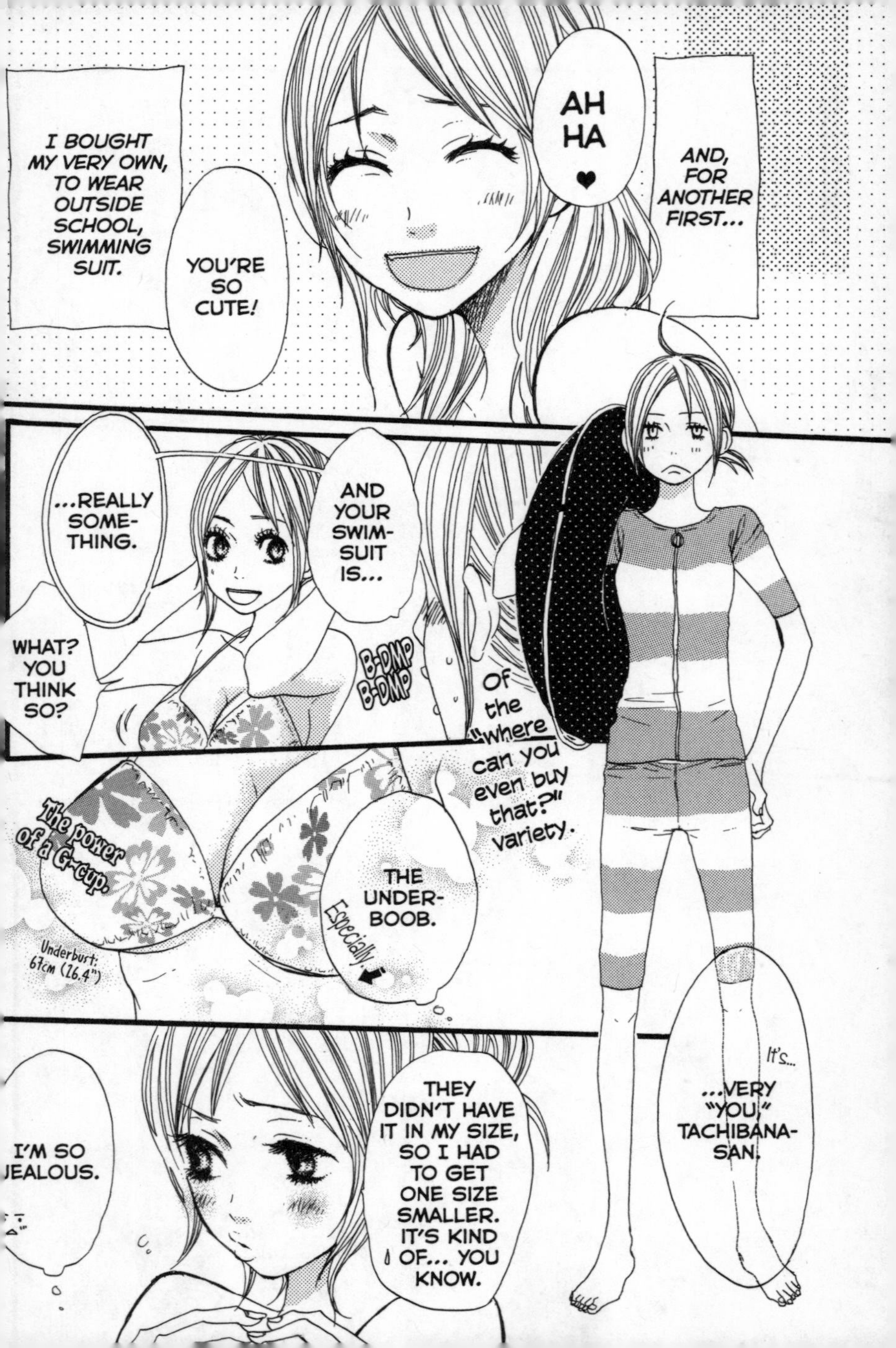
AND, FOR ANOTHER FIRST...
AH HA ♥
YOU'RE SO CUTE!
I BOUGHT MY VERY OWN, TO WEAR OUTSIDE SCHOOL, SWIMMING SUIT.
Of the "where can you even buy that?" variety.
It's...
...VERY "YOU," TACHIBANA-SAN.
AND YOUR SWIM-SUIT IS...
...REALLY SOME-THING.
B-DMP B-DMP
WHAT? YOU THINK SO?
THE UNDER-BOOB.
Especially.
The power of a G-cup.
Underbust: 67cm (26.4")
THEY DIDN'T HAVE IT IN MY SIZE, SO I HAD TO GET ONE SIZE SMALLER. IT'S KIND OF... YOU KNOW.
I'M SO JEALOUS.

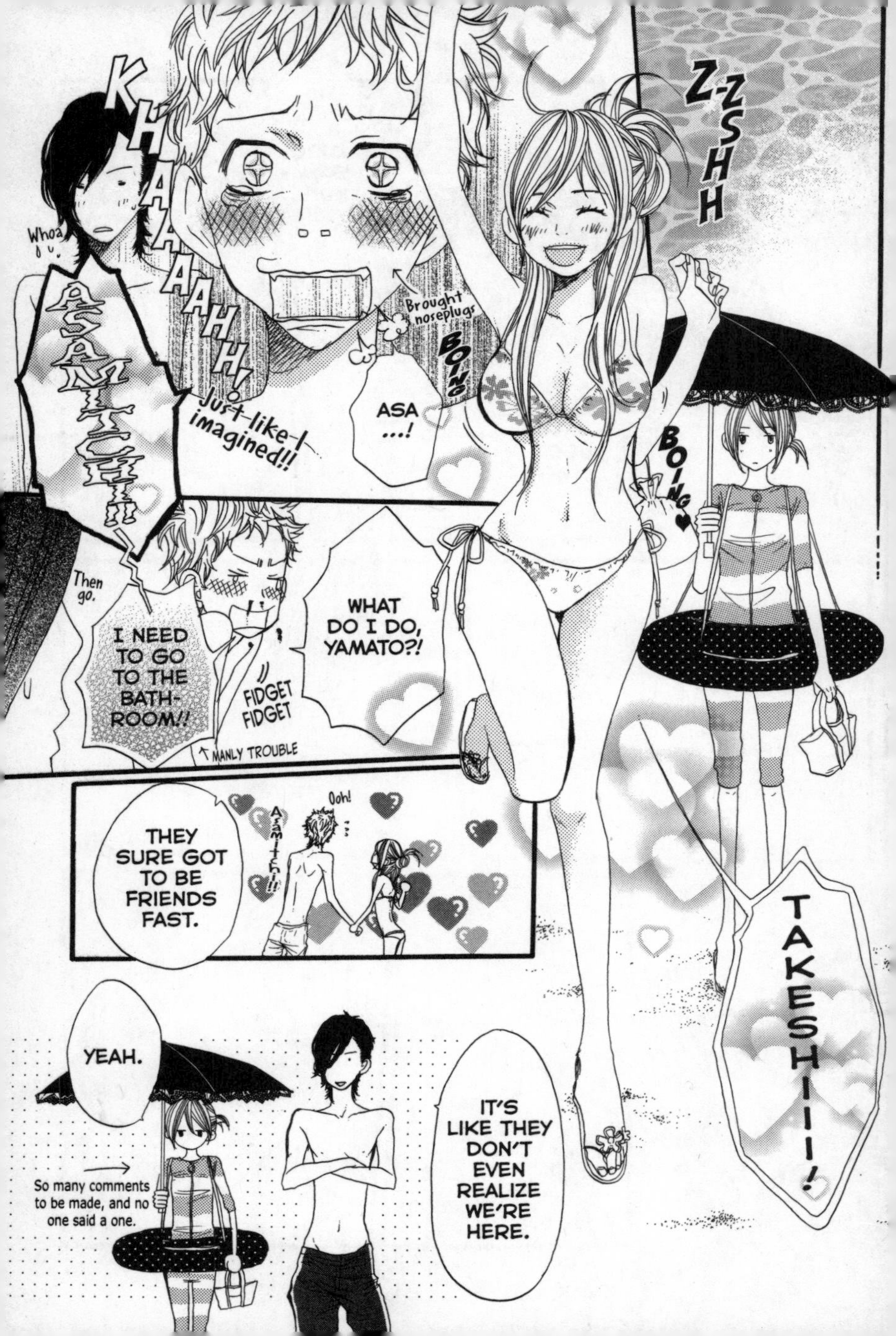

Z-ZSHH
TAKESHIIII!
BOING
BOING ♥
ASA ...!
KHAAAAAHH!
Just-like-I imagined!!
Brought noseplugs
Whoa
ASAMITCH!!
Then go.
WHAT DO I DO, YAMATO?!
FIDGET FIDGET
I NEED TO GO TO THE BATH-ROOM!!
MANLY TROUBLE
Ooh!
Asamitch!!
THEY SURE GOT TO BE FRIENDS FAST.
IT'S LIKE THEY DON'T EVEN REALIZE WE'RE HERE.
YEAH.
So many comments to be made, and no one said a one.

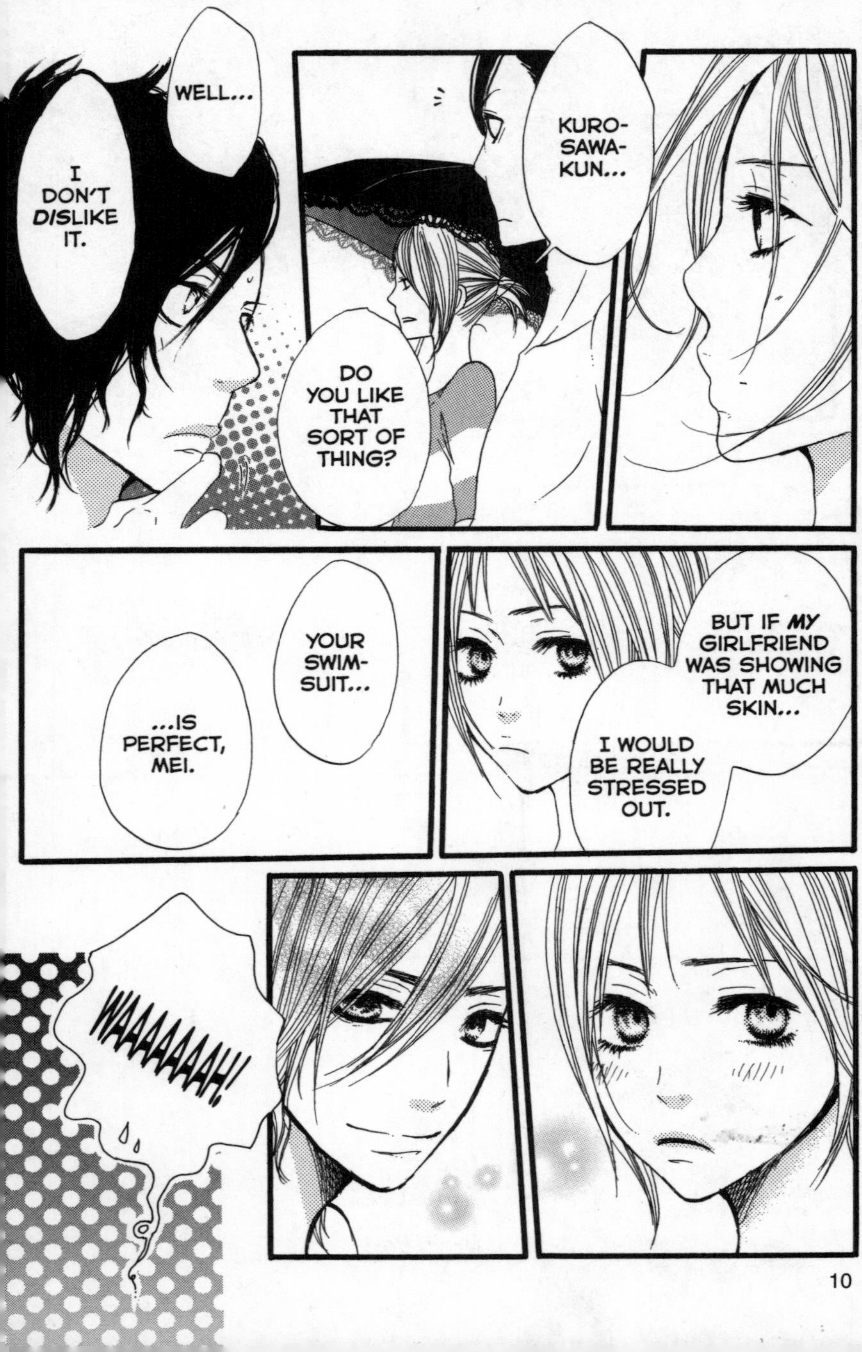
KURO-SAWA-KUN...
DO YOU LIKE THAT SORT OF THING?
WELL...
I DON'T *DIS*LIKE IT.
BUT IF *MY* GIRLFRIEND WAS SHOWING THAT MUCH SKIN...
I WOULD BE REALLY STRESSED OUT.
YOUR SWIM-SUIT...
...IS PERFECT, MEI.
WAAAAAAAH!

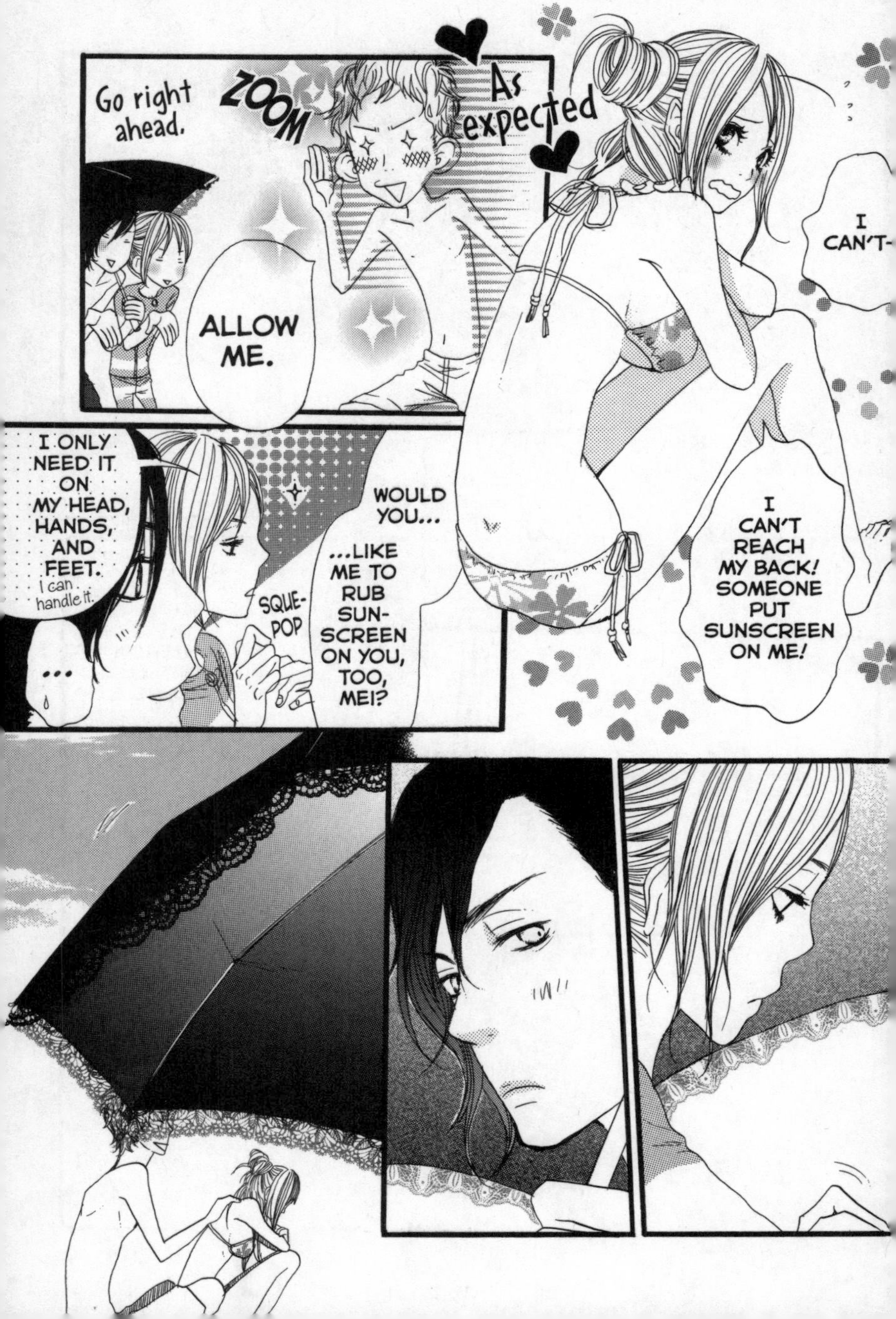

I CAN'T-
I CAN'T REACH MY BACK! SOMEONE PUT SUNSCREEN ON ME!
As expected
ZOOM
ALLOW ME.
Go right ahead.
WOULD YOU...
...LIKE ME TO RUB SUN-SCREEN ON YOU, TOO, MEI?
SQUE-POP
I ONLY NEED IT ON MY HEAD, HANDS, AND FEET.
I can handle it.
...

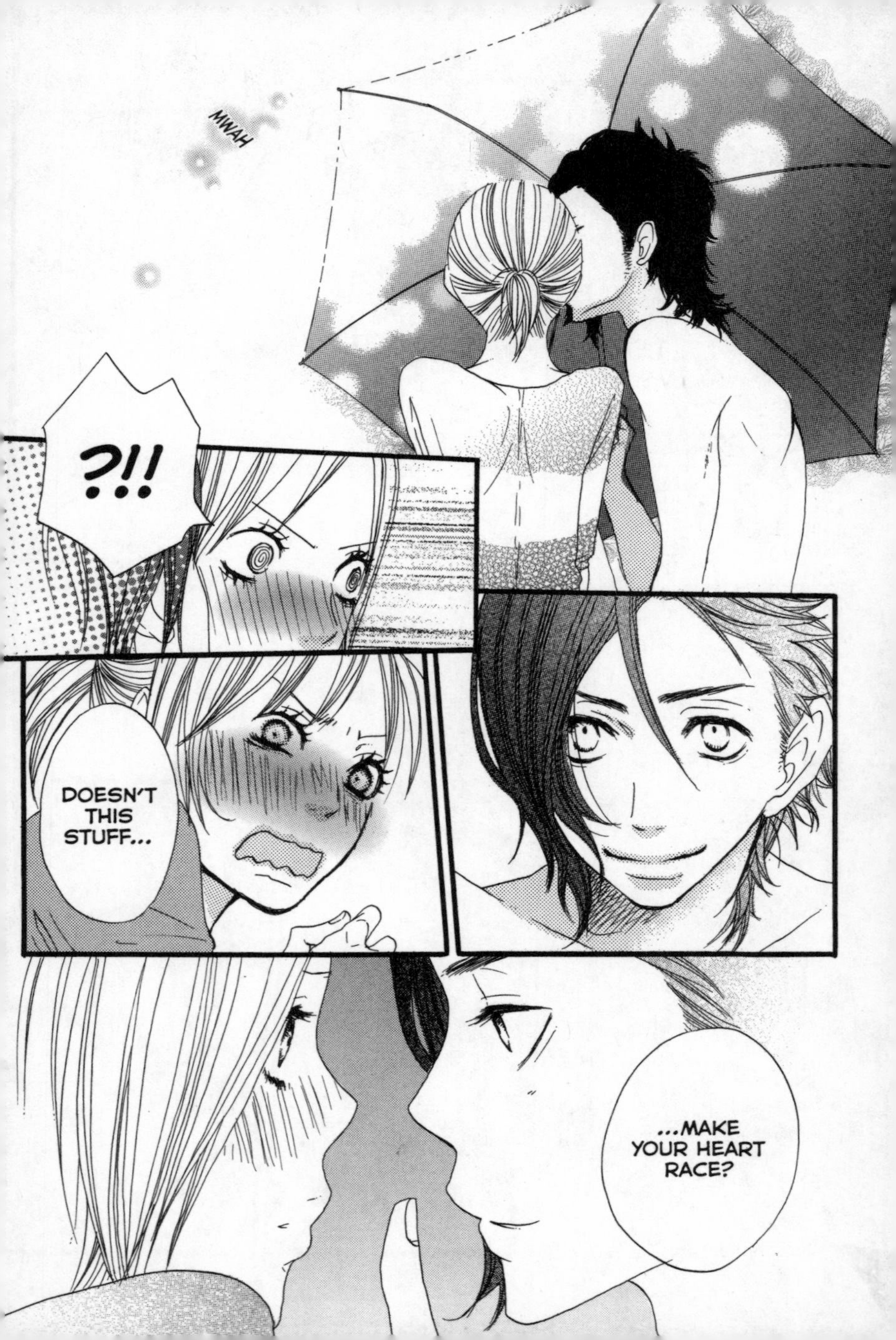
MWAH
?!!
DOESN'T THIS STUFF...
...MAKE YOUR HEART RACE?

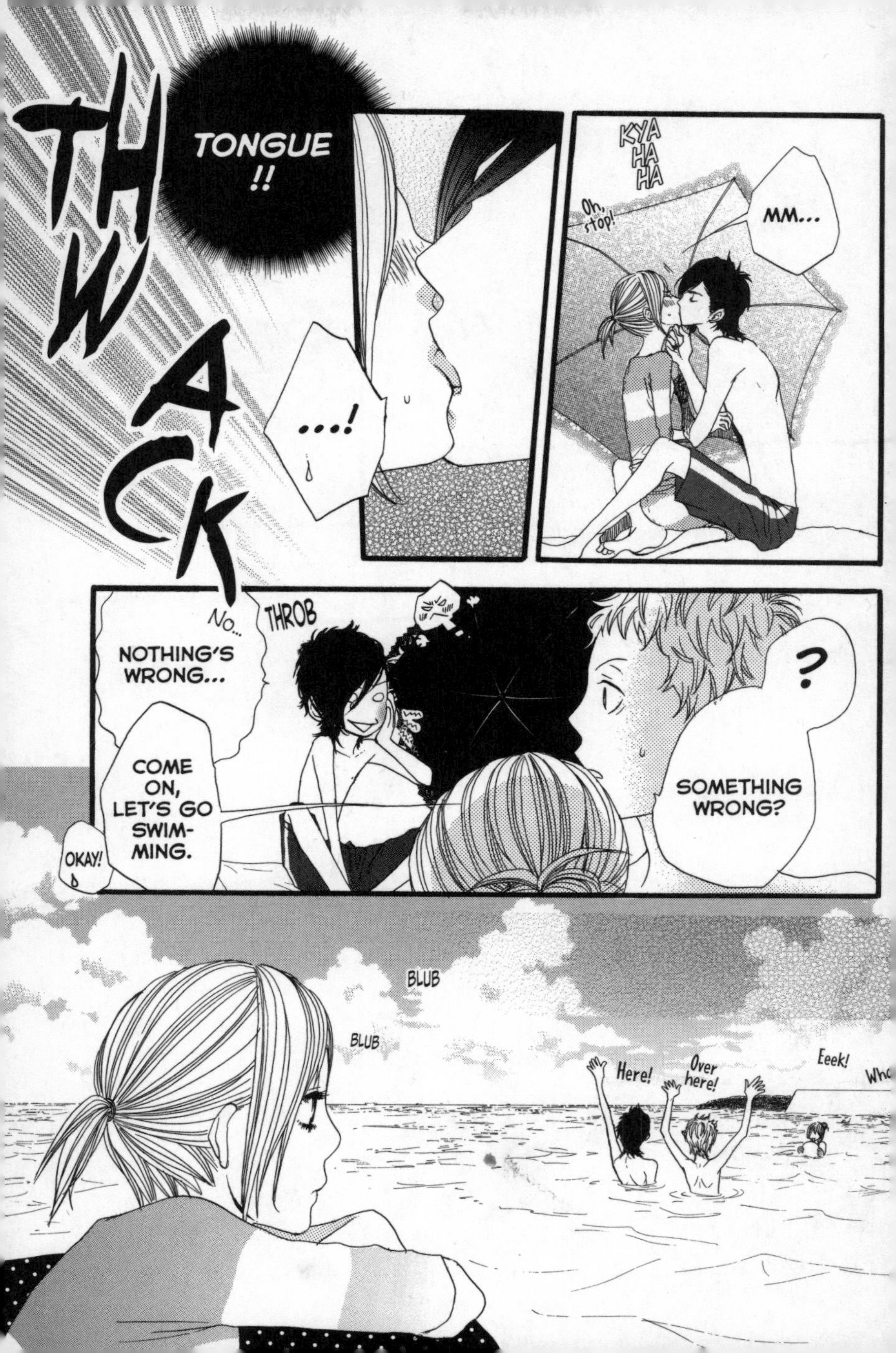

KYA HA HA
Oh, stop!
MM...
...!
TONGUE !!
THWACK
?
SOMETHING WRONG?
THROB
No... NOTHING'S WRONG...
COME ON, LET'S GO SWIMMING.
OKAY!
Eeek!
Over here!
Here!
BLUB
BLUB

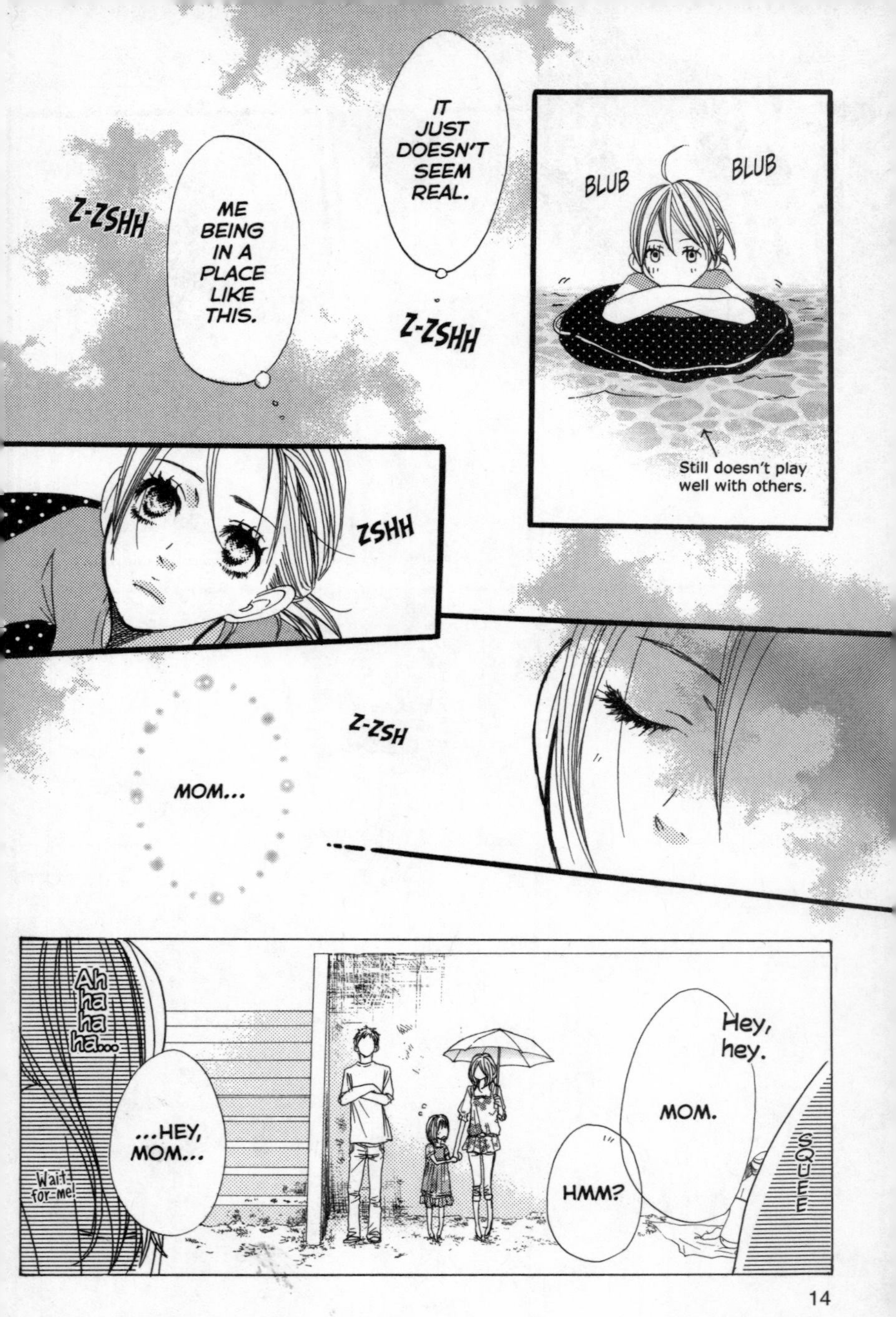
BLUB
BLUB
Still doesn't play well with others.
IT JUST DOESN'T SEEM REAL.
Z-ZSHH
ME BEING IN A PLACE LIKE THIS.
Z-ZSHH
ZSHH
Z-ZSH
MOM...
Hey, hey.
MOM.
SQUEE
HMM?
...HEY, MOM...
Ah ha ha ha...
Wait for me!

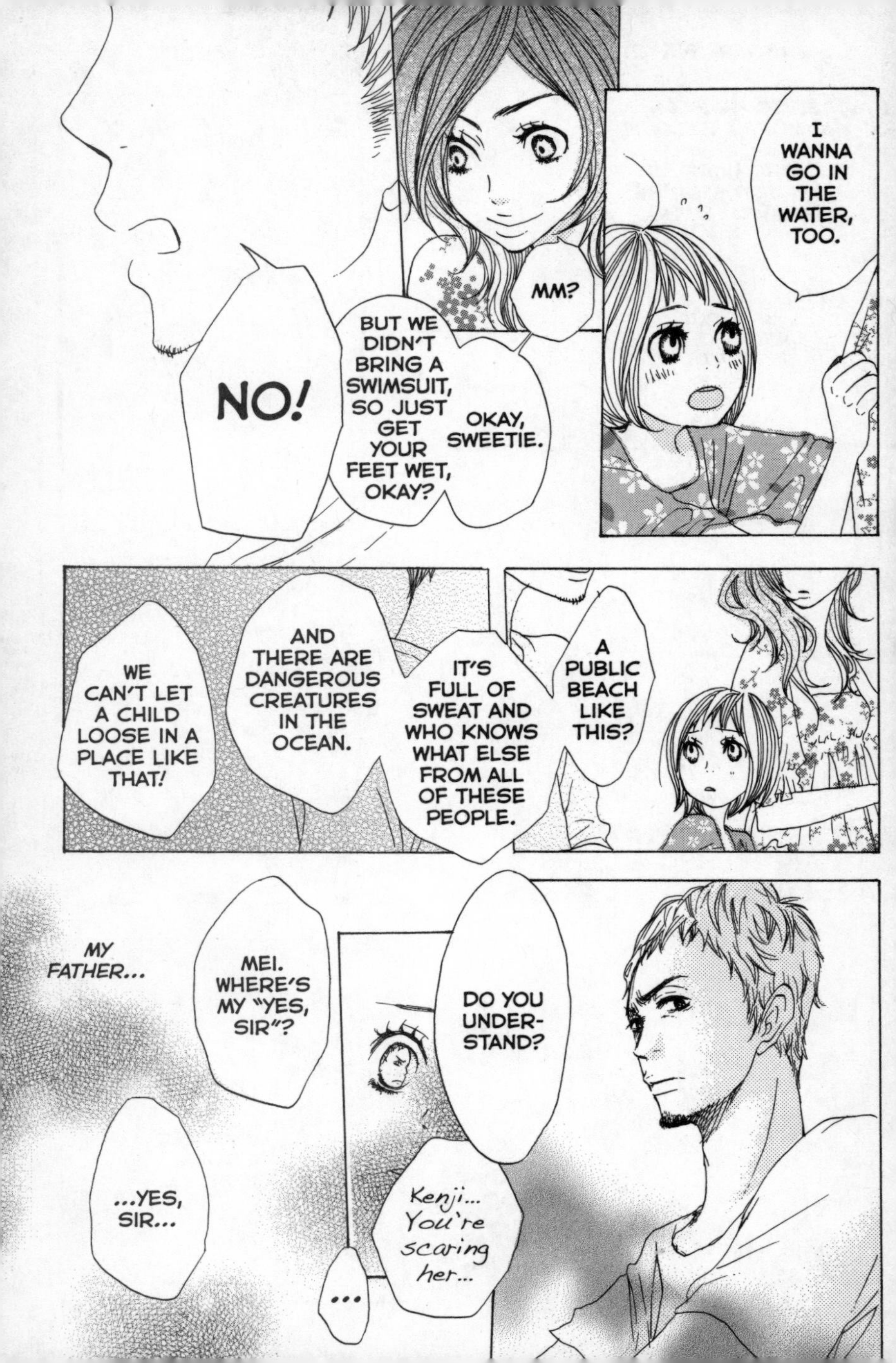
I WANNA GO IN THE WATER, TOO.
MM?
OKAY, SWEETIE.
BUT WE DIDN'T BRING A SWIMSUIT, SO JUST GET YOUR FEET WET, OKAY?
NO!
A PUBLIC BEACH LIKE THIS?
IT'S FULL OF SWEAT AND WHO KNOWS WHAT ELSE FROM ALL OF THESE PEOPLE.
AND THERE ARE DANGEROUS CREATURES IN THE OCEAN.
WE CAN'T LET A CHILD LOOSE IN A PLACE LIKE THAT!
DO YOU UNDER-STAND?
Kenji... You're scaring her...
...
MEI. WHERE'S MY "YES, SIR"?
MY FATHER...
...YES, SIR...

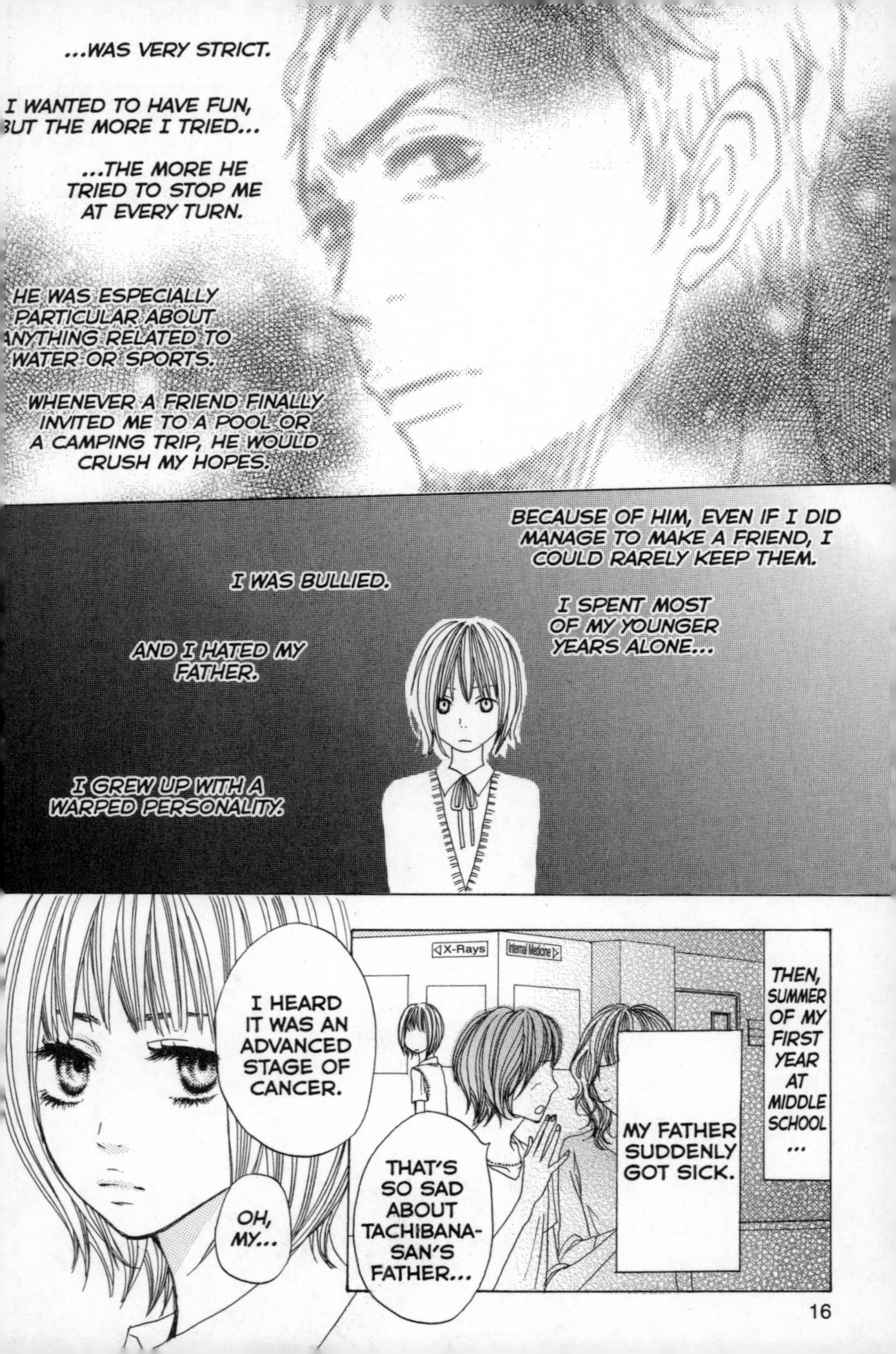
...WAS VERY STRICT.
I WANTED TO HAVE FUN, BUT THE MORE I TRIED...
...THE MORE HE TRIED TO STOP ME AT EVERY TURN.
HE WAS ESPECIALLY PARTICULAR ABOUT ANYTHING RELATED TO WATER OR SPORTS.
WHENEVER A FRIEND FINALLY INVITED ME TO A POOL OR A CAMPING TRIP, HE WOULD CRUSH MY HOPES.
BECAUSE OF HIM, EVEN IF I DID MANAGE TO MAKE A FRIEND, I COULD RARELY KEEP THEM.
I SPENT MOST OF MY YOUNGER YEARS ALONE...
I WAS BULLIED.
AND I HATED MY FATHER.
I GREW UP WITH A WARPED PERSONALITY.
THEN, SUMMER OF MY FIRST YEAR AT MIDDLE SCHOOL...
X-Rays
Internal Medicine
MY FATHER SUDDENLY GOT SICK.
I HEARD IT WAS AN ADVANCED STAGE OF CANCER.
THAT'S SO SAD ABOUT TACHIBANA-SAN'S FATHER...
OH, MY...

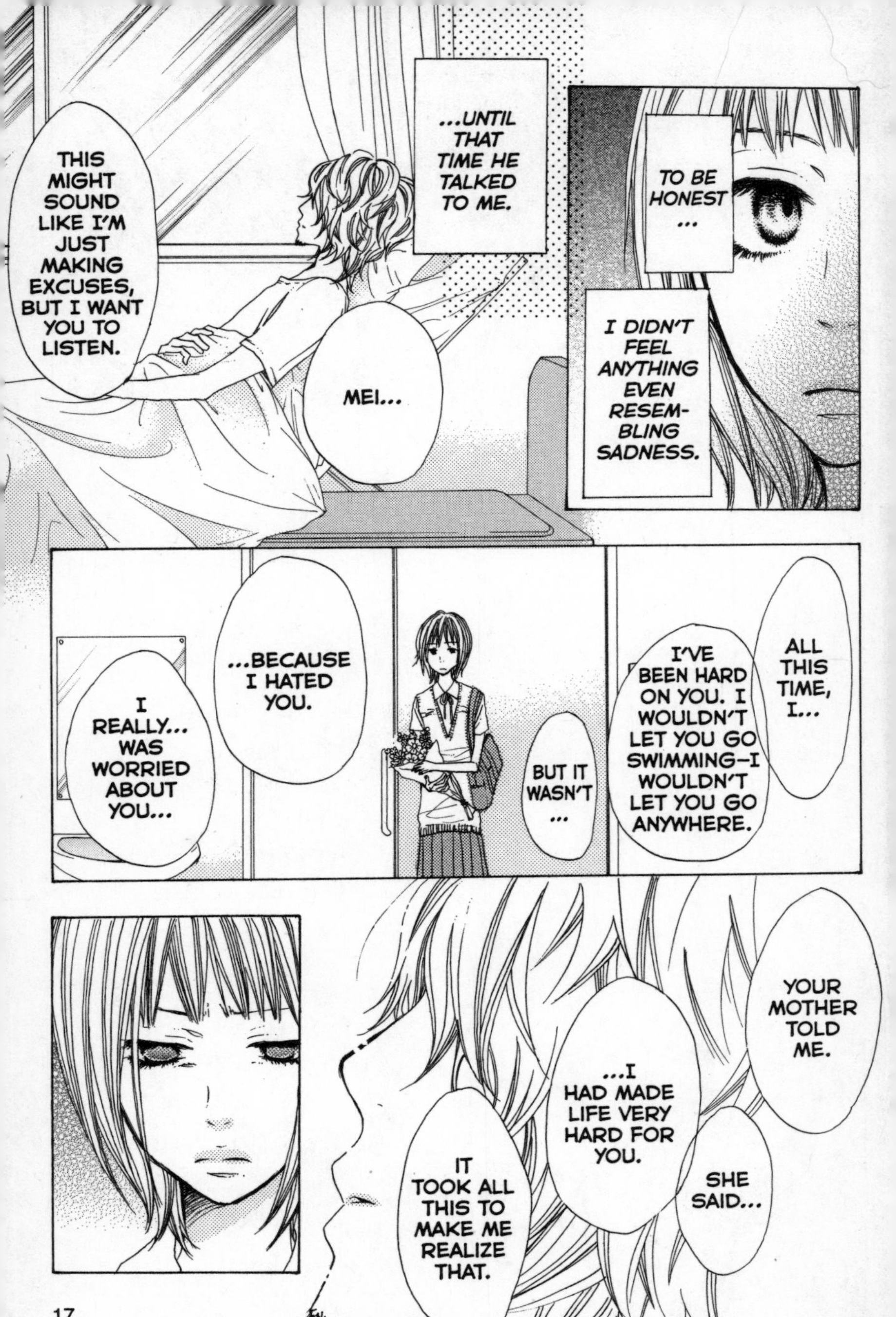
TO BE HONEST ...
I DIDN'T FEEL ANYTHING EVEN RESEMBLING SADNESS.
...UNTIL THAT TIME HE TALKED TO ME.
MEI...
THIS MIGHT SOUND LIKE I'M JUST MAKING EXCUSES, BUT I WANT YOU TO LISTEN.
ALL THIS TIME, I...
I'VE BEEN HARD ON YOU. I WOULDN'T LET YOU GO SWIMMING—I WOULDN'T LET YOU GO ANYWHERE.
BUT IT WASN'T ...
...BECAUSE I HATED YOU.
I REALLY... WAS WORRIED ABOUT YOU...
YOUR MOTHER TOLD ME.
SHE SAID...
...I HAD MADE LIFE VERY HARD FOR YOU.
IT TOOK ALL THIS TO MAKE ME REALIZE THAT.

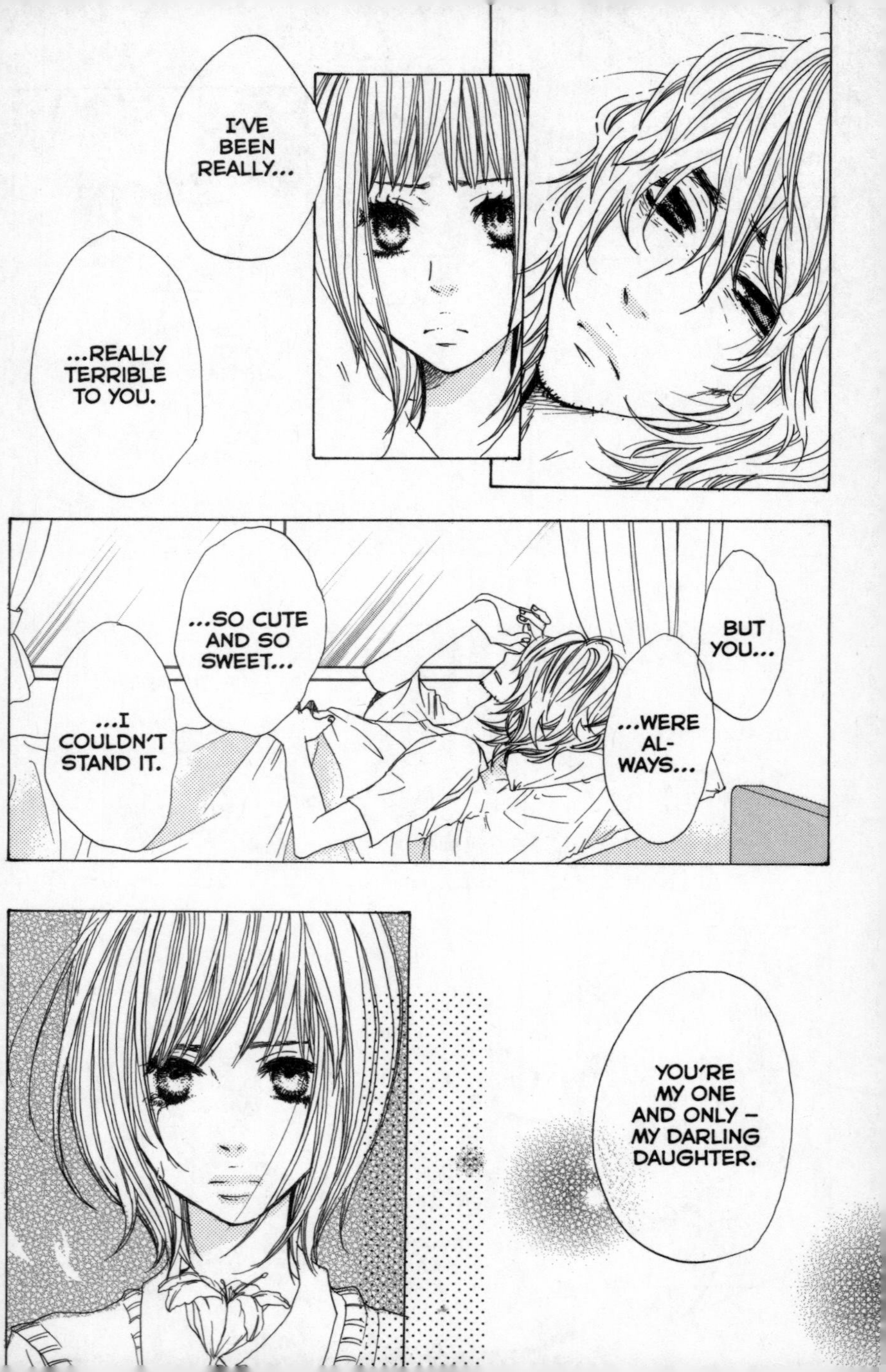
I'VE BEEN REALLY...
...REALLY TERRIBLE TO YOU.
BUT YOU...
...WERE ALWAYS...
...SO CUTE AND SO SWEET...
...I COULDN'T STAND IT.
YOU'RE MY ONE AND ONLY – MY DARLING DAUGHTER.

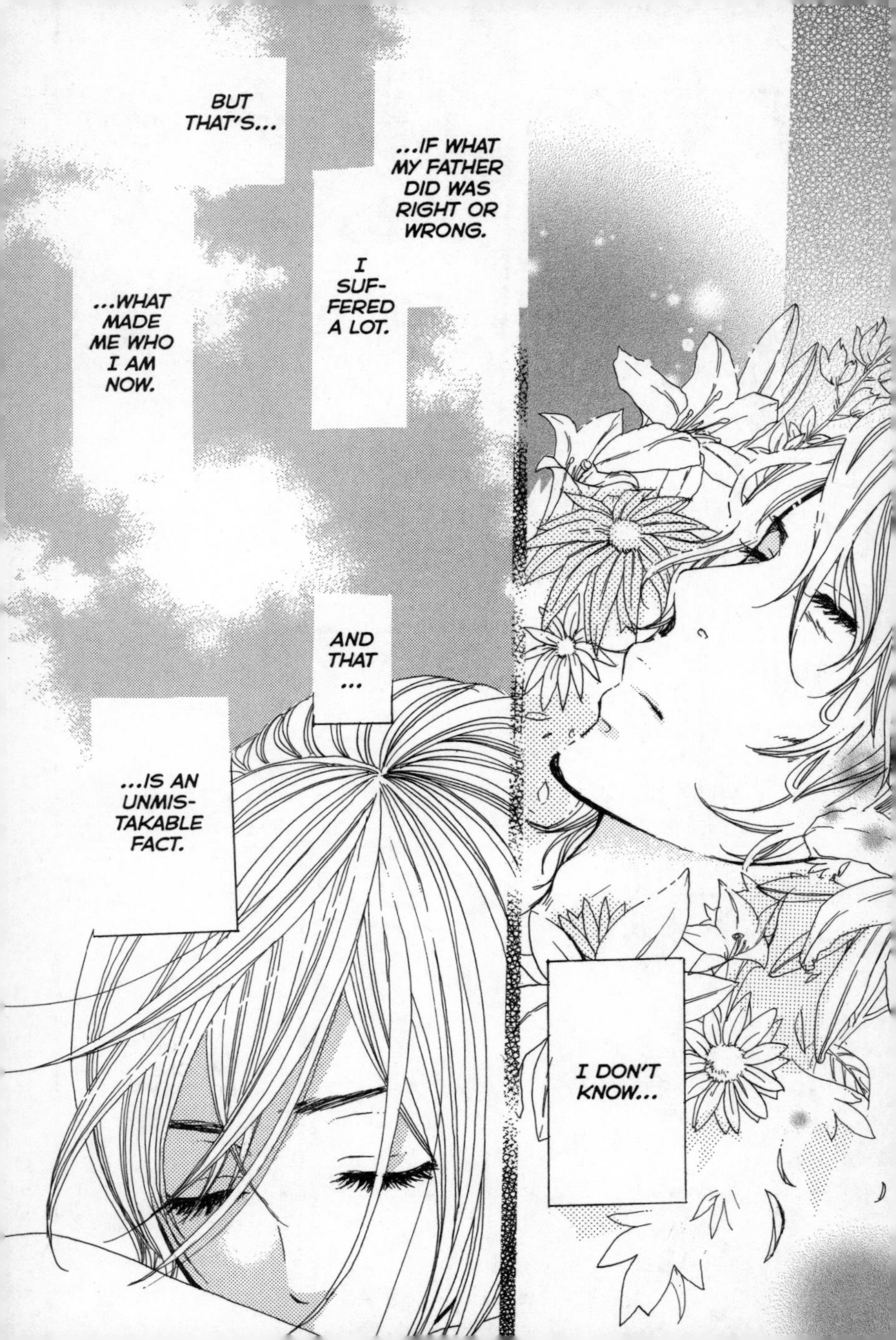
I DON'T KNOW...
...IF WHAT MY FATHER DID WAS RIGHT OR WRONG.
BUT THAT'S...
I SUF-FERED A LOT.
...WHAT MADE ME WHO I AM NOW.
AND THAT...
...IS AN UNMIS-TAKABLE FACT.

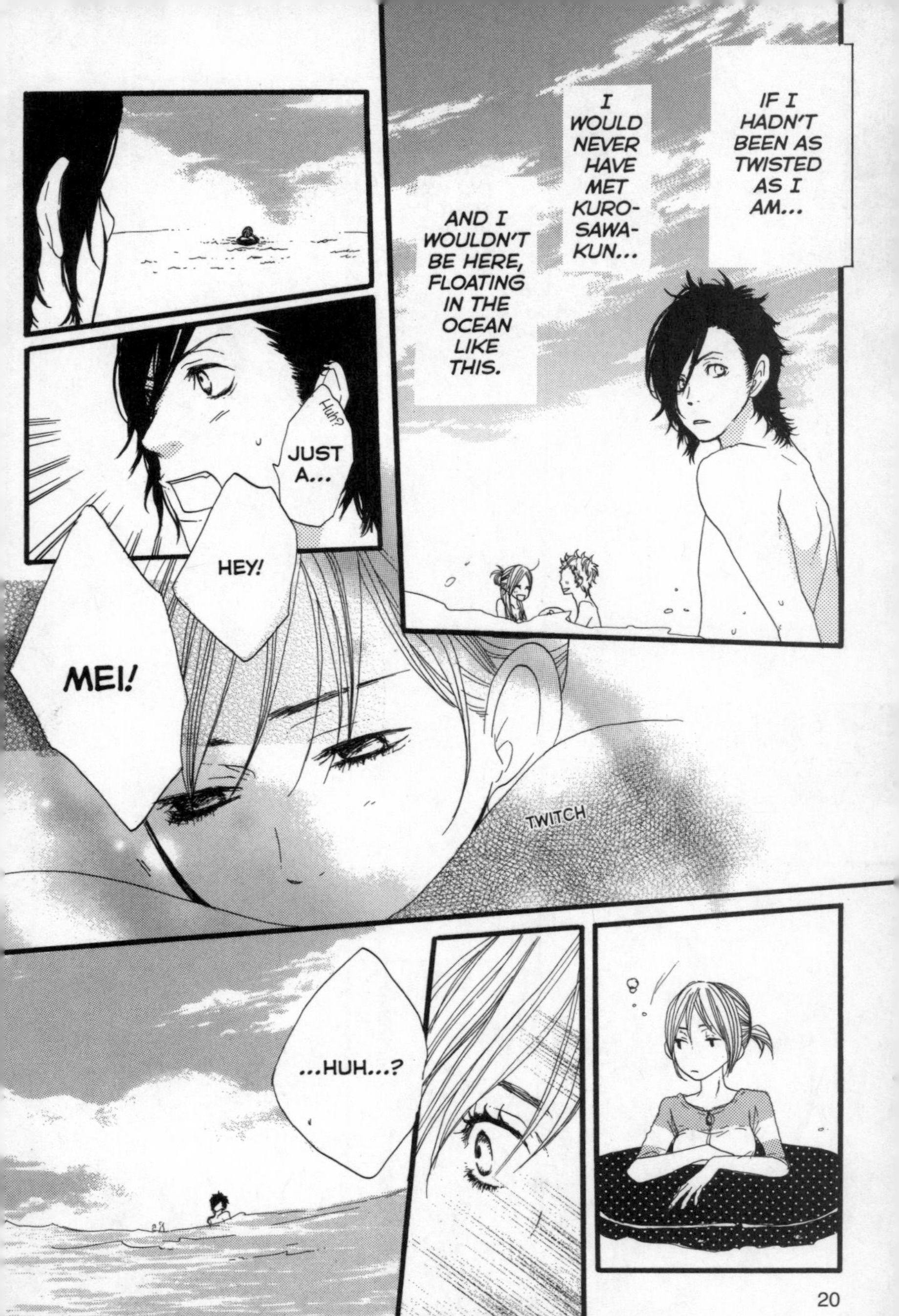
IF I HADN'T BEEN AS TWISTED AS I AM...
I WOULD NEVER HAVE MET KURO-SAWA-KUN...
AND I WOULDN'T BE HERE, FLOATING IN THE OCEAN LIKE THIS.
Huh?
JUST A...
HEY!
MEI!
TWITCH
...HUH...?

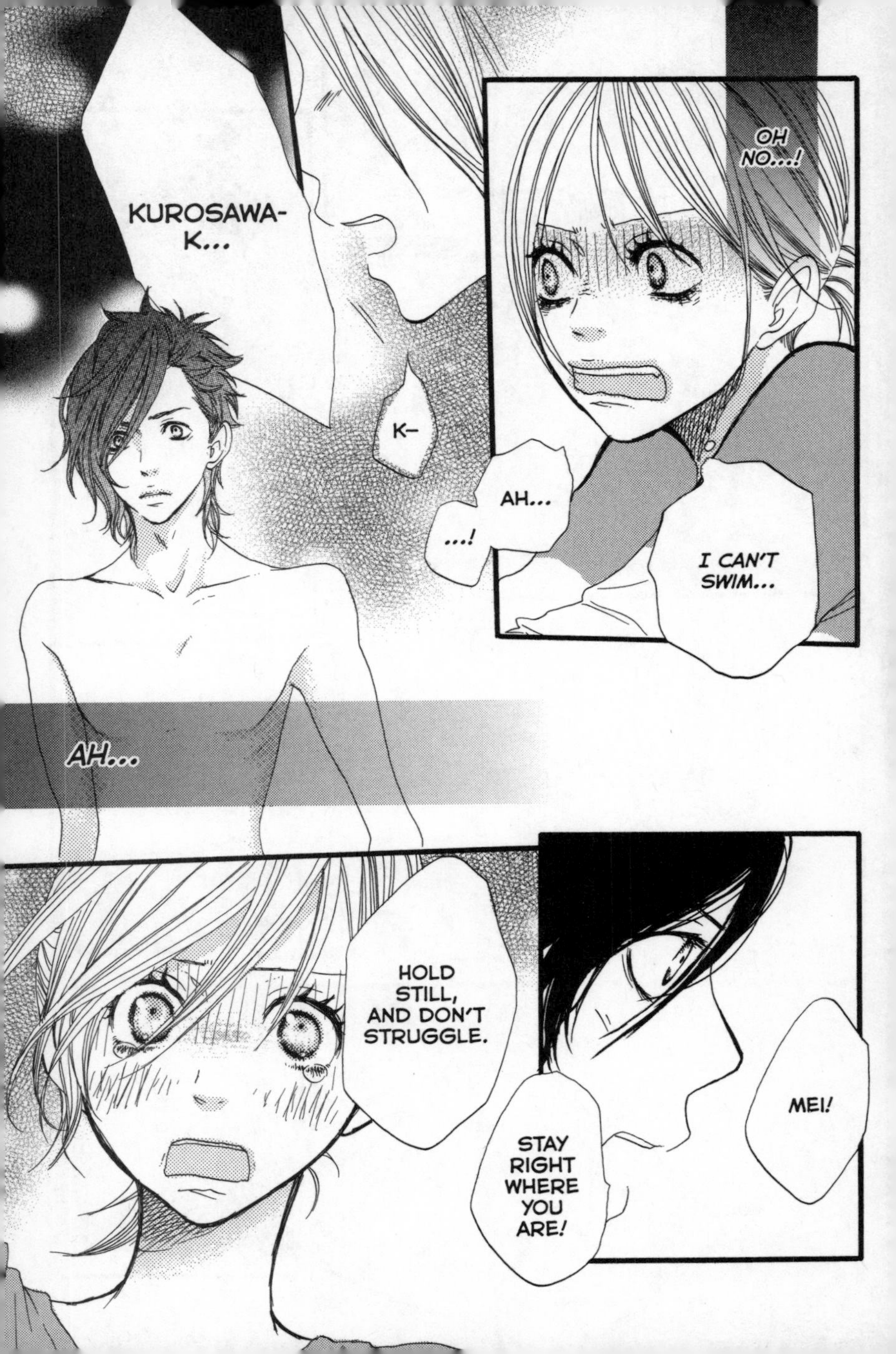
OH NO...!
AH...
I CAN'T SWIM...
...!
KUROSAWA-K...
K–
AH...
MEI!
STAY RIGHT WHERE YOU ARE!
HOLD STILL, AND DON'T STRUGGLE.

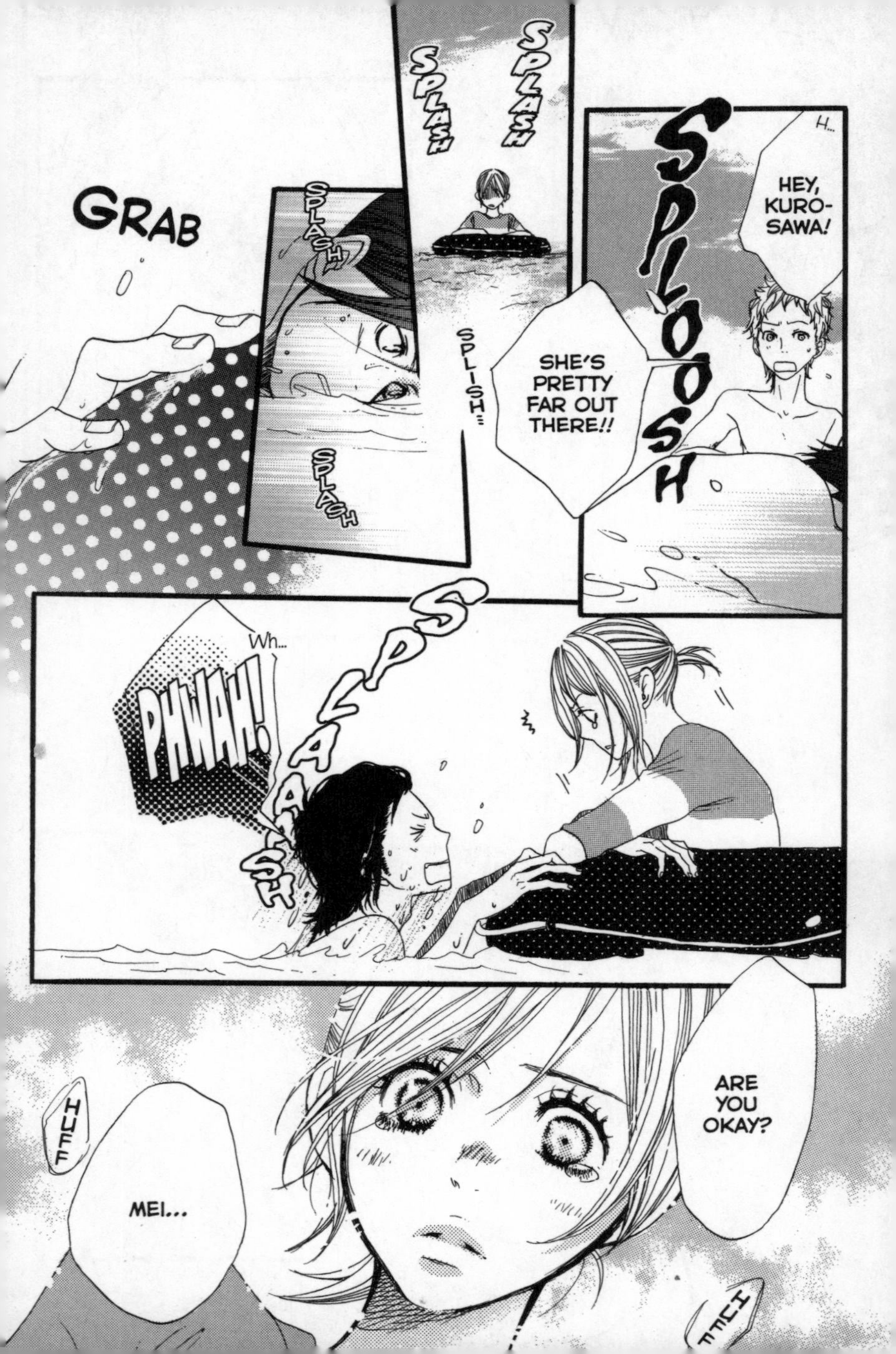

H...
HEY, KURO-SAWA!
SPLOOSH
SHE'S PRETTY FAR OUT THERE!!
SPLASH
SPLASH
SPLISH...
SPLASH
SPLASH
GRAB
SPLAAASH
Wh...
PHWAH!
ARE YOU OKAY?
HUFF
MEI...

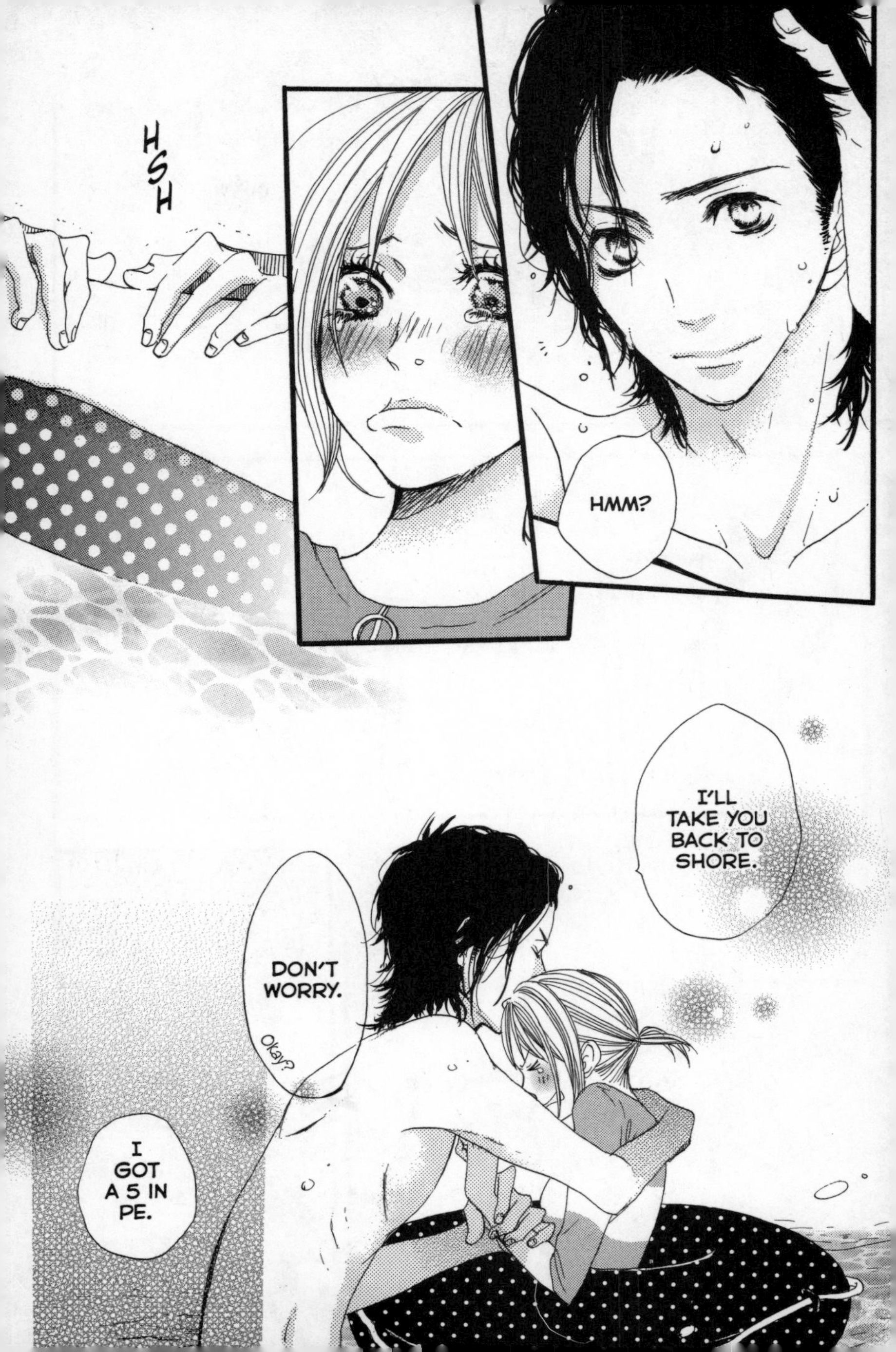
HMM?
HSH
I'LL TAKE YOU BACK TO SHORE.
DON'T WORRY.
Okay?
I GOT A 5 IN PE.

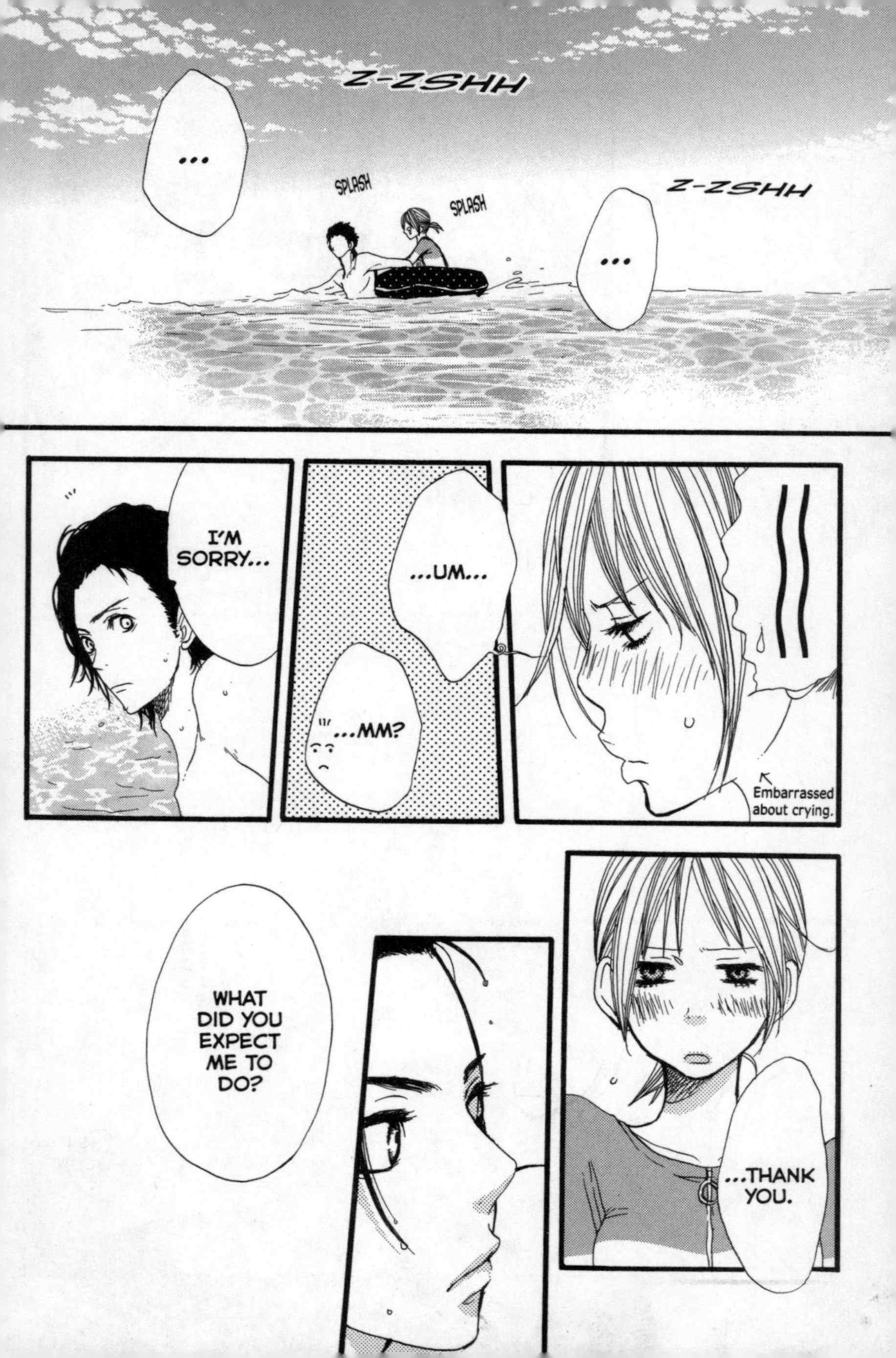
Z-ZSHH
Z-ZSHH
...
SPLASH
SPLASH
...
Embarrassed about crying.
...UM...
...MM?
I'M SORRY...
...THANK YOU.
WHAT DID YOU EXPECT ME TO DO?

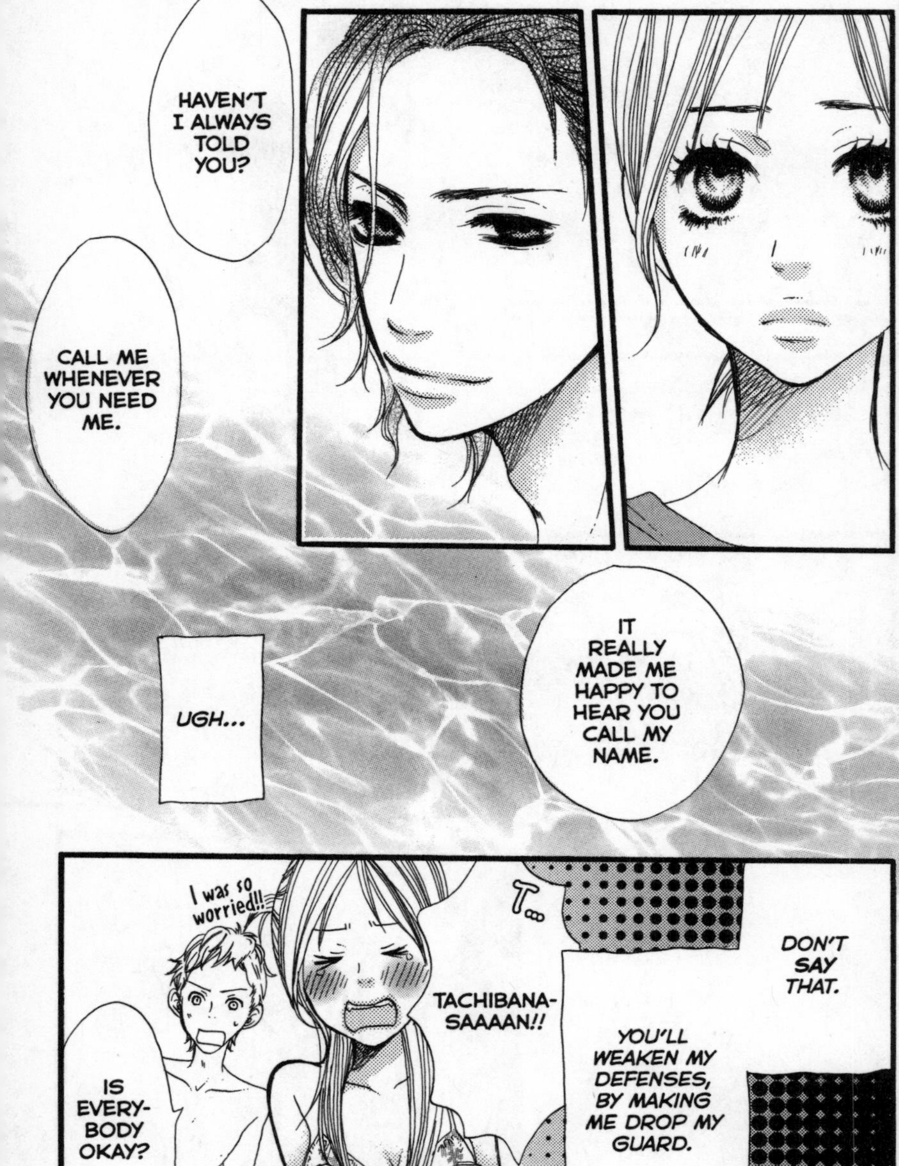
HAVEN'T I ALWAYS TOLD YOU?
CALL ME WHENEVER YOU NEED ME.
IT REALLY MADE ME HAPPY TO HEAR YOU CALL MY NAME.
UGH...
DON'T SAY THAT.
YOU'LL WEAKEN MY DEFENSES, BY MAKING ME DROP MY GUARD.
T...
TACHIBANA-SAAAAN!!
I was so worried!!
IS EVERY-BODY OKAY?

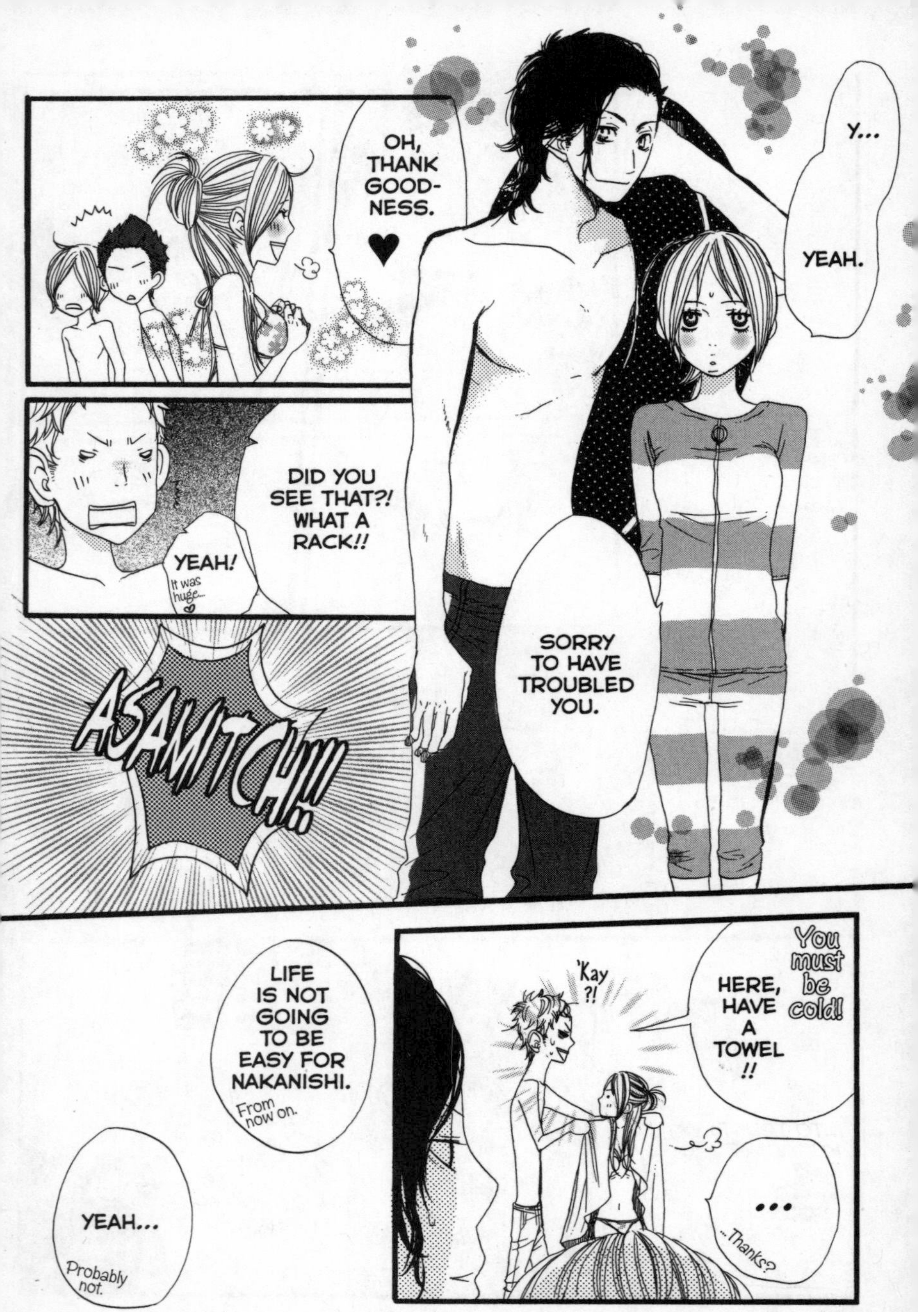
Y... YEAH.
OH, THANK GOODNESS. ♥
SORRY TO HAVE TROUBLED YOU.
DID YOU SEE THAT?! WHAT A RACK!!
YEAH! It was huge...
ASAMITCH!!!
You must be cold!
HERE, HAVE A TOWEL!!
'Kay?!
...
...Thanks?
LIFE IS NOT GOING TO BE EASY FOR NAKANISHI. From now on.
YEAH... Probably not.

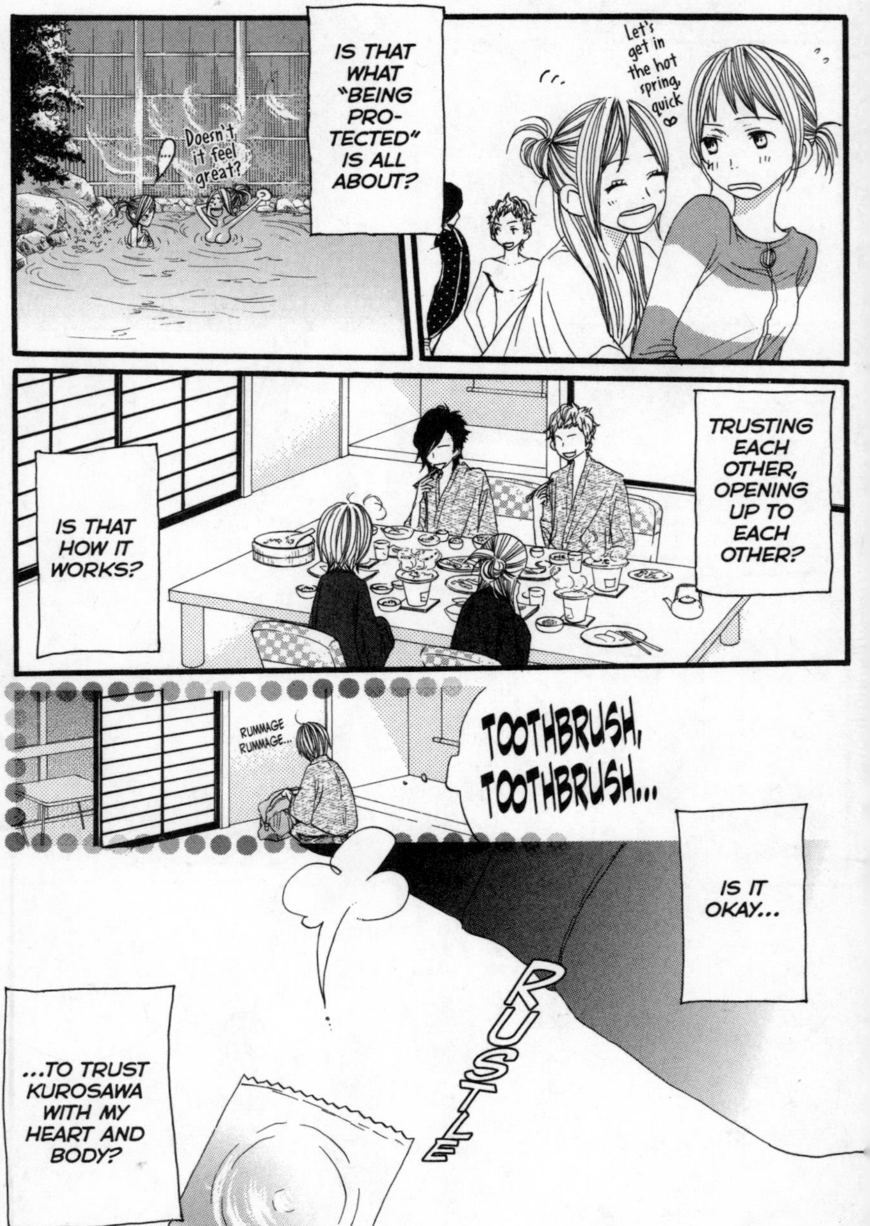
Let's get in the hot spring, quick
IS THAT WHAT "BEING PRO-TECTED" IS ALL ABOUT?
Doesn't it feel great?
TRUSTING EACH OTHER, OPENING UP TO EACH OTHER?
IS THAT HOW IT WORKS?
TOOTHBRUSH, TOOTHBRUSH...
RUMMAGE RUMMAGE...
IS IT OKAY...
RUSTLE
...TO TRUST KUROSAWA WITH MY HEART AND BODY?

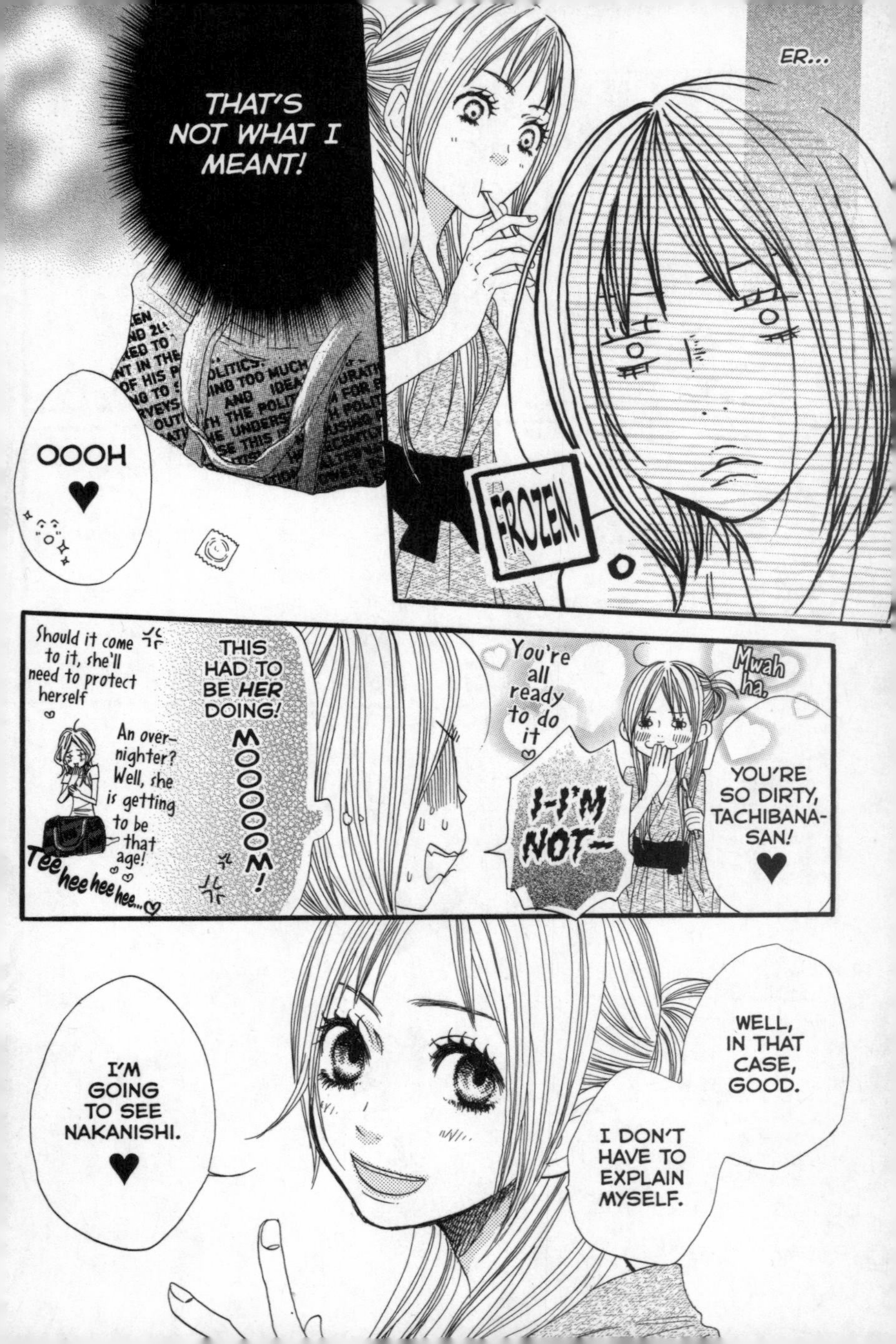
ER...
FROZEN.
THAT'S NOT WHAT I MEANT!
OOOH ♥
Mwah ha.
YOU'RE SO DIRTY, TACHIBANA-SAN! ♥
You're all ready to do it
I-I'M NOT–
THIS HAD TO BE HER DOING!
MOOOOOOM!
Should it come to it, she'll need to protect herself
An over-nighter? Well, she is getting to be that age!
Tee hee hee hee...
WELL, IN THAT CASE, GOOD.
I DON'T HAVE TO EXPLAIN MYSELF.
I'M GOING TO SEE NAKANISHI. ♥

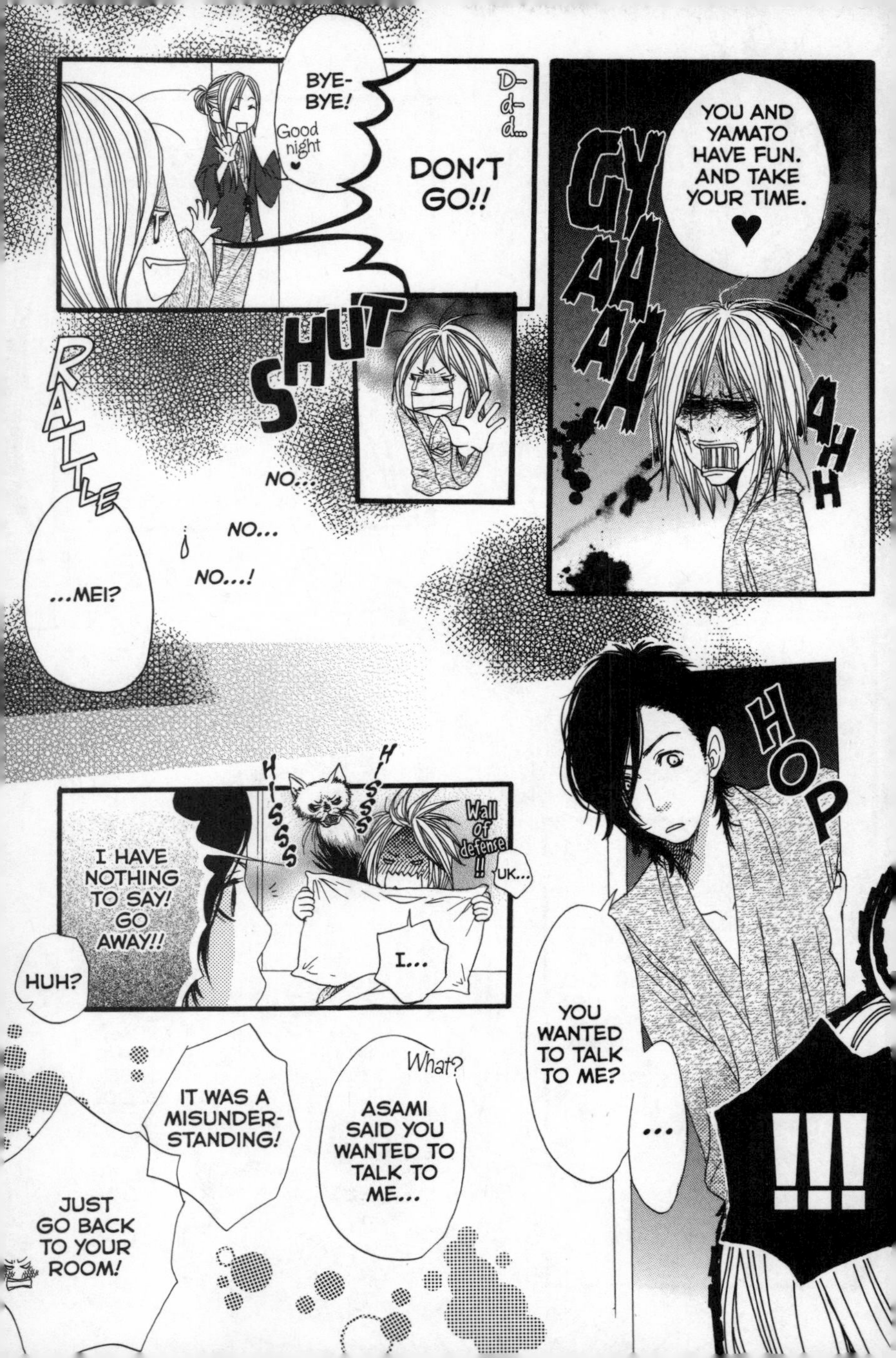
YOU AND YAMATO HAVE FUN. AND TAKE YOUR TIME. ♥
GYAAAAAHHH
BYE-BYE!
Good night ♥
D-d-d...
DON'T GO!!
SHUT
RATTLE
NO...
NO...
NO...!
...MEI?
HOP
YOU WANTED TO TALK TO ME?
...
!!!
What?
ASAMI SAID YOU WANTED TO TALK TO ME...
IT WAS A MISUNDERSTANDING!
JUST GO BACK TO YOUR ROOM!
HISSS
HISSS
Wall of defense!!
UK...
I...
I HAVE NOTHING TO SAY! GO AWAY!!
HUH?

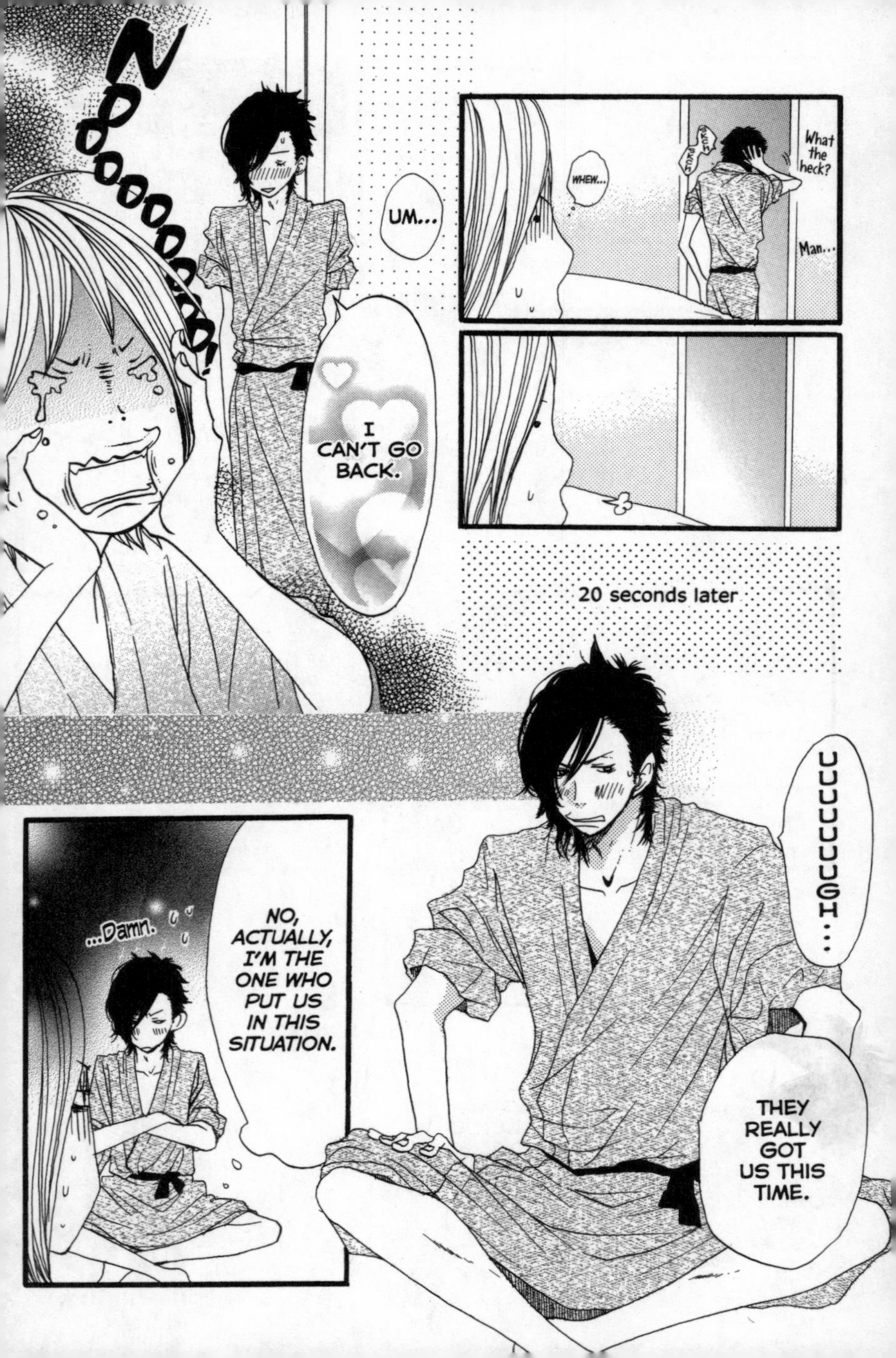
What the heck?
SKCH SKCH
Man...
WHEW...
NOOOOOOOOOOOO!
UM...
I CAN'T GO BACK.
20 seconds later
UUUUUUUGH...
THEY REALLY GOT US THIS TIME.
...Damn.
NO, ACTUALLY, I'M THE ONE WHO PUT US IN THIS SITUATION.

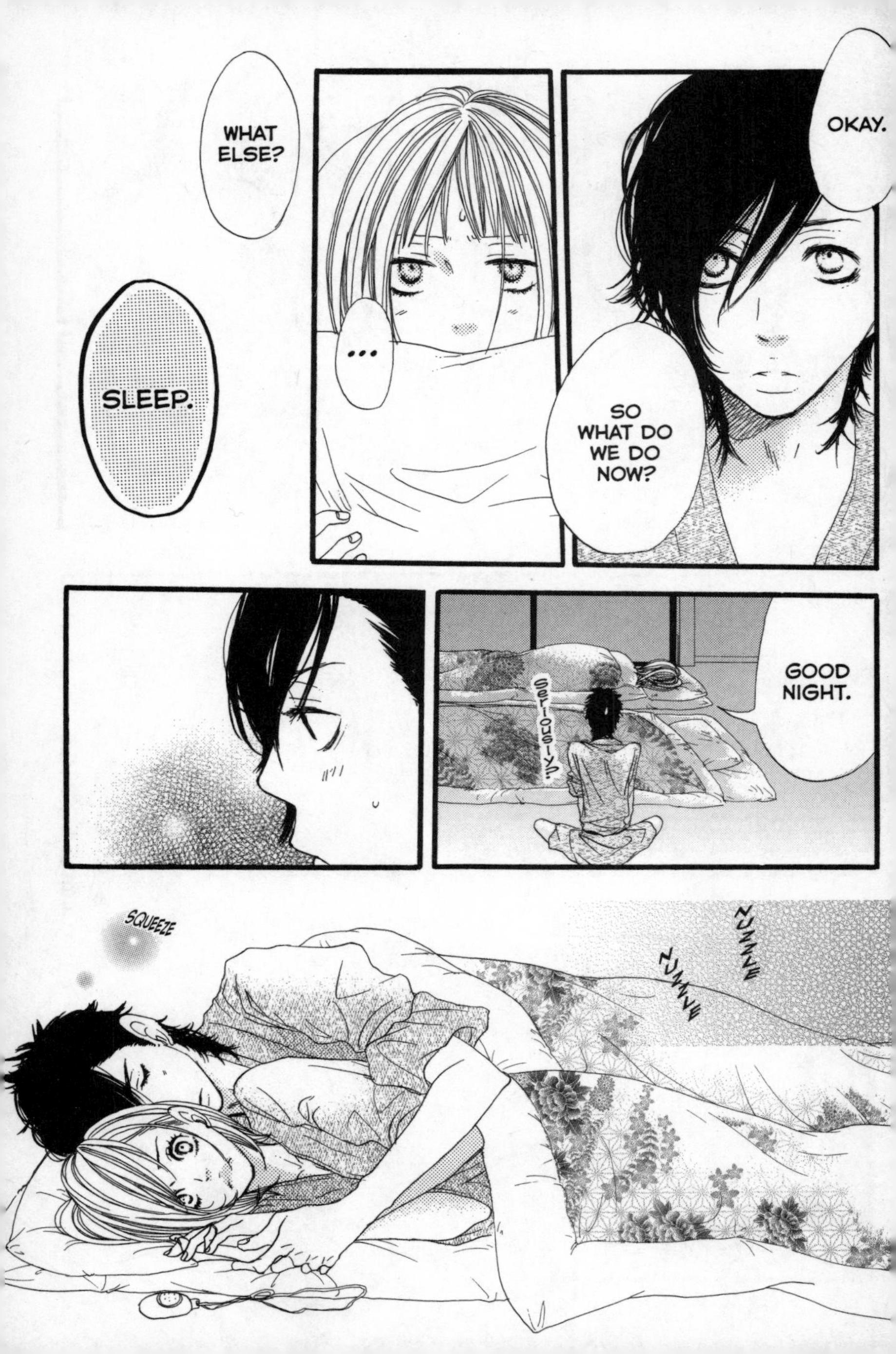
OKAY.
SO WHAT DO WE DO NOW?
...
WHAT ELSE?
SLEEP.
GOOD NIGHT.
Seriously?
SQUEEZE

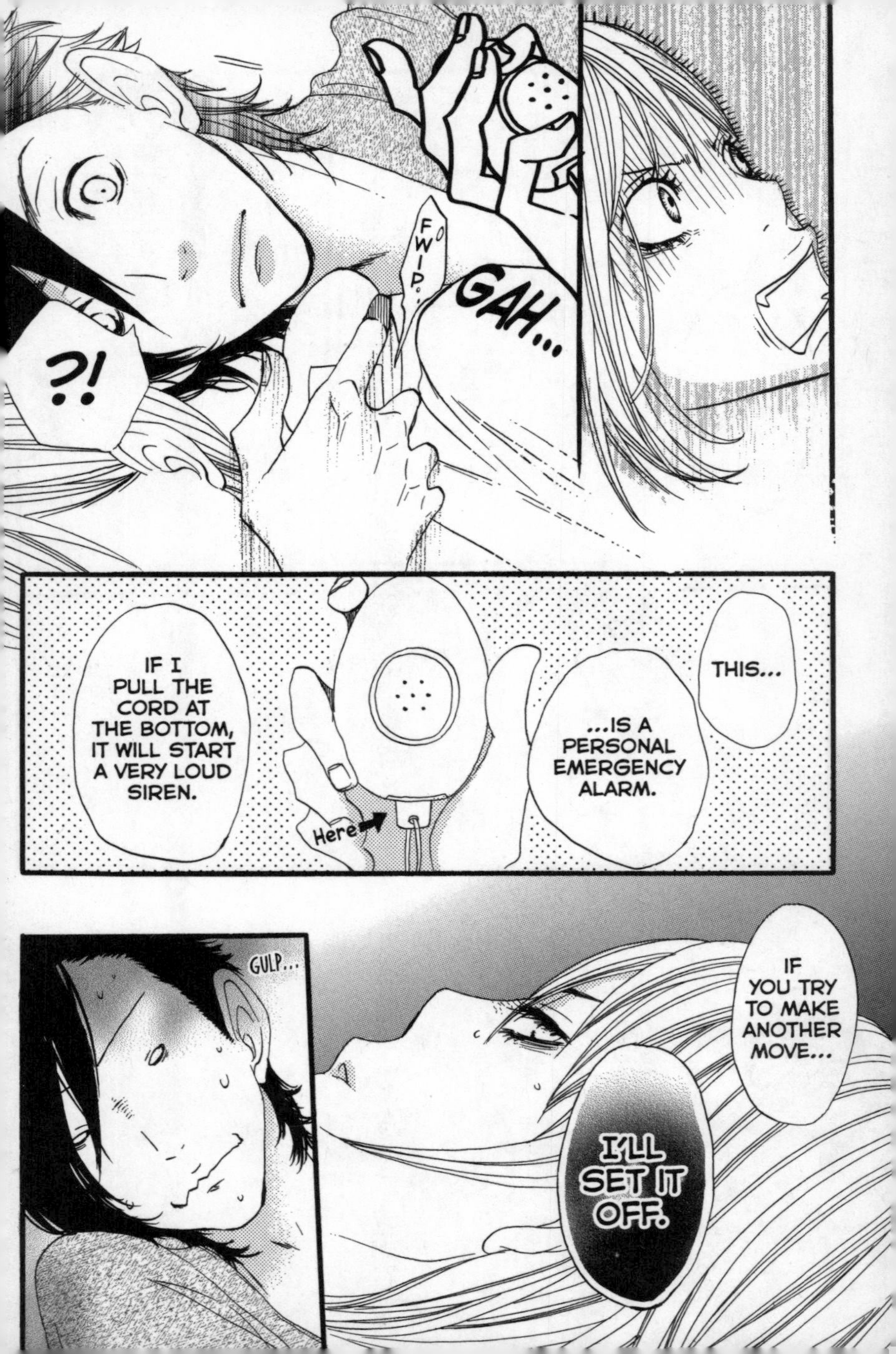
GAH...
FWIP
?!
THIS...
...IS A PERSONAL EMERGENCY ALARM.
IF I PULL THE CORD AT THE BOTTOM, IT WILL START A VERY LOUD SIREN.
Here
IF YOU TRY TO MAKE ANOTHER MOVE...
I'LL SET IT OFF.
GULP...

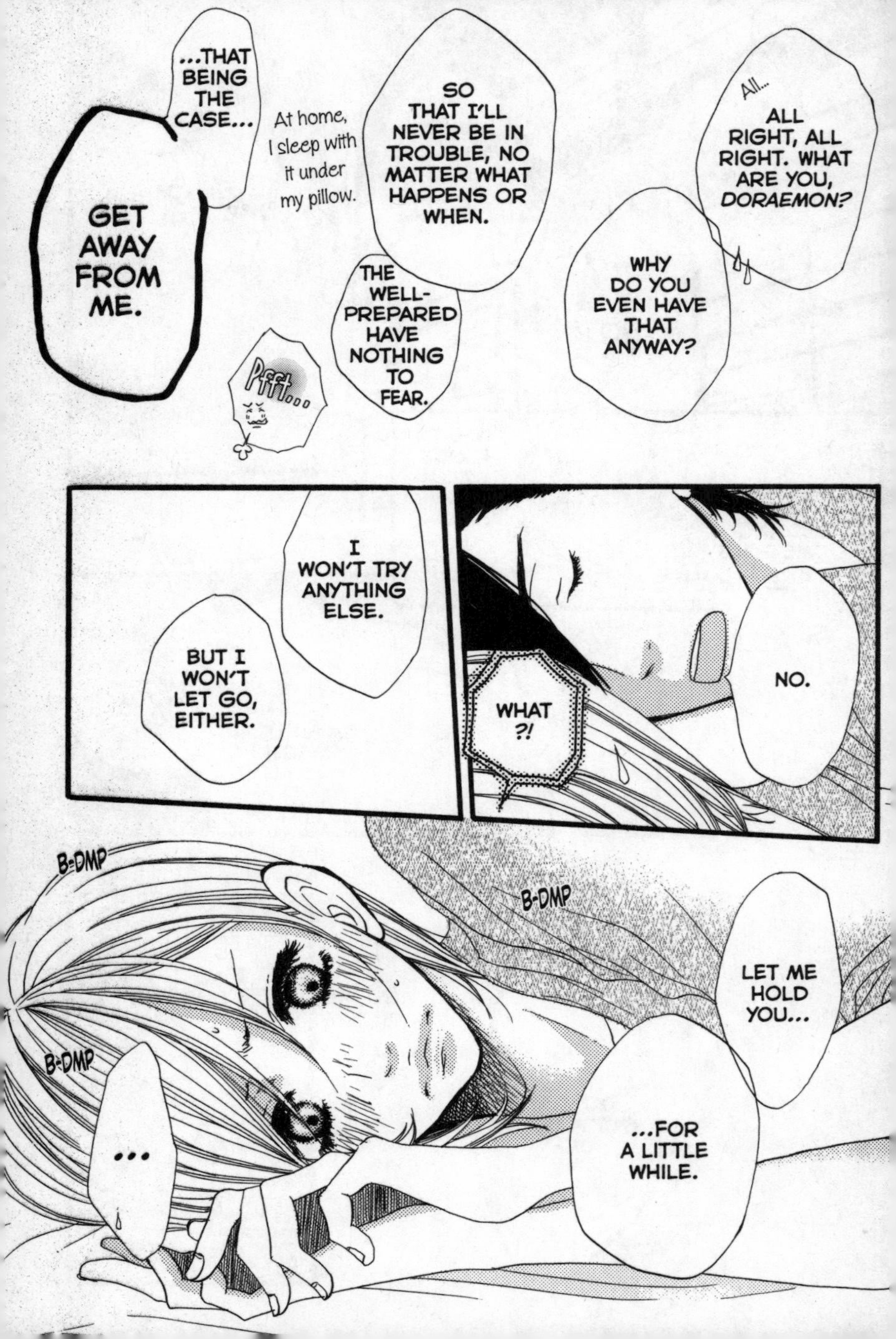
All...
ALL RIGHT, ALL RIGHT. WHAT ARE YOU, *DORAEMON?*
WHY DO YOU EVEN HAVE THAT ANYWAY?
SO THAT I'LL NEVER BE IN TROUBLE, NO MATTER WHAT HAPPENS OR WHEN.
THE WELL-PREPARED HAVE NOTHING TO FEAR.
At home, I sleep with it under my pillow.
Pffft...
...THAT BEING THE CASE...
GET AWAY FROM ME.
NO.
WHAT?!
I WON'T TRY ANYTHING ELSE.
BUT I WON'T LET GO, EITHER.
LET ME HOLD YOU...
...FOR A LITTLE WHILE.
B-DMP
B-DMP
B-DMP
...

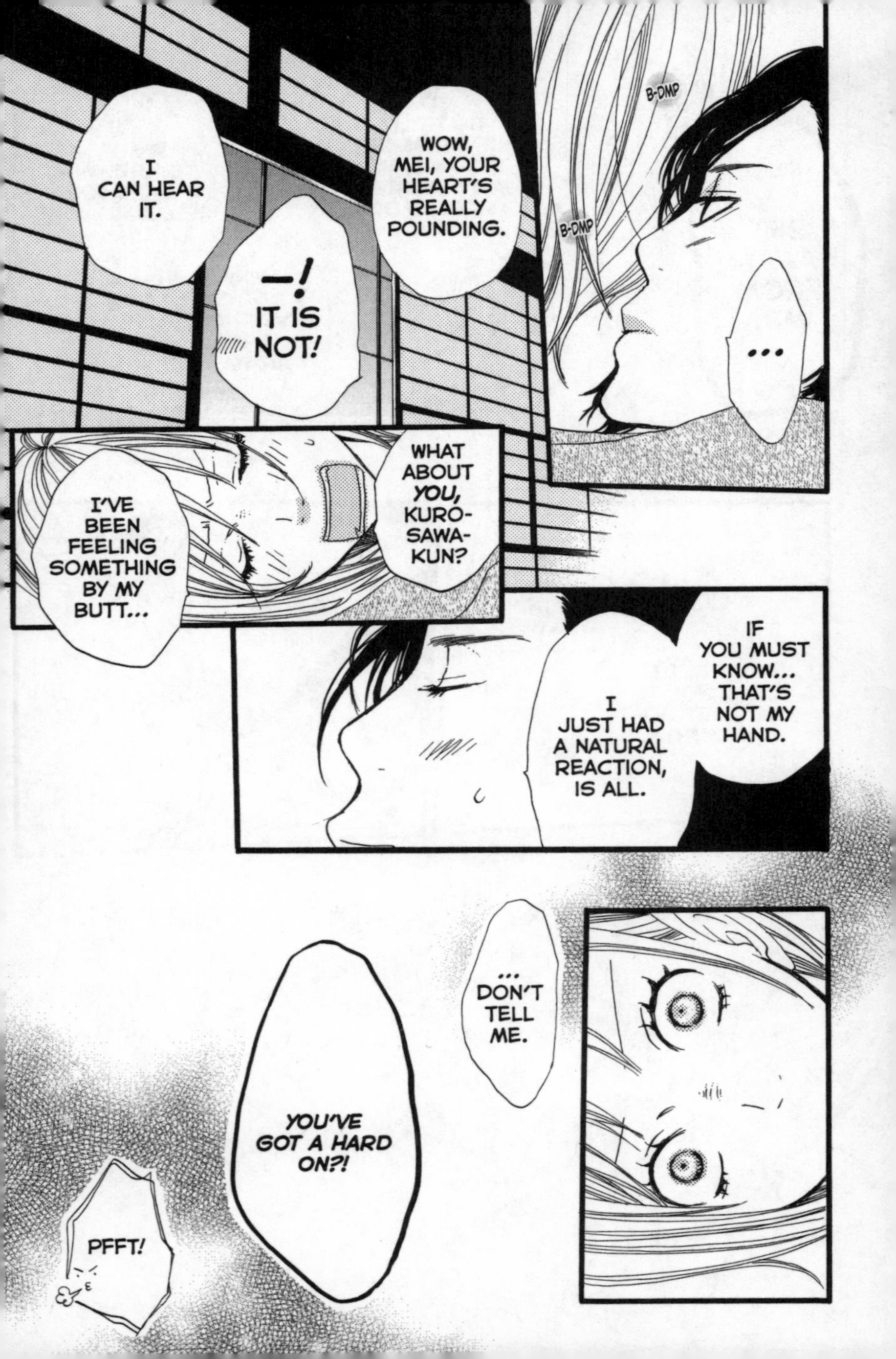
B-DMP
B-DMP
...
WOW, MEI, YOUR HEART'S REALLY POUNDING.
—! IT IS NOT!
I CAN HEAR IT.
WHAT ABOUT *YOU*, KURO-SAWA-KUN?
I'VE BEEN FEELING SOMETHING BY MY BUTT...
IF YOU MUST KNOW... THAT'S NOT MY HAND.
I JUST HAD A NATURAL REACTION, IS ALL.
...DON'T TELL ME.
YOU'VE GOT A HARD ON?!
PFFT!

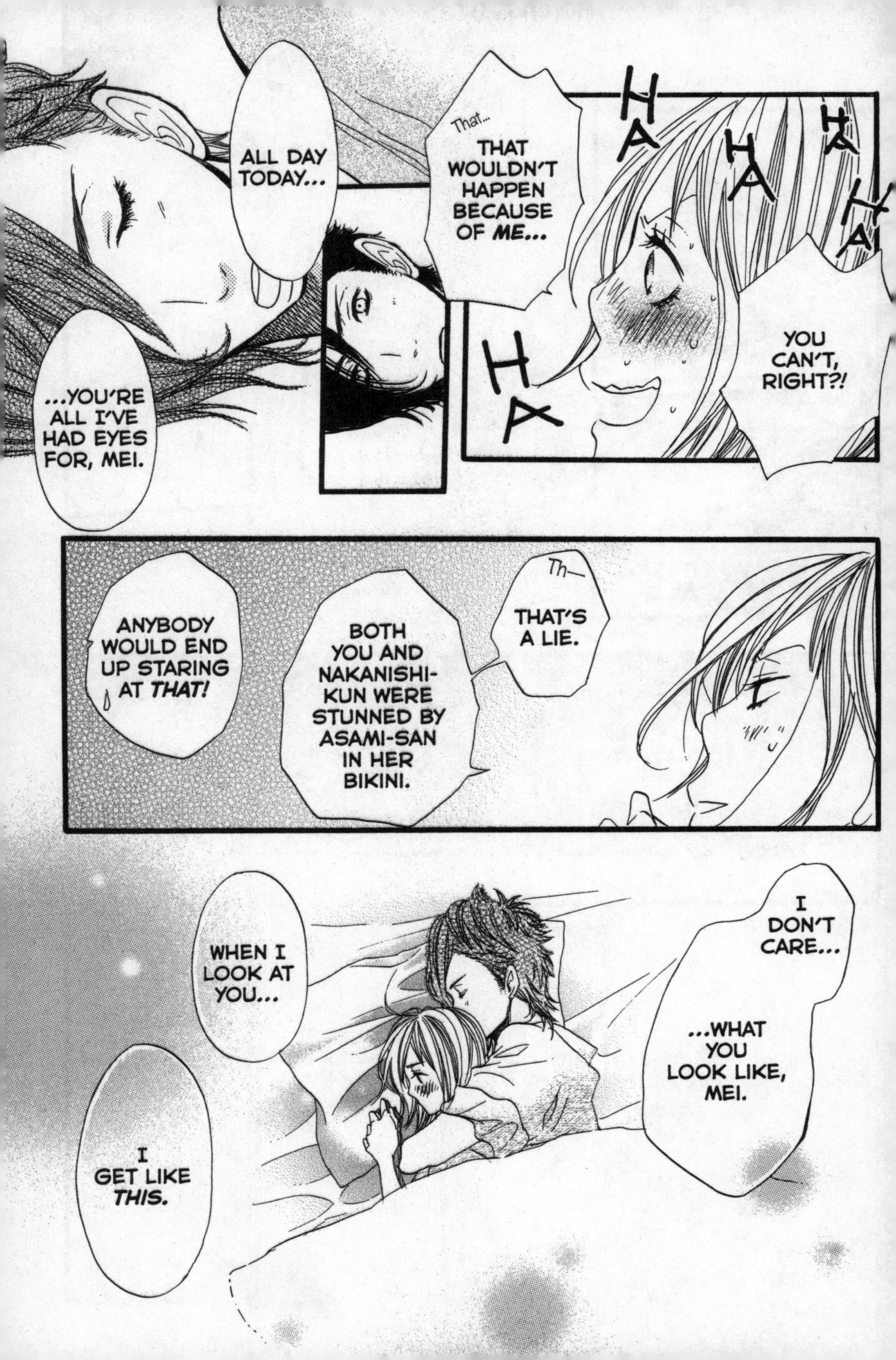
HA HA HA HA
YOU CAN'T, RIGHT?!
HA HA
That...
THAT WOULDN'T HAPPEN BECAUSE OF *ME*...
ALL DAY TODAY...
...YOU'RE ALL I'VE HAD EYES FOR, MEI.
Th—
THAT'S A LIE.
BOTH YOU AND NAKANISHI-KUN WERE STUNNED BY ASAMI-SAN IN HER BIKINI.
ANYBODY WOULD END UP STARING AT *THAT!*
I DON'T CARE...
...WHAT YOU LOOK LIKE, MEI.
WHEN I LOOK AT YOU...
I GET LIKE *THIS.*

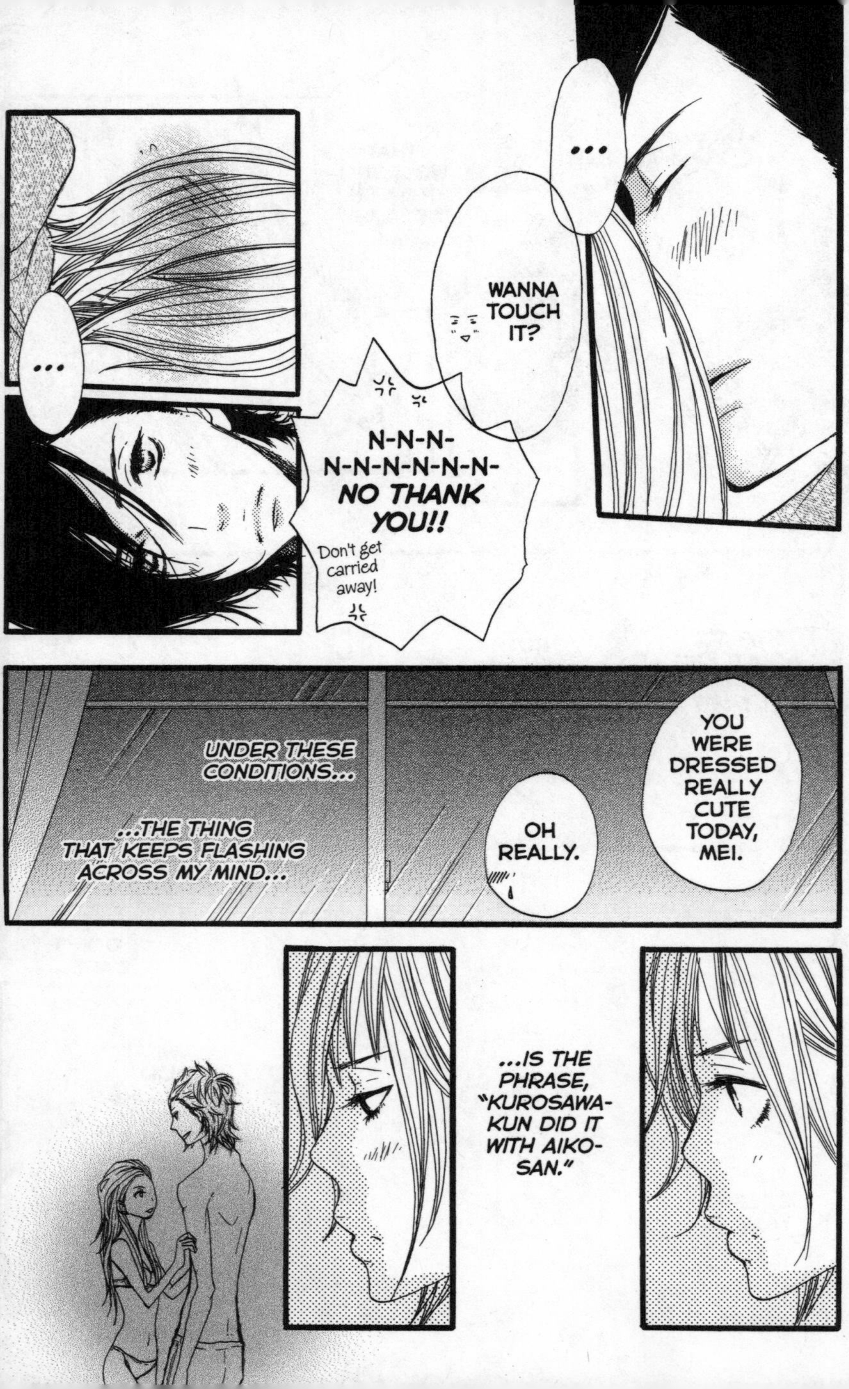
...
WANNA TOUCH IT?
...
N-N-N- N-N-N-N-N-N- NO THANK YOU!!
Don't get carried away!
YOU WERE DRESSED REALLY CUTE TODAY, MEI.
OH REALLY.
UNDER THESE CONDITIONS...
...THE THING THAT KEEPS FLASHING ACROSS MY MIND...
...IS THE PHRASE, "KUROSAWA-KUN DID IT WITH AIKO-SAN."

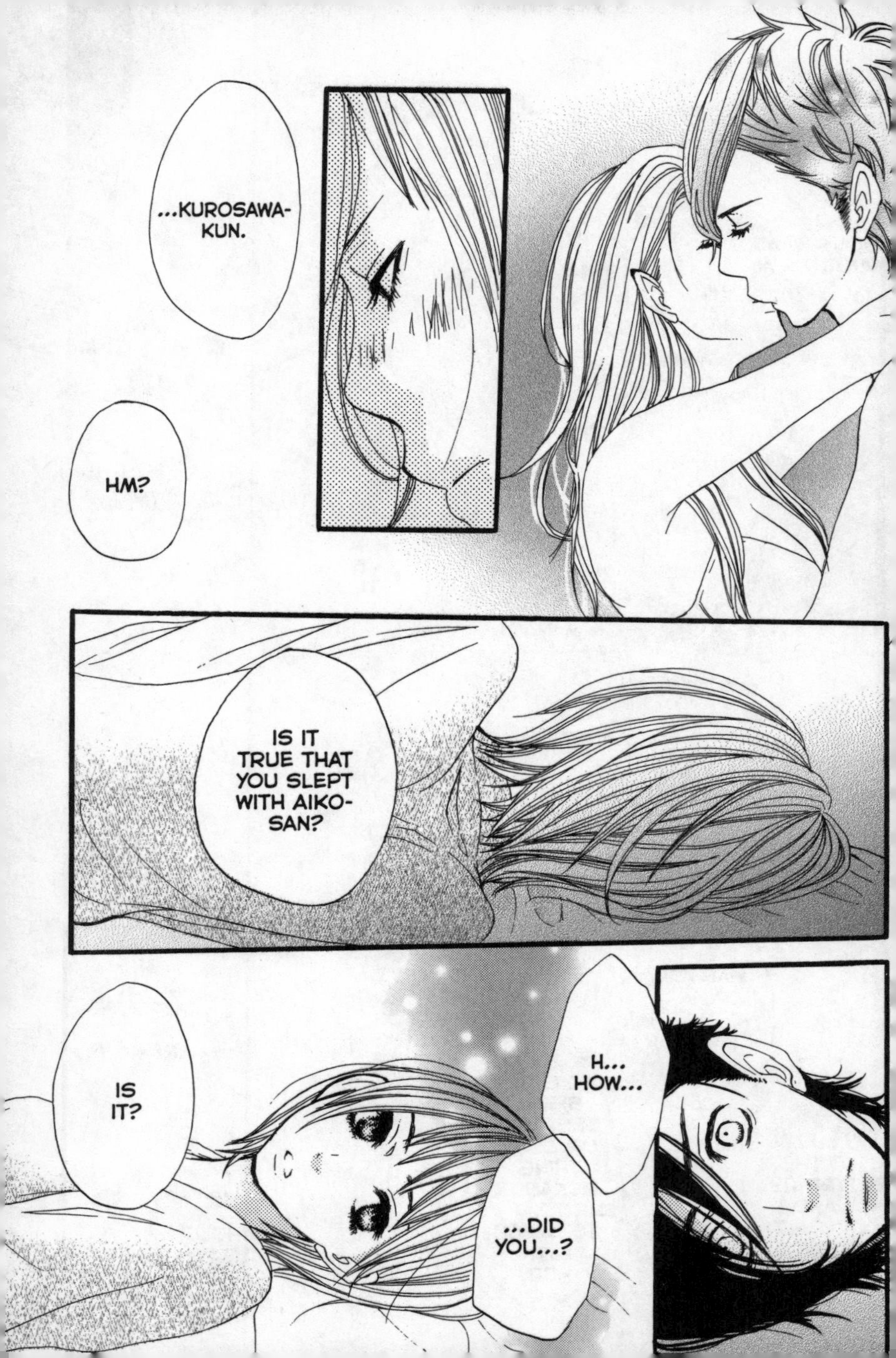
...KUROSAWA-KUN.
HM?
IS IT TRUE THAT YOU SLEPT WITH AIKO-SAN?
H... HOW...
...DID YOU...?
IS IT?

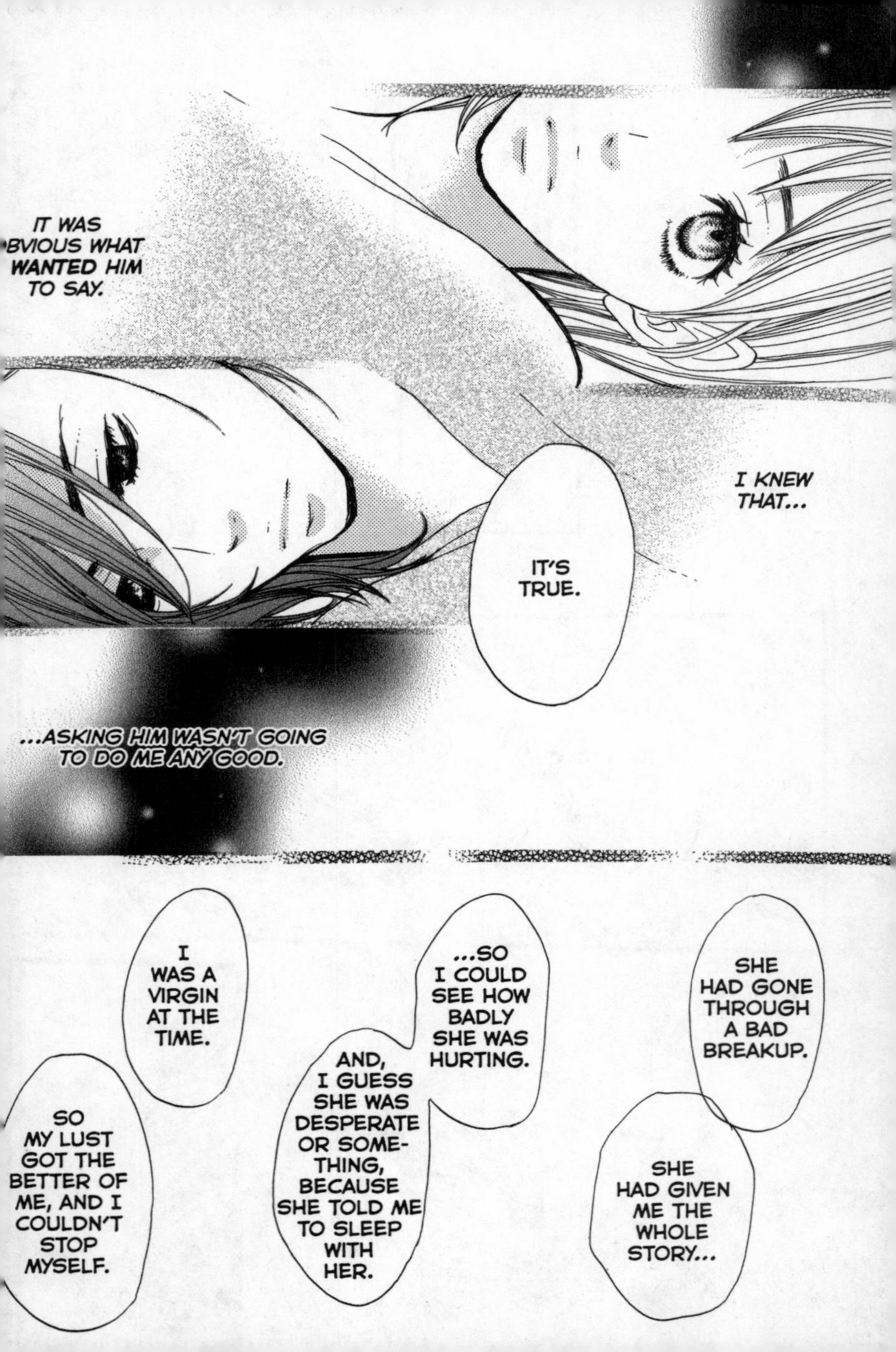
IT WAS BVIOUS WHAT WANTED HIM TO SAY.
I KNEW THAT...
IT'S TRUE.
...ASKING HIM WASN'T GOING TO DO ME ANY GOOD.
SHE HAD GONE THROUGH A BAD BREAKUP.
SHE HAD GIVEN ME THE WHOLE STORY...
...SO I COULD SEE HOW BADLY SHE WAS HURTING.
AND, I GUESS SHE WAS DESPERATE OR SOME-THING, BECAUSE SHE TOLD ME TO SLEEP WITH HER.
I WAS A VIRGIN AT THE TIME.
SO MY LUST GOT THE BETTER OF ME, AND I COULDN'T STOP MYSELF.

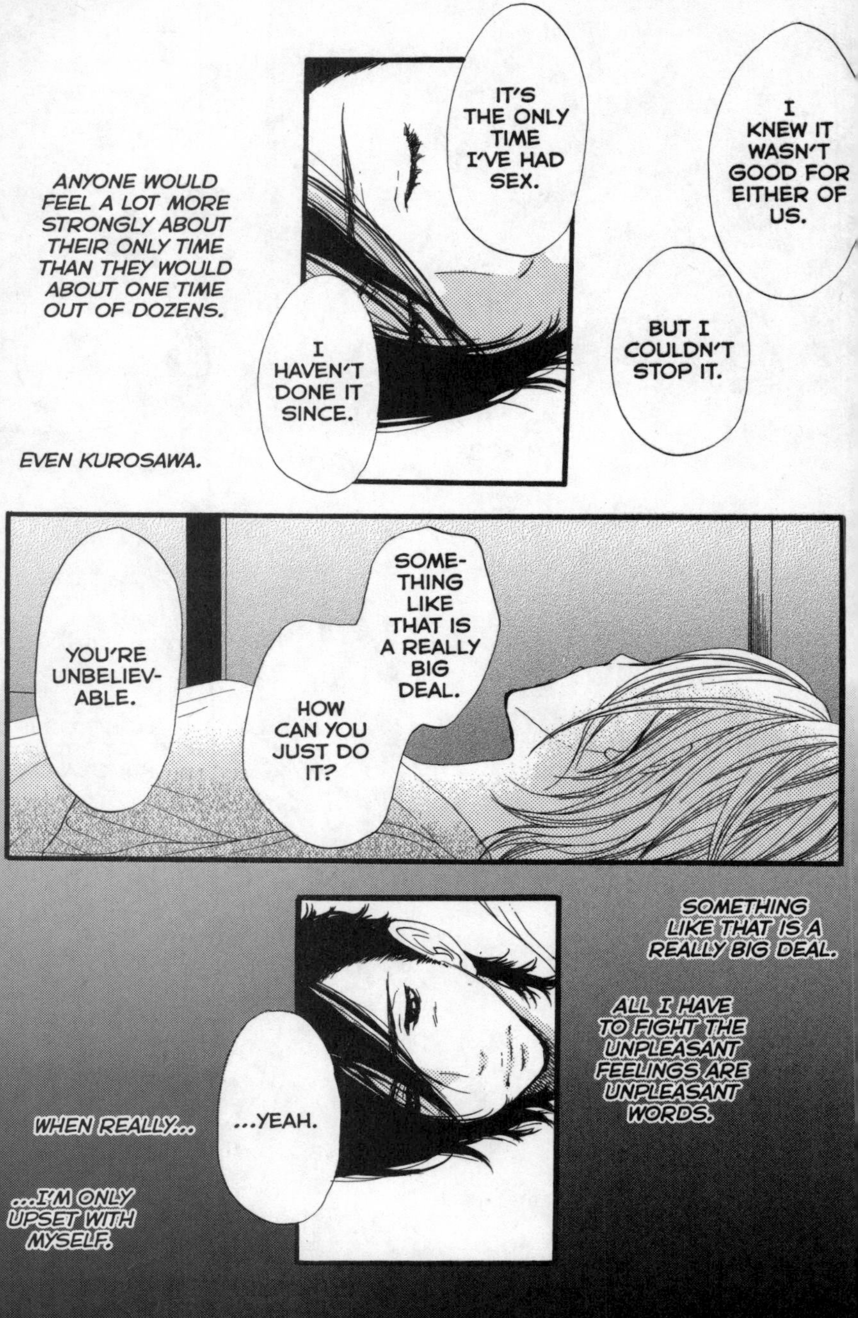
I KNEW IT WASN'T GOOD FOR EITHER OF US.
BUT I COULDN'T STOP IT.
IT'S THE ONLY TIME I'VE HAD SEX.
I HAVEN'T DONE IT SINCE.
ANYONE WOULD FEEL A LOT MORE STRONGLY ABOUT THEIR ONLY TIME THAN THEY WOULD ABOUT ONE TIME OUT OF DOZENS.
EVEN KUROSAWA.
SOME-THING LIKE THAT IS A REALLY BIG DEAL.
HOW CAN YOU JUST DO IT?
YOU'RE UNBELIEV-ABLE.
SOMETHING LIKE THAT IS A REALLY BIG DEAL.
ALL I HAVE TO FIGHT THE UNPLEASANT FEELINGS ARE UNPLEASANT WORDS.
...YEAH.
WHEN REALLY...
...I'M ONLY UPSET WITH MYSELF.

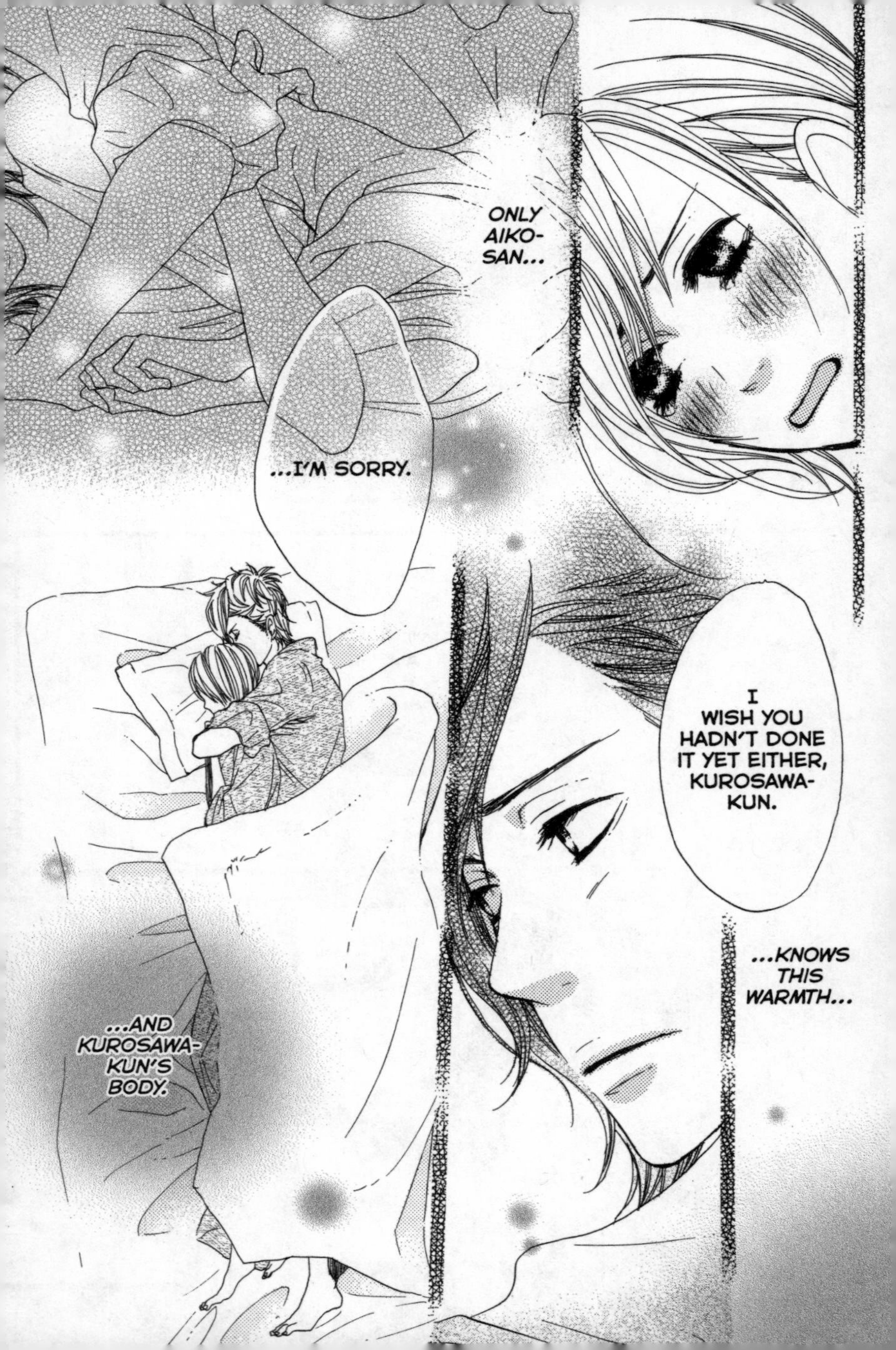
ONLY AIKO-SAN...
...I'M SORRY.
I WISH YOU HADN'T DONE IT YET EITHER, KUROSAWA-KUN.
...KNOWS THIS WARMTH...
...AND KUROSAWA-KUN'S BODY.

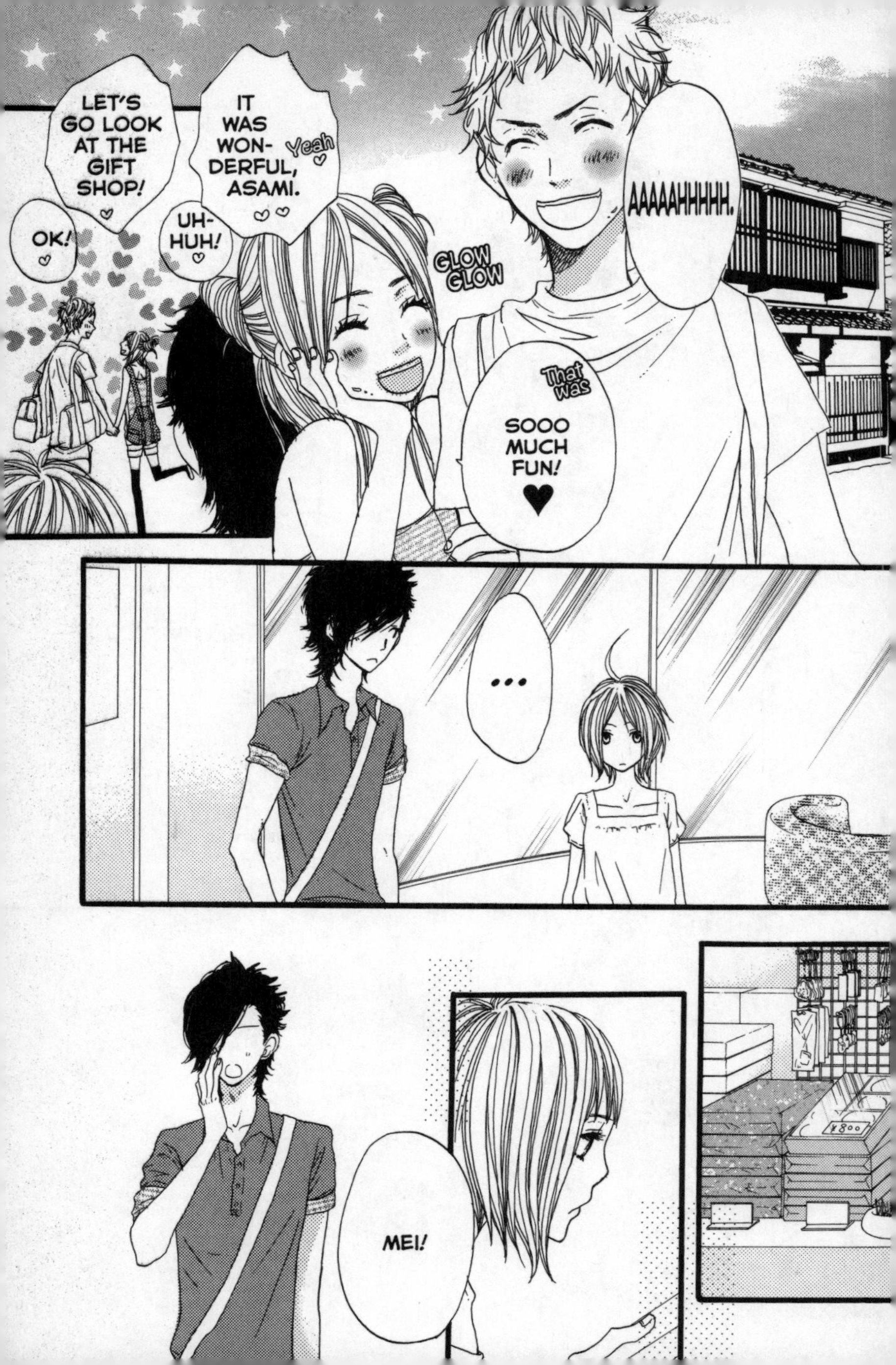
AAAAAHHHHH.
That was SOOO MUCH FUN! ♥
GLOW GLOW
IT WAS WONDERFUL, ASAMI.
Yeah
UH-HUH!
LET'S GO LOOK AT THE GIFT SHOP!
OK!
...
MEI!

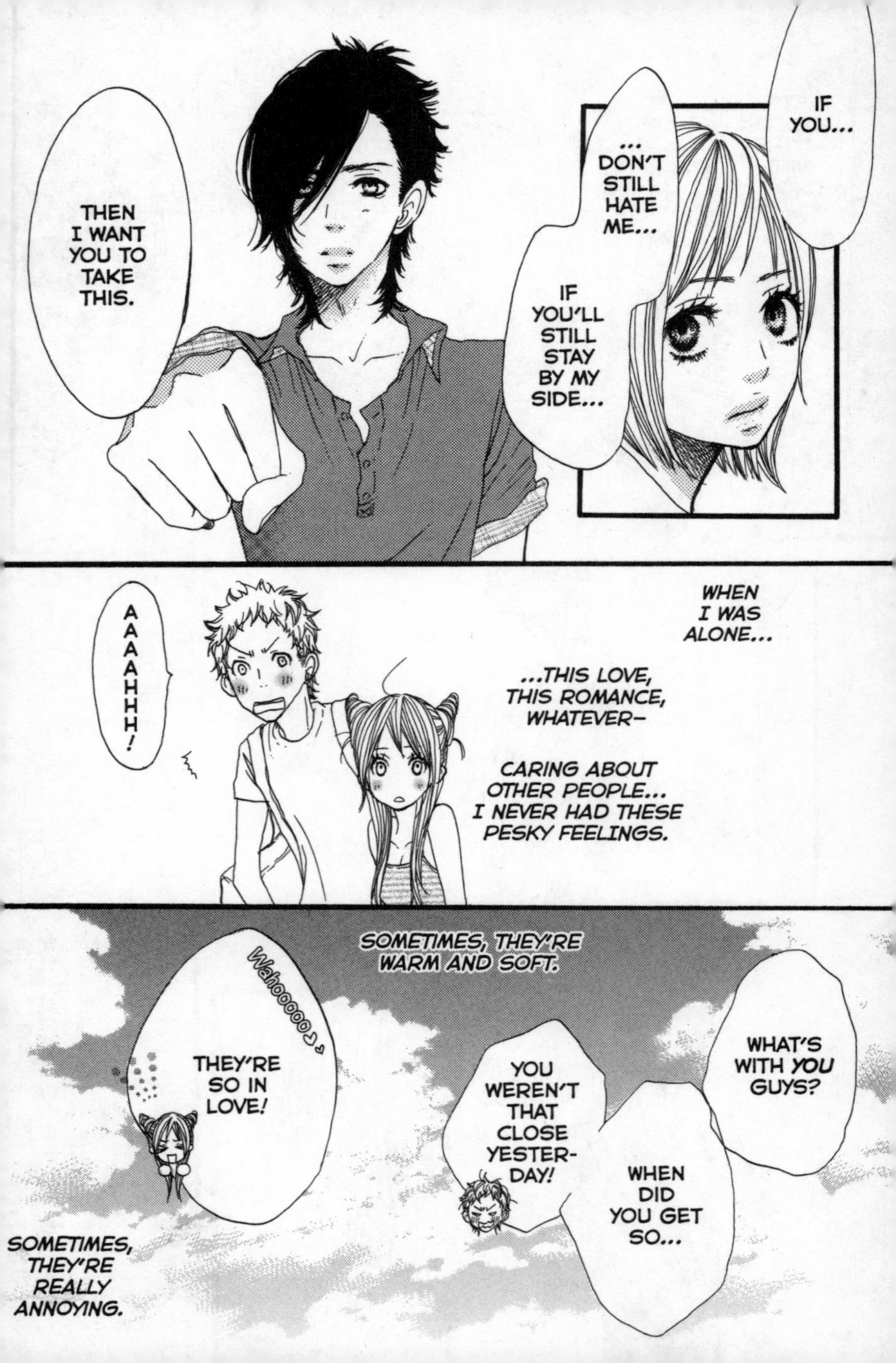

IF YOU...
...DON'T STILL HATE ME...
IF YOU'LL STILL STAY BY MY SIDE...
THEN I WANT YOU TO TAKE THIS.
WHEN I WAS ALONE...
...THIS LOVE, THIS ROMANCE, WHATEVER–
CARING ABOUT OTHER PEOPLE... I NEVER HAD THESE PESKY FEELINGS.
AAAAHHH!
SOMETIMES, THEY'RE WARM AND SOFT.
WHAT'S WITH *YOU* GUYS?
WHEN DID YOU GET SO...
YOU WEREN'T THAT CLOSE YESTER-DAY!
Wahooooo♪
THEY'RE SO IN LOVE!
SOMETIMES, THEY'RE REALLY ANNOYING.

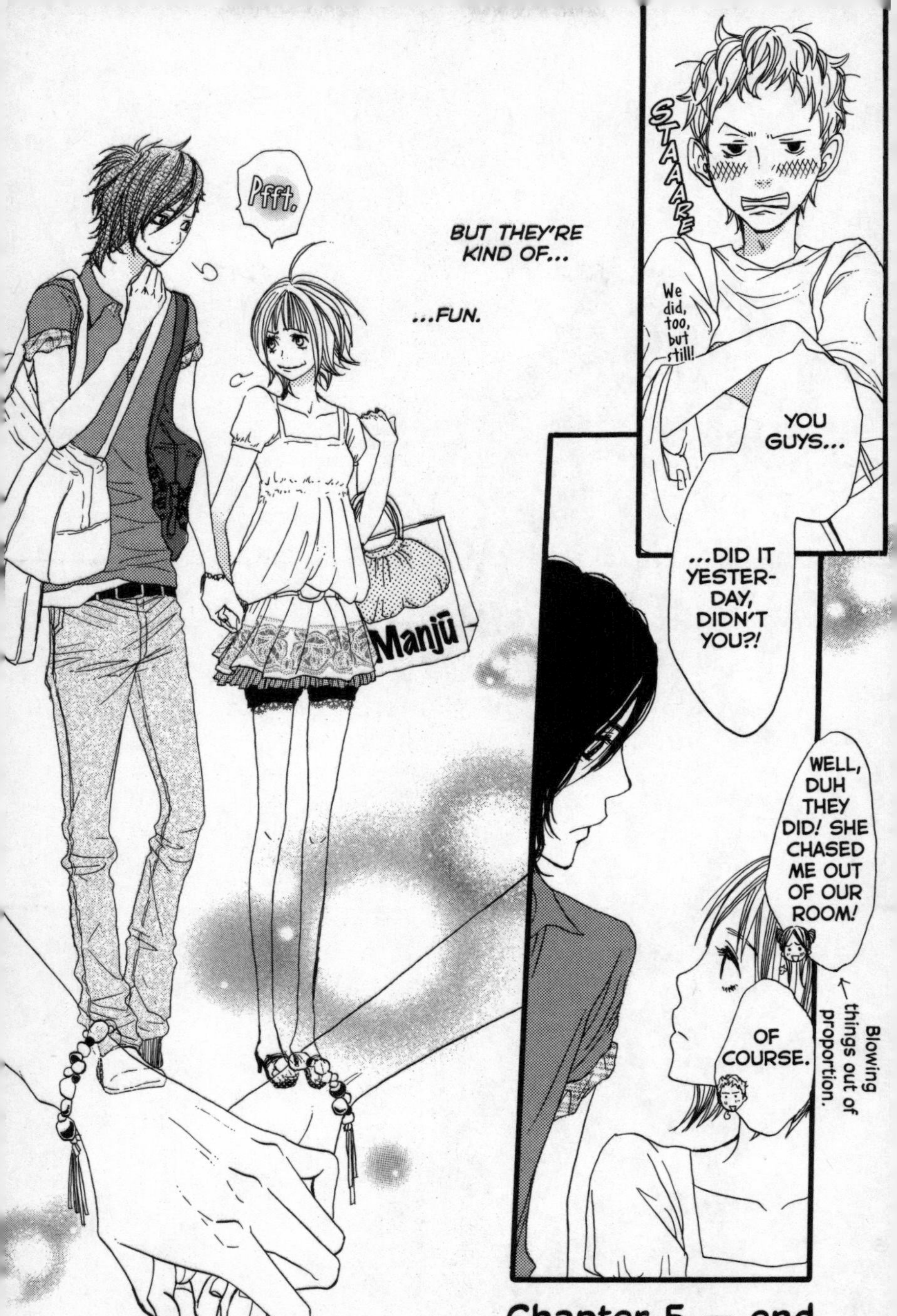
STAAARE
We did, too, but still!
YOU GUYS...
...DID IT YESTERDAY, DIDN'T YOU?!
WELL, DUH THEY DID! SHE CHASED ME OUT OF OUR ROOM!
Blowing things out of proportion.
OF COURSE.
Pfft.
BUT THEY'RE KIND OF...
...FUN.
Manjū

Chapter 5 — end

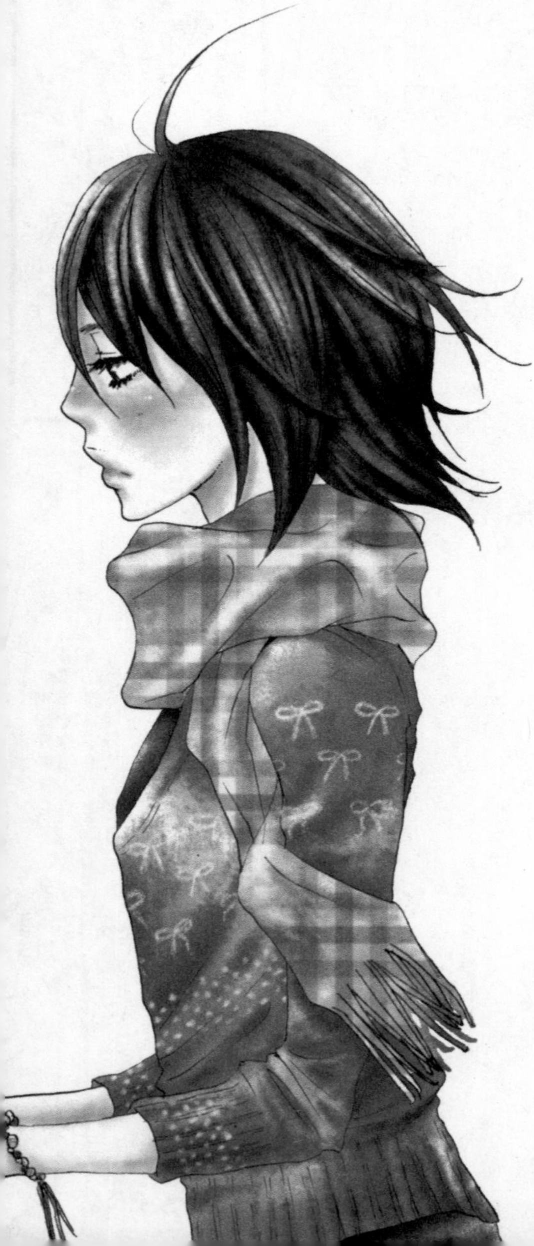

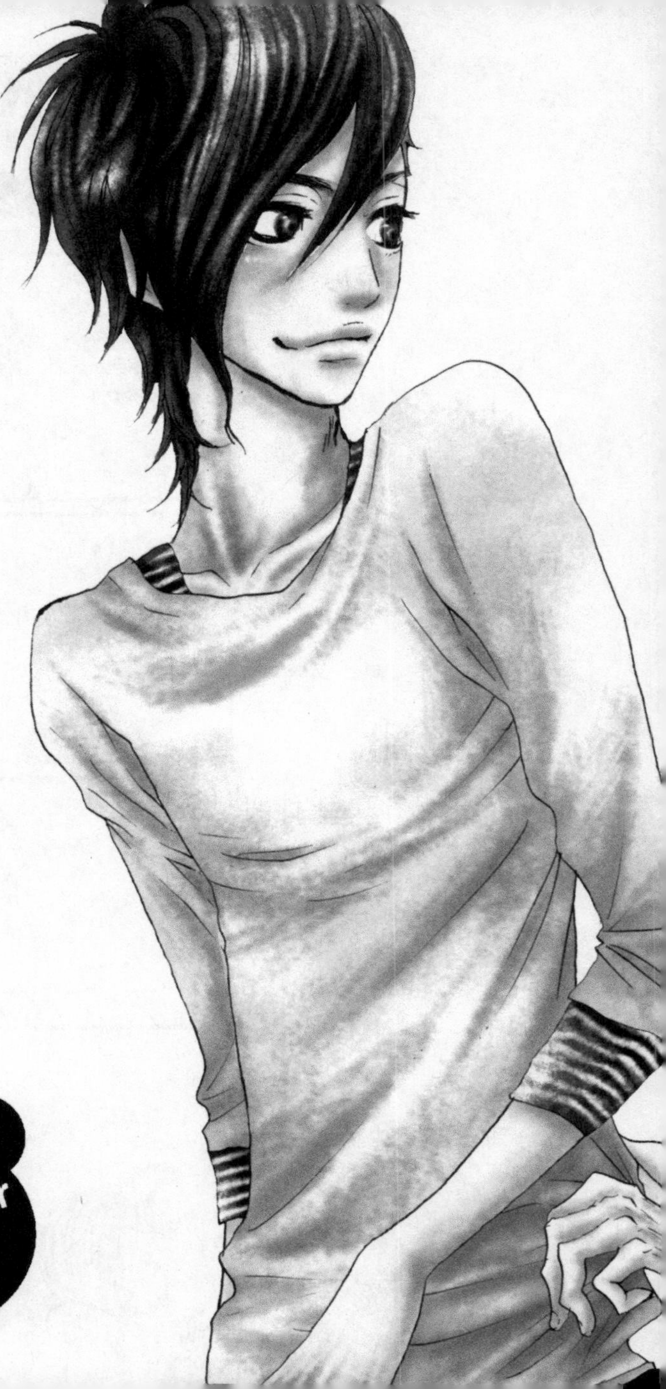

Chapter 6

What Mei Loves

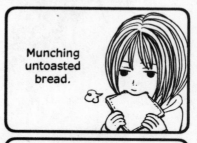

Munching untoasted bread.

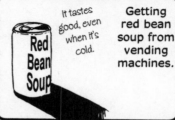

Getting red bean soup from vending machines.
It tastes good, even when it's cold.
Red Bean Soup

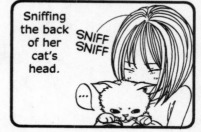

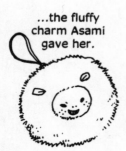

Sniffing the back of her cat's head.
SNIFF SNIFF
...

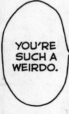

And...

...the fluffy charm Asami gave her.

I LIKE EATING YAKINIKU SAUCE ON WHITE RICE, TOO.
STEAM STEAM
YOU'RE SUCH A WEIRDO.

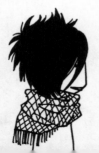

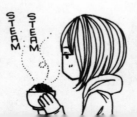

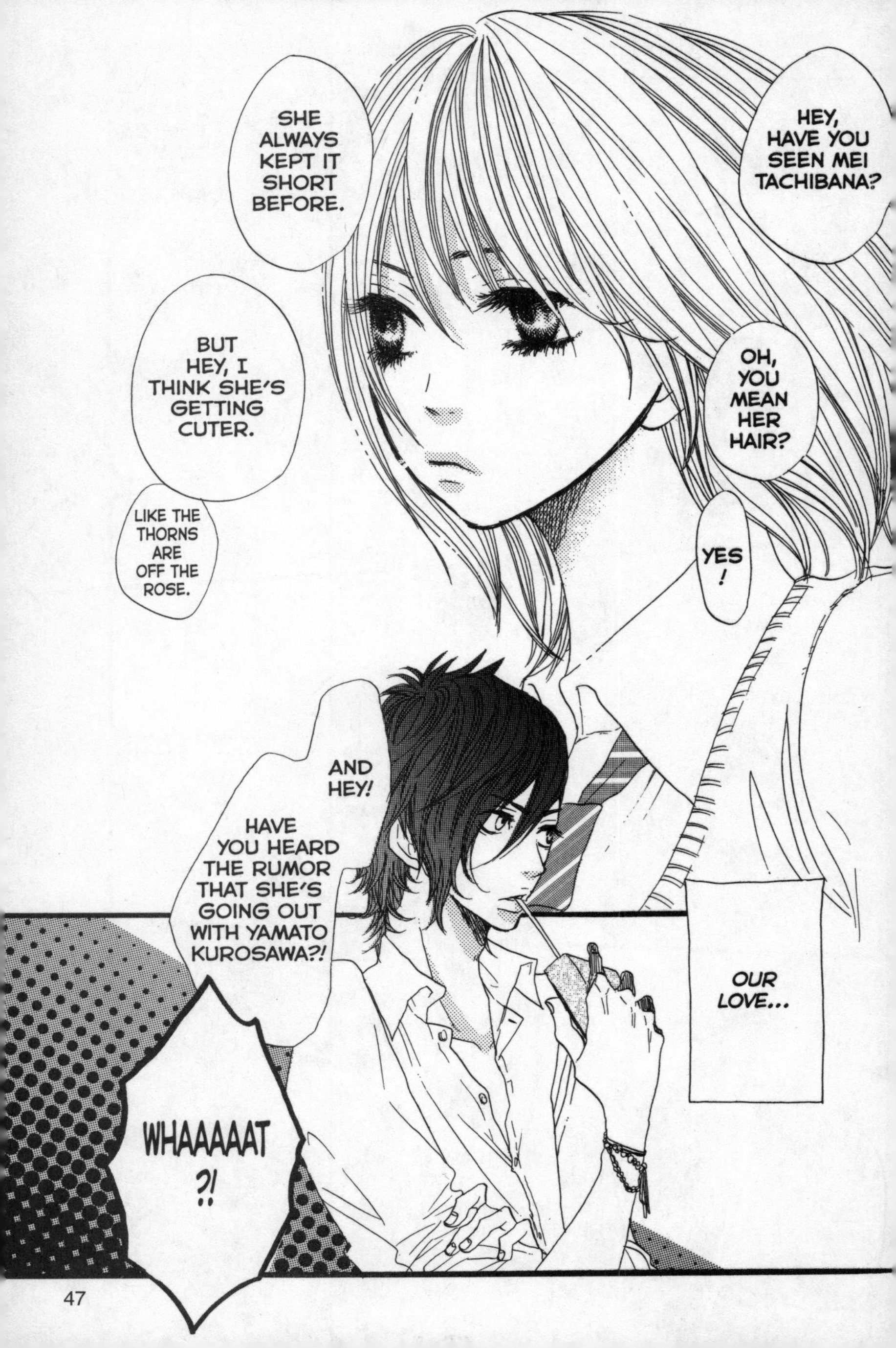
HEY, HAVE YOU SEEN MEI TACHIBANA?
OH, YOU MEAN HER HAIR?
YES!
SHE ALWAYS KEPT IT SHORT BEFORE.
BUT HEY, I THINK SHE'S GETTING CUTER.
LIKE THE THORNS ARE OFF THE ROSE.
AND HEY!
HAVE YOU HEARD THE RUMOR THAT SHE'S GOING OUT WITH YAMATO KUROSAWA?!
OUR LOVE...
WHAAAAAT ?!

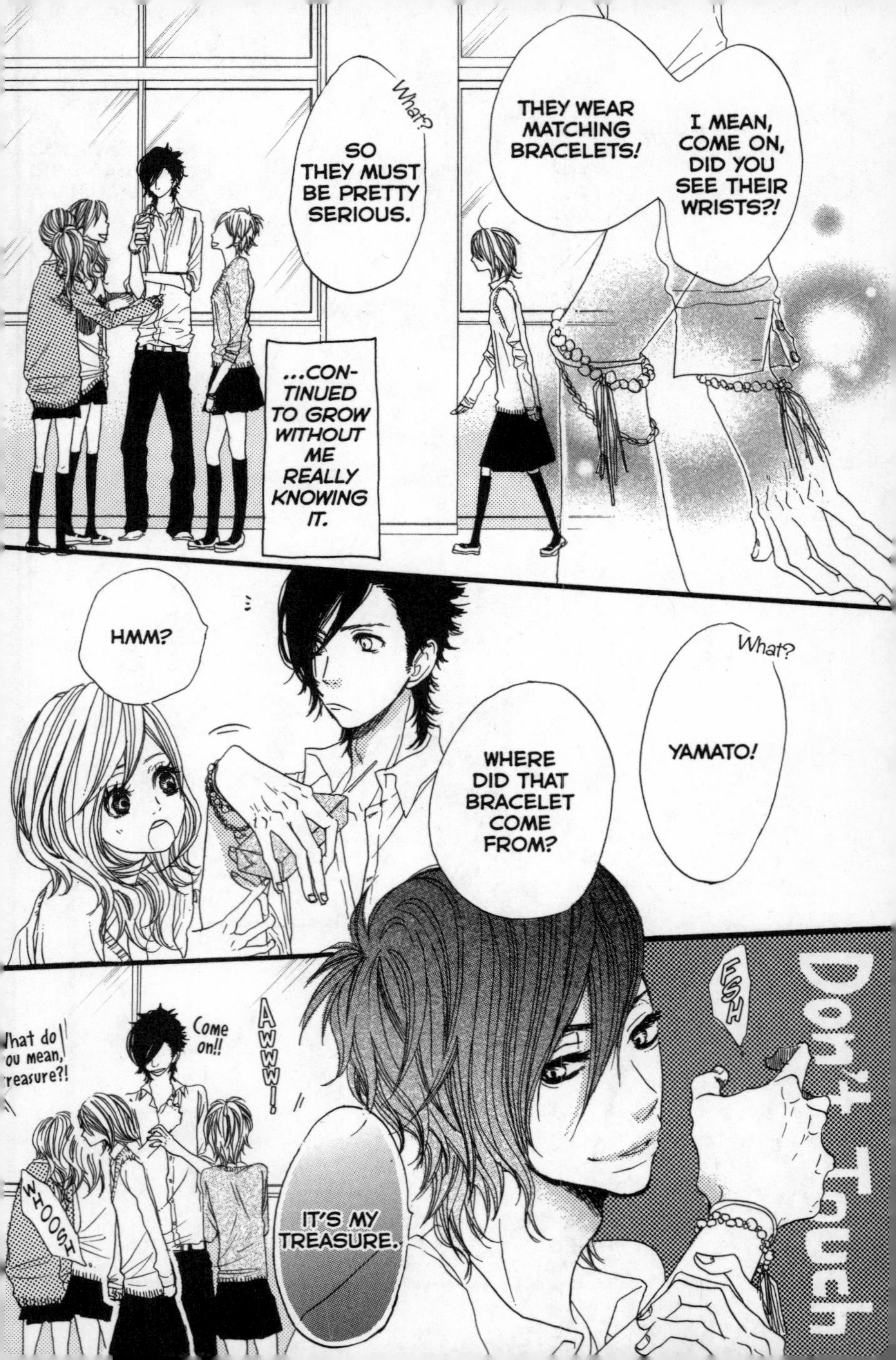
I MEAN, COME ON, DID YOU SEE THEIR WRISTS?!
THEY WEAR MATCHING BRACELETS!
What?
SO THEY MUST BE PRETTY SERIOUS.
...CON-TINUED TO GROW WITHOUT ME REALLY KNOWING IT.
What?
YAMATO!
WHERE DID THAT BRACELET COME FROM?
HMM?
FSH
Don't Touch
IT'S MY TREASURE.
AWWW!
Come on!!
hat do ou mean, reasure?!
WHOOSH

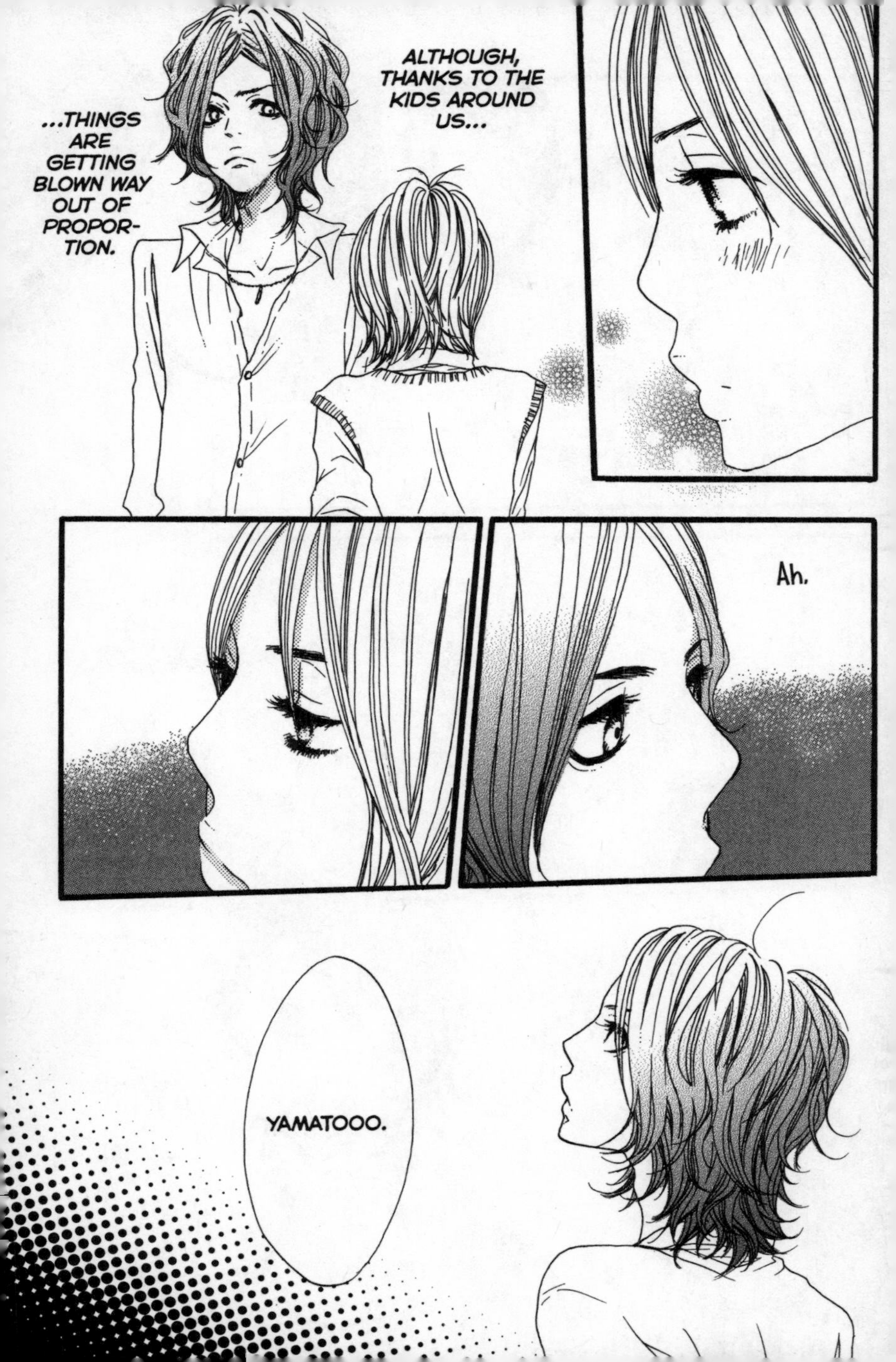

ALTHOUGH, THANKS TO THE KIDS AROUND US...
...THINGS ARE GETTING BLOWN WAY OUT OF PROPORTION.
Ah.
YAMATOOO.

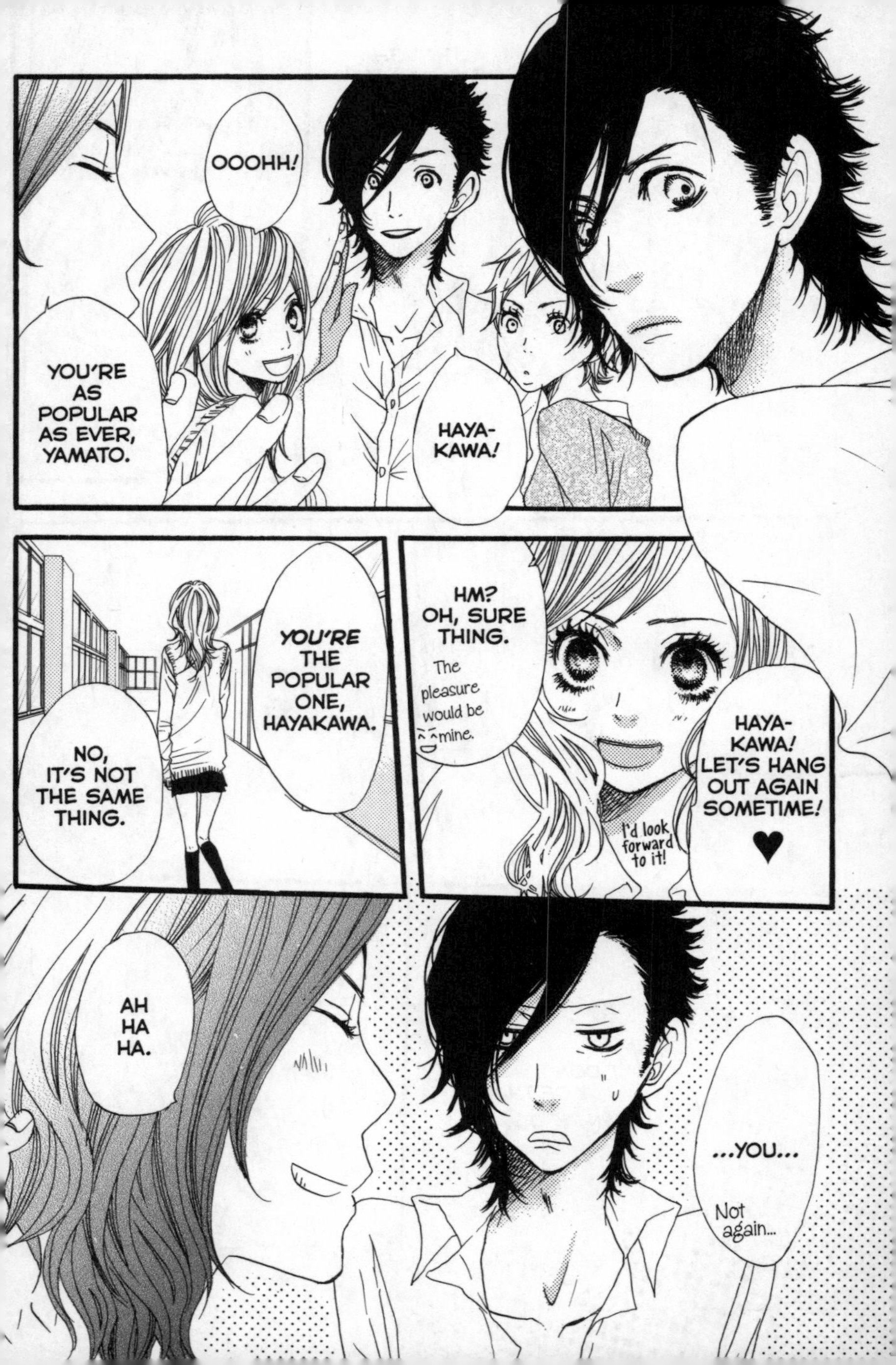
HAYA-KAWA!
OOOHH!
YOU'RE AS POPULAR AS EVER, YAMATO.
HAYA-KAWA! LET'S HANG OUT AGAIN SOMETIME! ♥
I'd look forward to it!
HM? OH, SURE THING.
The pleasure would be mine.
YOU'RE THE POPULAR ONE, HAYAKAWA.
NO, IT'S NOT THE SAME THING.
...YOU...
Not again...
AH HA HA.

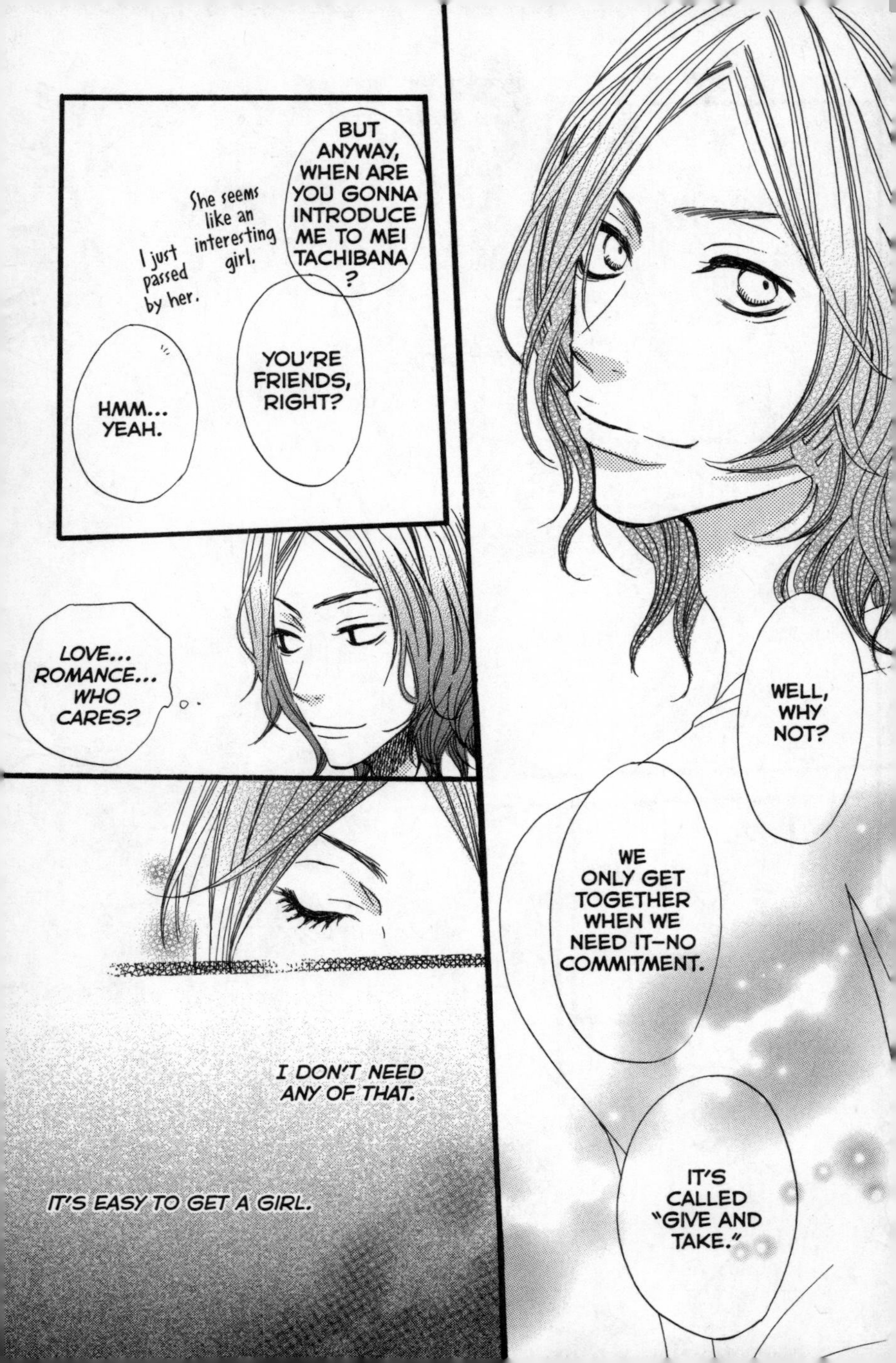
WELL, WHY NOT?
WE ONLY GET TOGETHER WHEN WE NEED IT—NO COMMITMENT.
IT'S CALLED "GIVE AND TAKE."
BUT ANYWAY, WHEN ARE YOU GONNA INTRODUCE ME TO MEI TACHIBANA?
She seems like an interesting girl.
I just passed by her.
YOU'RE FRIENDS, RIGHT?
HMM... YEAH.
LOVE... ROMANCE... WHO CARES?
I DON'T NEED ANY OF THAT.
IT'S EASY TO GET A GIRL.

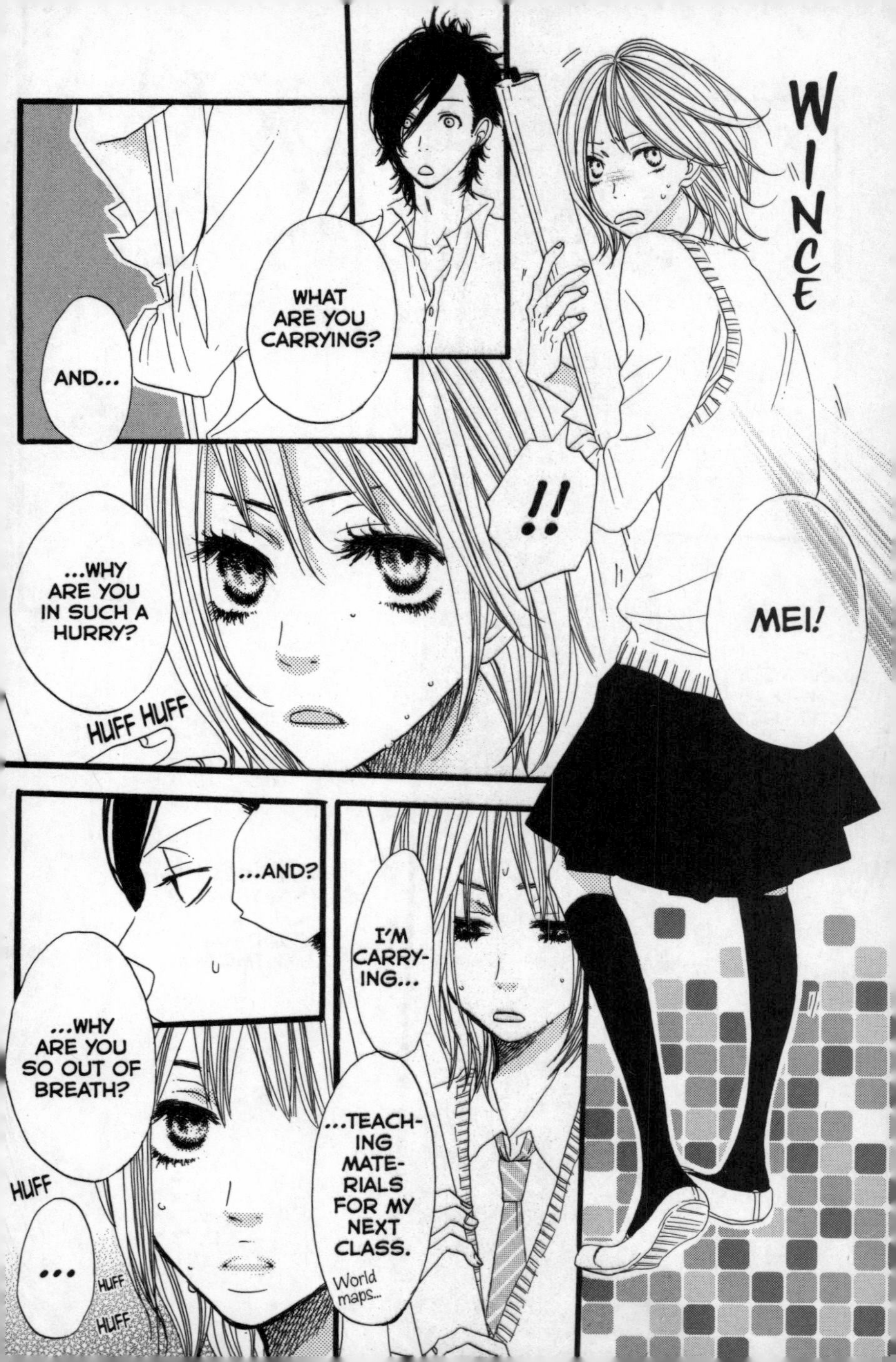
WINCE
MEI!
!!
WHAT ARE YOU CARRYING?
AND...
...WHY ARE YOU IN SUCH A HURRY?
HUFF HUFF
I'M CARRYING...
...TEACHING MATERIALS FOR MY NEXT CLASS.
World maps...
...AND?
...WHY ARE YOU SO OUT OF BREATH?
HUFF
...
HUFF
HUFF

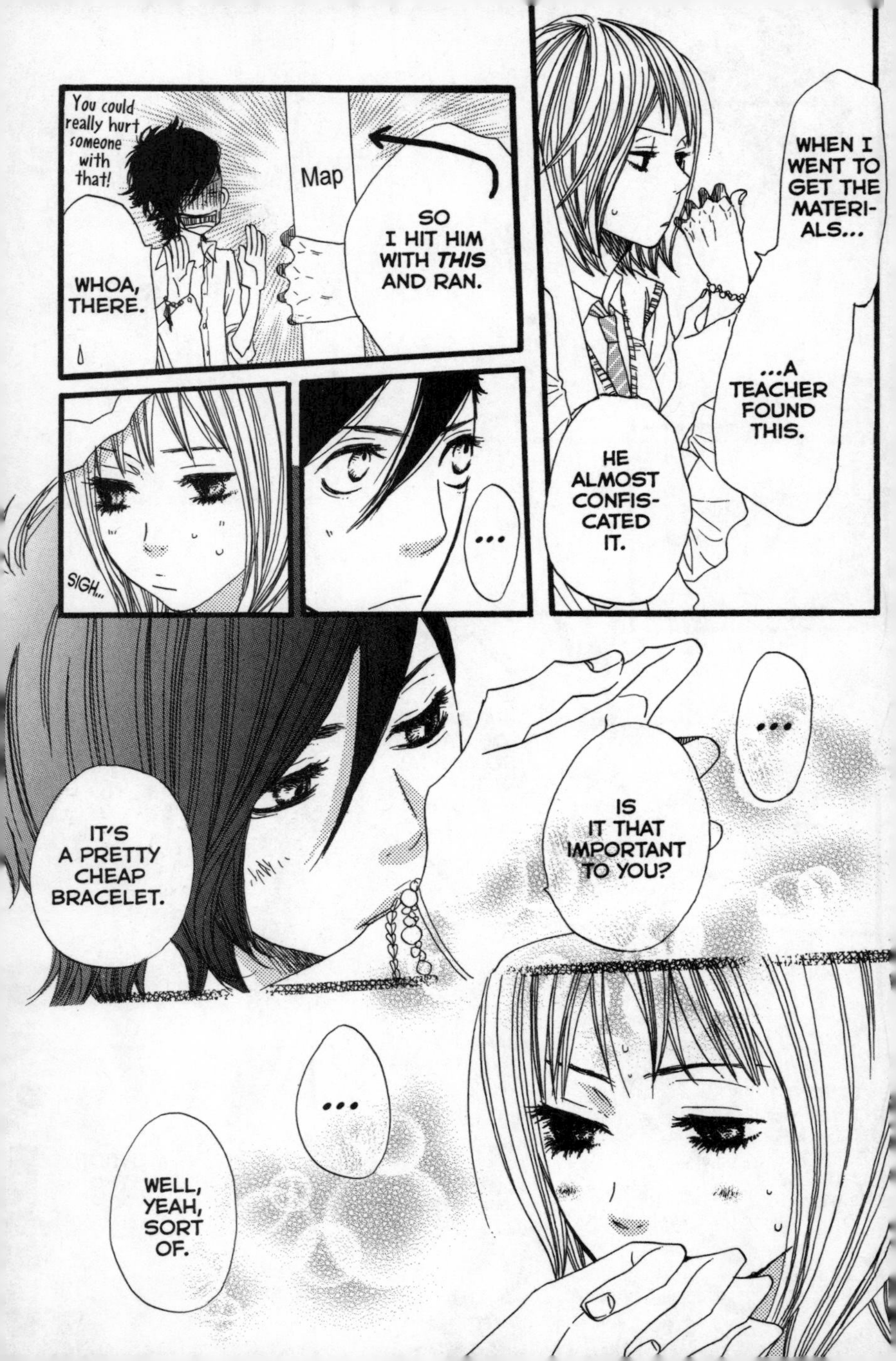
WHEN I WENT TO GET THE MATERIALS...
...A TEACHER FOUND THIS.
HE ALMOST CONFISCATED IT.
SO I HIT HIM WITH *THIS* AND RAN.
Map
You could really hurt someone with that!
WHOA, THERE.
...
SIGH...
...
IS IT THAT IMPORTANT TO YOU?
IT'S A PRETTY CHEAP BRACELET.
...
WELL, YEAH, SORT OF.

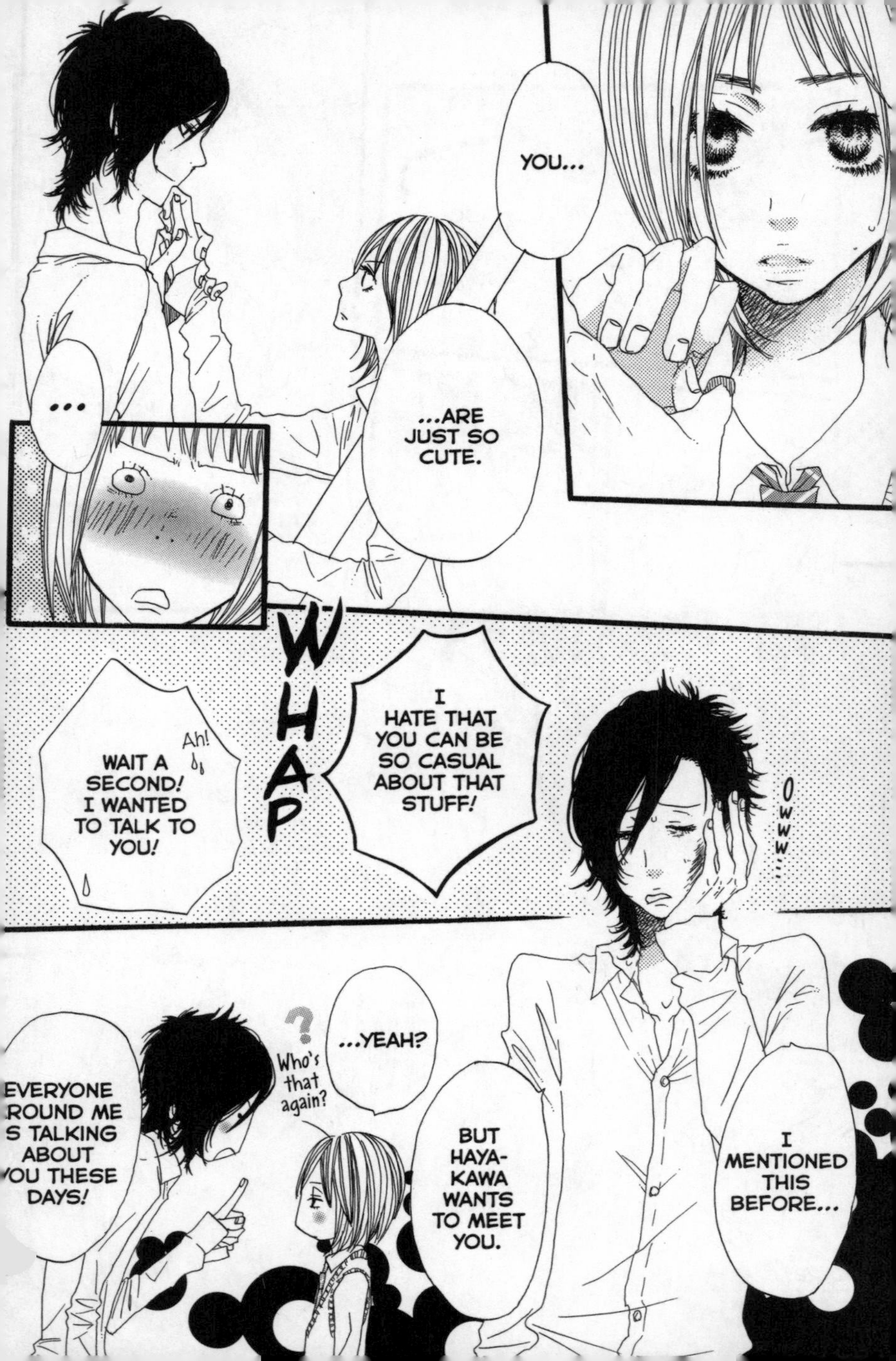
YOU...
...ARE JUST SO CUTE.
...
OWWW...
I HATE THAT YOU CAN BE SO CASUAL ABOUT THAT STUFF!
WHAP
Ah!
WAIT A SECOND! I WANTED TO TALK TO YOU!
I MENTIONED THIS BEFORE...
BUT HAYA-KAWA WANTS TO MEET YOU.
...YEAH?
?
Who's that again?
EVERYONE ROUND ME S TALKING ABOUT OU THESE DAYS!

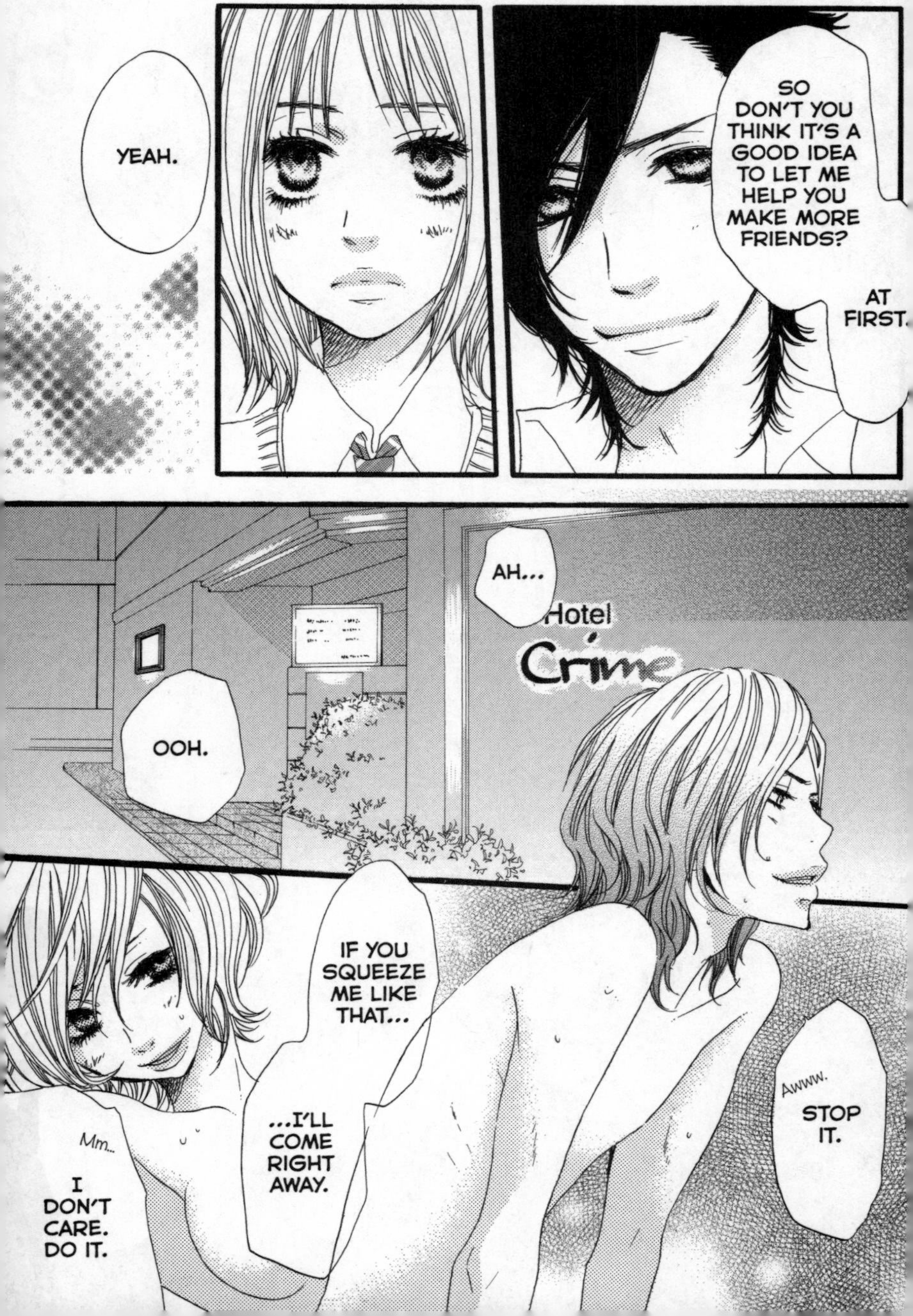
SO DON'T YOU THINK IT'S A GOOD IDEA TO LET ME HELP YOU MAKE MORE FRIENDS?
AT FIRST.
YEAH.
AH...
Hotel
Crime
OOH.
Awww.
STOP IT.
IF YOU SQUEEZE ME LIKE THAT...
...I'LL COME RIGHT AWAY.
Mm...
I DON'T CARE. DO IT.

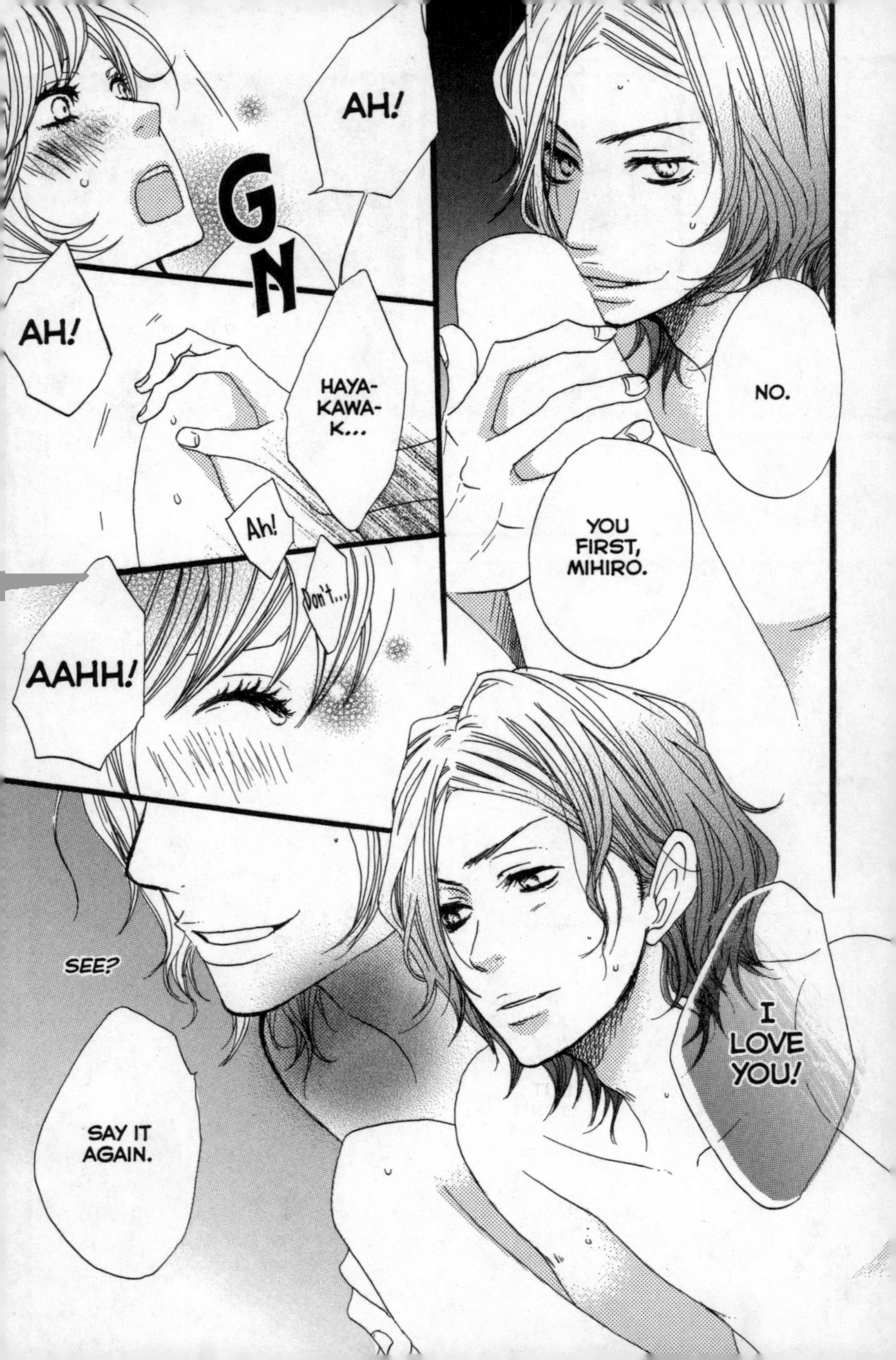
NO.
YOU FIRST, MIHIRO.
AH!
GN
AH!
HAYA-KAWAK...
Ah!
Don't...
AAHH!
I LOVE YOU!
SEE?
SAY IT AGAIN.

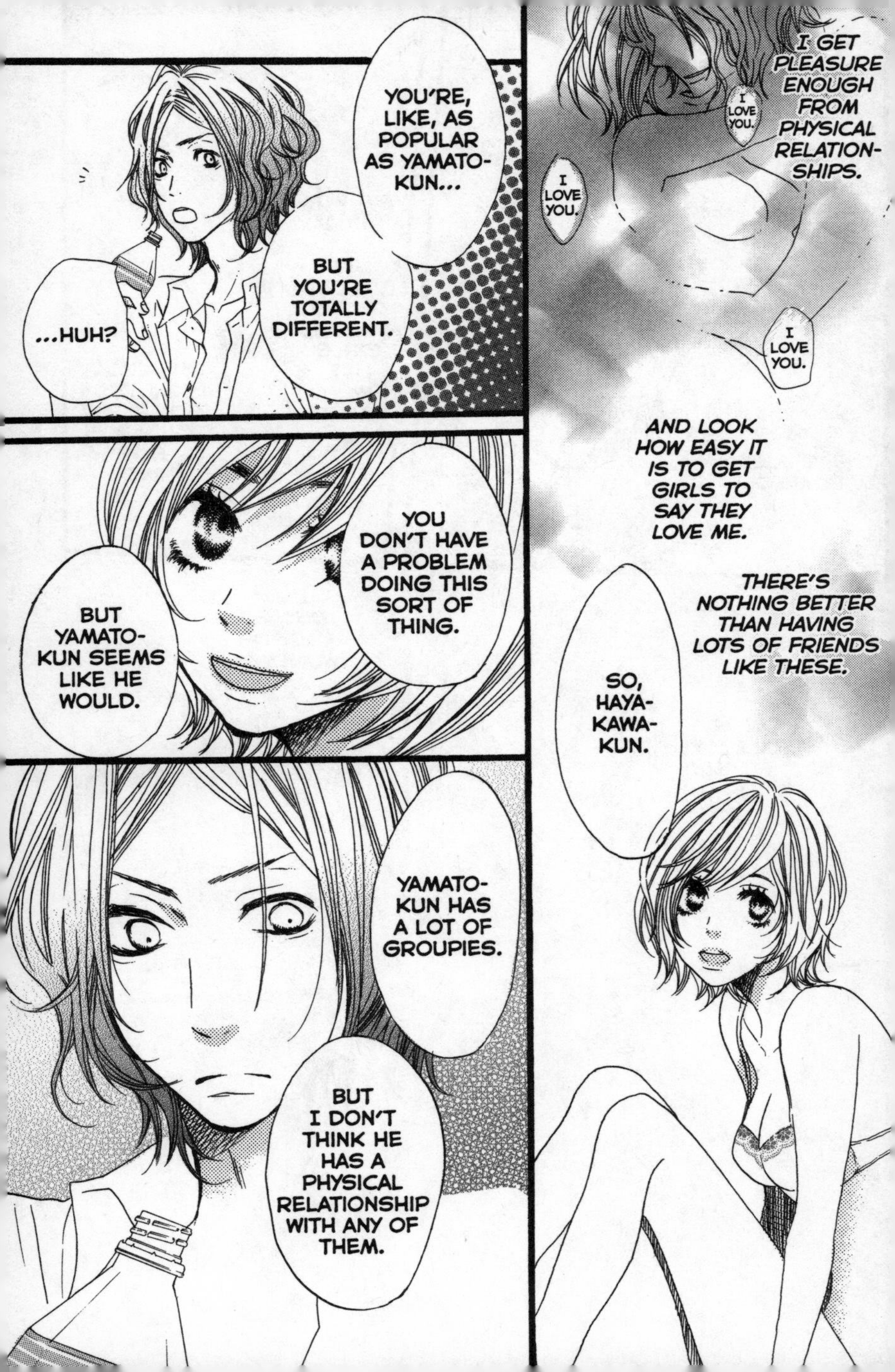

I GET PLEASURE ENOUGH FROM PHYSICAL RELATION-SHIPS.
I LOVE YOU.
I LOVE YOU.
I LOVE YOU.
AND LOOK HOW EASY IT IS TO GET GIRLS TO SAY THEY LOVE ME.
THERE'S NOTHING BETTER THAN HAVING LOTS OF FRIENDS LIKE THESE.
SO, HAYA-KAWA-KUN.
YOU'RE, LIKE, AS POPULAR AS YAMATO-KUN...
BUT YOU'RE TOTALLY DIFFERENT.
...HUH?
YOU DON'T HAVE A PROBLEM DOING THIS SORT OF THING.
BUT YAMATO-KUN SEEMS LIKE HE WOULD.
YAMATO-KUN HAS A LOT OF GROUPIES.
BUT I DON'T THINK HE HAS A PHYSICAL RELATIONSHIP WITH ANY OF THEM.

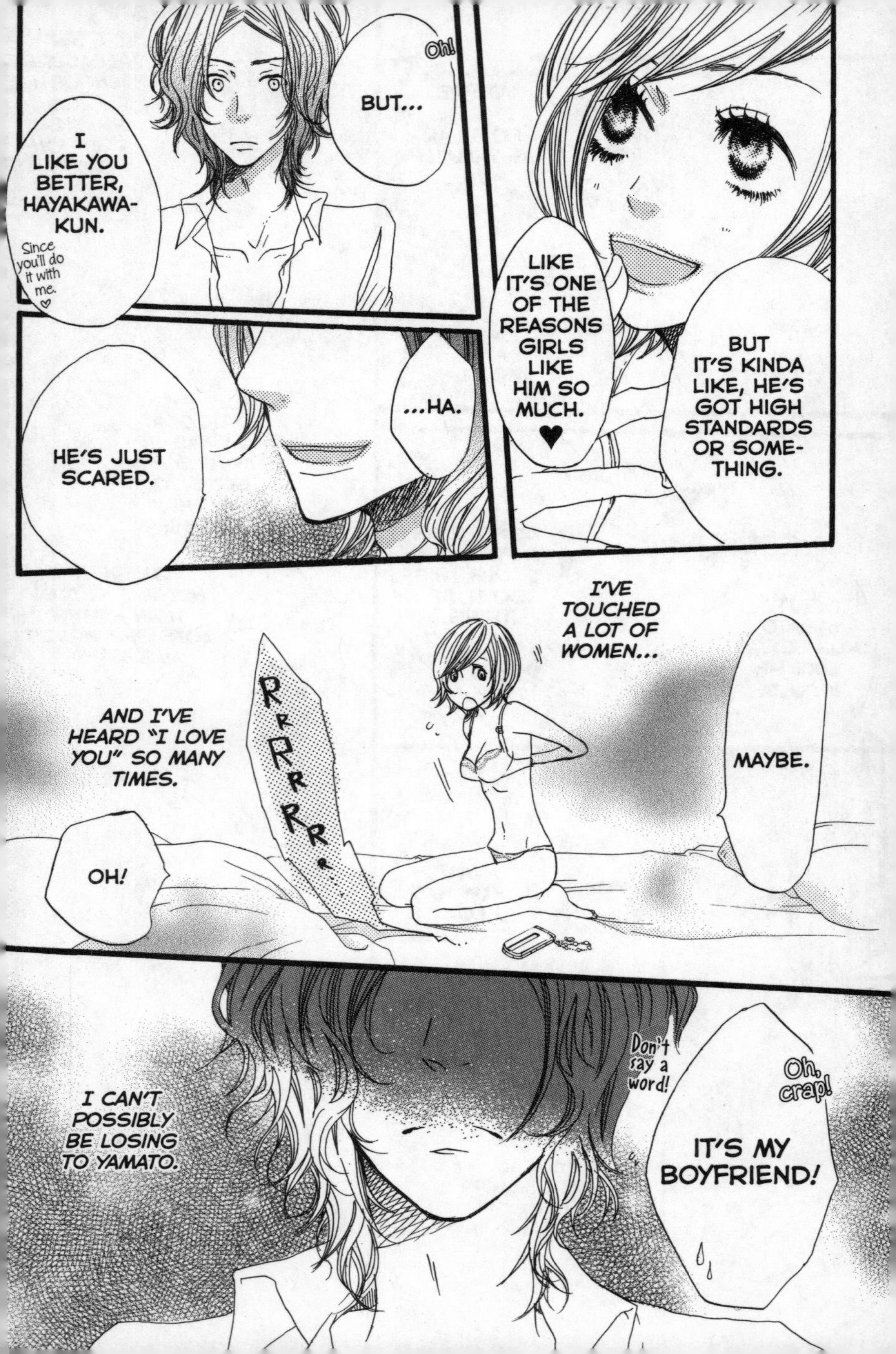
BUT IT'S KINDA LIKE, HE'S GOT HIGH STANDARDS OR SOME-THING.
LIKE IT'S ONE OF THE REASONS GIRLS LIKE HIM SO MUCH. ♥
Oh!
BUT...
I LIKE YOU BETTER, HAYAKAWA-KUN.
Since you'll do it with me. ♡
...HA.
HE'S JUST SCARED.
MAYBE.
I'VE TOUCHED A LOT OF WOMEN...
AND I'VE HEARD "I LOVE YOU" SO MANY TIMES.
RRRRRRR
OH!
Oh, crap!
IT'S MY BOYFRIEND!
Don't say a word!
I CAN'T POSSIBLY BE LOSING TO YAMATO.

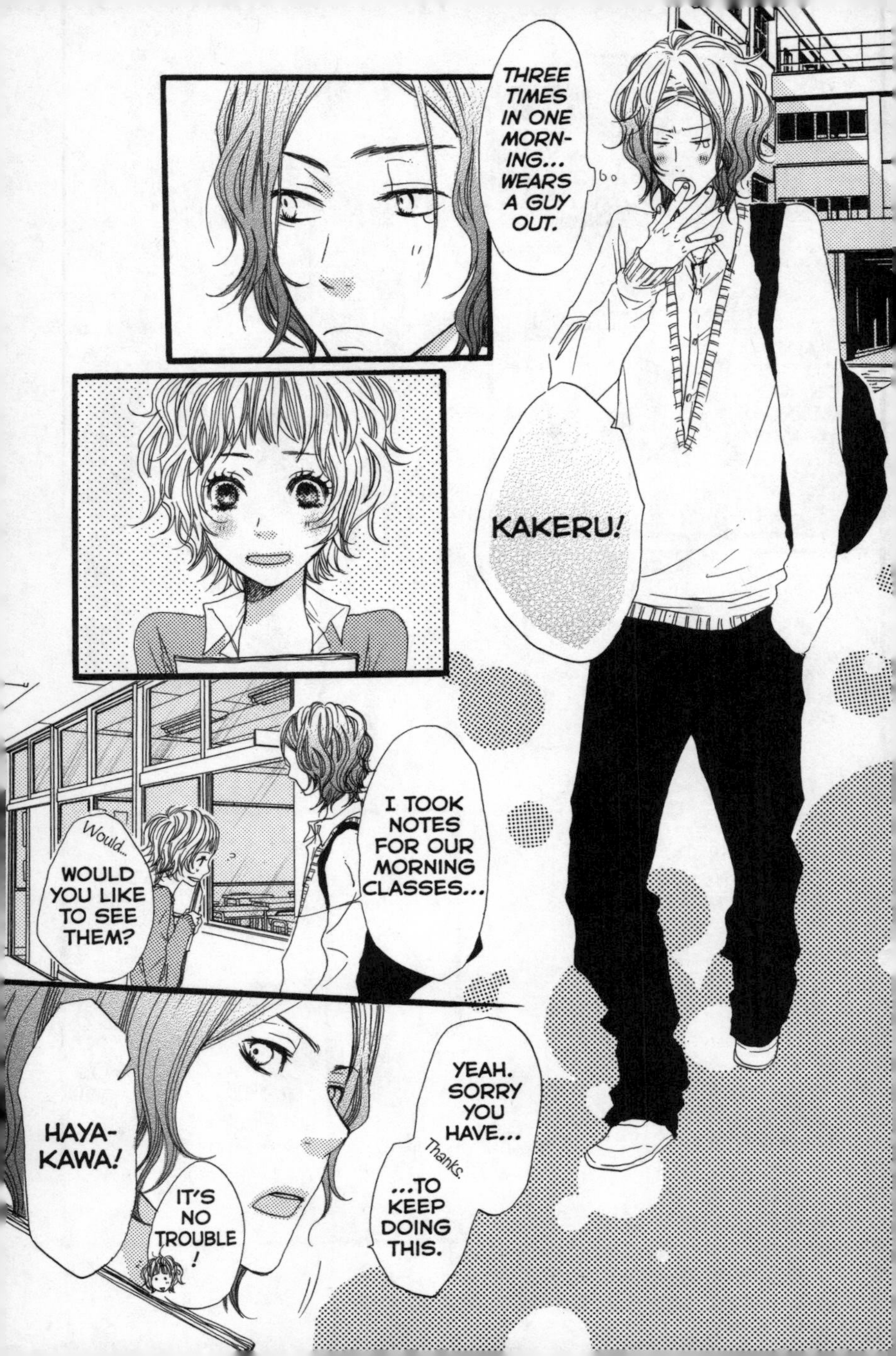
THREE TIMES IN ONE MORNING... WEARS A GUY OUT.
KAKERU!
I TOOK NOTES FOR OUR MORNING CLASSES...
Would...
WOULD YOU LIKE TO SEE THEM?
YEAH. SORRY YOU HAVE...
Thanks.
...TO KEEP DOING THIS.
HAYA-KAWA!
IT'S NO TROUBLE!

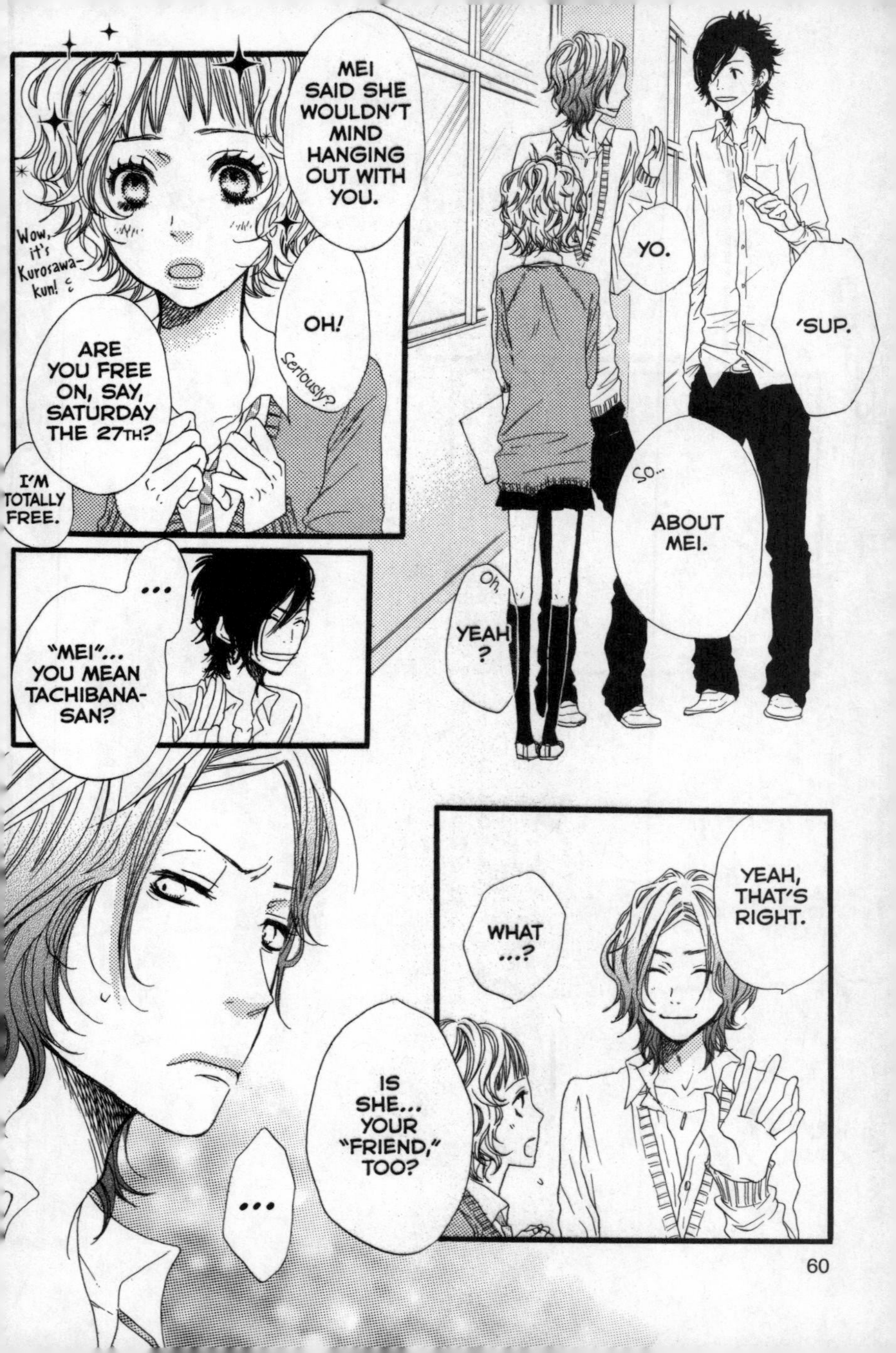
'SUP.
YO.
SO...
ABOUT MEI.
Oh,
YEAH?
MEI SAID SHE WOULDN'T MIND HANGING OUT WITH YOU.
OH!
Seriously?
Wow, it's Kurosawa-kun!
ARE YOU FREE ON, SAY, SATURDAY THE 27TH?
I'M TOTALLY FREE.
...
"MEI"... YOU MEAN TACHIBANA-SAN?
YEAH, THAT'S RIGHT.
WHAT...?
IS SHE... YOUR "FRIEND," TOO?
...

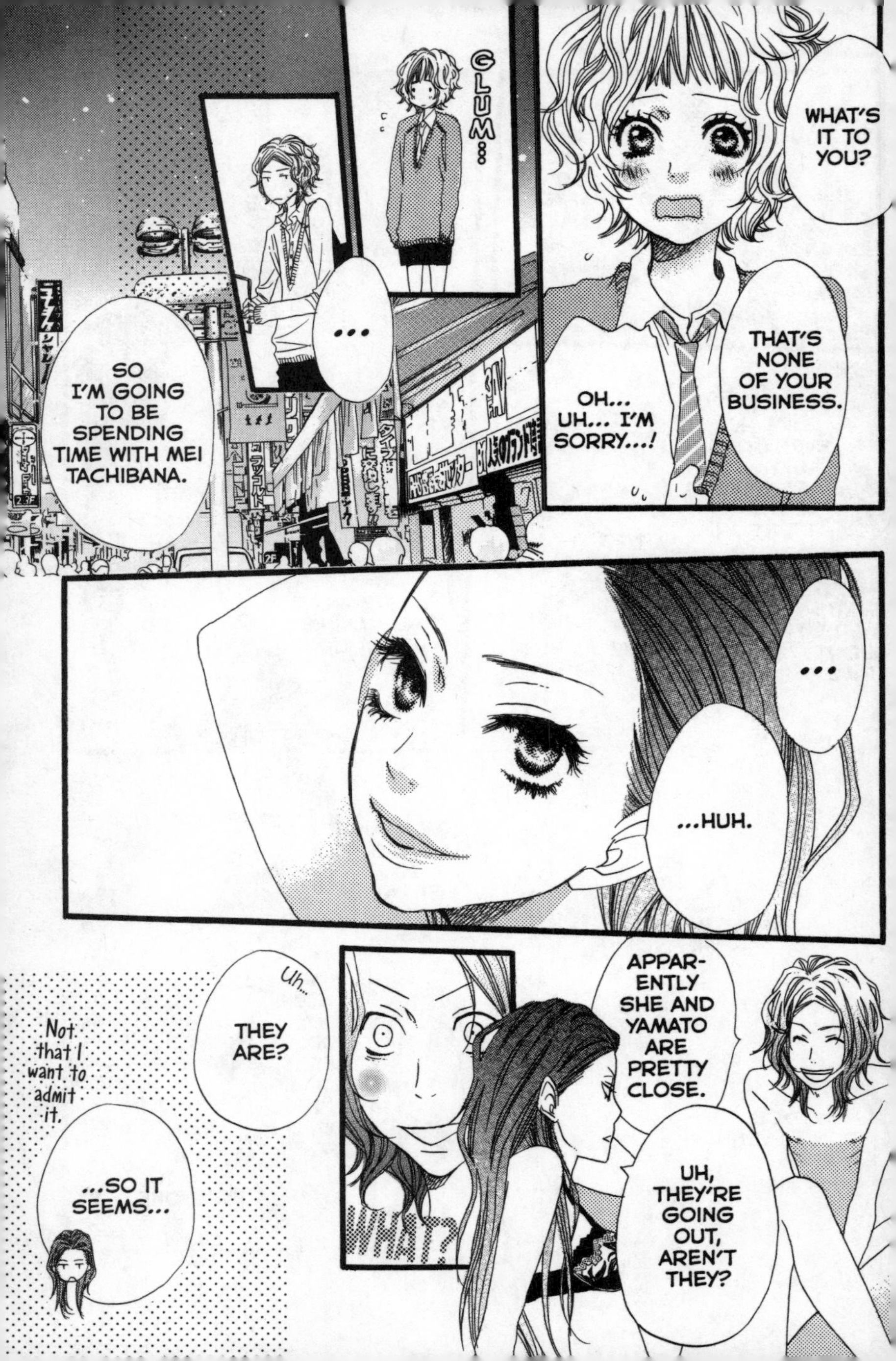
WHAT'S IT TO YOU?
THAT'S NONE OF YOUR BUSINESS.
OH... UH... I'M SORRY...!
GLUM...
...
SO I'M GOING TO BE SPENDING TIME WITH MEI TACHIBANA.
...
...HUH.
APPARENTLY SHE AND YAMATO ARE PRETTY CLOSE.
UH, THEY'RE GOING OUT, AREN'T THEY?
WHAT?
Uh...
THEY ARE?
Not that I want to admit it.
...SO IT SEEMS...

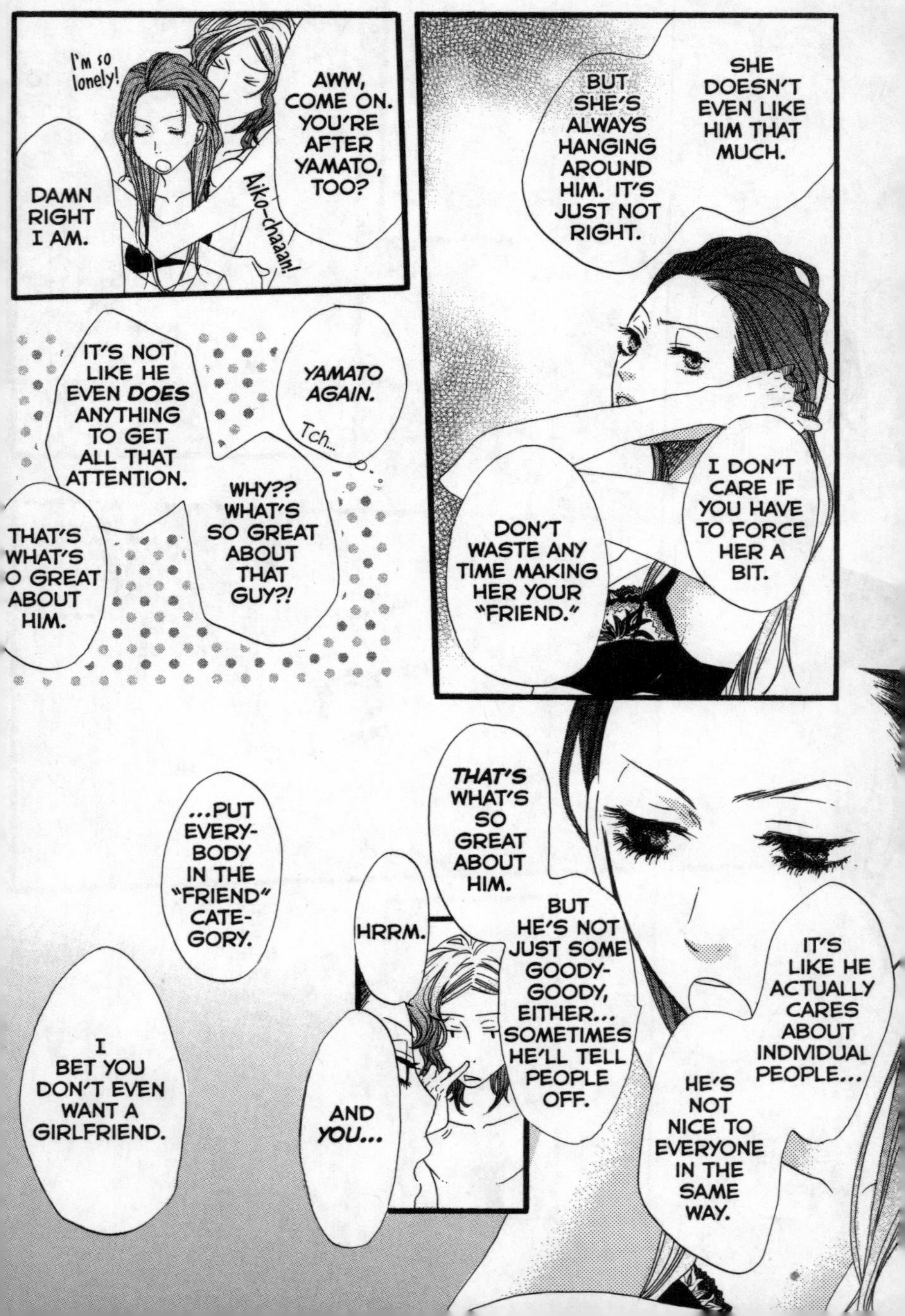
SHE DOESN'T EVEN LIKE HIM THAT MUCH.
BUT SHE'S ALWAYS HANGING AROUND HIM. IT'S JUST NOT RIGHT.
I DON'T CARE IF YOU HAVE TO FORCE HER A BIT.
DON'T WASTE ANY TIME MAKING HER YOUR "FRIEND."
I'm so lonely!
AWW, COME ON. YOU'RE AFTER YAMATO, TOO?
Aiko-chaaan!
DAMN RIGHT I AM.
YAMATO AGAIN.
Tch...
IT'S NOT LIKE HE EVEN DOES ANYTHING TO GET ALL THAT ATTENTION.
WHY?? WHAT'S SO GREAT ABOUT THAT GUY?!
THAT'S WHAT'S O GREAT ABOUT HIM.
THAT'S WHAT'S SO GREAT ABOUT HIM.
IT'S LIKE HE ACTUALLY CARES ABOUT INDIVIDUAL PEOPLE...
HE'S NOT NICE TO EVERYONE IN THE SAME WAY.
BUT HE'S NOT JUST SOME GOODY-GOODY, EITHER... SOMETIMES HE'LL TELL PEOPLE OFF.
HRRM.
AND YOU...
...PUT EVERYBODY IN THE "FRIEND" CATEGORY.
I BET YOU DON'T EVEN WANT A GIRLFRIEND.

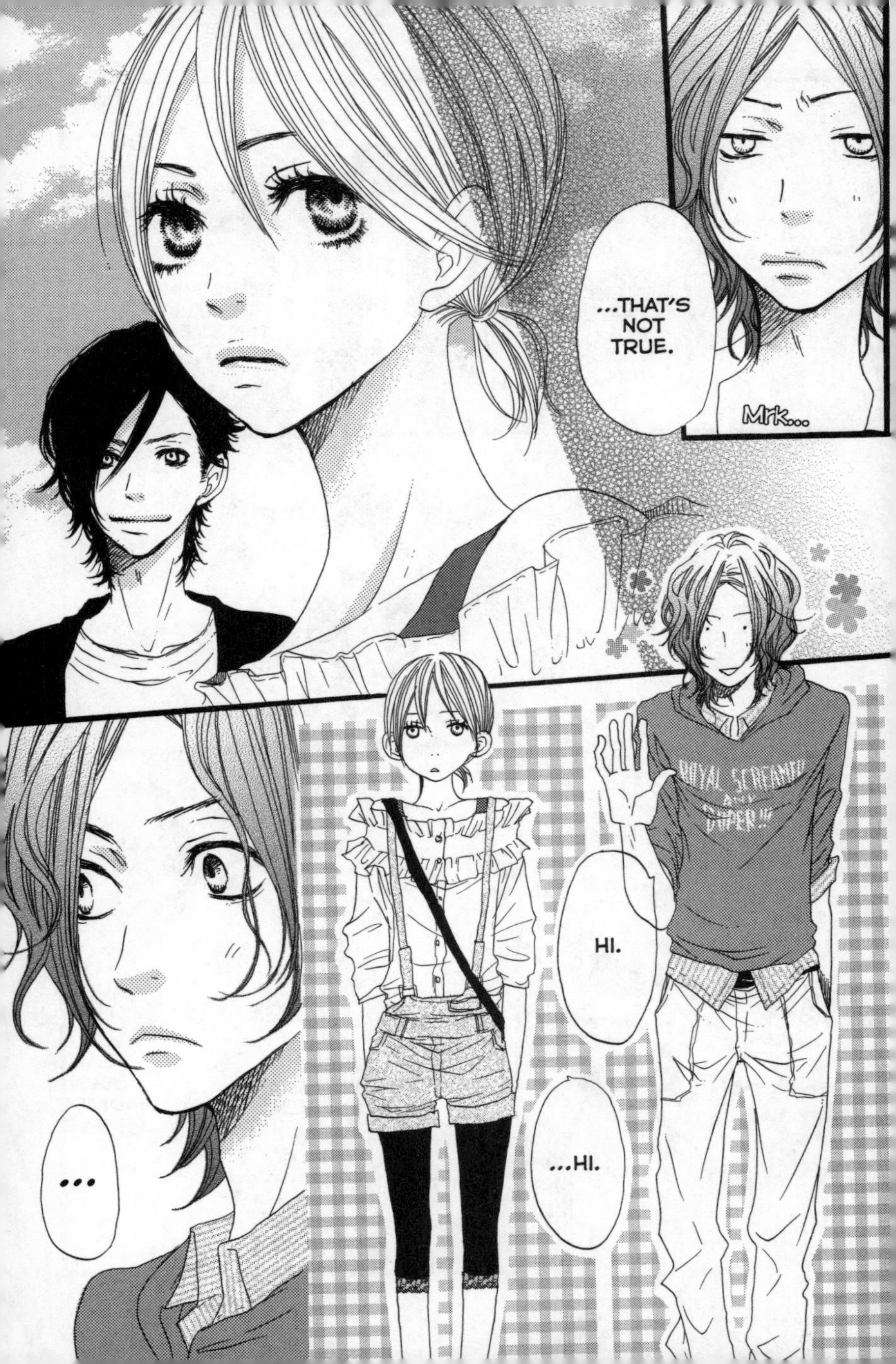
...THAT'S NOT TRUE.
Mrk...
HI.
...HI.
...

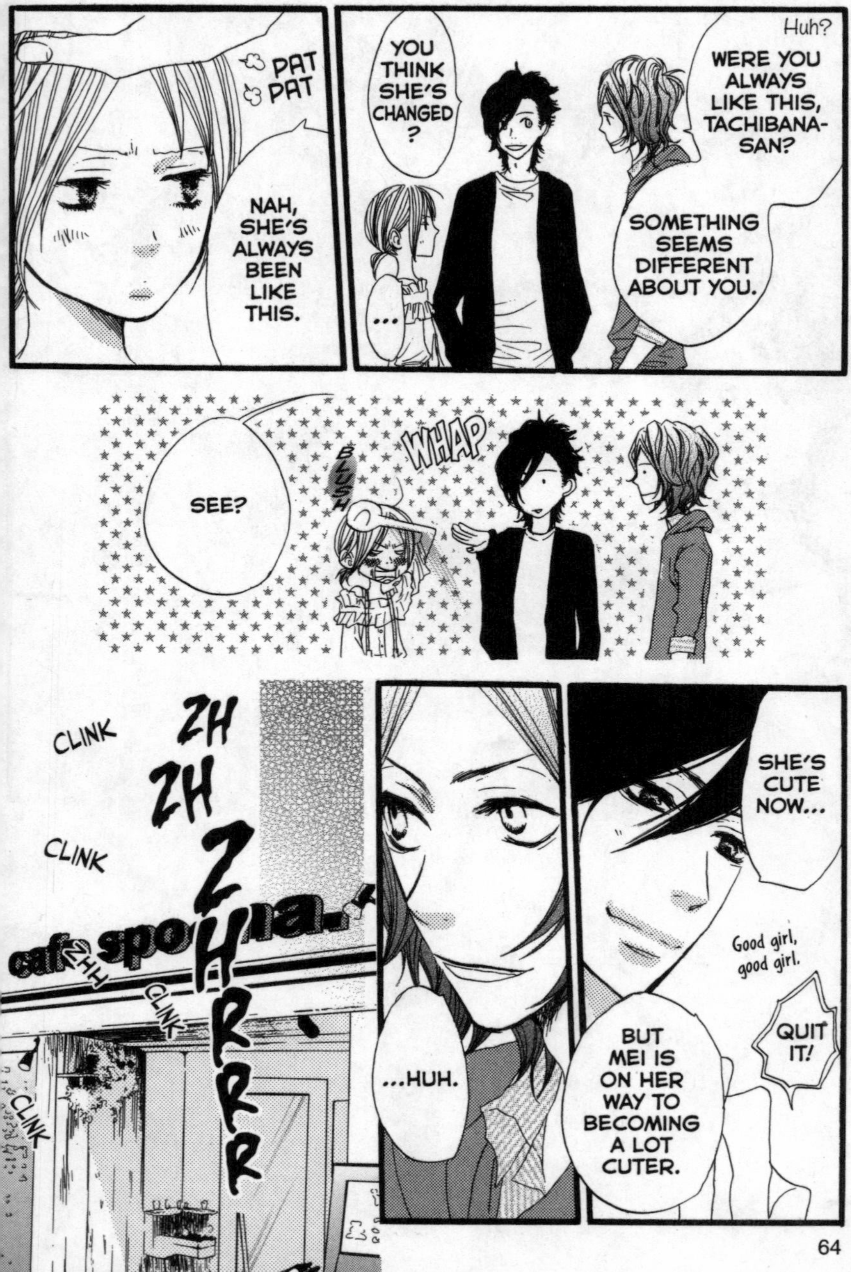
Huh?
WERE YOU ALWAYS LIKE THIS, TACHIBANA-SAN?
SOMETHING SEEMS DIFFERENT ABOUT YOU.
YOU THINK SHE'S CHANGED?
...
PAT PAT
NAH, SHE'S ALWAYS BEEN LIKE THIS.
WHAP
BLUSH
SEE?
SHE'S CUTE NOW...
Good girl, good girl.
QUIT IT!
BUT MEI IS ON HER WAY TO BECOMING A LOT CUTER.
...HUH.
CLINK
ZH ZH
CLINK
ZHHRRR
ZHH
CLINK
CLINK

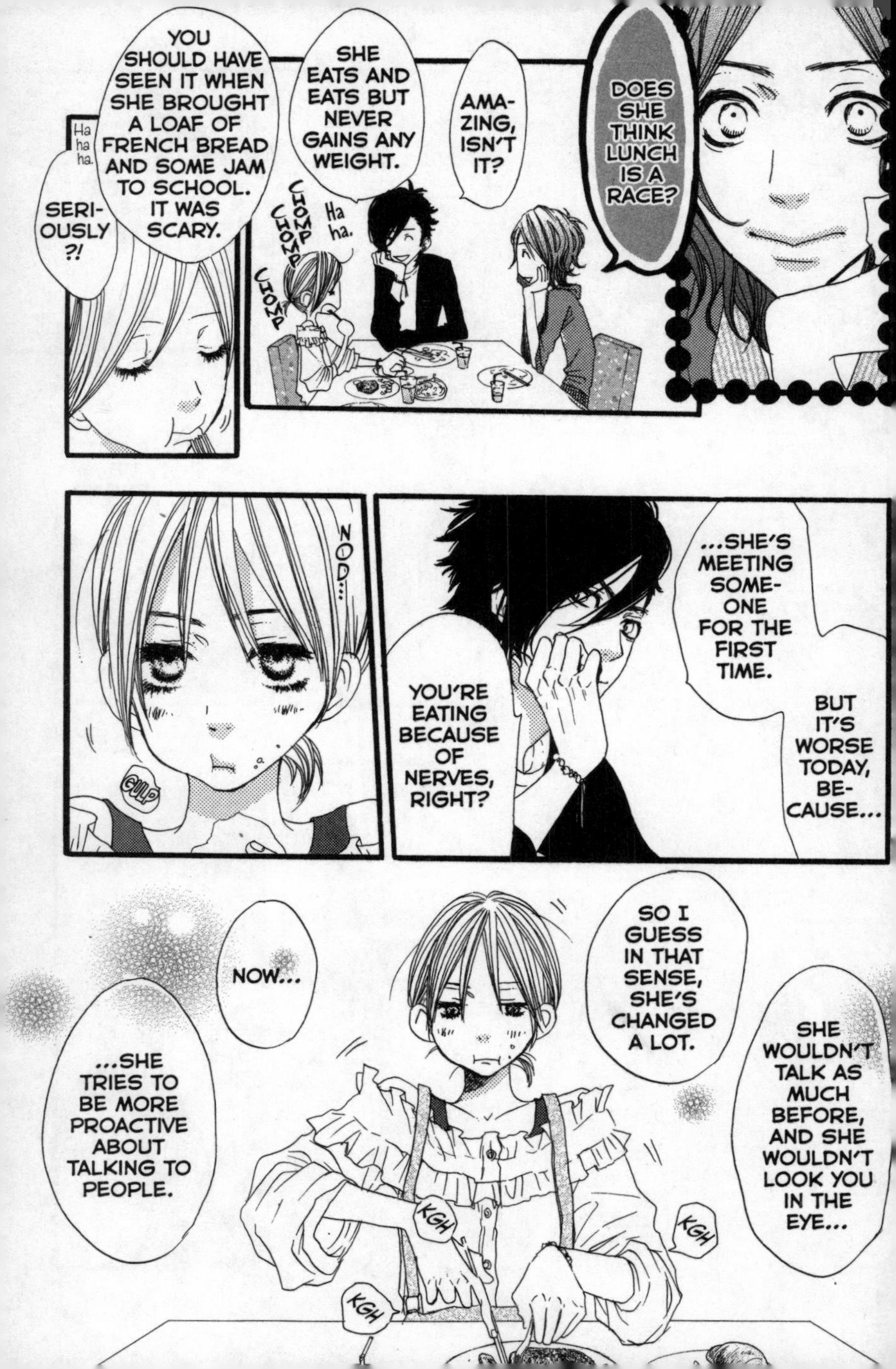
DOES SHE THINK LUNCH IS A RACE?
AMA-ZING, ISN'T IT?
SHE EATS AND EATS BUT NEVER GAINS ANY WEIGHT.
Ha ha.
CHOMP CHOMP CHOMP
YOU SHOULD HAVE SEEN IT WHEN SHE BROUGHT A LOAF OF FRENCH BREAD AND SOME JAM TO SCHOOL. IT WAS SCARY.
Ha ha ha.
SERI-OUSLY ?!
...SHE'S MEETING SOME-ONE FOR THE FIRST TIME.
BUT IT'S WORSE TODAY, BE-CAUSE...
YOU'RE EATING BECAUSE OF NERVES, RIGHT?
NOD...
GULP
SHE WOULDN'T TALK AS MUCH BEFORE, AND SHE WOULDN'T LOOK YOU IN THE EYE...
SO I GUESS IN THAT SENSE, SHE'S CHANGED A LOT.
NOW...
...SHE TRIES TO BE MORE PROACTIVE ABOUT TALKING TO PEOPLE.
KGH
KGH
KGH

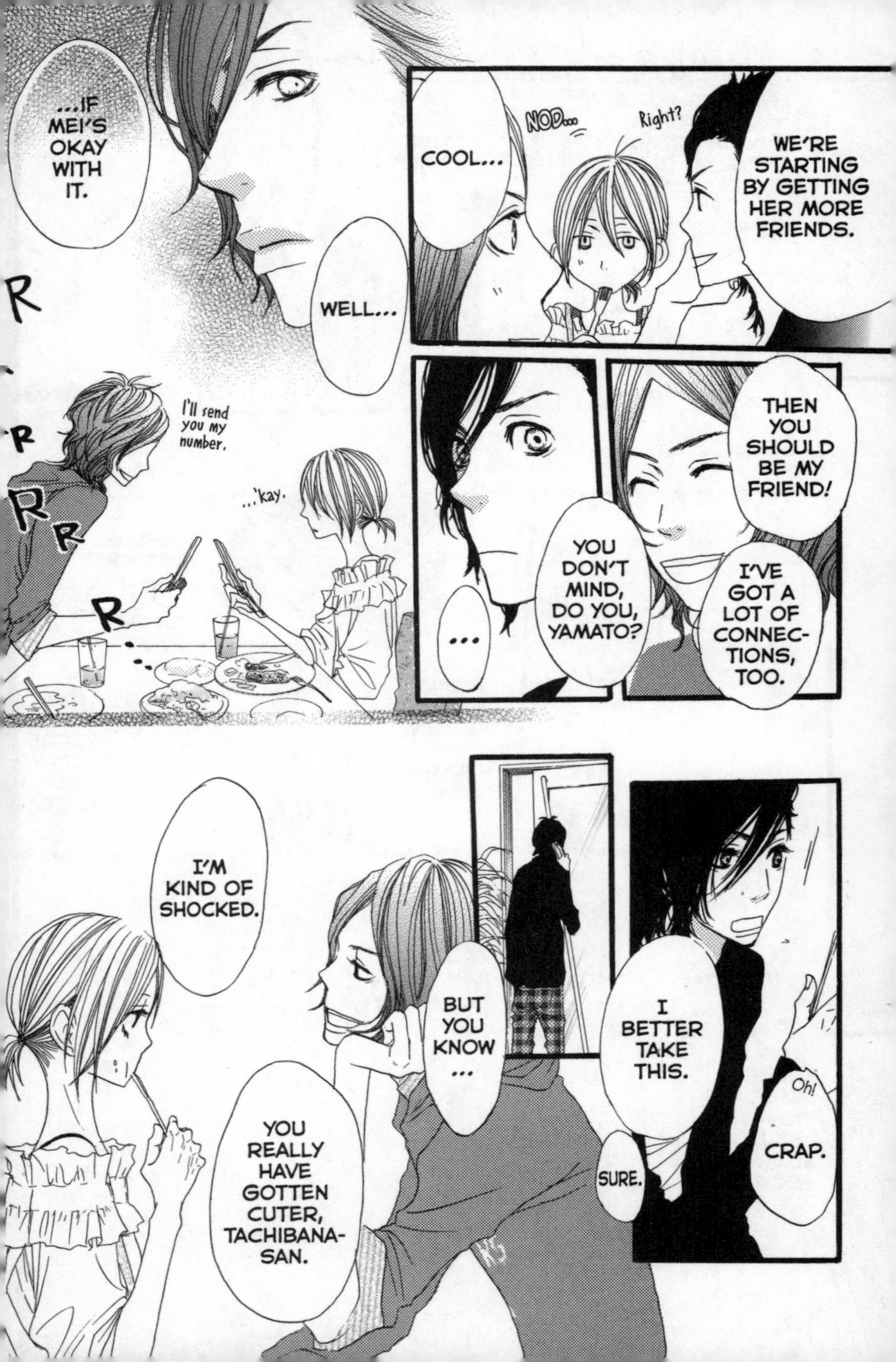
NOD...
Right?
WE'RE STARTING BY GETTING HER MORE FRIENDS.
COOL...
WELL...
...IF MEI'S OKAY WITH IT.
THEN YOU SHOULD BE MY FRIEND!
I'VE GOT A LOT OF CONNEC-TIONS, TOO.
YOU DON'T MIND, DO YOU, YAMATO?
...
I'll send you my number.
...'kay.
R
R
R
R
R
Oh!
CRAP.
I BETTER TAKE THIS.
SURE.
I'M KIND OF SHOCKED.
BUT YOU KNOW...
YOU REALLY HAVE GOTTEN CUTER, TACHIBANA-SAN.

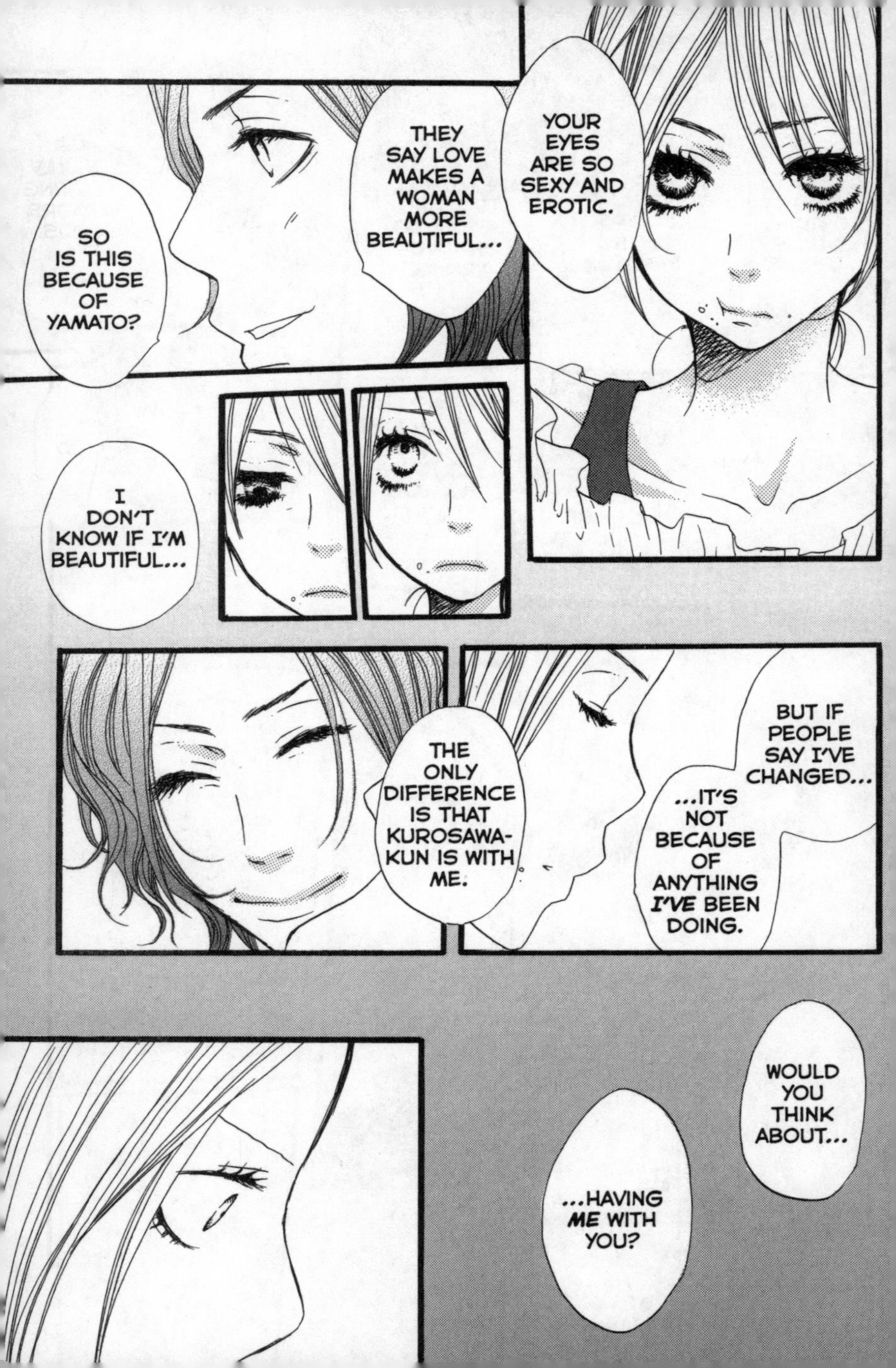
YOUR EYES ARE SO SEXY AND EROTIC.
THEY SAY LOVE MAKES A WOMAN MORE BEAUTIFUL...
SO IS THIS BECAUSE OF YAMATO?
I DON'T KNOW IF I'M BEAUTIFUL...
BUT IF PEOPLE SAY I'VE CHANGED...
...IT'S NOT BECAUSE OF ANYTHING *I'VE* BEEN DOING.
THE ONLY DIFFERENCE IS THAT KUROSAWA-KUN IS WITH ME.
WOULD YOU THINK ABOUT...
...HAVING *ME* WITH YOU?

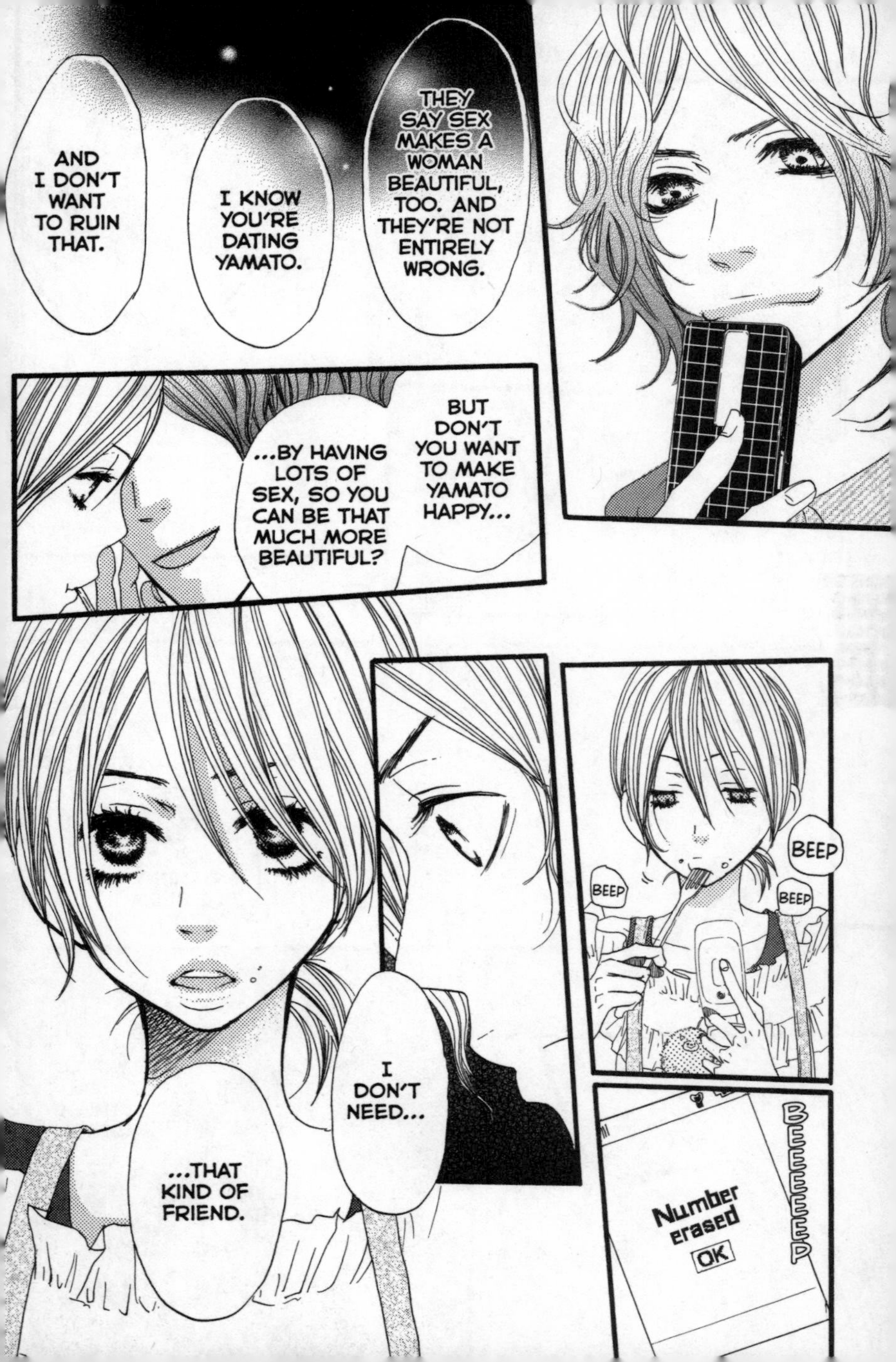
THEY SAY SEX MAKES A WOMAN BEAUTIFUL, TOO. AND THEY'RE NOT ENTIRELY WRONG.
I KNOW YOU'RE DATING YAMATO.
AND I DON'T WANT TO RUIN THAT.
BUT DON'T YOU WANT TO MAKE YAMATO HAPPY...
...BY HAVING LOTS OF SEX, SO YOU CAN BE THAT MUCH MORE BEAUTIFUL?
BEEP
BEEP
BEEP
BEEEEEEEP
Number erased
OK
I DON'T NEED...
...THAT KIND OF FRIEND.

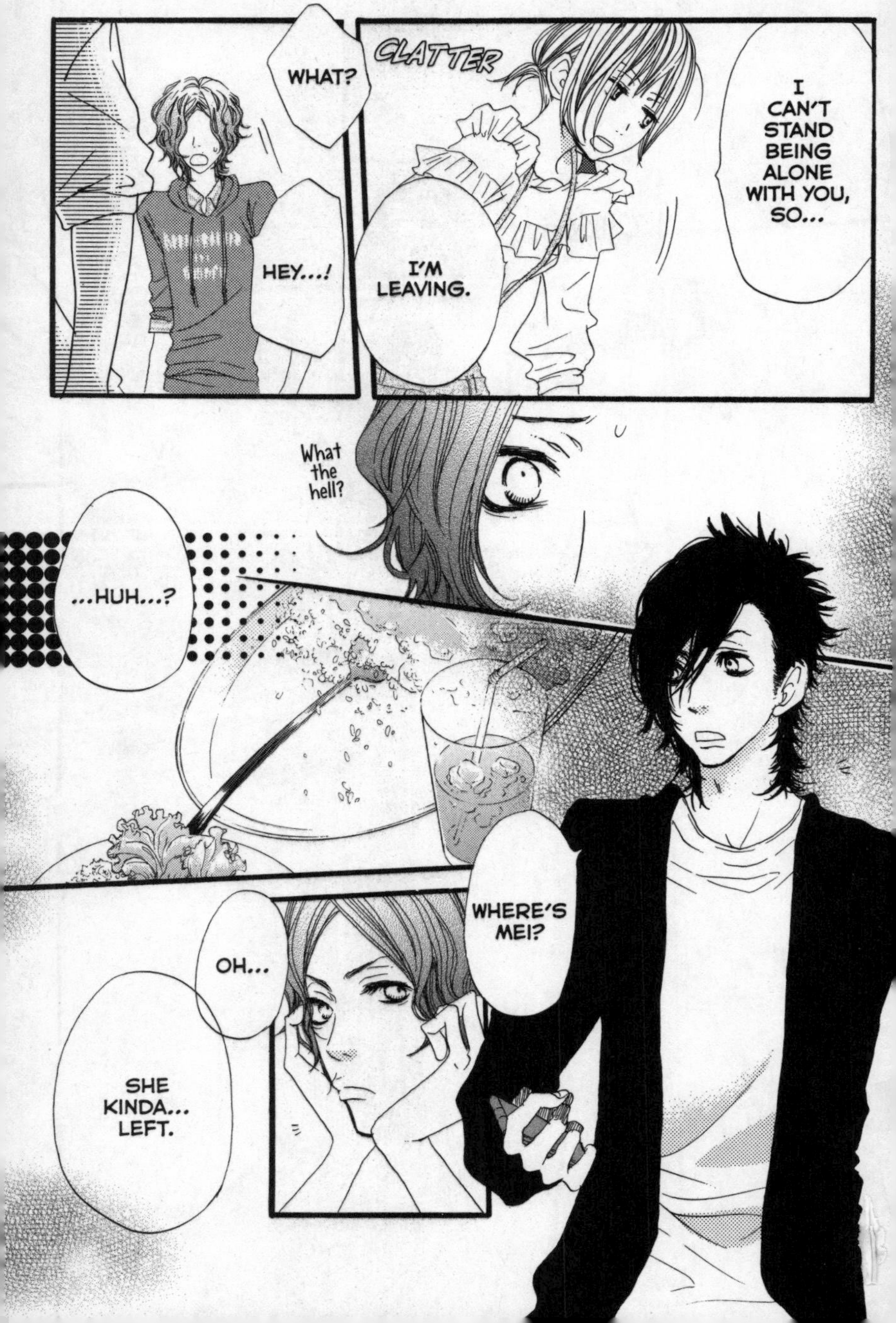
I CAN'T STAND BEING ALONE WITH YOU, SO...
CLATTER
I'M LEAVING.
WHAT?
HEY...!
What the hell?
...HUH...?
WHERE'S MEI?
OH...
SHE KINDA... LEFT.

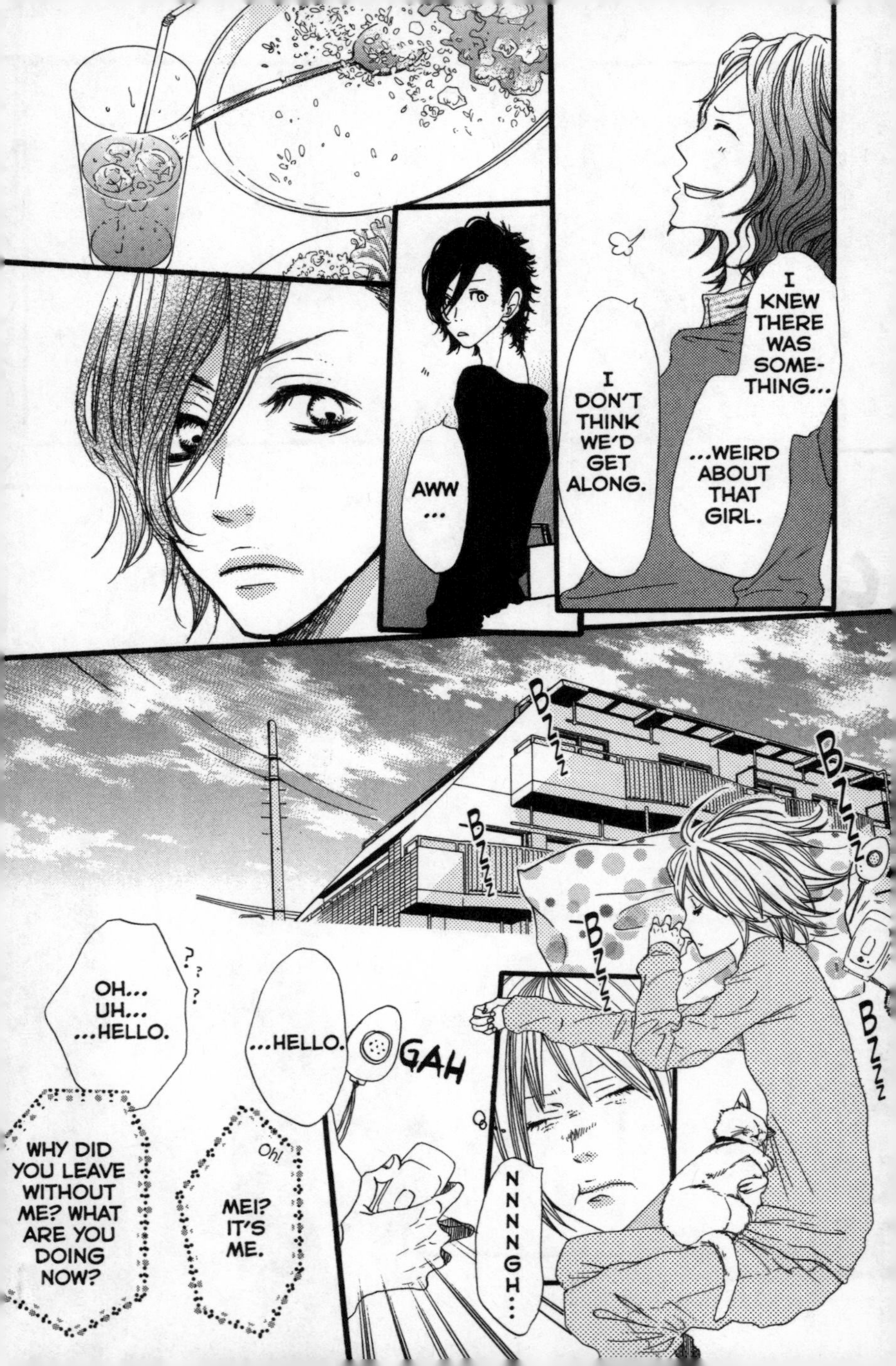
I KNEW THERE WAS SOMETHING...
...WEIRD ABOUT THAT GIRL.
I DON'T THINK WE'D GET ALONG.
AWW...
BZZZ
BZZZZ
BZZZ
BZZZ
BZZZ
NNNNGH...
GAH
...HELLO.
OH... UH... ...HELLO.
Oh!
MEI? IT'S ME.
WHY DID YOU LEAVE WITHOUT ME? WHAT ARE YOU DOING NOW?

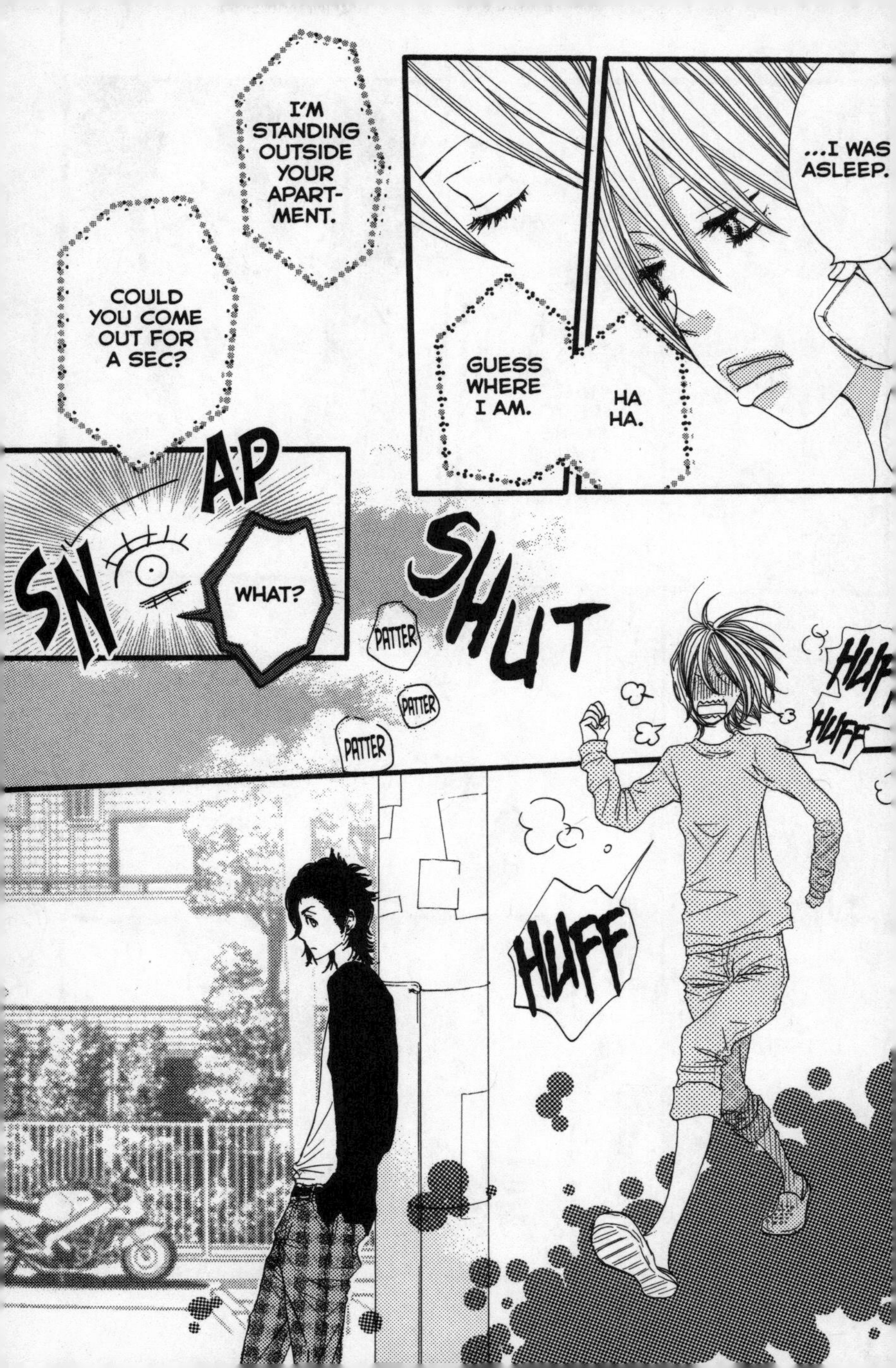
...I WAS ASLEEP.
GUESS WHERE I AM.
HA HA.
I'M STANDING OUTSIDE YOUR APARTMENT.
COULD YOU COME OUT FOR A SEC?
SNAP
WHAT?
SHUT
PATTER
PATTER
PATTER
HUFF, HUFF
HUFF

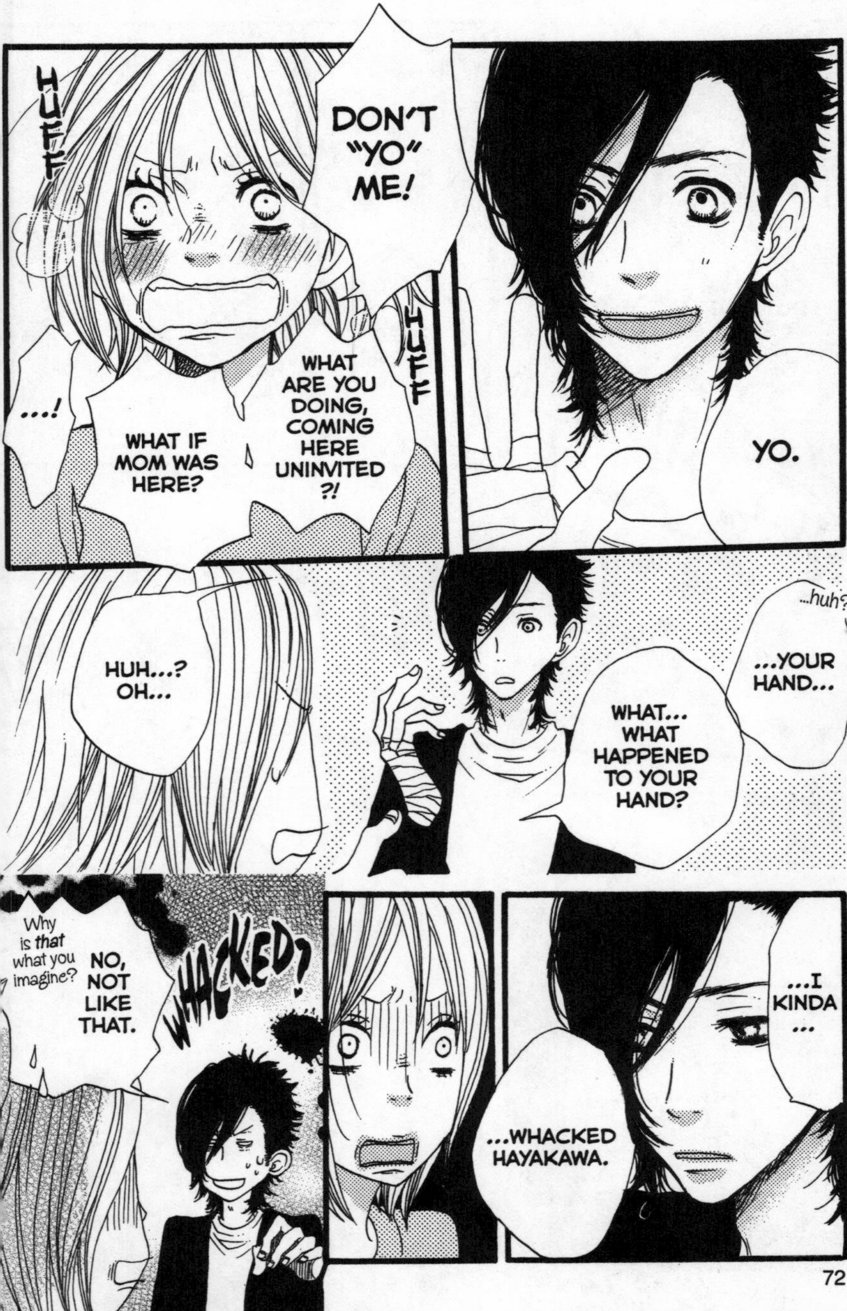
YO.
DON'T "YO" ME!
HUFF
HUFF
WHAT ARE YOU DOING, COMING HERE UNINVITED ?!
WHAT IF MOM WAS HERE?
...!
...huh?
...YOUR HAND...
WHAT... WHAT HAPPENED TO YOUR HAND?
HUH...? OH...
...I KINDA ...
...WHACKED HAYAKAWA.
WHACKED?
NO, NOT LIKE THAT.
Why is *that* what you imagine?

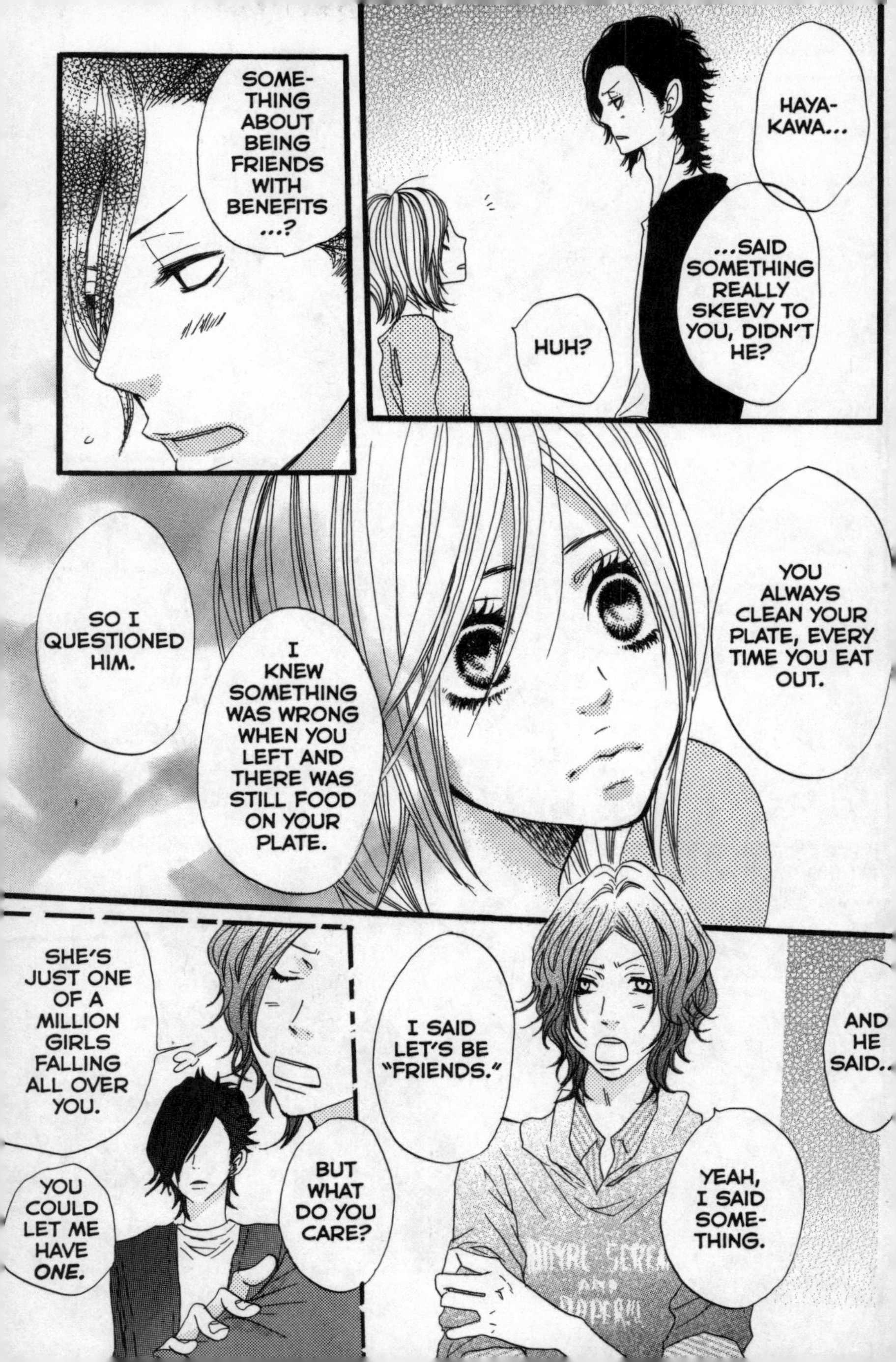
HAYA-KAWA...
...SAID SOMETHING REALLY SKEEVY TO YOU, DIDN'T HE?
HUH?
SOME-THING ABOUT BEING FRIENDS WITH BENEFITS ...?
YOU ALWAYS CLEAN YOUR PLATE, EVERY TIME YOU EAT OUT.
I KNEW SOMETHING WAS WRONG WHEN YOU LEFT AND THERE WAS STILL FOOD ON YOUR PLATE.
SO I QUESTIONED HIM.
AND HE SAID..
I SAID LET'S BE "FRIENDS."
YEAH, I SAID SOME-THING.
SHE'S JUST ONE OF A MILLION GIRLS FALLING ALL OVER YOU.
BUT WHAT DO YOU CARE?
YOU COULD LET ME HAVE *ONE*.

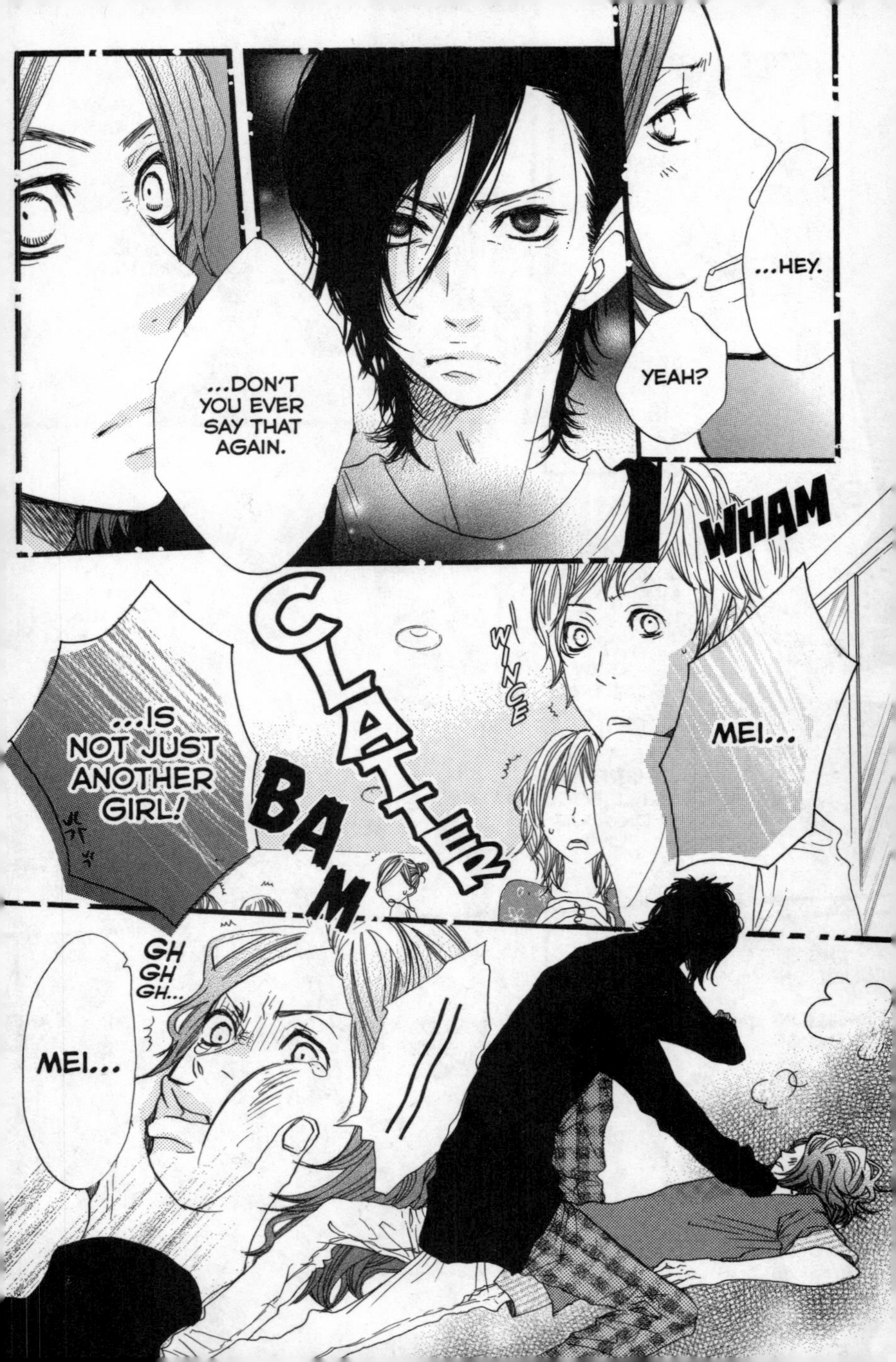
...HEY.
YEAH?
...DON'T YOU EVER SAY THAT AGAIN.
WHAM
MEI...
WINCE
CLATTER
...IS NOT JUST ANOTHER GIRL!
BAM
GH GH GH...
MEI...

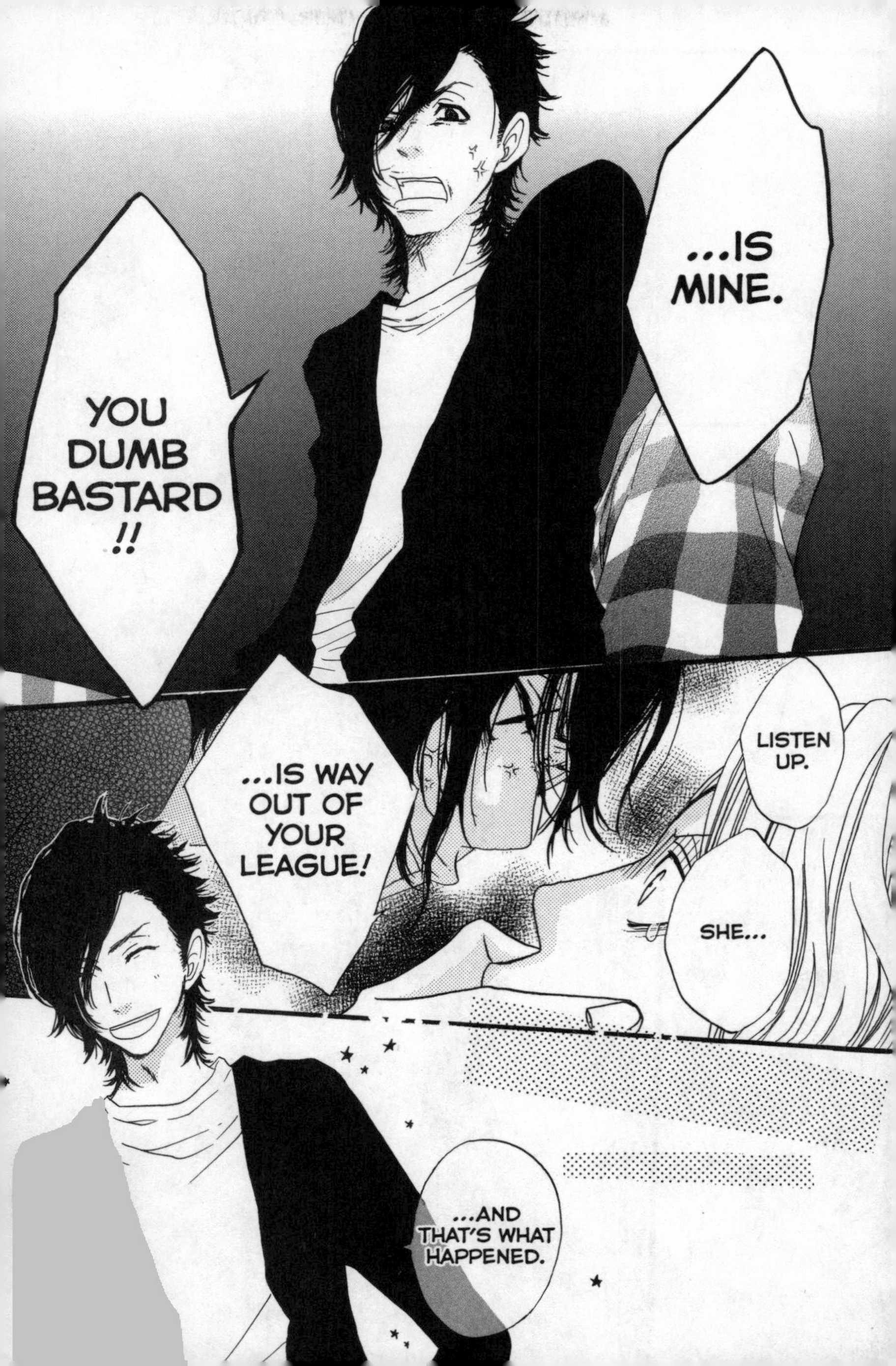
...IS MINE.
YOU DUMB BASTARD!!
LISTEN UP.
SHE...
...IS WAY OUT OF YOUR LEAGUE!
...AND THAT'S WHAT HAPPENED.

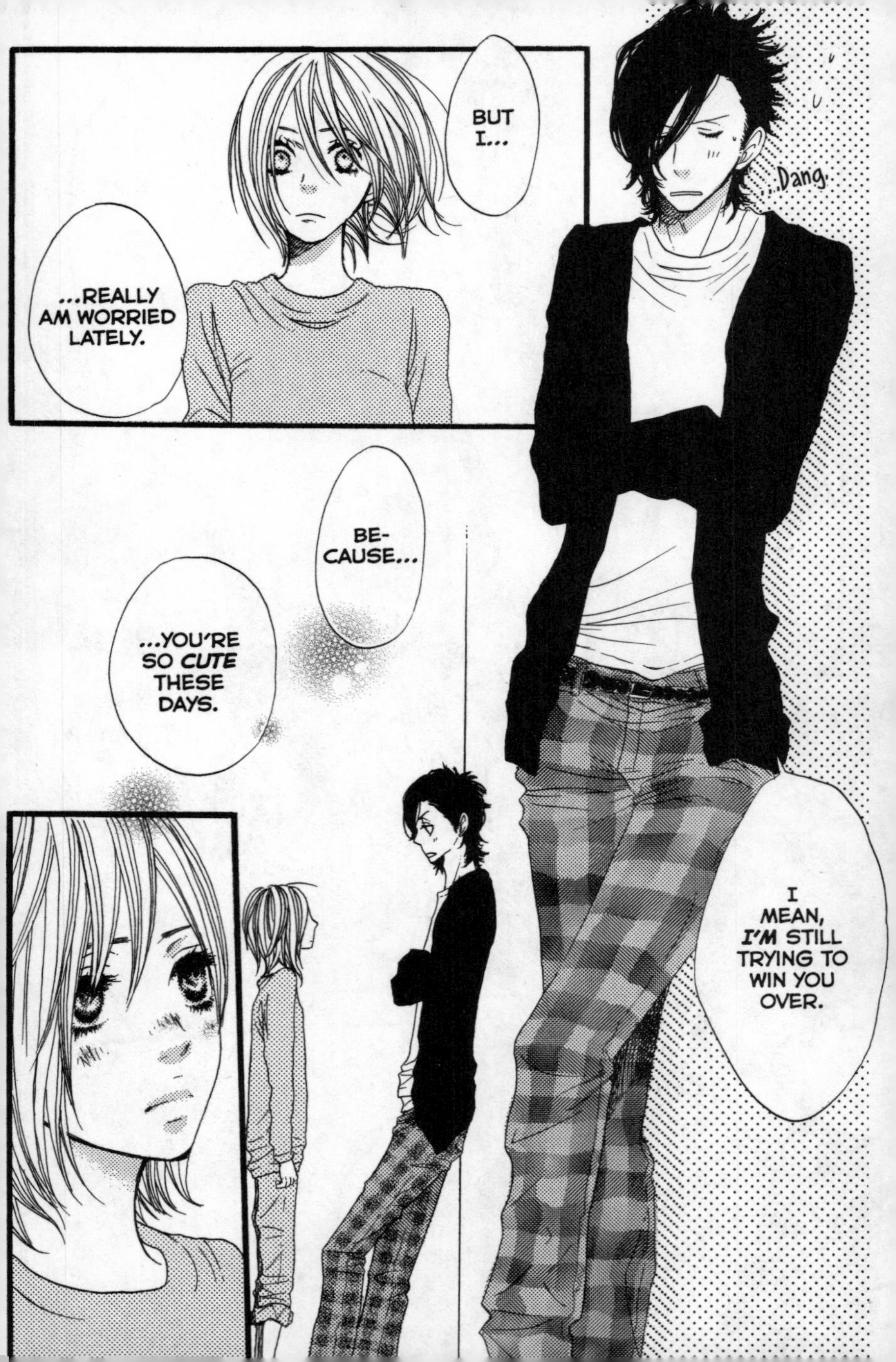
...Dang
I MEAN, *I'M* STILL TRYING TO WIN YOU OVER.
BUT I...
...REALLY AM WORRIED LATELY.
BE-CAUSE...
...YOU'RE SO *CUTE* THESE DAYS.

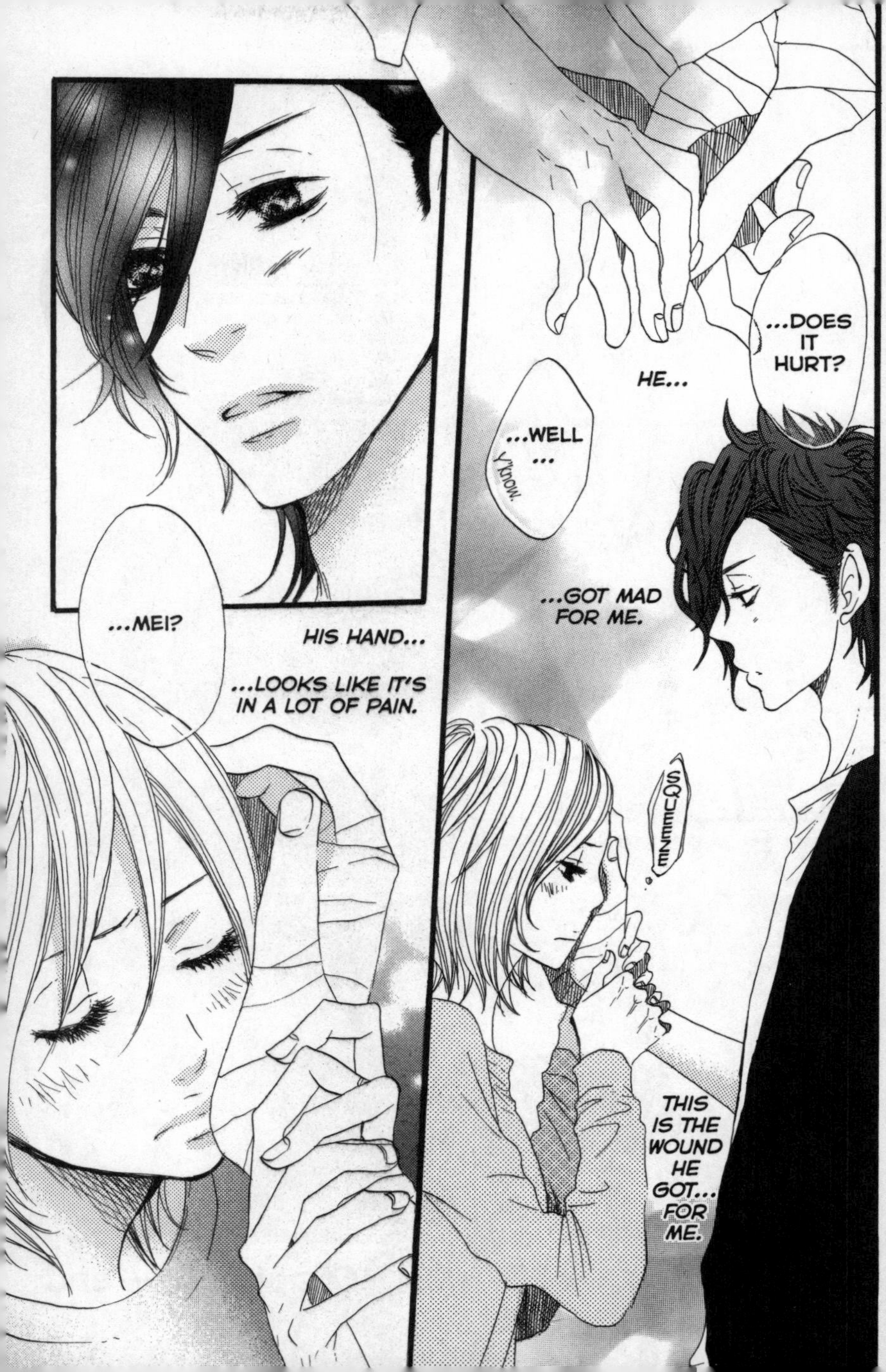
...DOES IT HURT?
HE...
...WELL ...
y'know.
...GOT MAD FOR ME.
SQUEEEZE
THIS IS THE WOUND HE GOT... FOR ME.
HIS HAND...
...LOOKS LIKE IT'S IN A LOT OF PAIN.
...MEI?

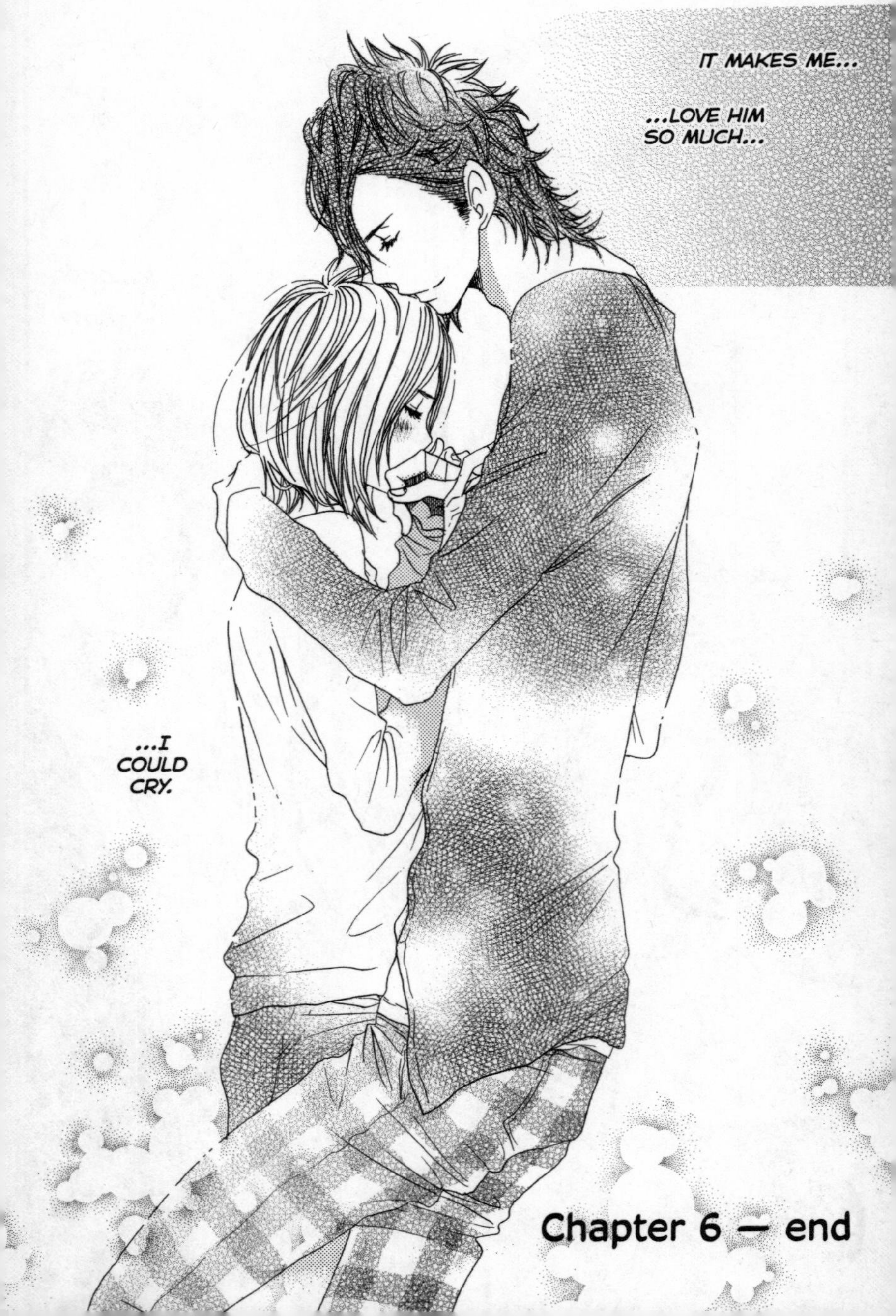
IT MAKES ME...
...LOVE HIM SO MUCH...
...I COULD CRY.

Chapter 6 — end

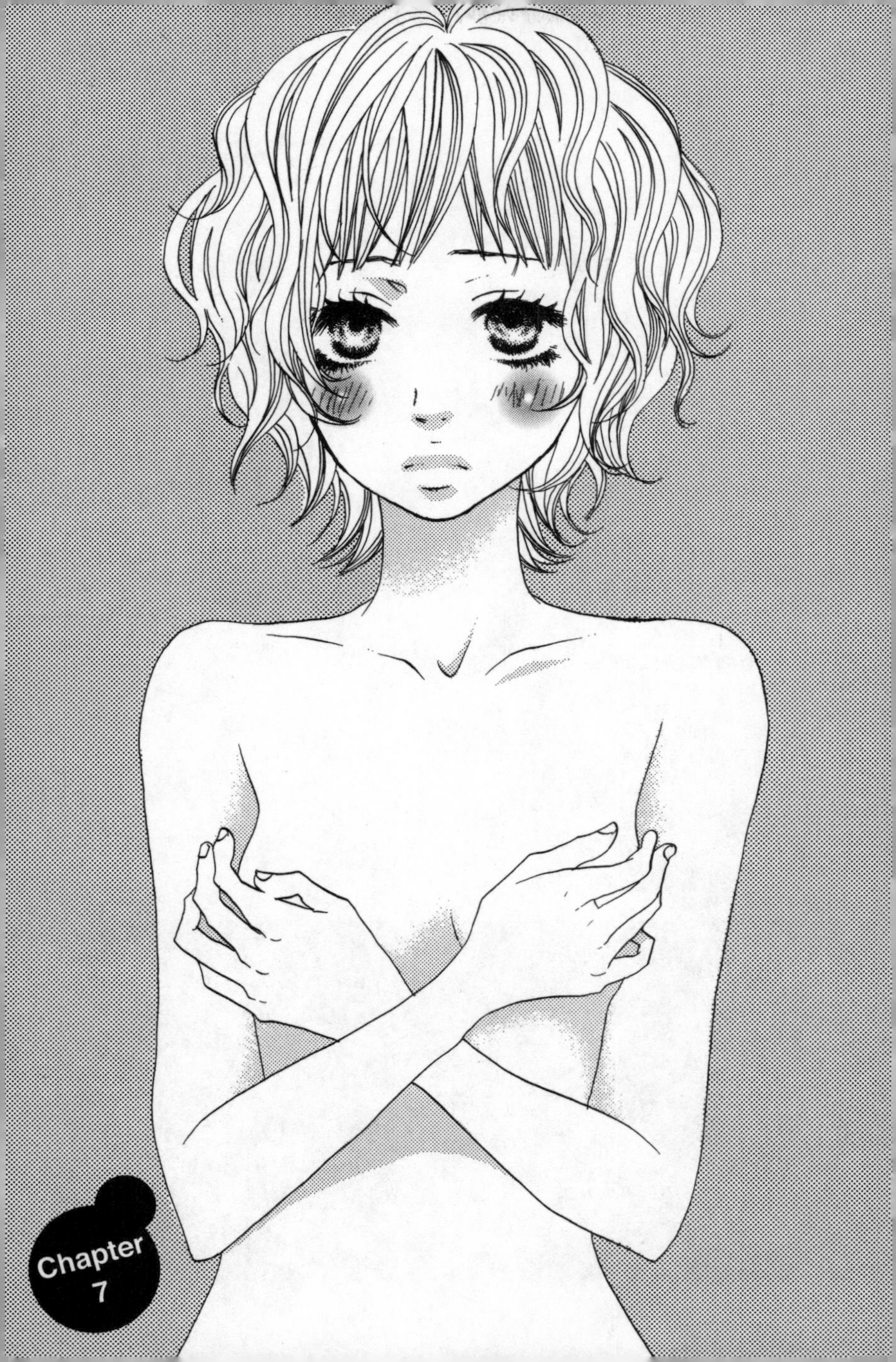
Chapter
7

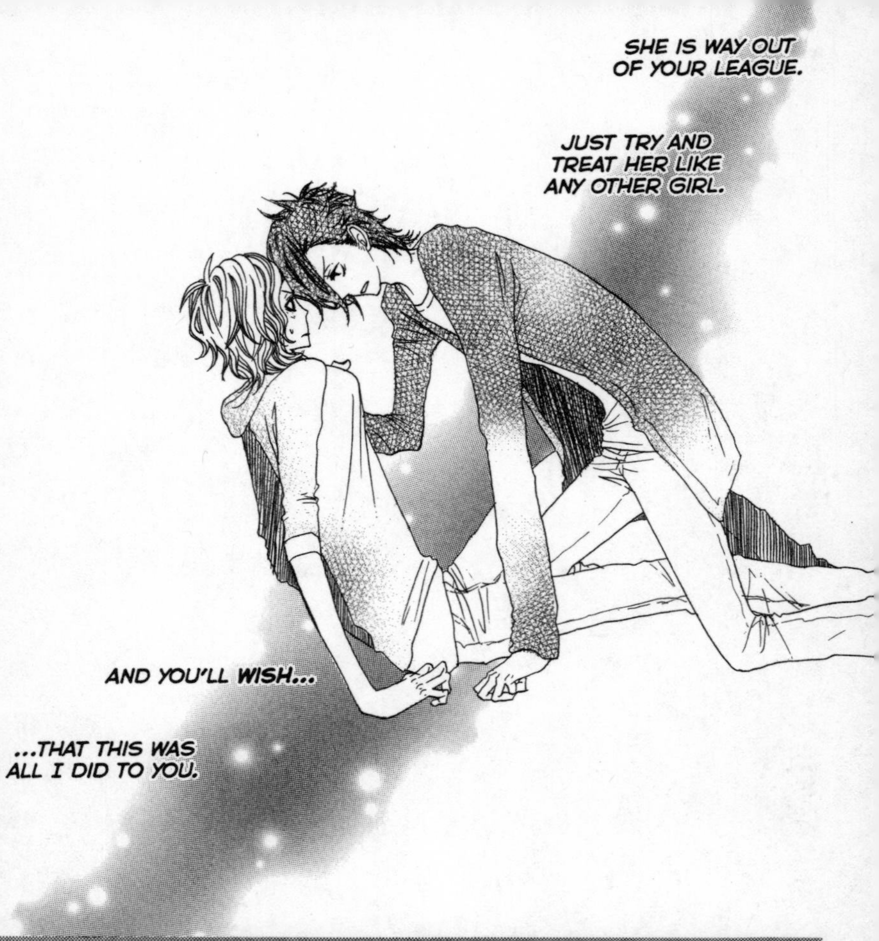
SHE IS WAY OUT OF YOUR LEAGUE.
JUST TRY AND TREAT HER LIKE ANY OTHER GIRL.
AND YOU'LL WISH...
...THAT THIS WAS ALL I DID TO YOU.

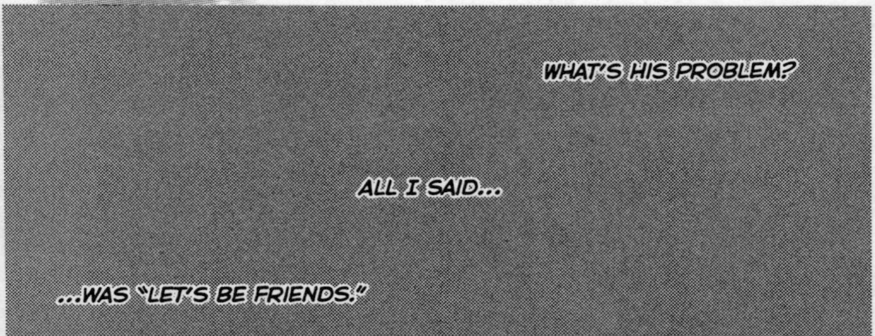
WHAT'S HIS PROBLEM?
ALL I SAID...
...WAS "LET'S BE FRIENDS."

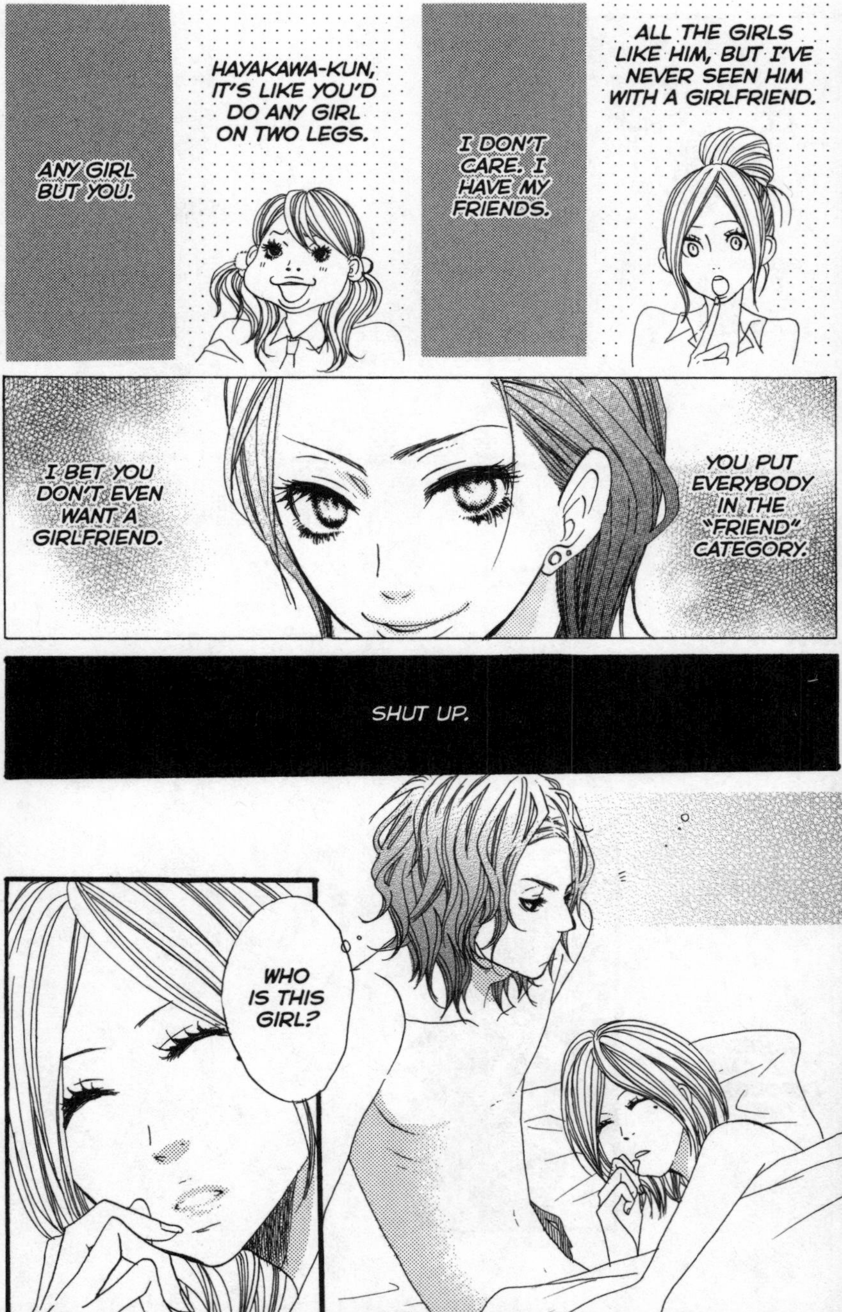
ALL THE GIRLS LIKE HIM, BUT I'VE NEVER SEEN HIM WITH A GIRLFRIEND.
I DON'T CARE. I HAVE MY FRIENDS.
HAYAKAWA-KUN, IT'S LIKE YOU'D DO ANY GIRL ON TWO LEGS.
ANY GIRL BUT YOU.
YOU PUT EVERYBODY IN THE "FRIEND" CATEGORY.
I BET YOU DON'T EVEN WANT A GIRLFRIEND.
SHUT UP.
WHO IS THIS GIRL?

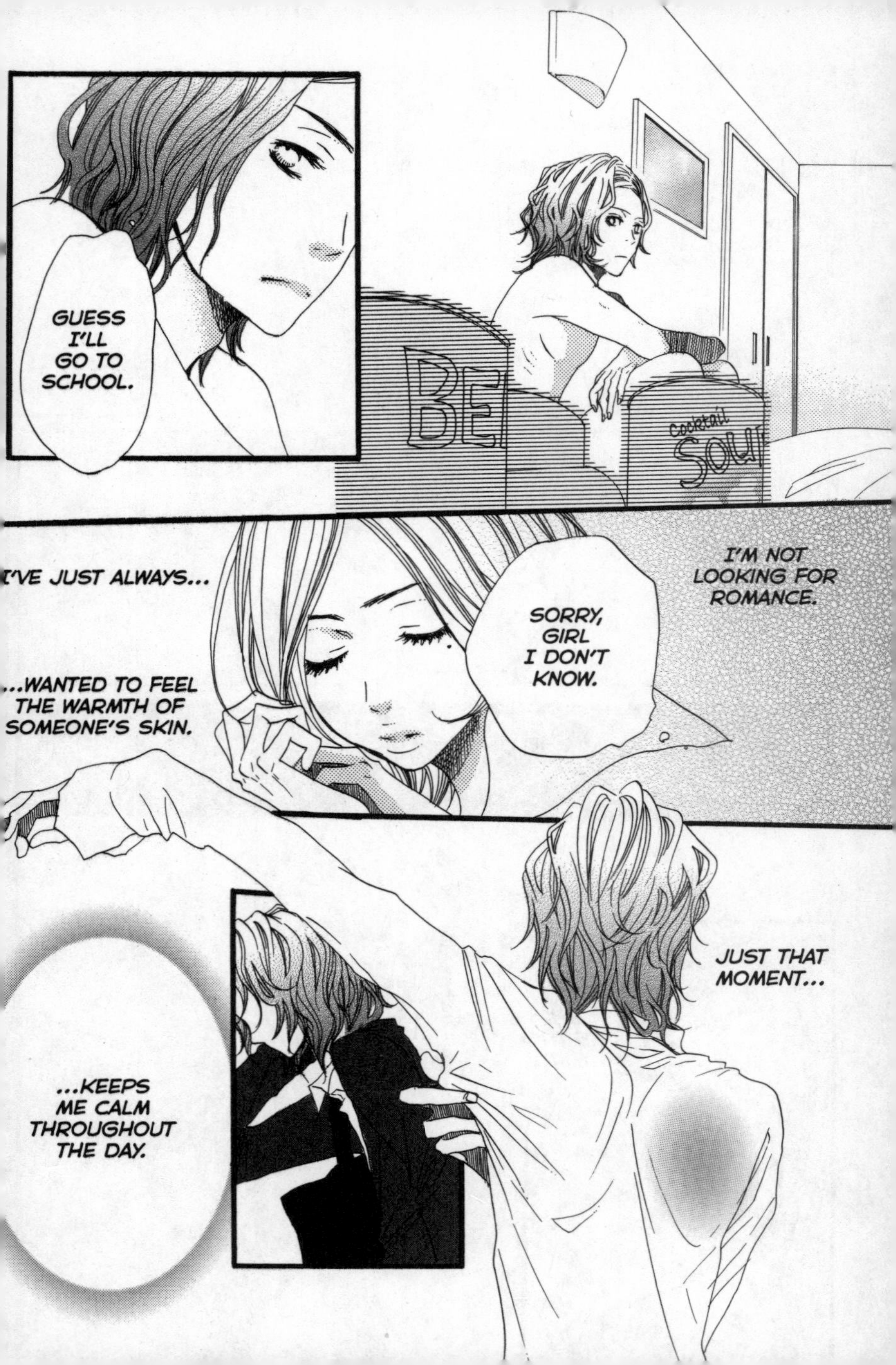
BE
Cocktail
SOU
GUESS I'LL GO TO SCHOOL.
I'M NOT LOOKING FOR ROMANCE.
SORRY, GIRL I DON'T KNOW.
I'VE JUST ALWAYS...
...WANTED TO FEEL THE WARMTH OF SOMEONE'S SKIN.
JUST THAT MOMENT...
...KEEPS ME CALM THROUGHOUT THE DAY.

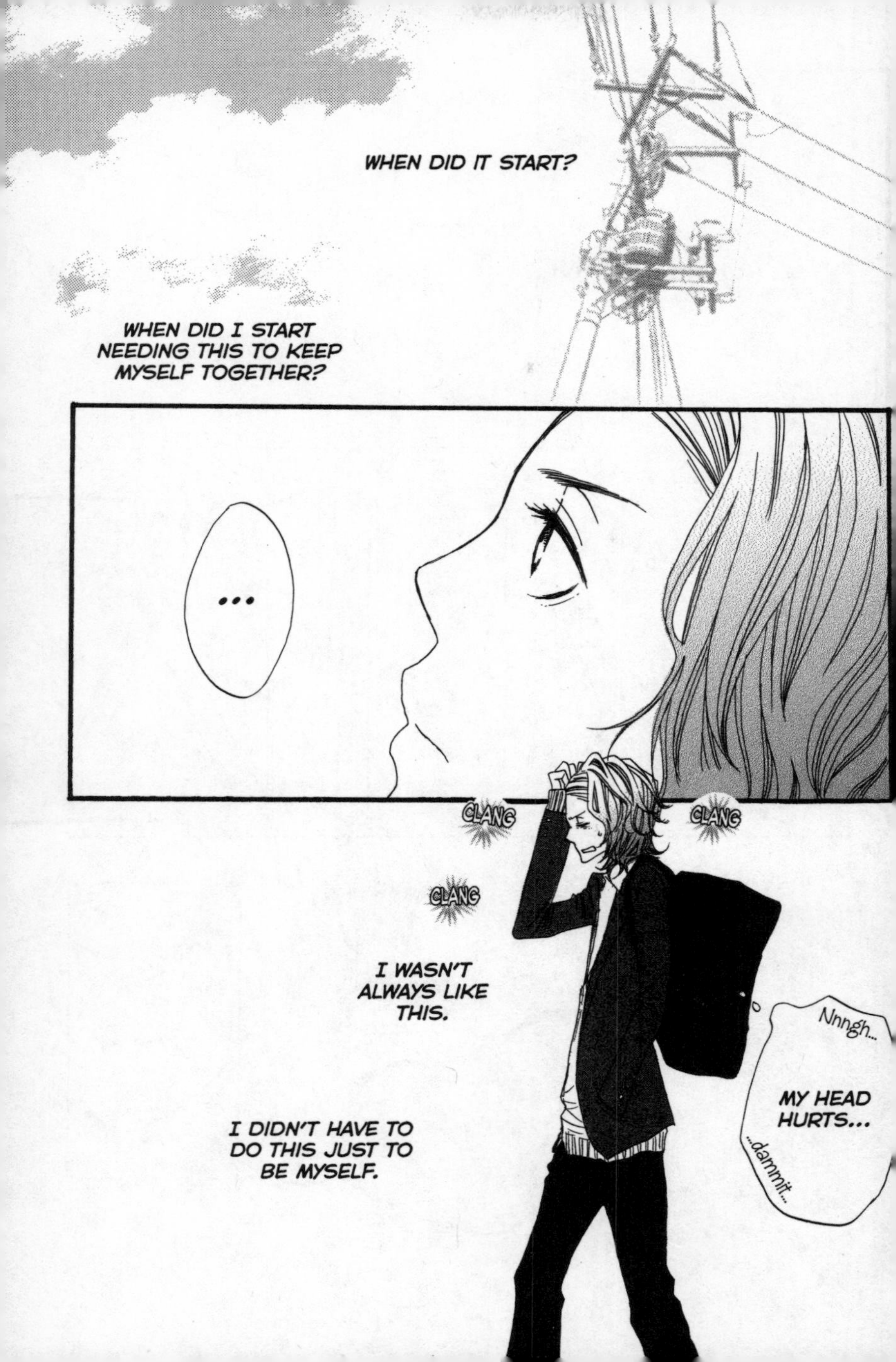
WHEN DID IT START?
WHEN DID I START NEEDING THIS TO KEEP MYSELF TOGETHER?
...
CLANG
CLANG
CLANG
Nnngh...
MY HEAD HURTS...
...dammit...
I WASN'T ALWAYS LIKE THIS.
I DIDN'T HAVE TO DO THIS JUST TO BE MYSELF.

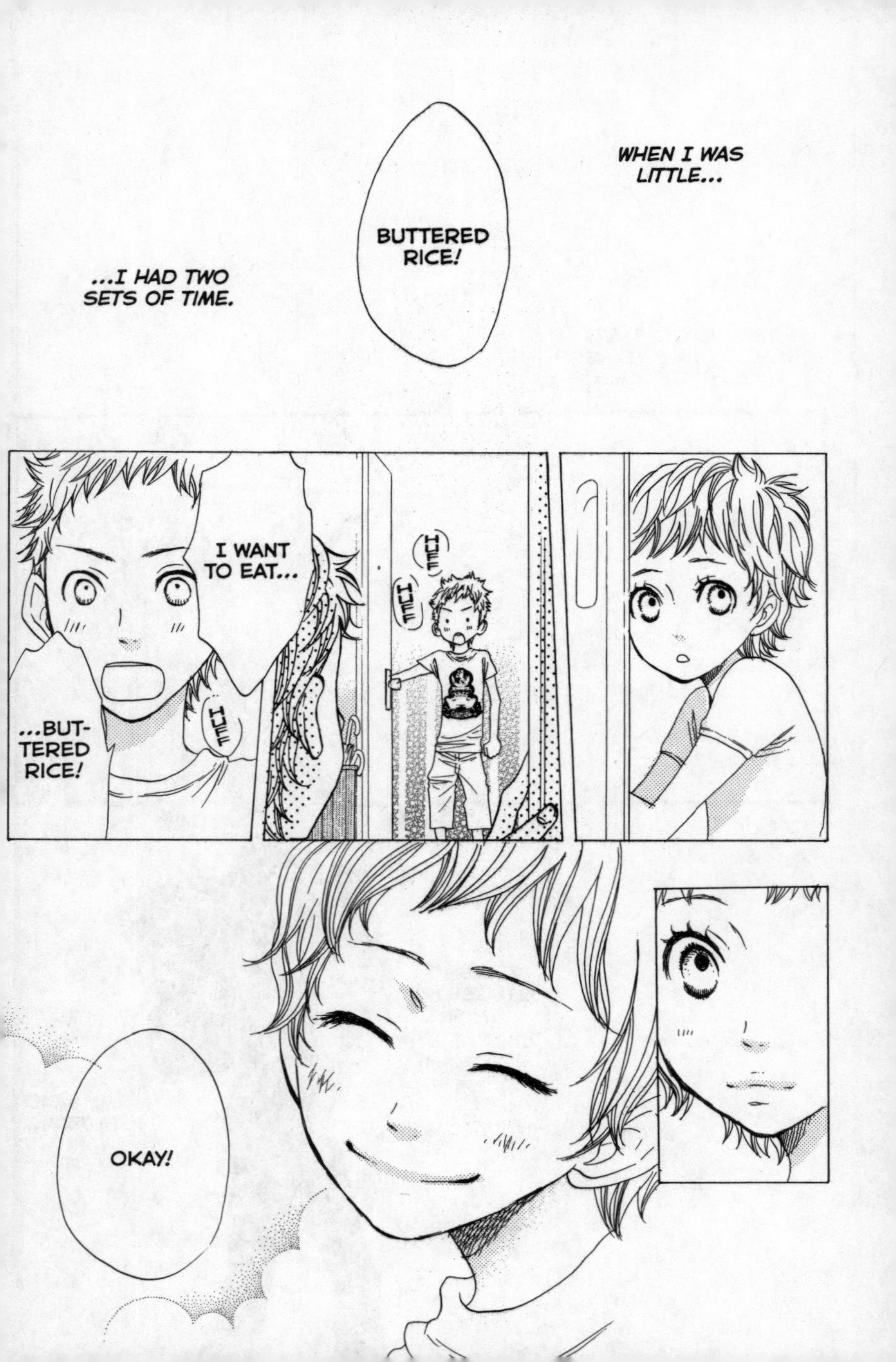
WHEN I WAS LITTLE...
BUTTERED RICE!
...I HAD TWO SETS OF TIME.
HUFF
HUFF
I WANT TO EAT...
HUFF
...BUT-TERED RICE!
OKAY!

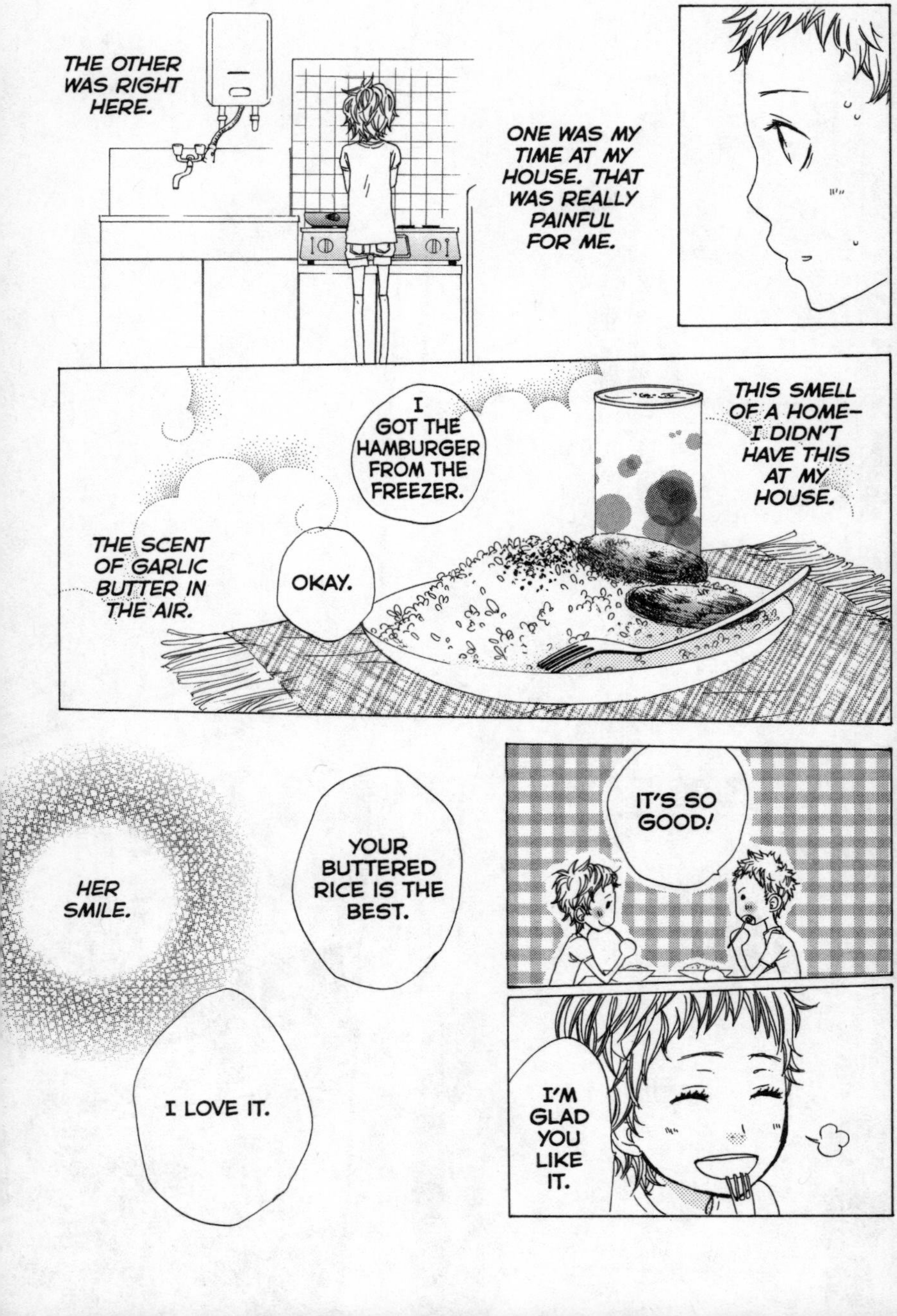
ONE WAS MY TIME AT MY HOUSE. THAT WAS REALLY PAINFUL FOR ME.
THE OTHER WAS RIGHT HERE.
THIS SMELL OF A HOME— I DIDN'T HAVE THIS AT MY HOUSE.
I GOT THE HAMBURGER FROM THE FREEZER.
OKAY.
THE SCENT OF GARLIC BUTTER IN THE AIR.
IT'S SO GOOD!
I'M GLAD YOU LIKE IT.
YOUR BUTTERED RICE IS THE BEST.
HER SMILE.
I LOVE IT.

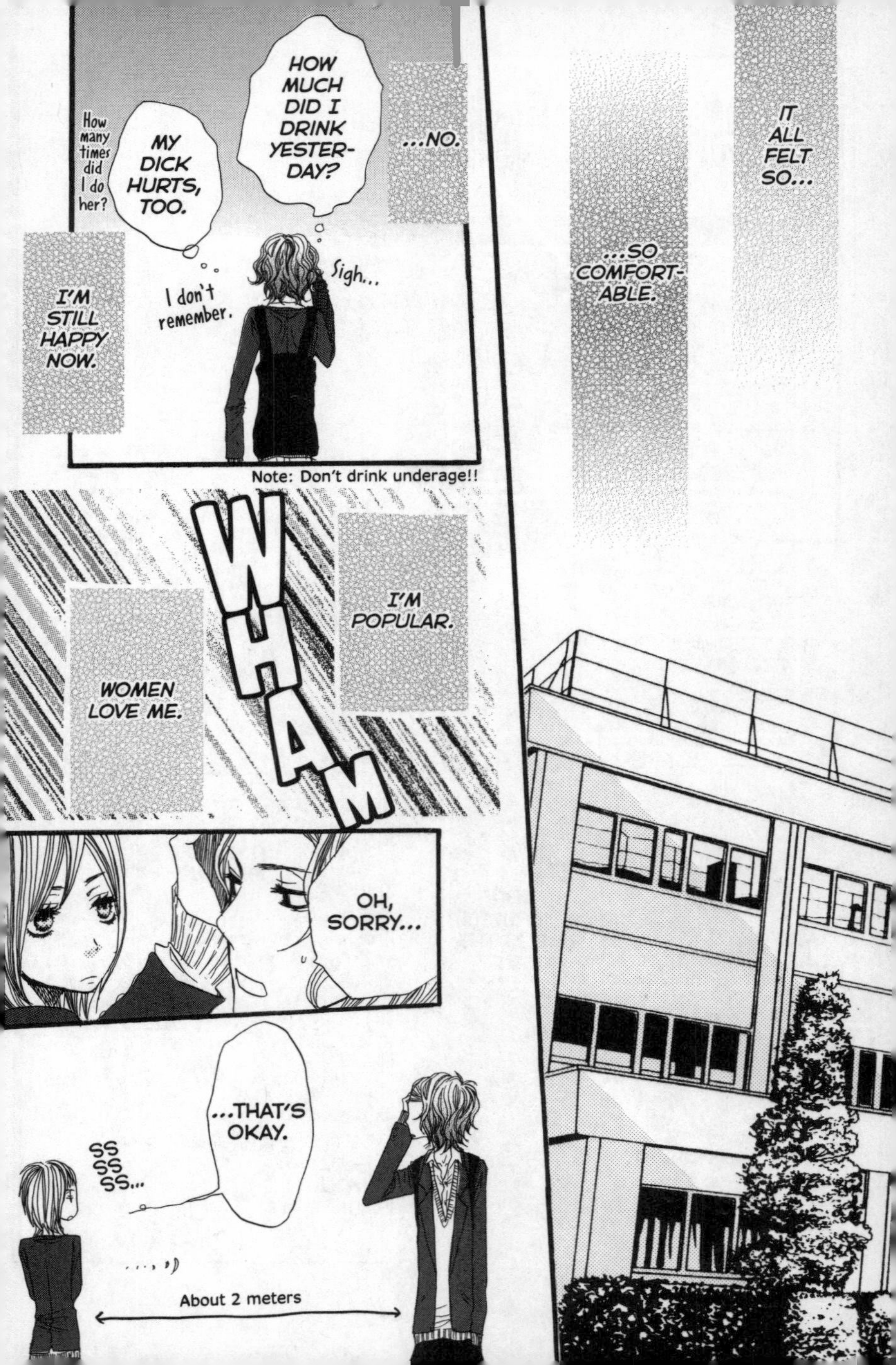
IT ALL FELT SO...
...SO COMFORTABLE.
...NO.
HOW MUCH DID I DRINK YESTERDAY?
MY DICK HURTS, TOO.
How many times did I do her?
Sigh...
I don't remember.
I'M STILL HAPPY NOW.
Note: Don't drink underage!!
I'M POPULAR.
WHAM
WOMEN LOVE ME.
OH, SORRY...
...THAT'S OKAY.
SS SS SS...
About 2 meters

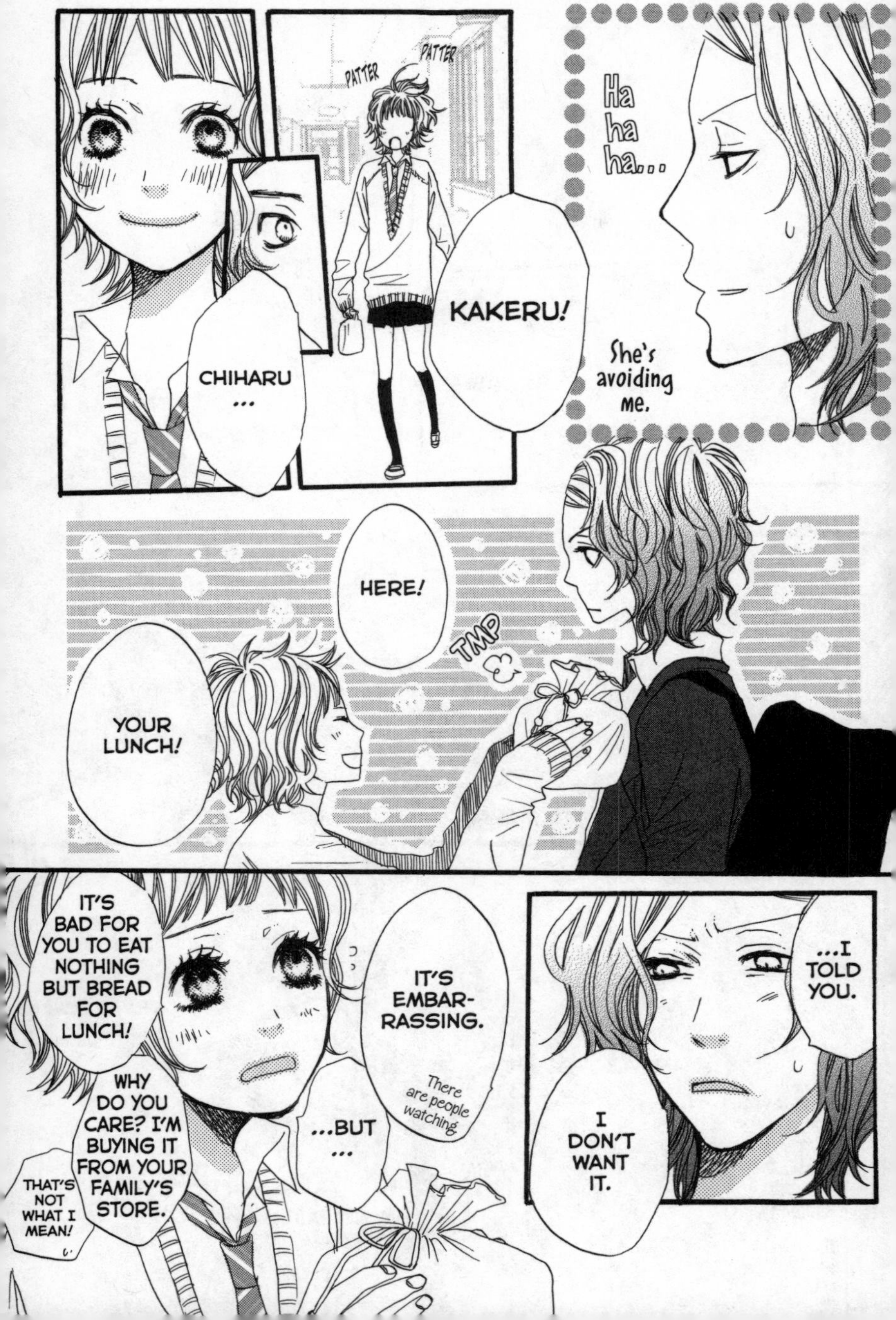
Ha ha ha...
She's avoiding me.
PATTER
PATTER
KAKERU!
CHIHARU ...
HERE!
TMP
YOUR LUNCH!
...I TOLD YOU.
I DON'T WANT IT.
IT'S EMBARRASSING.
There are people watching.
...BUT ...
IT'S BAD FOR YOU TO EAT NOTHING BUT BREAD FOR LUNCH!
WHY DO YOU CARE? I'M BUYING IT FROM YOUR FAMILY'S STORE.
THAT'S NOT WHAT I MEAN!

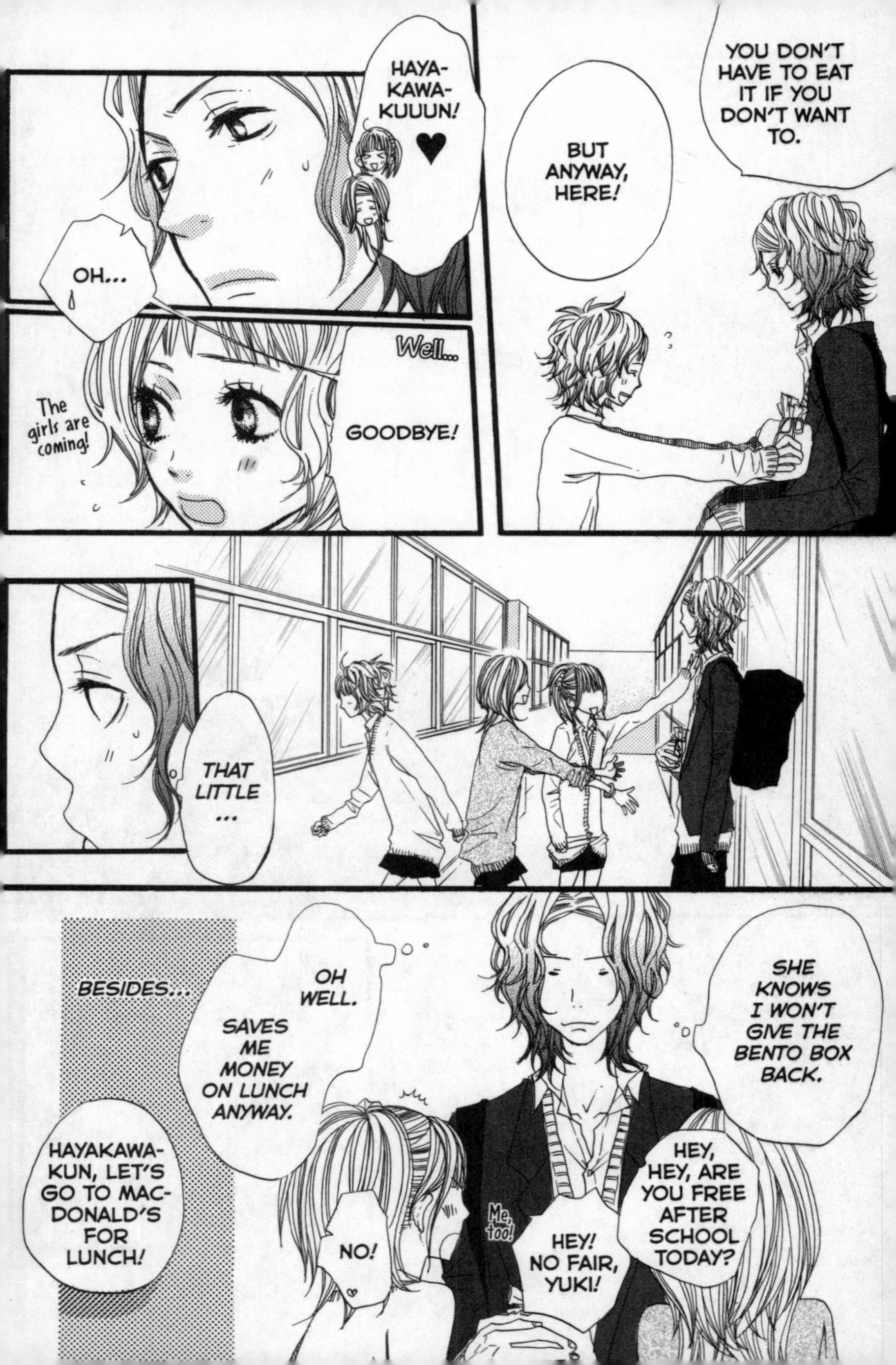
YOU DON'T HAVE TO EAT IT IF YOU DON'T WANT TO.
BUT ANYWAY, HERE!
HAYA-KAWA-KUUUN! ♥
OH...
Well...
GOODBYE!
The girls are coming!
THAT LITTLE ...
SHE KNOWS I WON'T GIVE THE BENTO BOX BACK.
OH WELL. SAVES ME MONEY ON LUNCH ANYWAY.
BESIDES...
HEY, HEY, ARE YOU FREE AFTER SCHOOL TODAY?
HEY! NO FAIR, YUKI!
Me, too!
NO!
HAYAKAWA-KUN, LET'S GO TO MAC-DONALD'S FOR LUNCH!

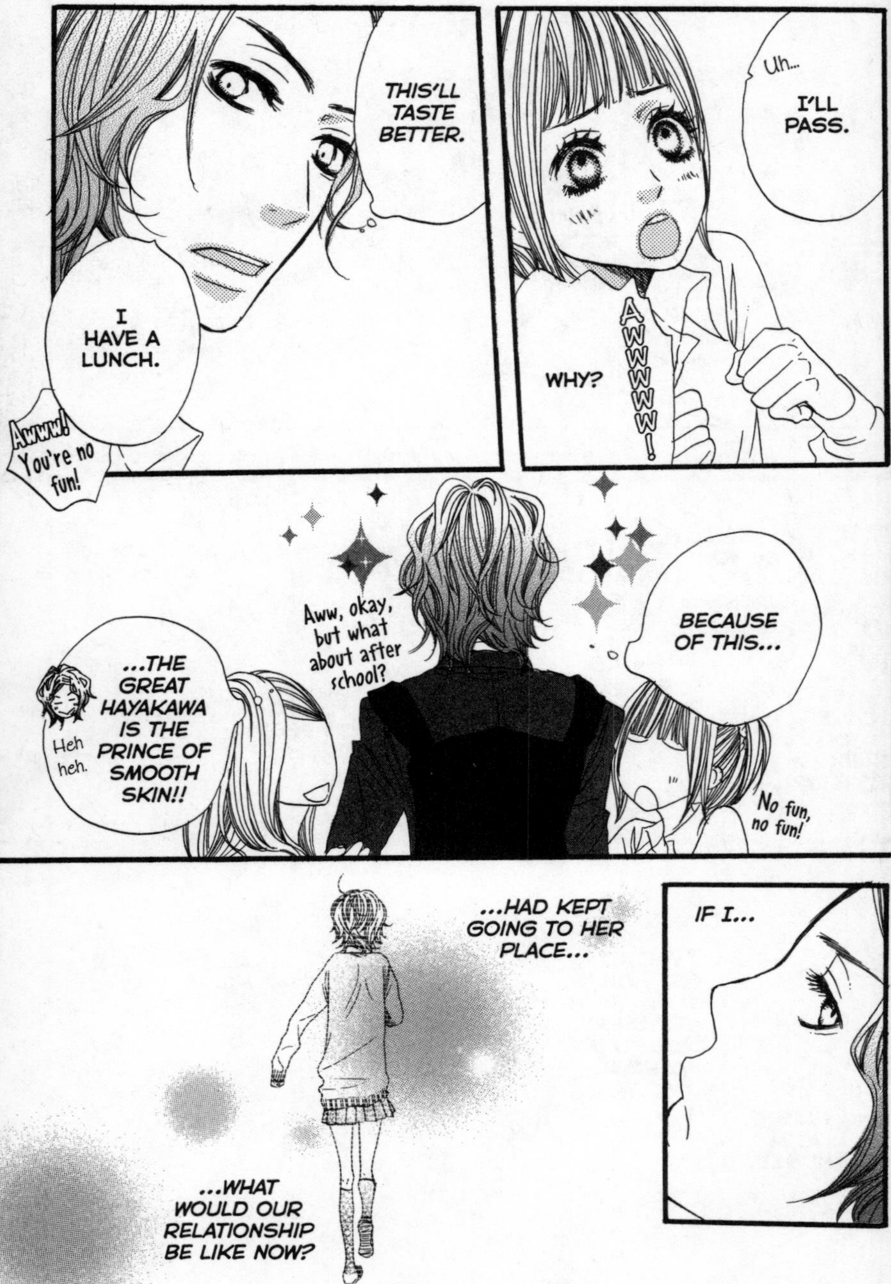
Uh... I'LL PASS.
AWWWWW!
WHY?
THIS'LL TASTE BETTER.
I HAVE A LUNCH.
Awww! You're no fun!
BECAUSE OF THIS...
No fun, no fun!
Aww, okay, but what about after school?
...THE GREAT HAYAKAWA IS THE PRINCE OF SMOOTH SKIN!!
Heh heh.
IF I...
...HAD KEPT GOING TO HER PLACE...
...WHAT WOULD OUR RELATIONSHIP BE LIKE NOW?

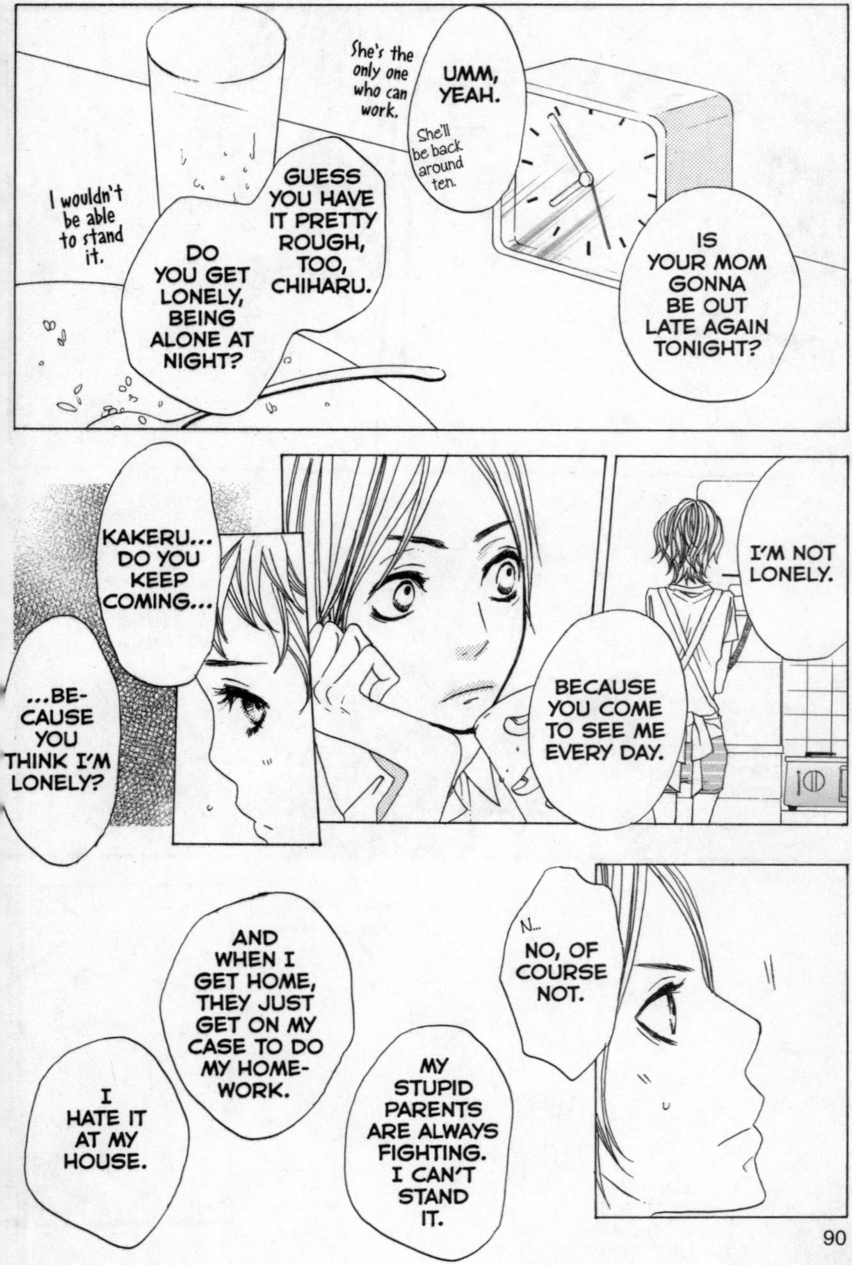
IS YOUR MOM GONNA BE OUT LATE AGAIN TONIGHT?
UMM, YEAH.
She'll be back around ten.
She's the only one who can work.
GUESS YOU HAVE IT PRETTY ROUGH, TOO, CHIHARU.
DO YOU GET LONELY, BEING ALONE AT NIGHT?
I wouldn't be able to stand it.
I'M NOT LONELY.
BECAUSE YOU COME TO SEE ME EVERY DAY.
KAKERU... DO YOU KEEP COMING...
...BE-CAUSE YOU THINK I'M LONELY?
N...
NO, OF COURSE NOT.
MY STUPID PARENTS ARE ALWAYS FIGHTING. I CAN'T STAND IT.
AND WHEN I GET HOME, THEY JUST GET ON MY CASE TO DO MY HOME-WORK.
I HATE IT AT MY HOUSE.

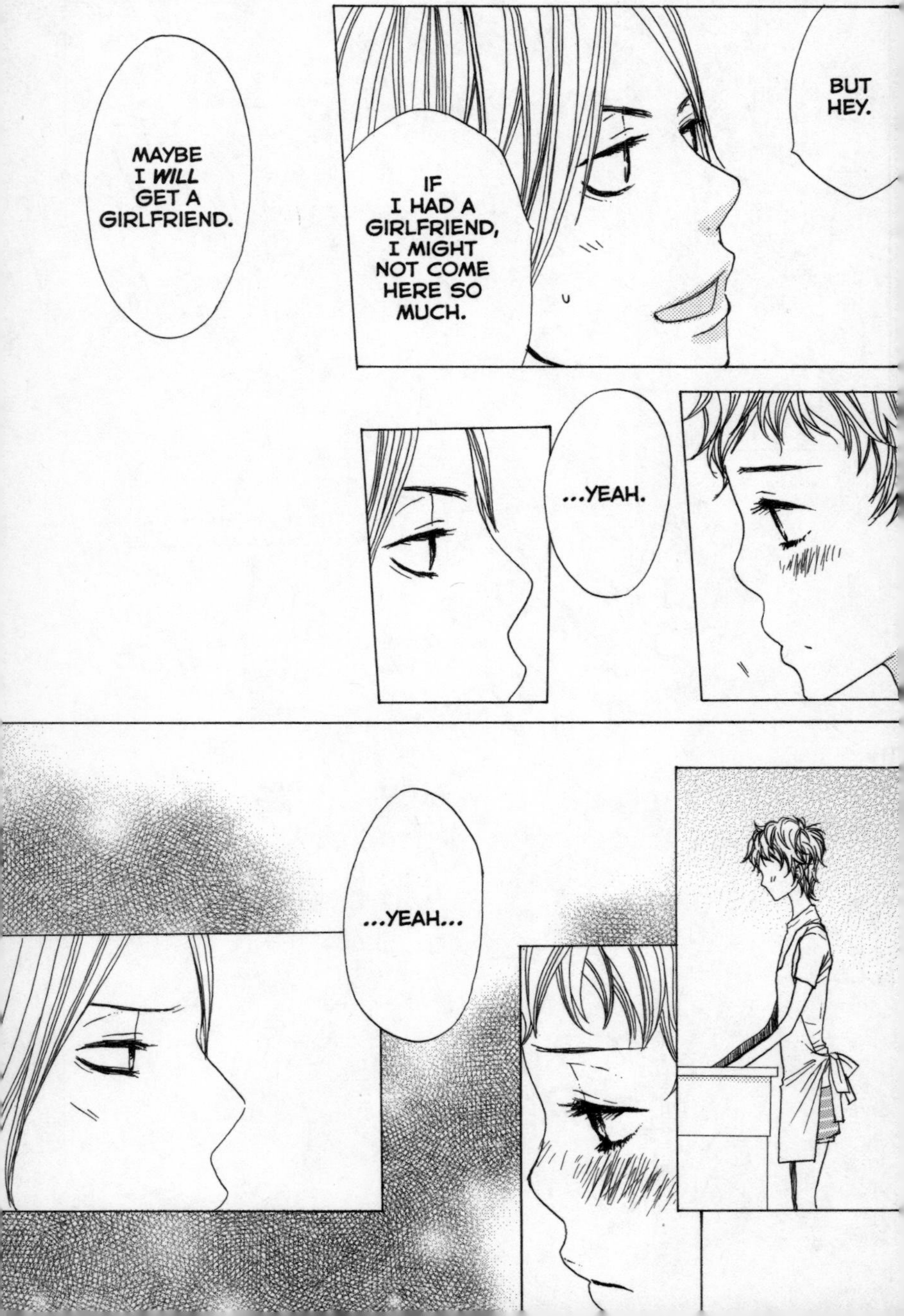
BUT HEY.
IF I HAD A GIRLFRIEND, I MIGHT NOT COME HERE SO MUCH.
MAYBE I *WILL* GET A GIRLFRIEND.
...YEAH.
...YEAH...

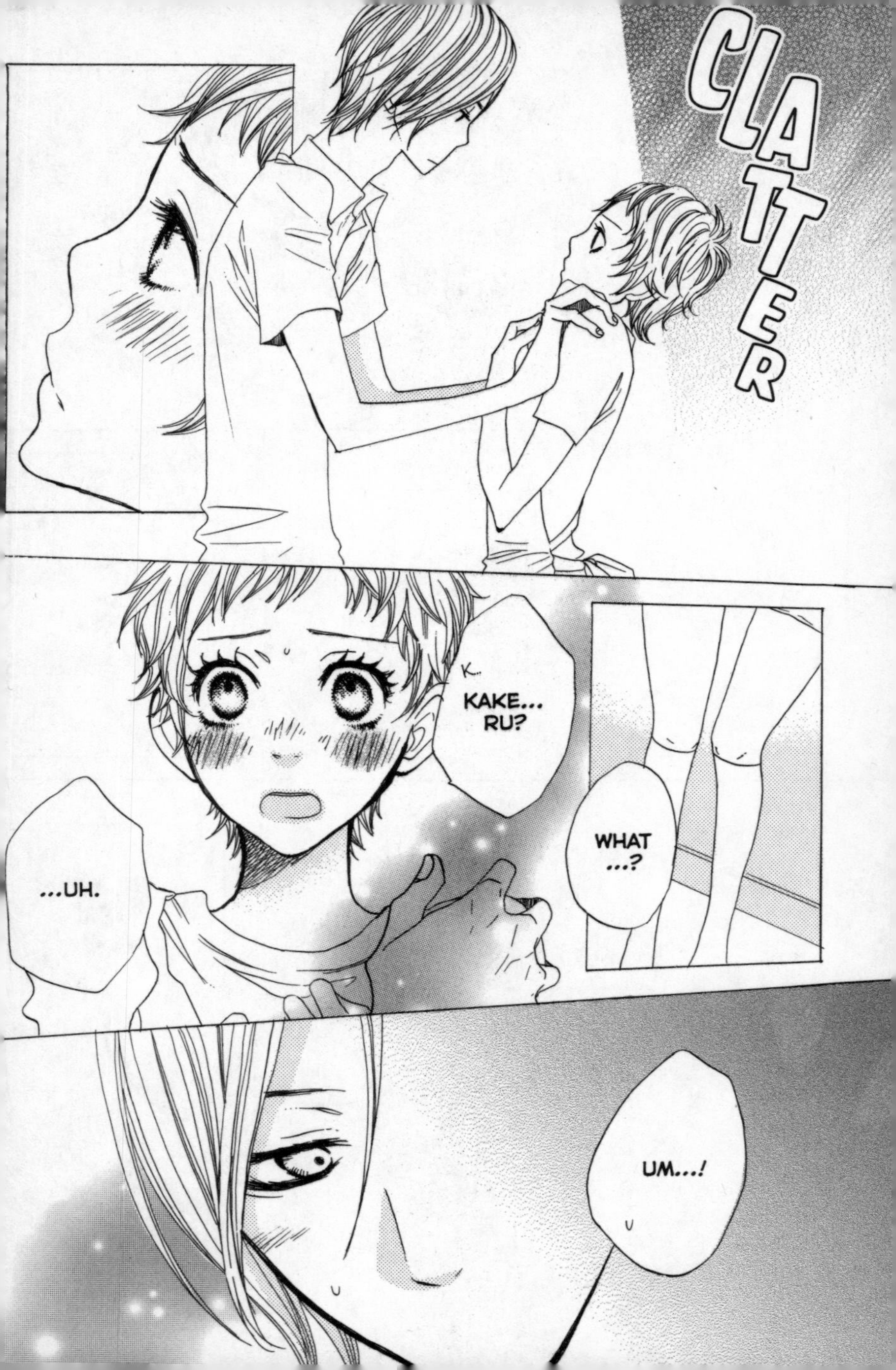
CLATTER
WHAT ...?
K... KAKE... RU?
...UH.
UM...!

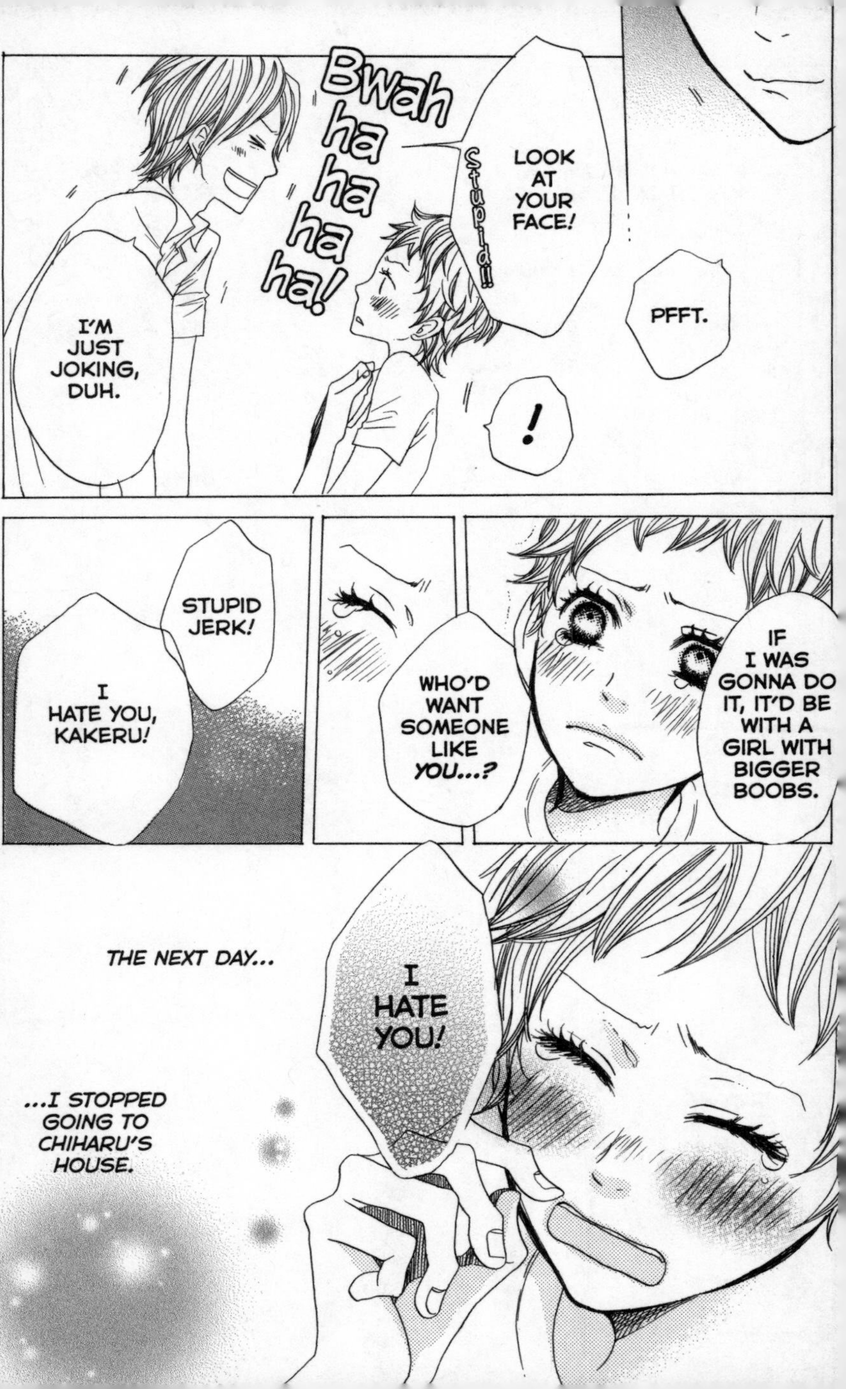
PFFT.
LOOK AT YOUR FACE!
Stupid!!
Bwah ha ha ha ha!
!
I'M JUST JOKING, DUH.
IF I WAS GONNA DO IT, IT'D BE WITH A GIRL WITH BIGGER BOOBS.
WHO'D WANT SOMEONE LIKE *YOU*...?
STUPID JERK!
I HATE YOU, KAKERU!
I HATE YOU!
THE NEXT DAY...
...I STOPPED GOING TO CHIHARU'S HOUSE.

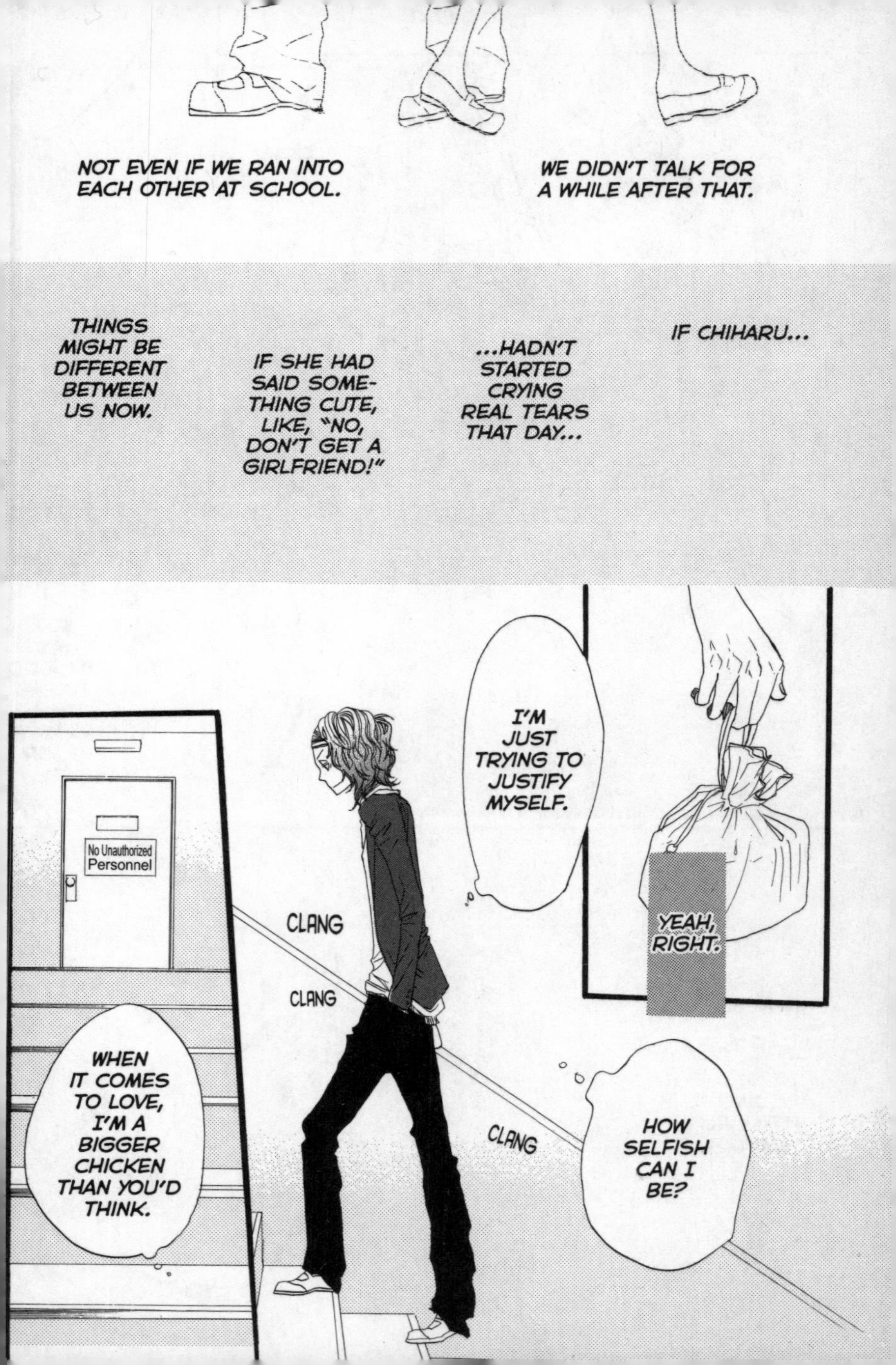
WE DIDN'T TALK FOR A WHILE AFTER THAT.
NOT EVEN IF WE RAN INTO EACH OTHER AT SCHOOL.
IF CHIHARU...
...HADN'T STARTED CRYING REAL TEARS THAT DAY...
IF SHE HAD SAID SOME-THING CUTE, LIKE, "NO, DON'T GET A GIRLFRIEND!"
THINGS MIGHT BE DIFFERENT BETWEEN US NOW.
I'M JUST TRYING TO JUSTIFY MYSELF.
YEAH, RIGHT.
CLANG
CLANG
HOW SELFISH CAN I BE?
CLANG
No Unauthorized Personnel
WHEN IT COMES TO LOVE, I'M A BIGGER CHICKEN THAN YOU'D THINK.

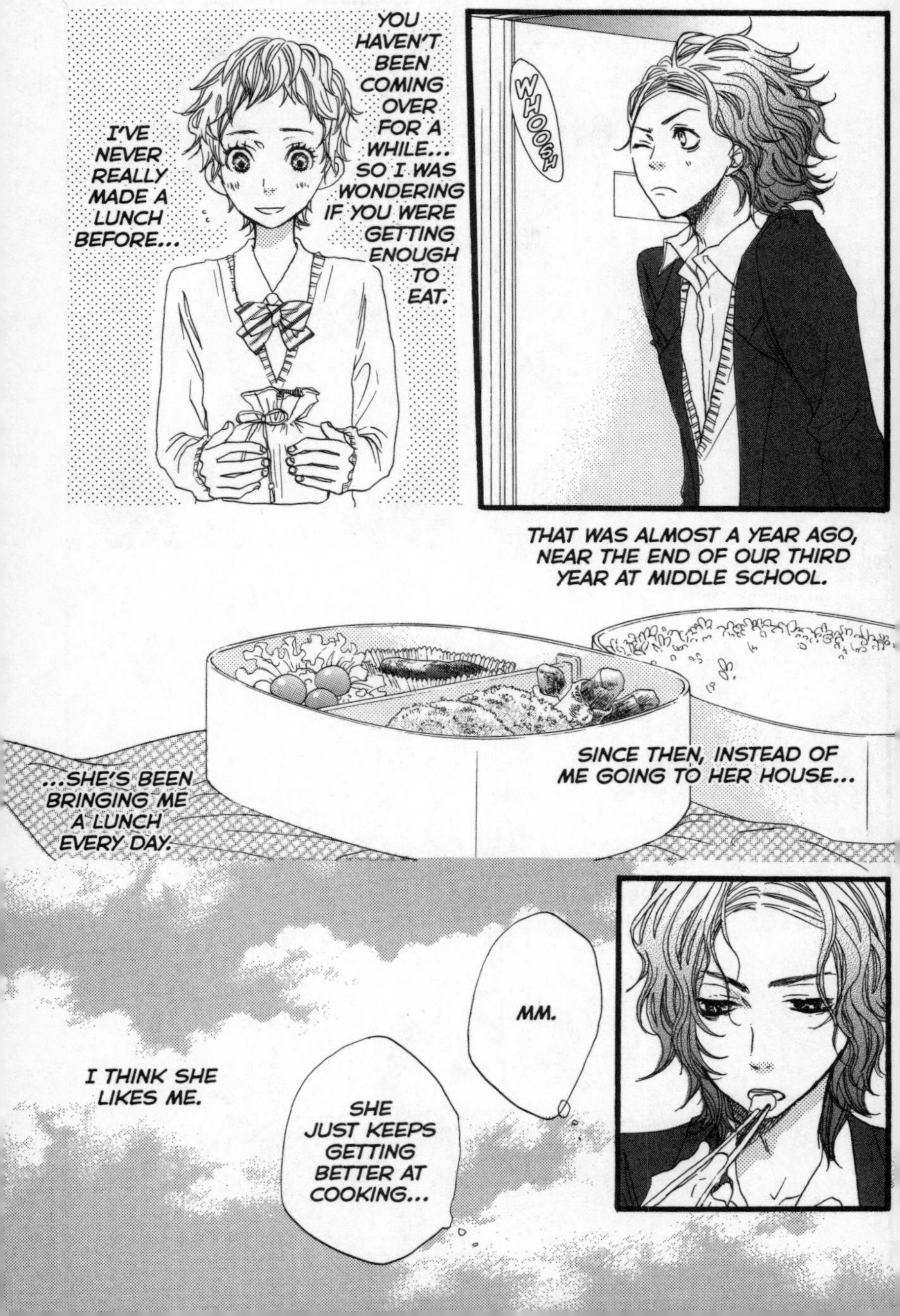
WHOOSH
YOU HAVEN'T BEEN COMING OVER FOR A WHILE... SO I WAS WONDERING IF YOU WERE GETTING ENOUGH TO EAT.
I'VE NEVER REALLY MADE A LUNCH BEFORE...
THAT WAS ALMOST A YEAR AGO, NEAR THE END OF OUR THIRD YEAR AT MIDDLE SCHOOL.
SINCE THEN, INSTEAD OF ME GOING TO HER HOUSE...
...SHE'S BEEN BRINGING ME A LUNCH EVERY DAY.
MM.
SHE JUST KEEPS GETTING BETTER AT COOKING...
I THINK SHE LIKES ME.

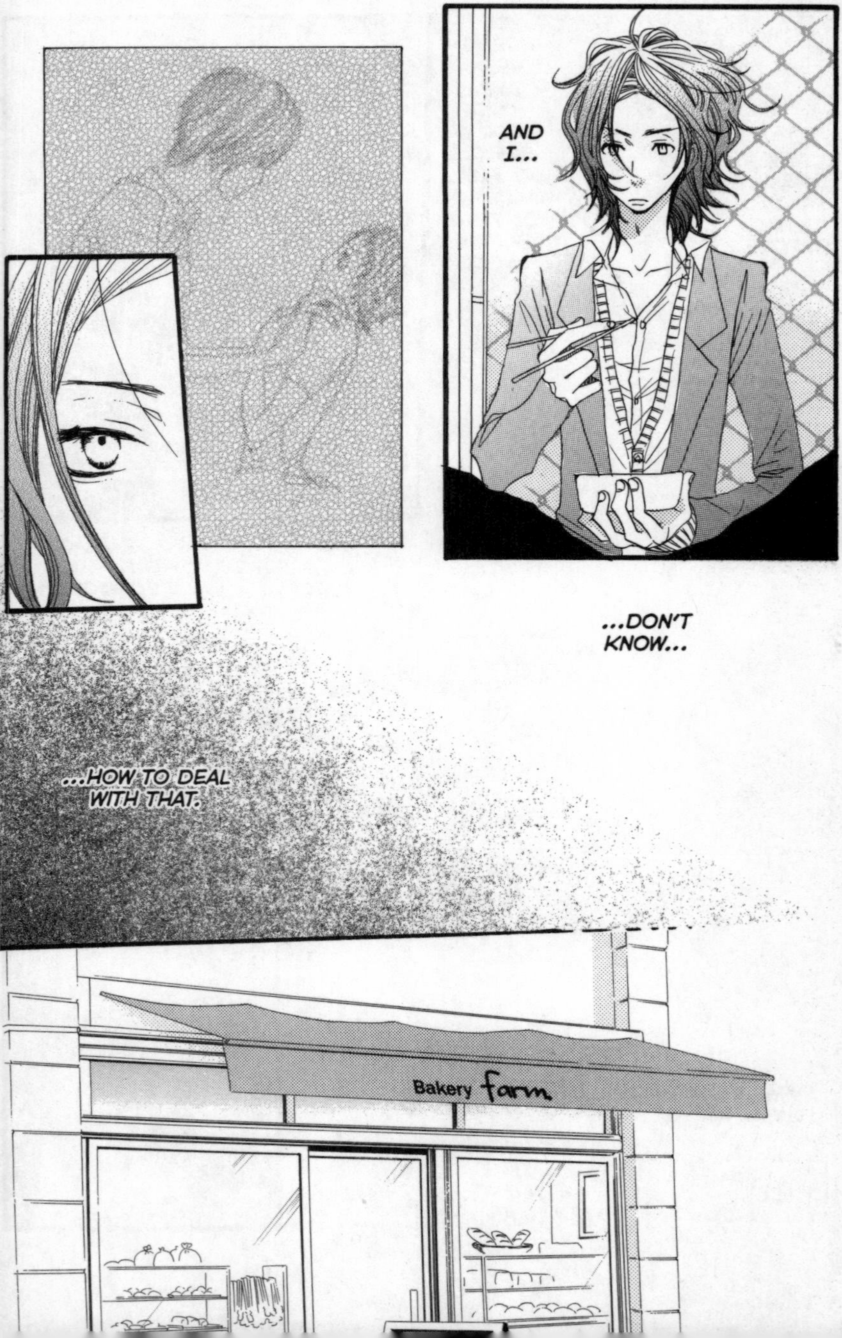
AND I...
...DON'T KNOW...
...HOW TO DEAL WITH THAT.
Bakery farm

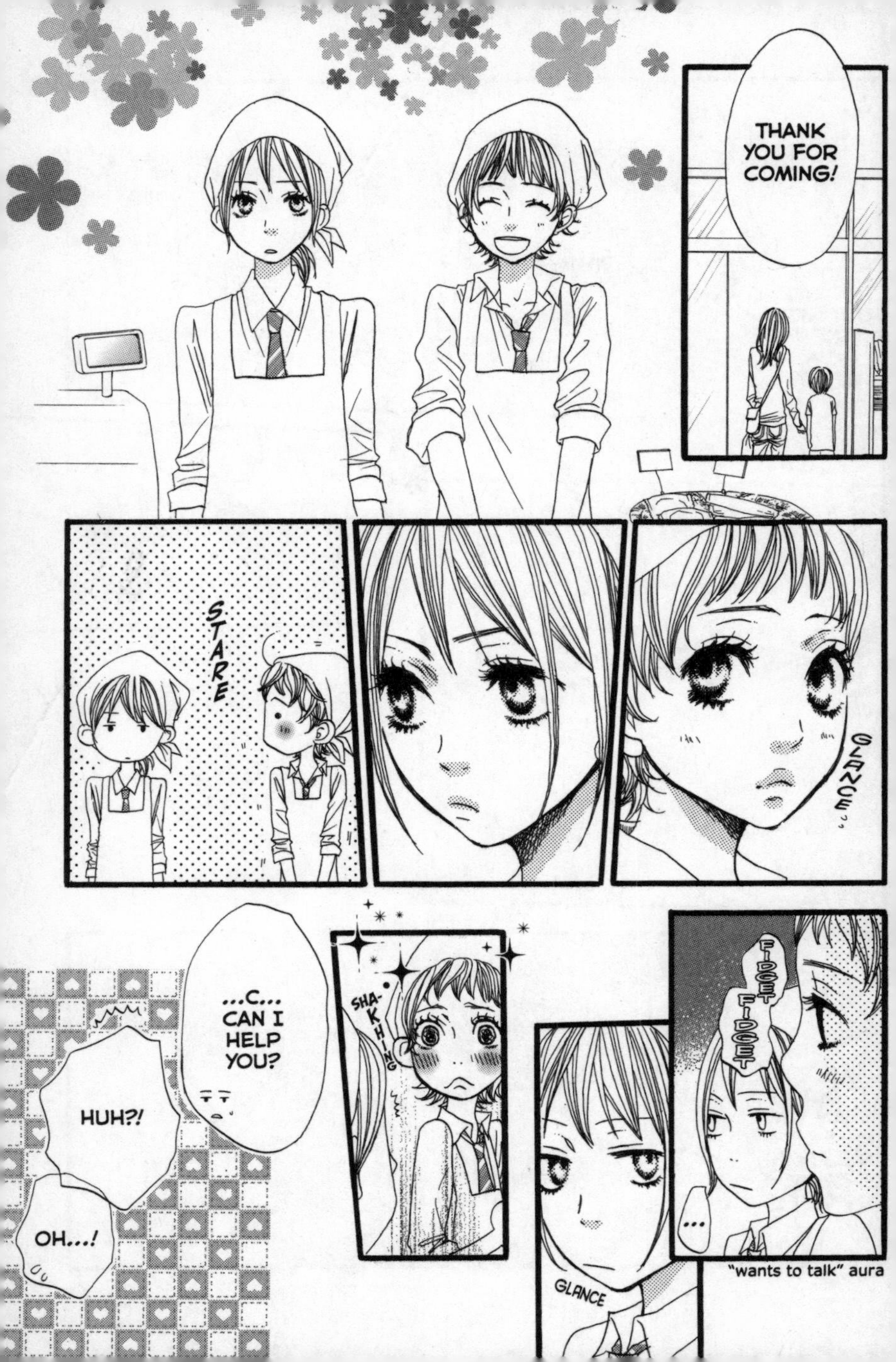
THANK YOU FOR COMING!
GLANCE
STARE
FIDGET FIDGET
...
"wants to talk" aura
GLANCE
SHA-KHING
...C... CAN I HELP YOU?
HUH?!
OH...!

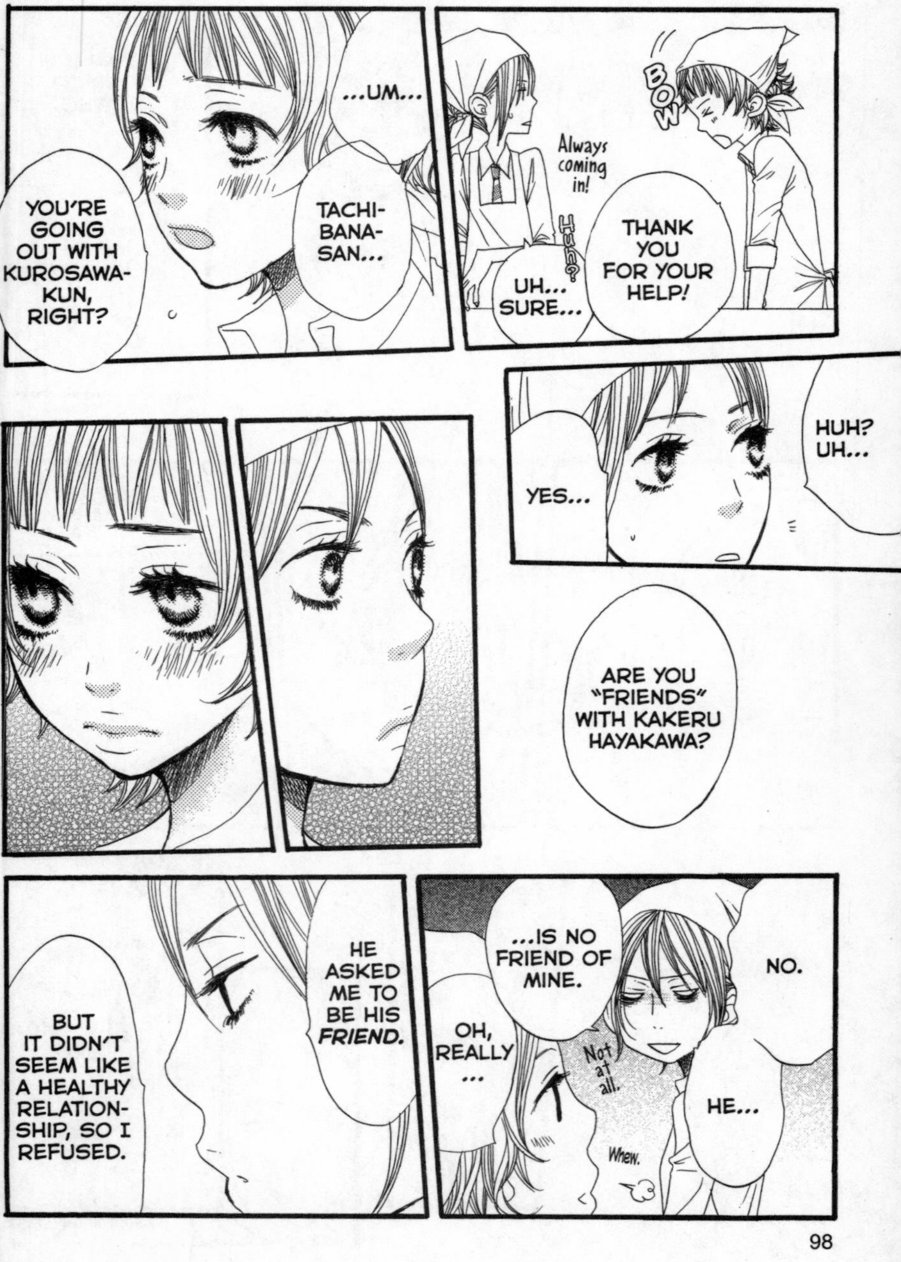
BOW
THANK YOU FOR YOUR HELP!
Always coming in!
Huh?
UH... SURE...
...UM...
TACHI-BANA-SAN...
YOU'RE GOING OUT WITH KUROSAWA-KUN, RIGHT?
HUH? UH...
YES...
ARE YOU "FRIENDS" WITH KAKERU HAYAKAWA?
NO.
HE...
...IS NO FRIEND OF MINE.
Not at all.
OH, REALLY...
Whew.
HE ASKED ME TO BE HIS *FRIEND.*
BUT IT DIDN'T SEEM LIKE A HEALTHY RELATIONSHIP, SO I REFUSED.

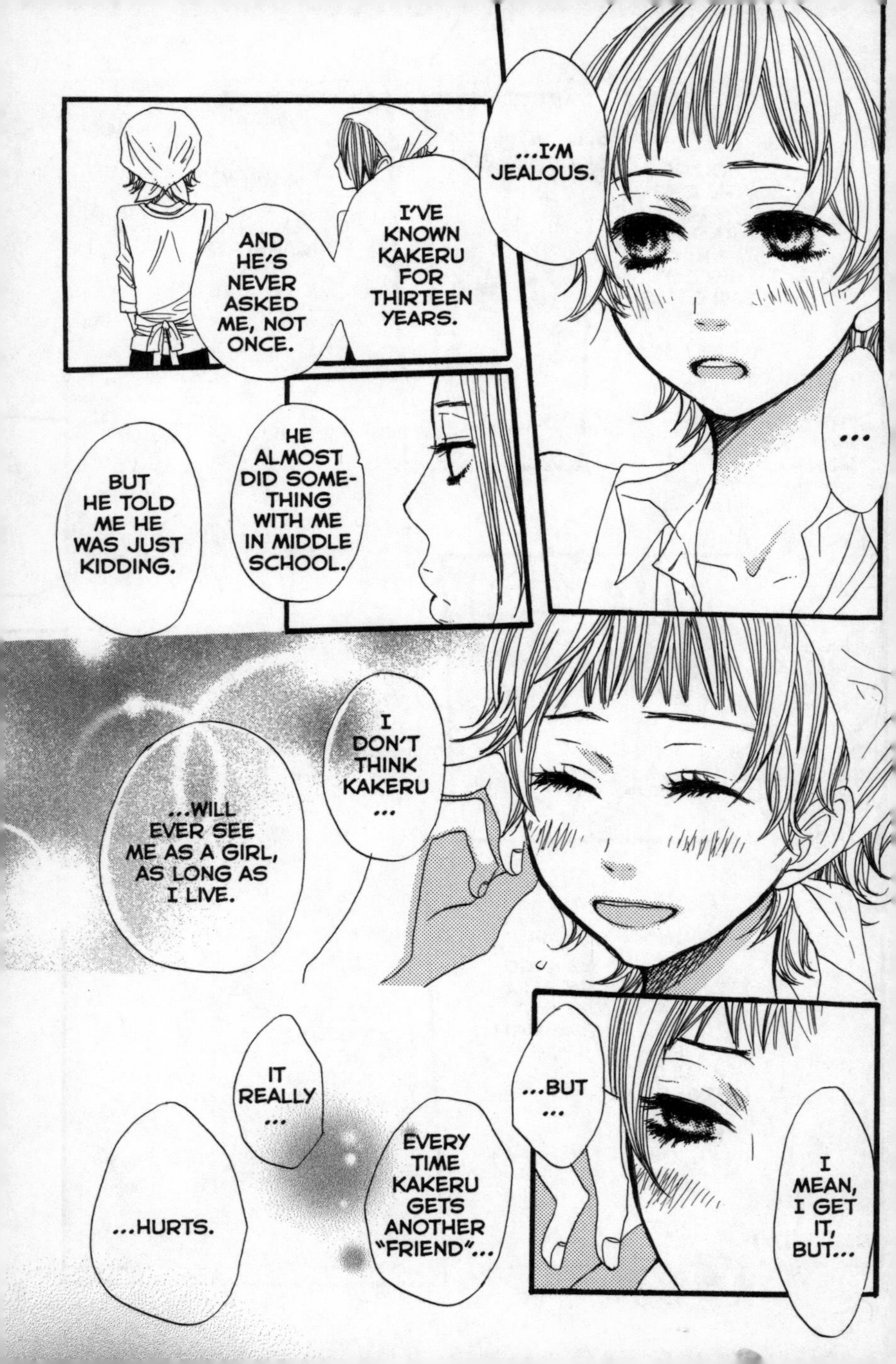
...I'M JEALOUS.
...
I'VE KNOWN KAKERU FOR THIRTEEN YEARS.
AND HE'S NEVER ASKED ME, NOT ONCE.
HE ALMOST DID SOMETHING WITH ME IN MIDDLE SCHOOL.
BUT HE TOLD ME HE WAS JUST KIDDING.
I DON'T THINK KAKERU...
...WILL EVER SEE ME AS A GIRL, AS LONG AS I LIVE.
...BUT...
I MEAN, I GET IT, BUT...
EVERY TIME KAKERU GETS ANOTHER "FRIEND"...
IT REALLY...
...HURTS.

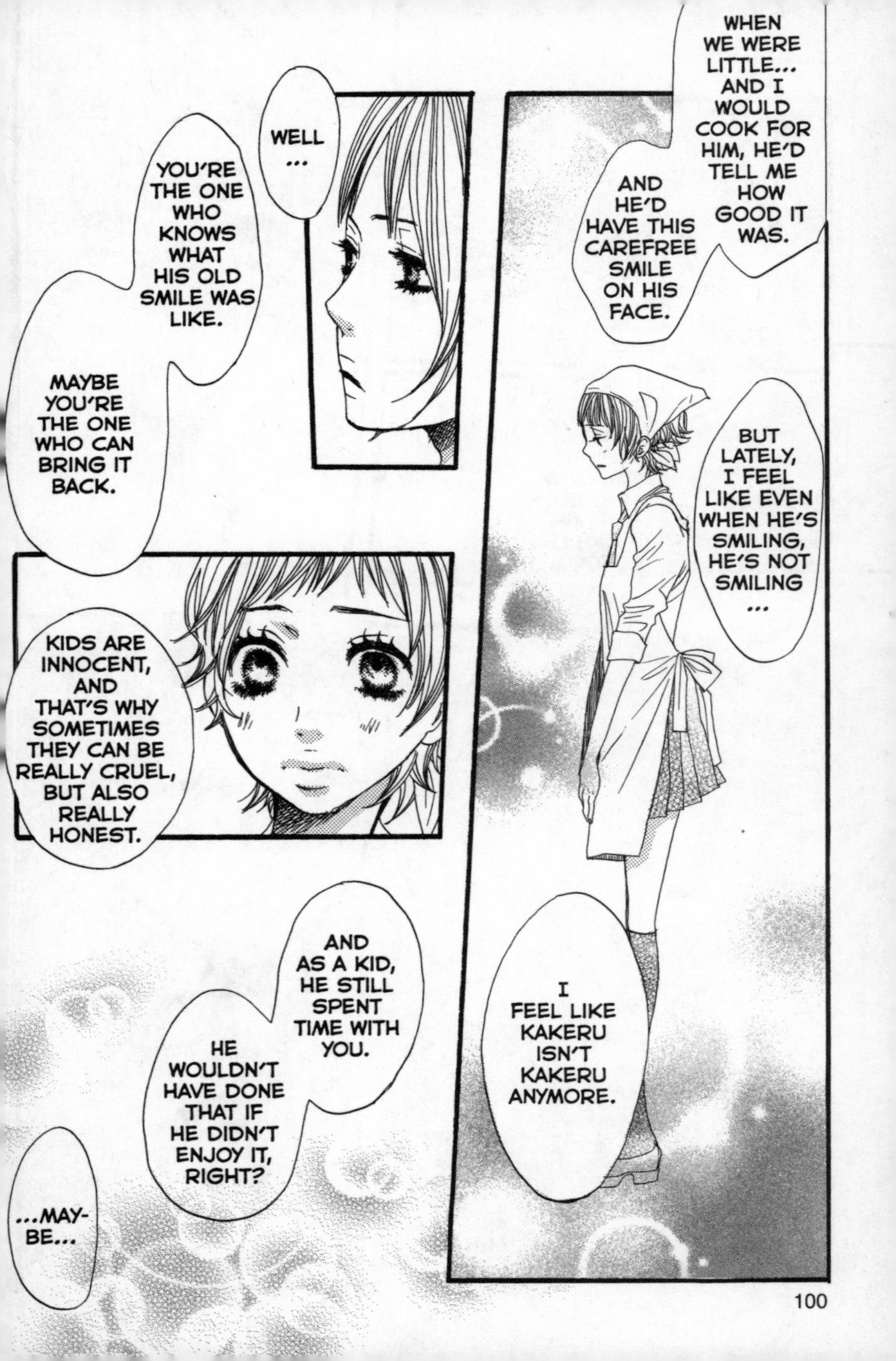
WHEN WE WERE LITTLE... AND I WOULD COOK FOR HIM, HE'D TELL ME HOW GOOD IT WAS.
AND HE'D HAVE THIS CAREFREE SMILE ON HIS FACE.
BUT LATELY, I FEEL LIKE EVEN WHEN HE'S SMILING, HE'S NOT SMILING...
I FEEL LIKE KAKERU ISN'T KAKERU ANYMORE.
WELL...
YOU'RE THE ONE WHO KNOWS WHAT HIS OLD SMILE WAS LIKE.
MAYBE YOU'RE THE ONE WHO CAN BRING IT BACK.
KIDS ARE INNOCENT, AND THAT'S WHY SOMETIMES THEY CAN BE REALLY CRUEL, BUT ALSO REALLY HONEST.
AND AS A KID, HE STILL SPENT TIME WITH YOU.
HE WOULDN'T HAVE DONE THAT IF HE DIDN'T ENJOY IT, RIGHT?
...MAY-BE...

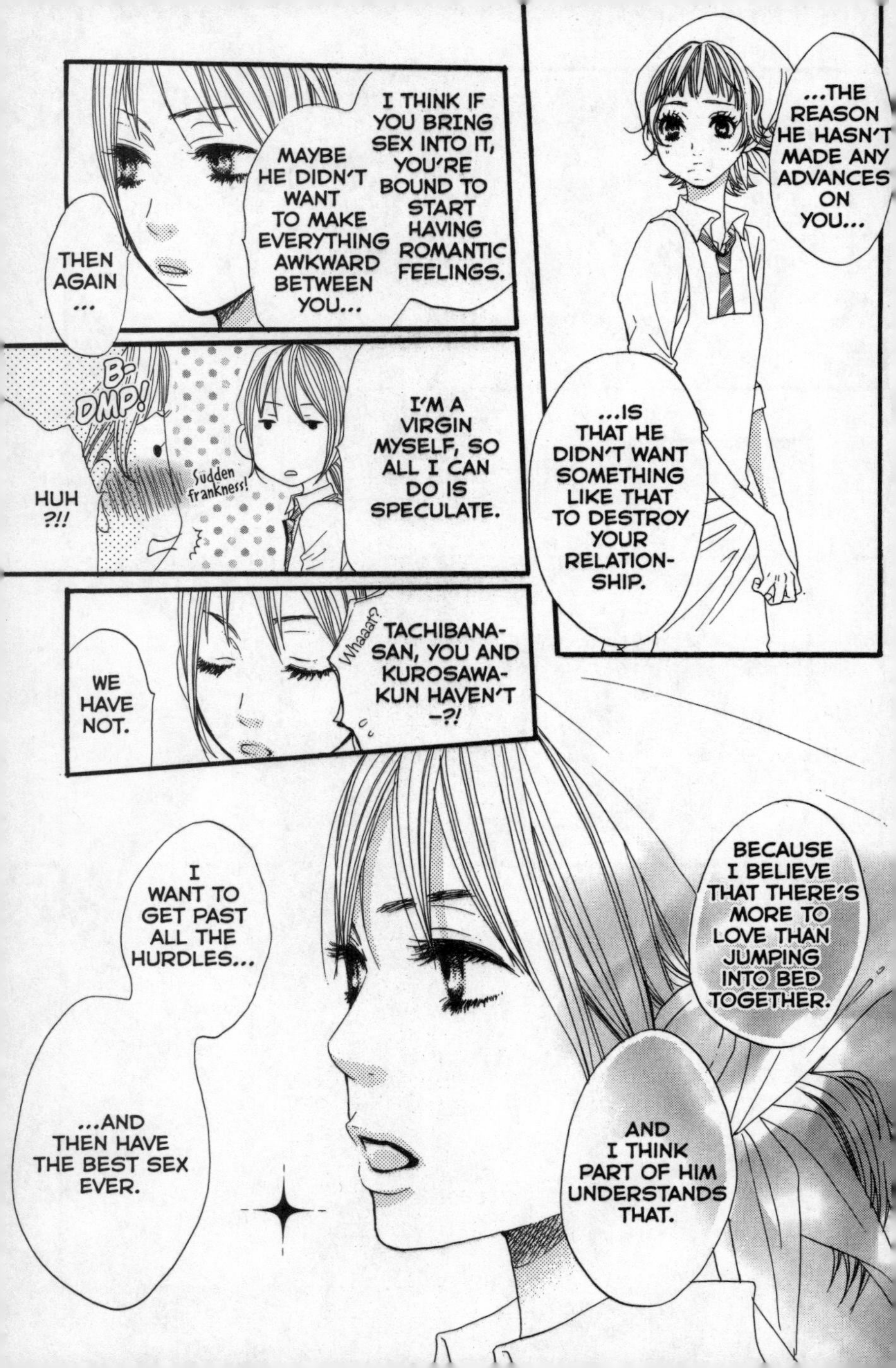
...THE REASON HE HASN'T MADE ANY ADVANCES ON YOU...
...IS THAT HE DIDN'T WANT SOMETHING LIKE THAT TO DESTROY YOUR RELATION-SHIP.
I THINK IF YOU BRING SEX INTO IT, YOU'RE BOUND TO START HAVING ROMANTIC FEELINGS.
MAYBE HE DIDN'T WANT TO MAKE EVERYTHING AWKWARD BETWEEN YOU...
THEN AGAIN...
I'M A VIRGIN MYSELF, SO ALL I CAN DO IS SPECULATE.
Sudden frankness!
B-DMP!
HUH ?!!
TACHIBANA-SAN, YOU AND KUROSAWA-KUN HAVEN'T -?!
Whaaat?
WE HAVE NOT.
BECAUSE I BELIEVE THAT THERE'S MORE TO LOVE THAN JUMPING INTO BED TOGETHER.
AND I THINK PART OF HIM UNDERSTANDS THAT.
I WANT TO GET PAST ALL THE HURDLES...
...AND THEN HAVE THE BEST SEX EVER.

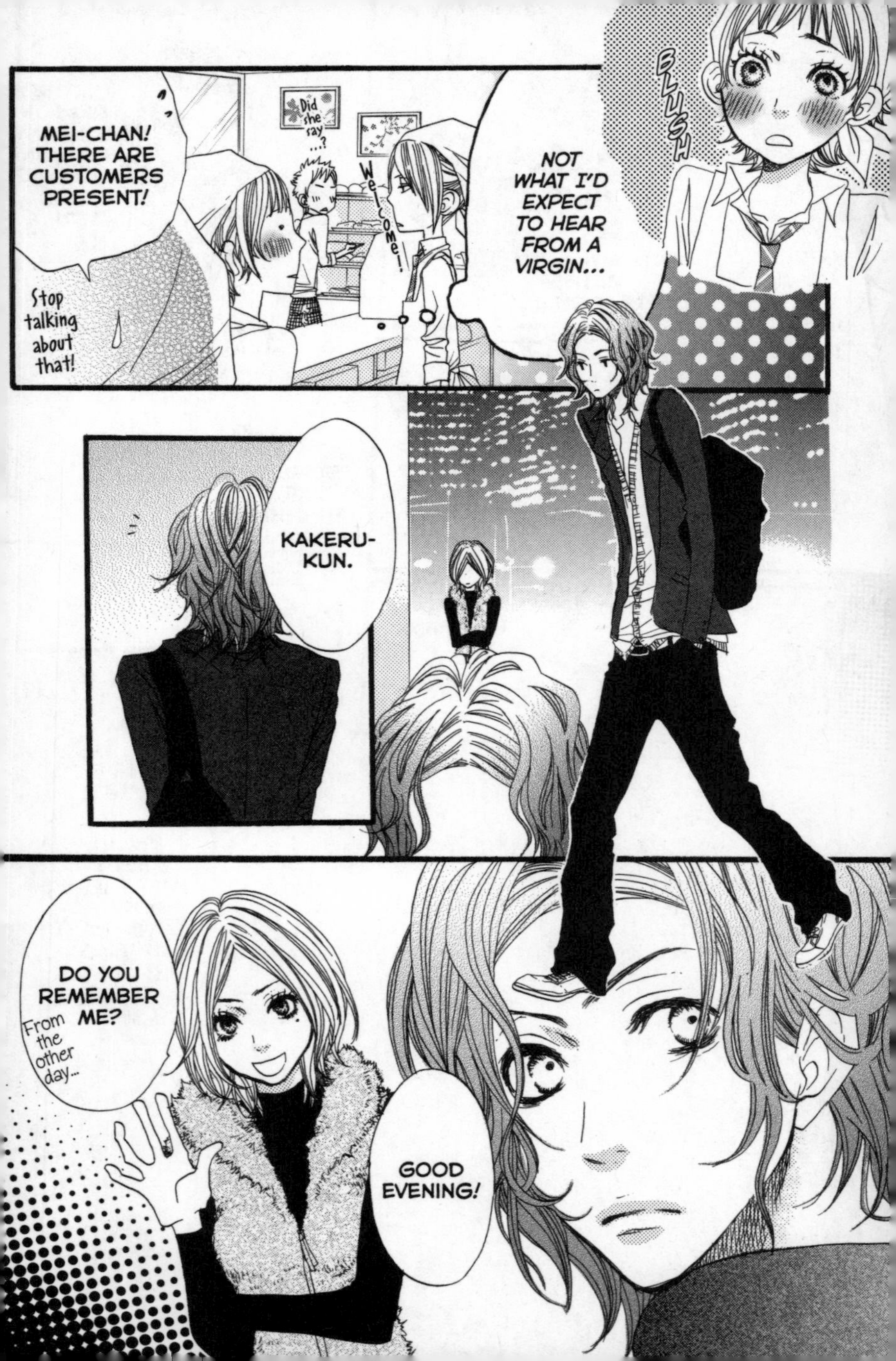
BLUSH
NOT WHAT I'D EXPECT TO HEAR FROM A VIRGIN...
Welcome!
Did she say ...?
MEI-CHAN! THERE ARE CUSTOMERS PRESENT!
Stop talking about that!
KAKERU-KUN.
GOOD EVENING!
DO YOU REMEMBER ME?
From the other day...

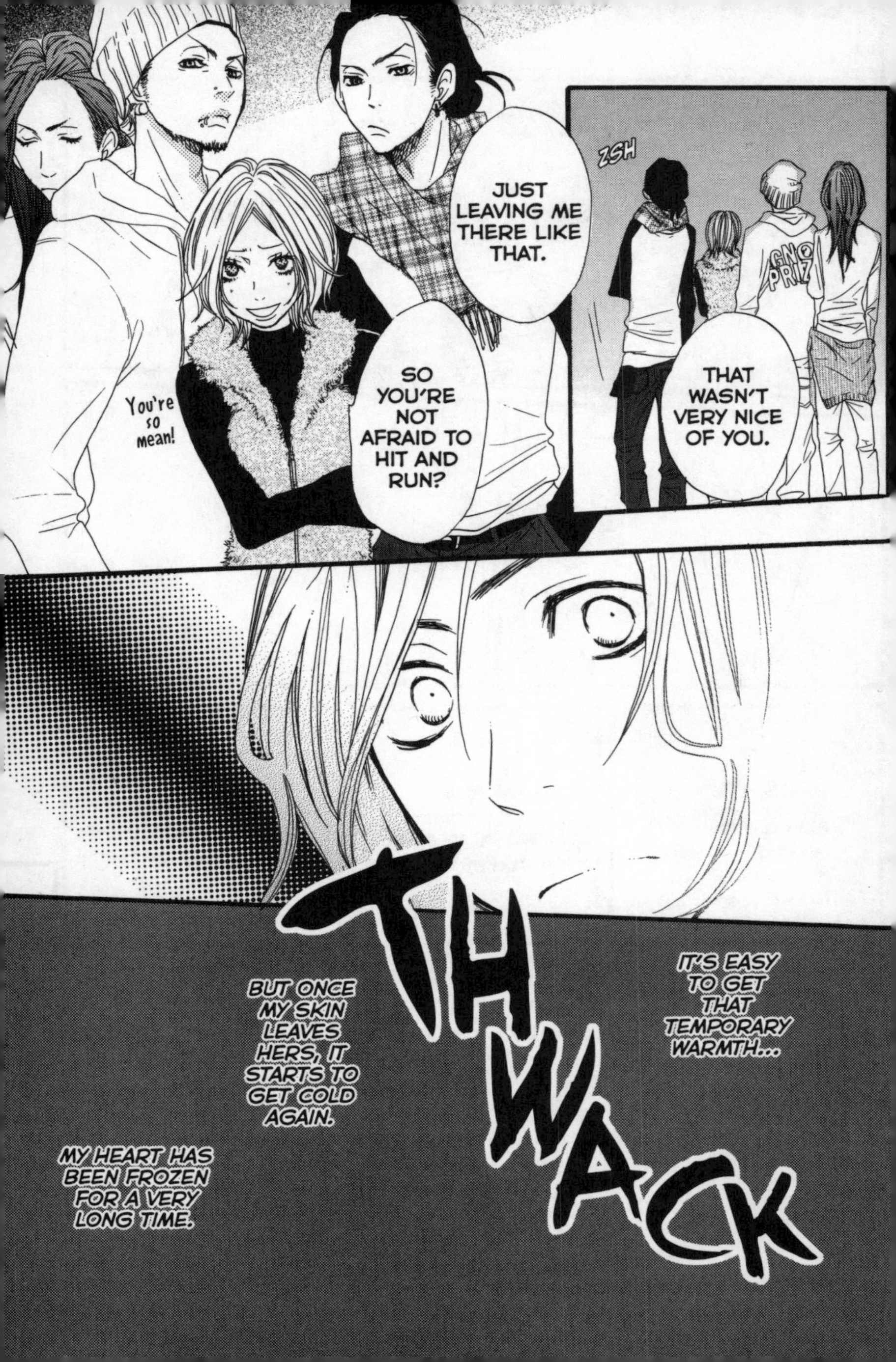
ZSH
THAT WASN'T VERY NICE OF YOU.
JUST LEAVING ME THERE LIKE THAT.
SO YOU'RE NOT AFRAID TO HIT AND RUN?
You're so mean!
THWACK
IT'S EASY TO GET THAT TEMPORARY WARMTH...
BUT ONCE MY SKIN LEAVES HERS, IT STARTS TO GET COLD AGAIN.
MY HEART HAS BEEN FROZEN FOR A VERY LONG TIME.

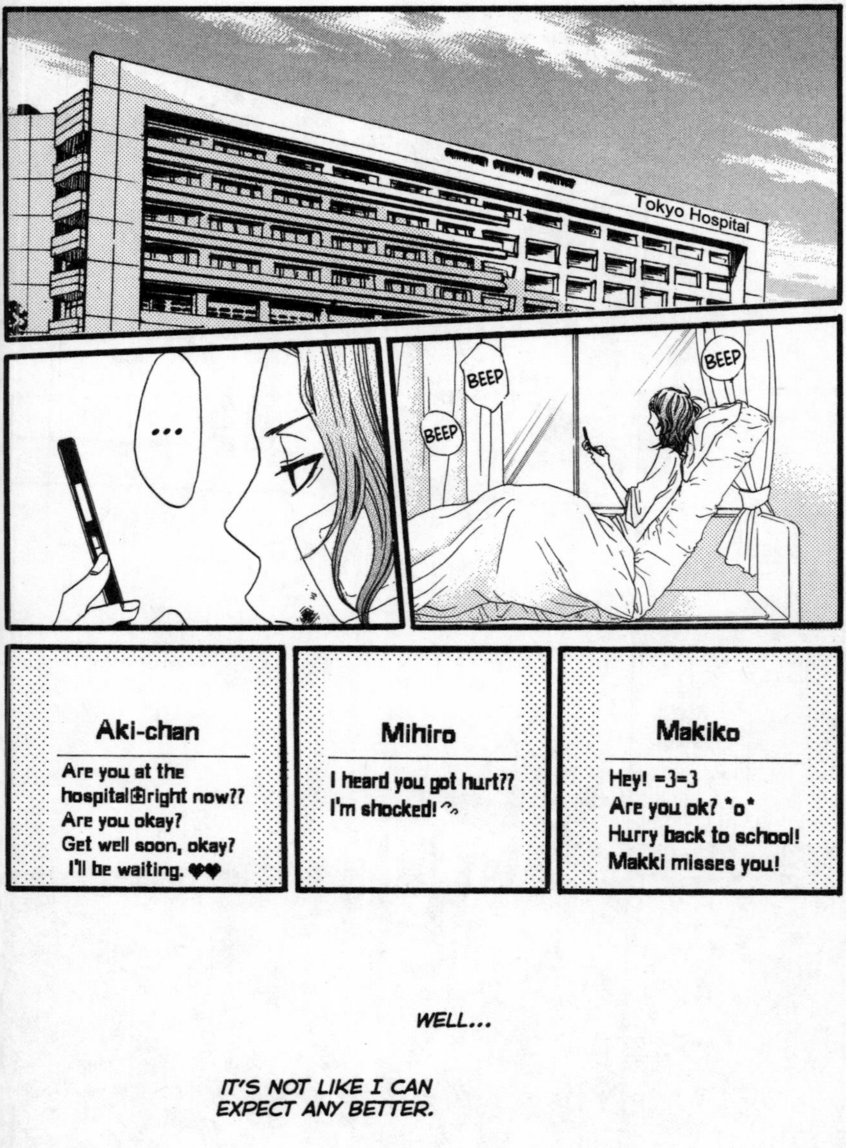
Tokyo Hospital
BEEP
BEEP
BEEP
...
Makiko
Hey! =3=3
Are you ok? *o*
Hurry back to school!
Makki misses you!
Mihiro
I heard you got hurt??
I'm shocked!
Aki-chan
Are you at the
hospital right now??
Are you okay?
Get well soon, okay?
I'll be waiting.
WELL...
IT'S NOT LIKE I CAN
EXPECT ANY BETTER.

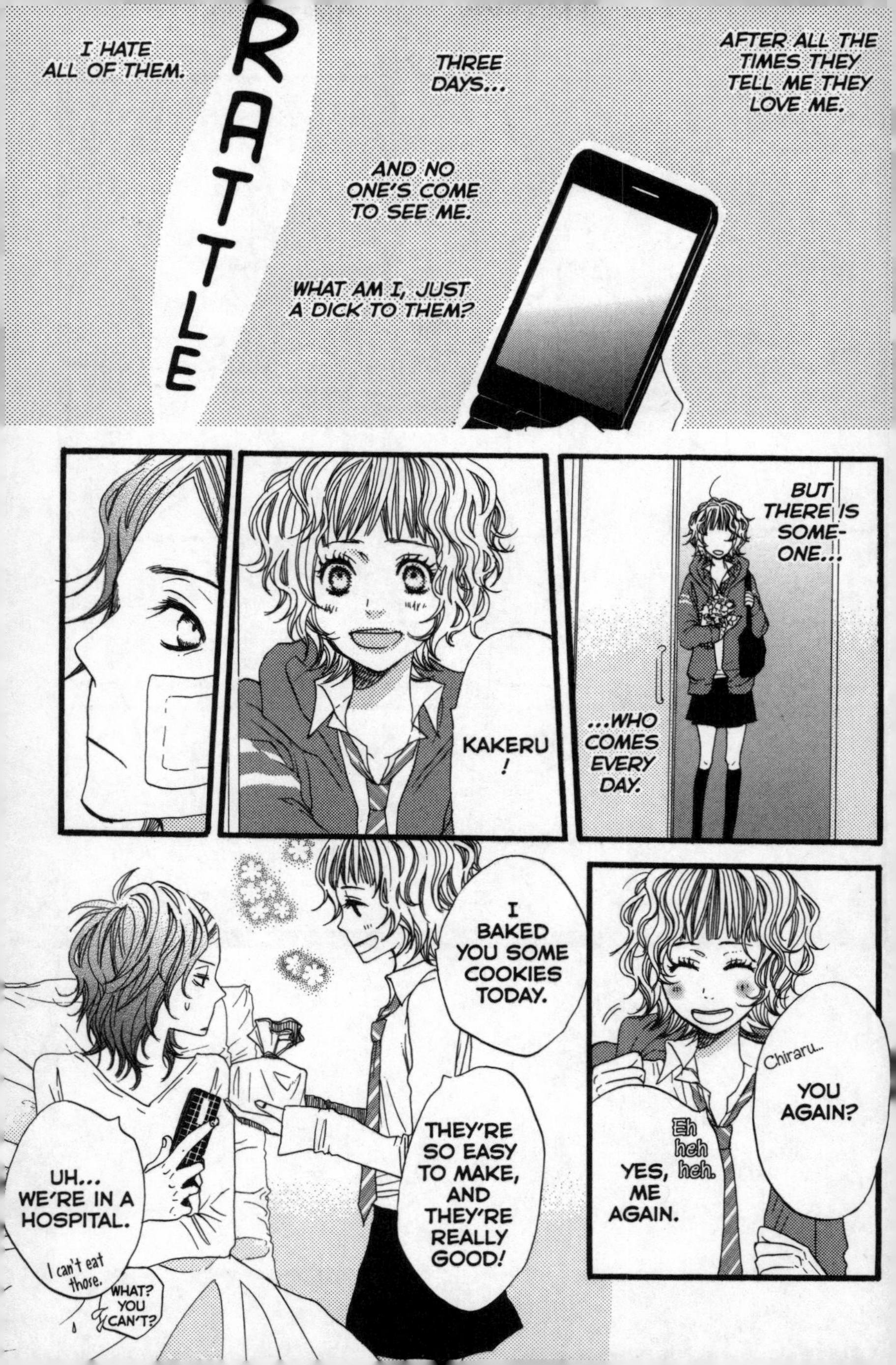
AFTER ALL THE TIMES THEY TELL ME THEY LOVE ME.
THREE DAYS...
AND NO ONE'S COME TO SEE ME.
WHAT AM I, JUST A DICK TO THEM?
RATTLE
I HATE ALL OF THEM.
BUT THERE IS SOME-ONE...
...WHO COMES EVERY DAY.
KAKERU!
Chiraru...
YOU AGAIN?
Eh heh heh.
YES, ME AGAIN.
I BAKED YOU SOME COOKIES TODAY.
THEY'RE SO EASY TO MAKE, AND THEY'RE REALLY GOOD!
UH... WE'RE IN A HOSPITAL.
I can't eat those.
WHAT? YOU CAN'T?

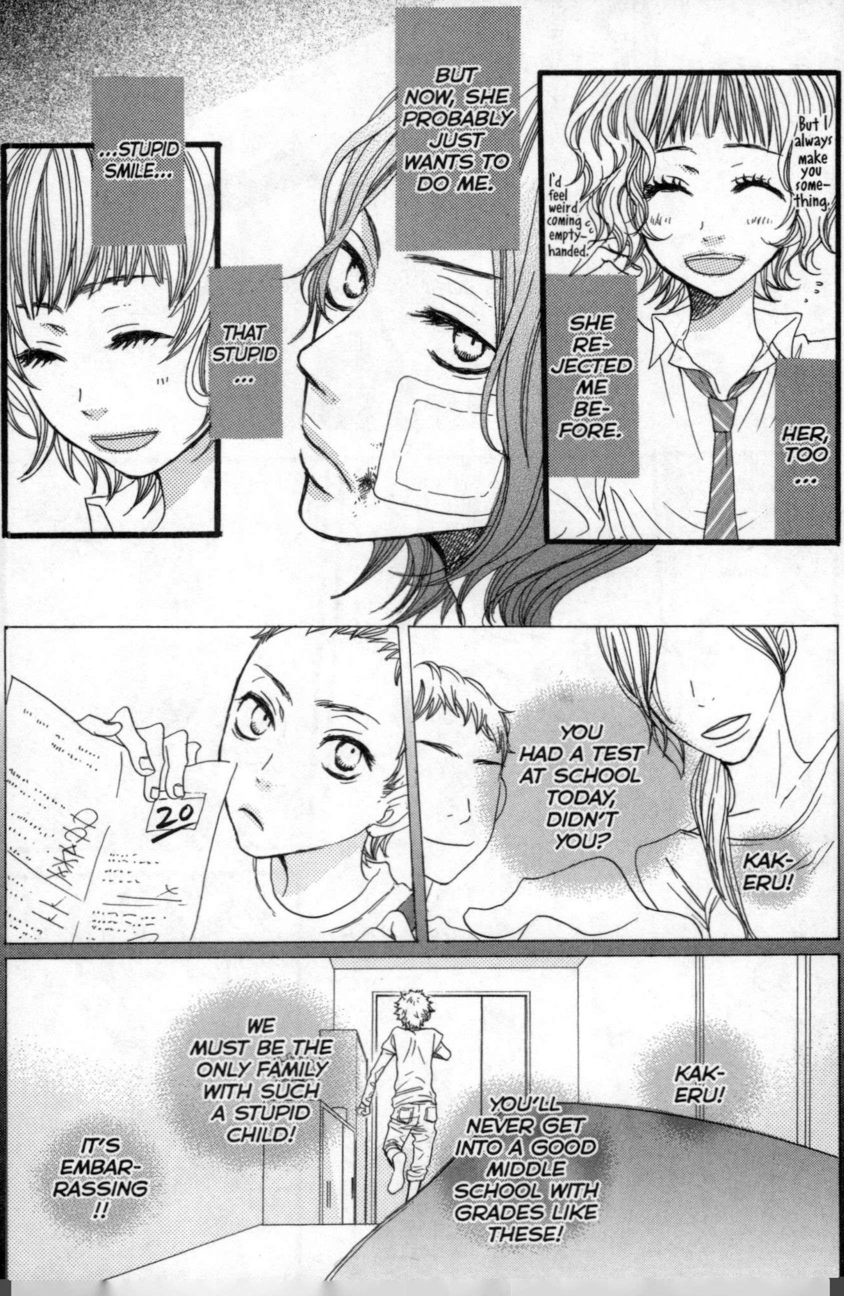
But I always make you something.
I'd feel weird coming empty-handed.
HER, TOO...
SHE REJECTED ME BEFORE.
BUT NOW, SHE PROBABLY JUST WANTS TO DO ME.
THAT STUPID...
...STUPID SMILE...
KAKERU!
YOU HAD A TEST AT SCHOOL TODAY, DIDN'T YOU?
20
KAKERU!
YOU'LL NEVER GET INTO A GOOD MIDDLE SCHOOL WITH GRADES LIKE THESE!
WE MUST BE THE ONLY FAMILY WITH SUCH A STUPID CHILD!
IT'S EMBARRASSING!!

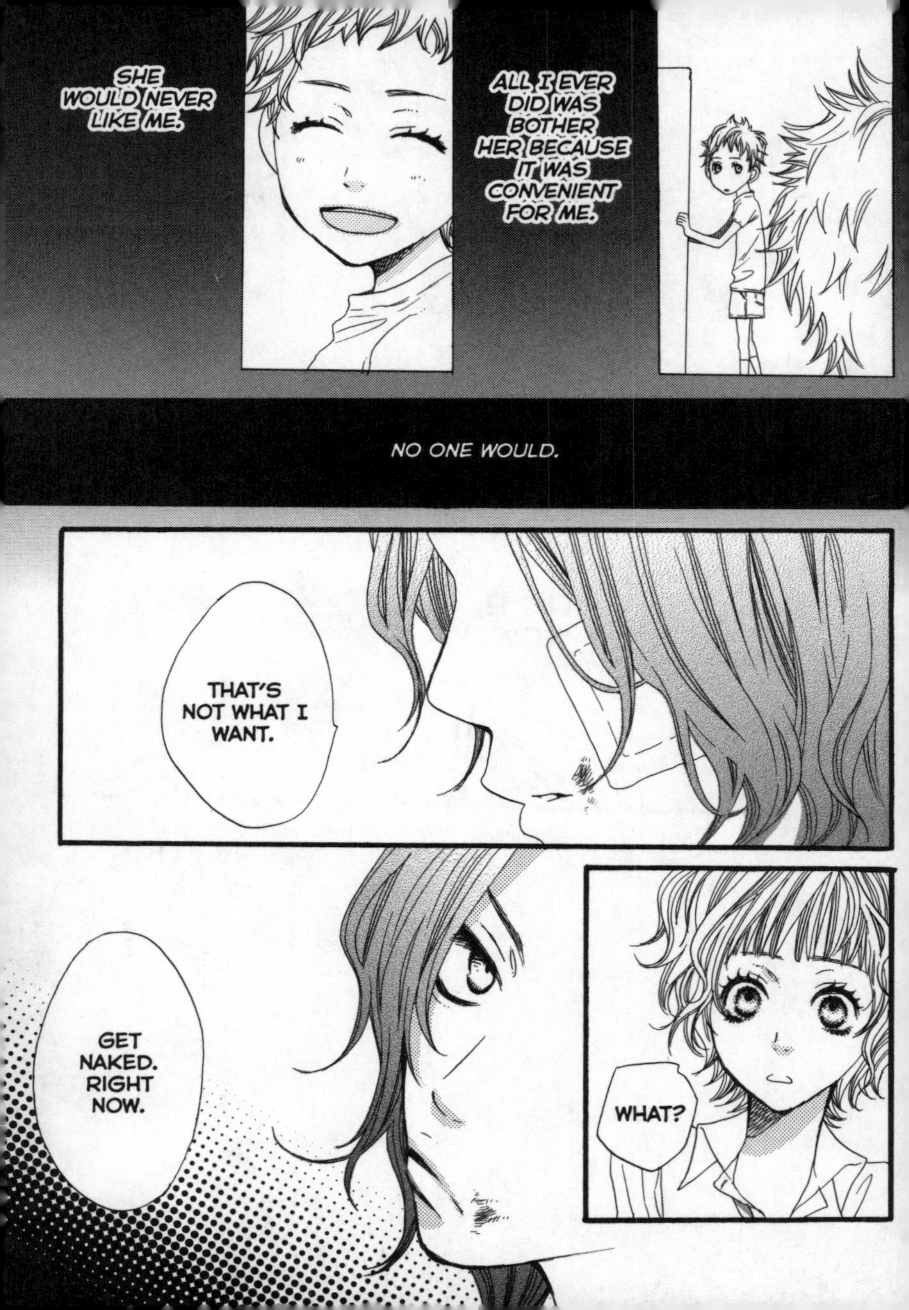
SHE WOULD NEVER LIKE ME.
ALL I EVER DID WAS BOTHER HER BECAUSE IT WAS CONVENIENT FOR ME.
NO ONE WOULD.
THAT'S NOT WHAT I WANT.
GET NAKED. RIGHT NOW.
WHAT?

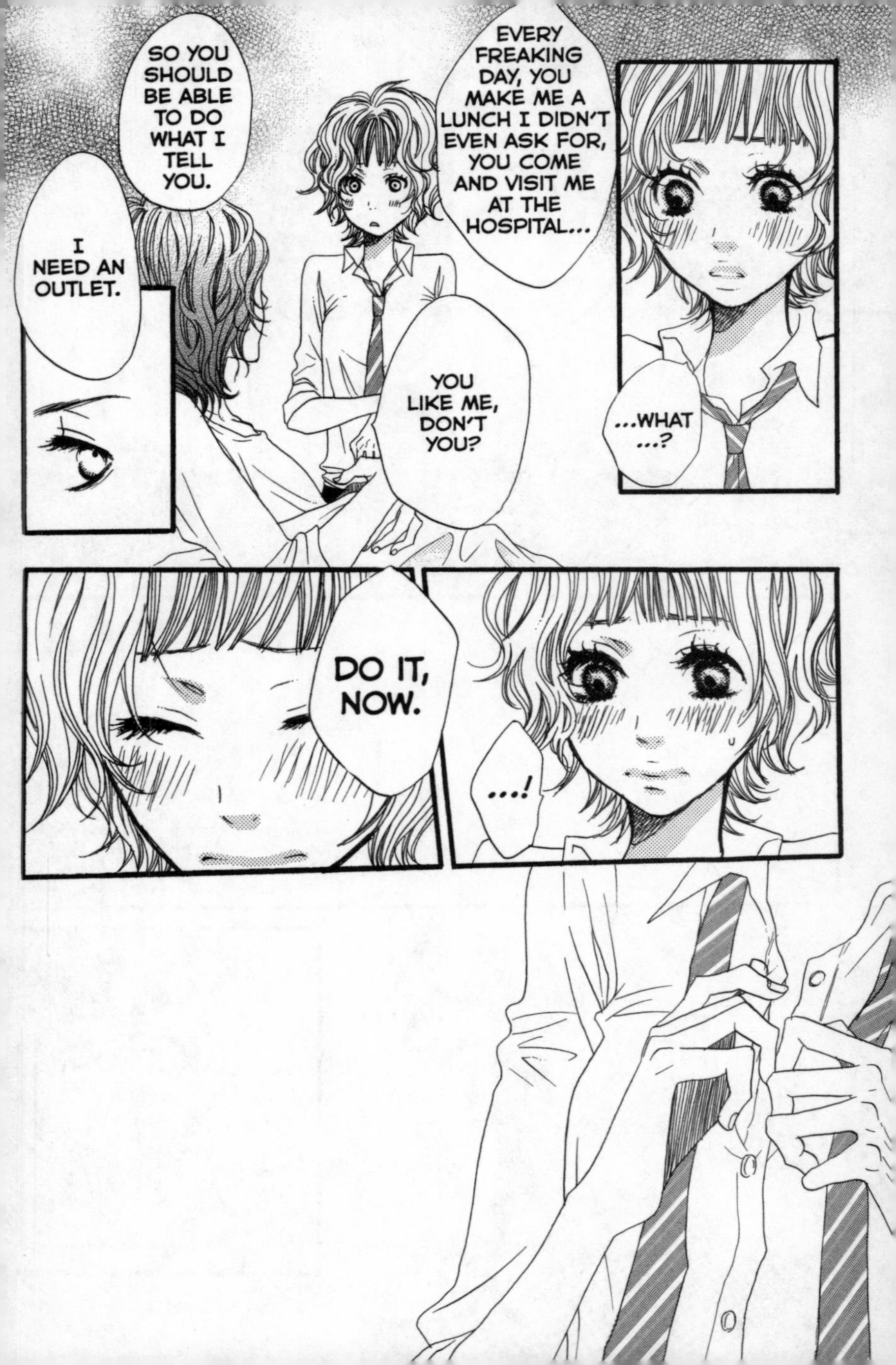
EVERY FREAKING DAY, YOU MAKE ME A LUNCH I DIDN'T EVEN ASK FOR, YOU COME AND VISIT ME AT THE HOSPITAL...
YOU LIKE ME, DON'T YOU?
...WHAT ...?
SO YOU SHOULD BE ABLE TO DO WHAT I TELL YOU.
I NEED AN OUTLET.
DO IT, NOW.
...!

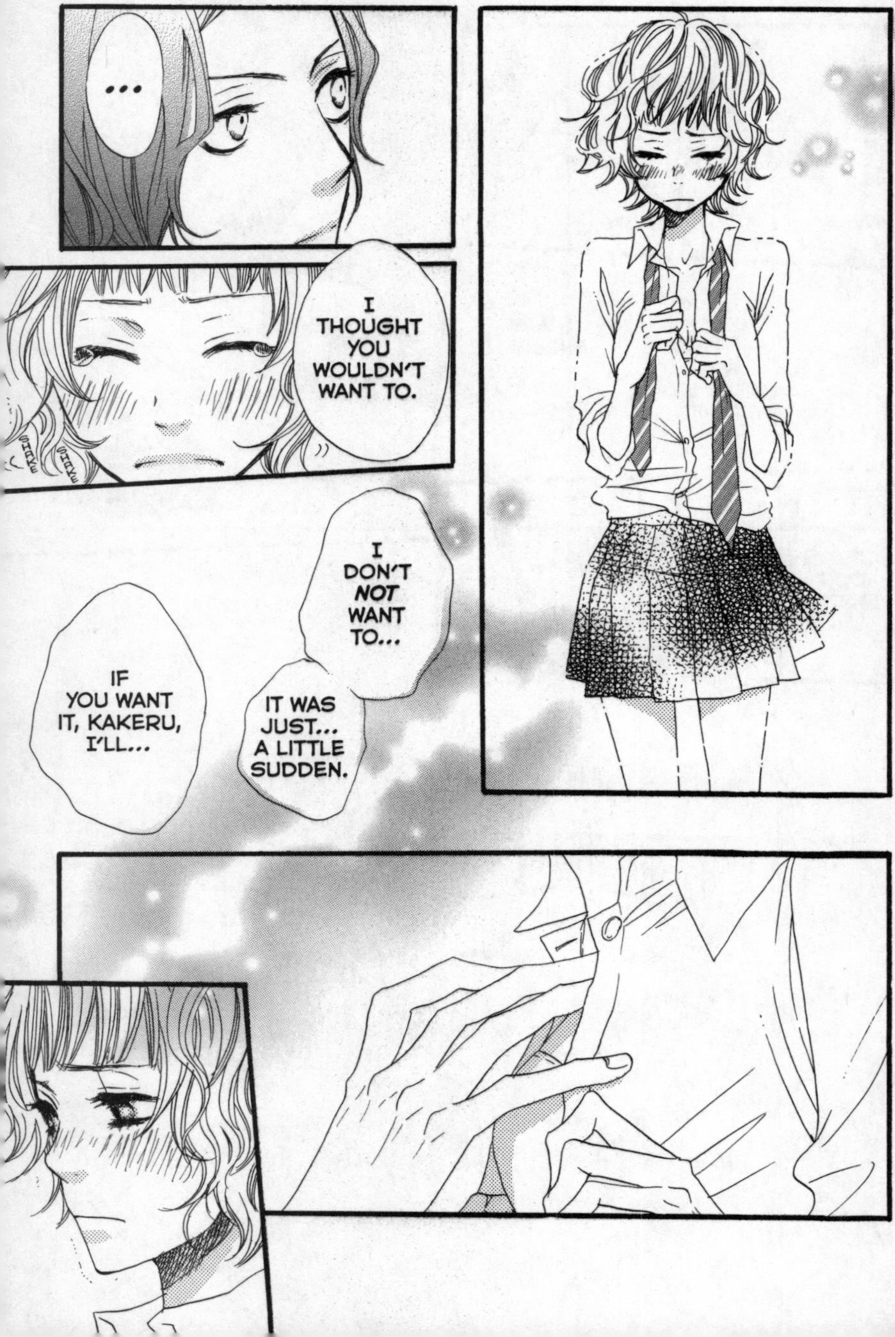
...
I THOUGHT YOU WOULDN'T WANT TO.
SHAKE SHAKE
I DON'T *NOT* WANT TO...
IT WAS JUST... A LITTLE SUDDEN.
IF YOU WANT IT, KAKERU, I'LL...

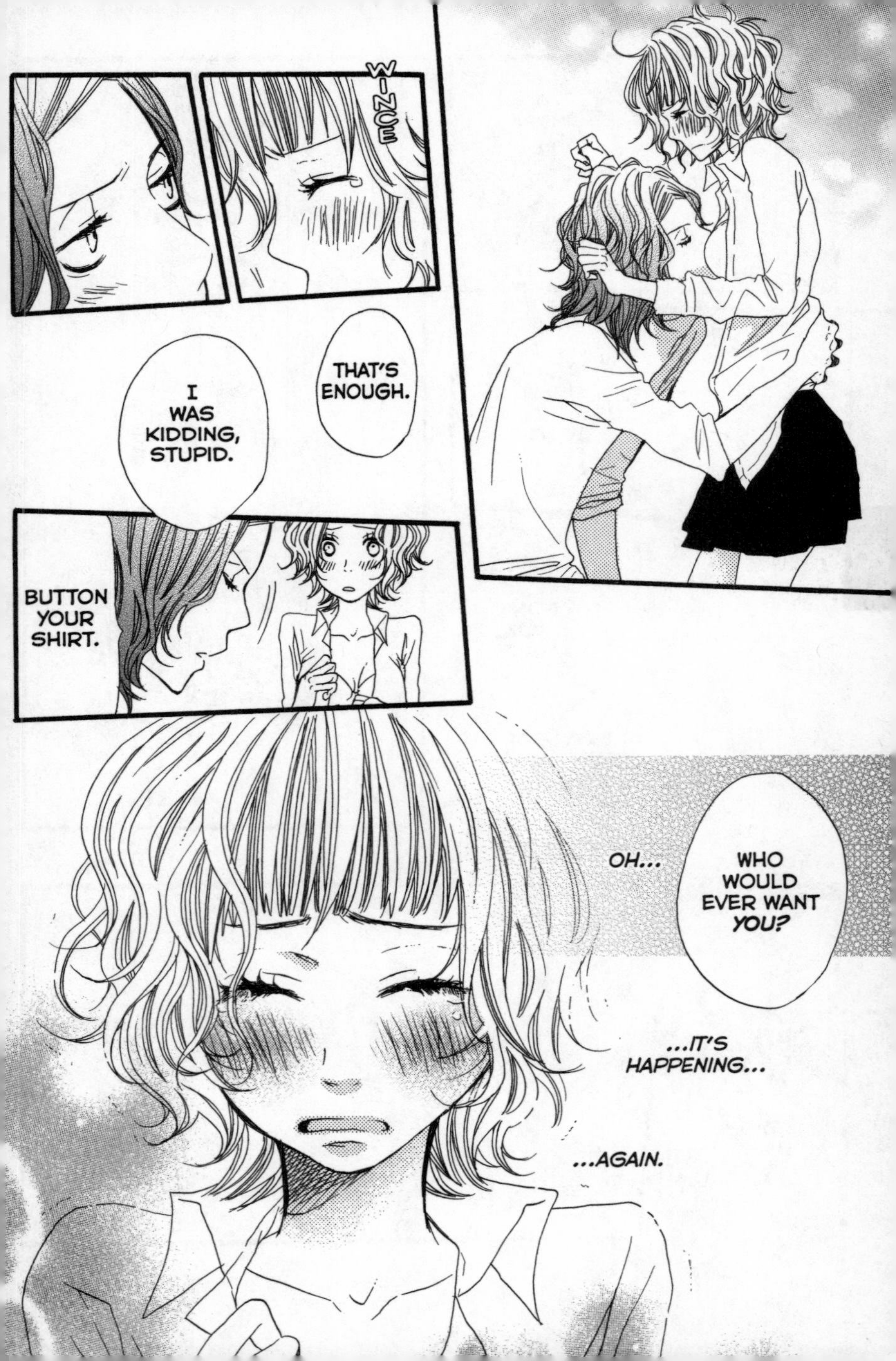
WINCE
THAT'S ENOUGH.
I WAS KIDDING, STUPID.
BUTTON YOUR SHIRT.
WHO WOULD EVER WANT *YOU?*
OH...
...IT'S HAPPENING...
...AGAIN.

DON'T HATE ME.

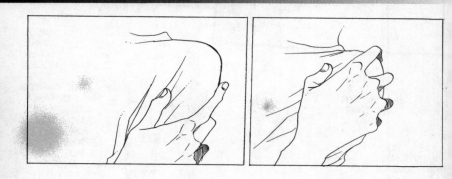

MY DAD HATES ME,
MY MOM HATES ME...

IF YOU HATE ME, TOO...

THEN I...

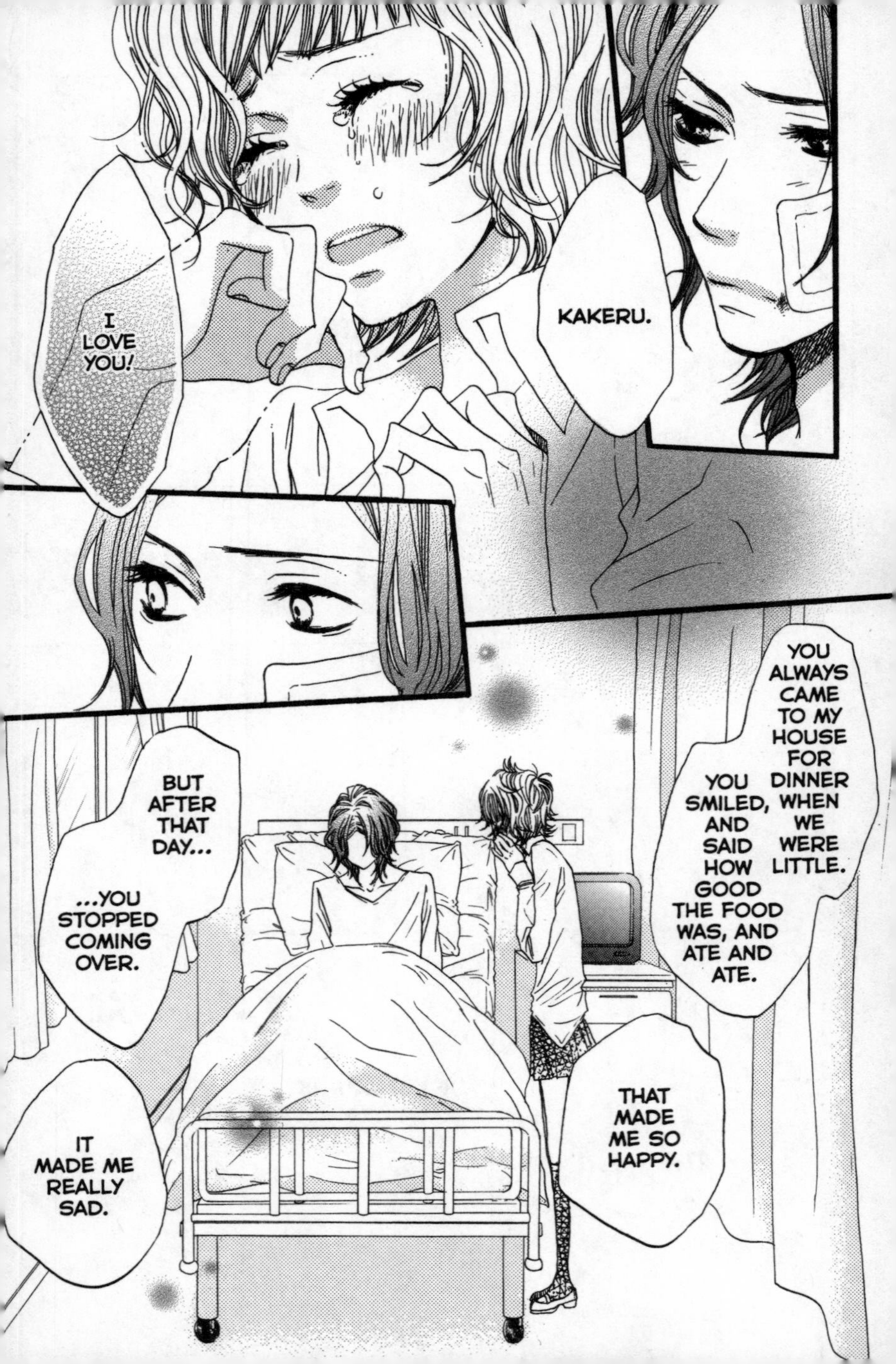
KAKERU.
I LOVE YOU!
YOU ALWAYS CAME TO MY HOUSE FOR DINNER WHEN WE WERE LITTLE.
YOU SMILED, AND SAID HOW GOOD THE FOOD WAS, AND ATE AND ATE.
THAT MADE ME SO HAPPY.
BUT AFTER THAT DAY...
...YOU STOPPED COMING OVER.
IT MADE ME REALLY SAD.

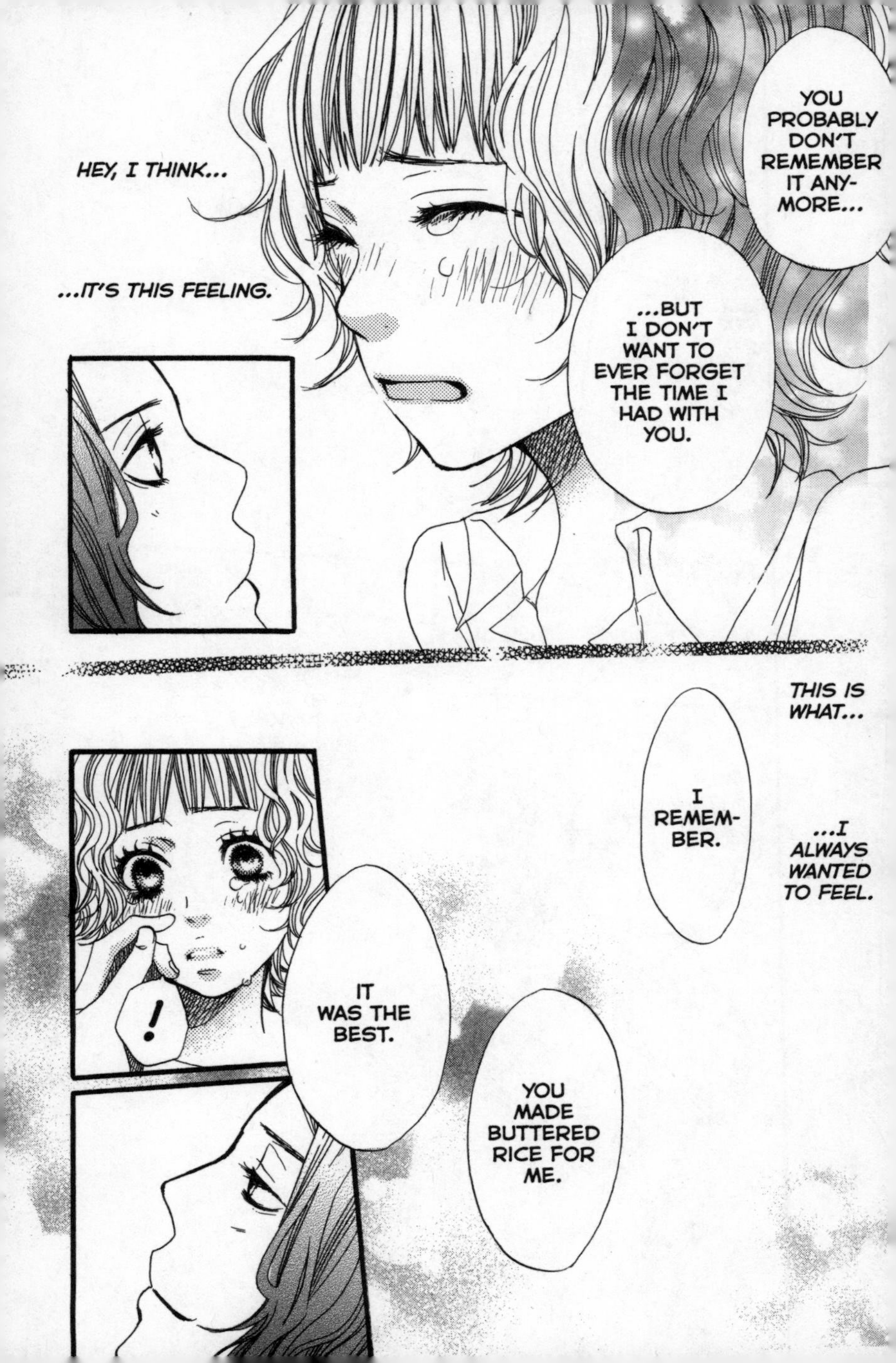
YOU PROBABLY DON'T REMEMBER IT ANY-MORE...
...BUT I DON'T WANT TO EVER FORGET THE TIME I HAD WITH YOU.
HEY, I THINK...
...IT'S THIS FEELING.
THIS IS WHAT...
I REMEM-BER.
...I ALWAYS WANTED TO FEEL.
YOU MADE BUTTERED RICE FOR ME.
IT WAS THE BEST.
!

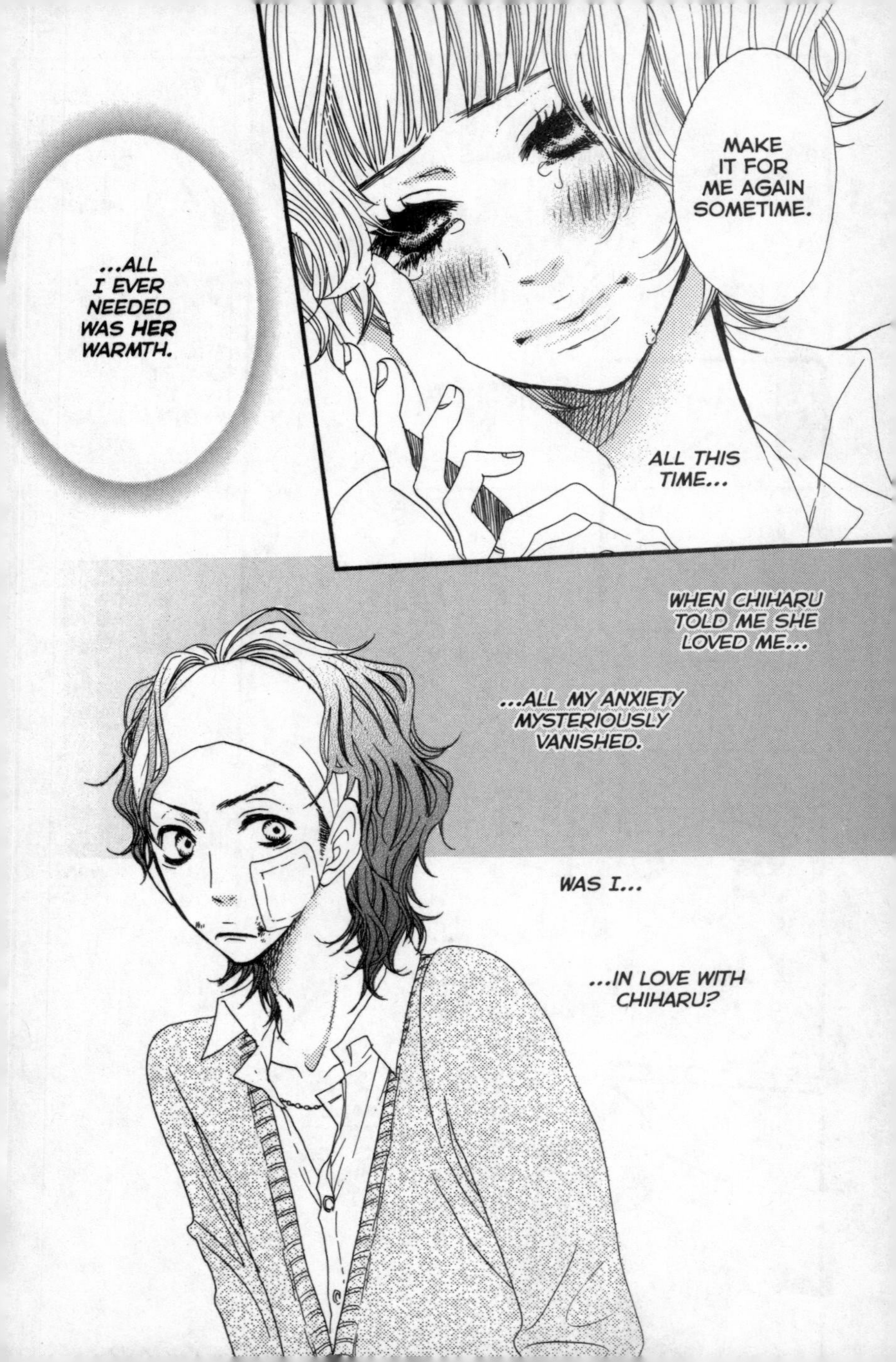
MAKE IT FOR ME AGAIN SOMETIME.
ALL THIS TIME...
...ALL I EVER NEEDED WAS HER WARMTH.
WHEN CHIHARU TOLD ME SHE LOVED ME...
...ALL MY ANXIETY MYSTERIOUSLY VANISHED.
WAS I...
...IN LOVE WITH CHIHARU?

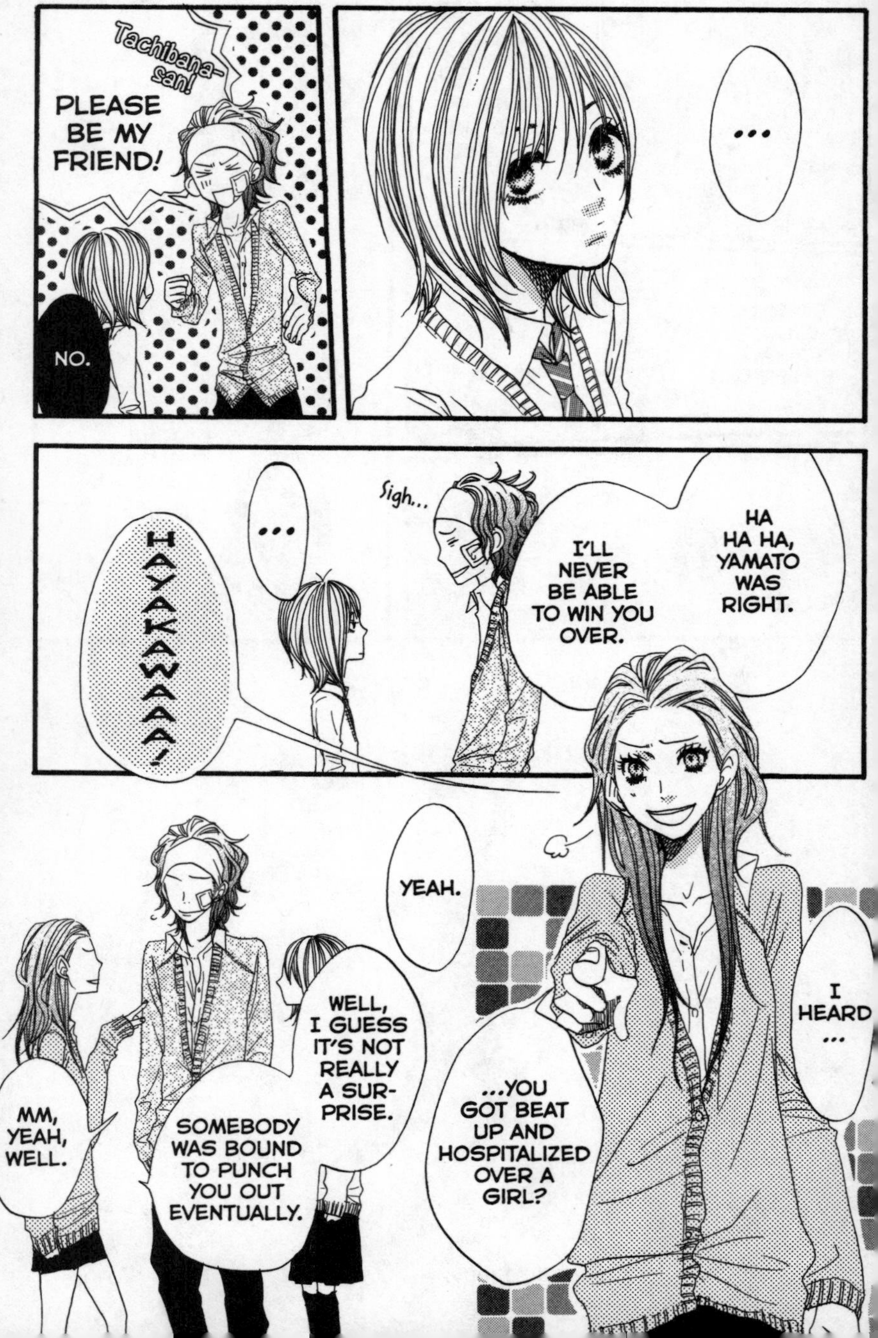
...
Tachibana-san!
PLEASE BE MY FRIEND!
NO.
HA HA HA, YAMATO WAS RIGHT.
I'LL NEVER BE ABLE TO WIN YOU OVER.
Sigh...
...
HAYAKAWAAA!
I HEARD...
...YOU GOT BEAT UP AND HOSPITALIZED OVER A GIRL?
YEAH.
WELL, I GUESS IT'S NOT REALLY A SURPRISE.
SOMEBODY WAS BOUND TO PUNCH YOU OUT EVENTUALLY.
MM, YEAH, WELL.

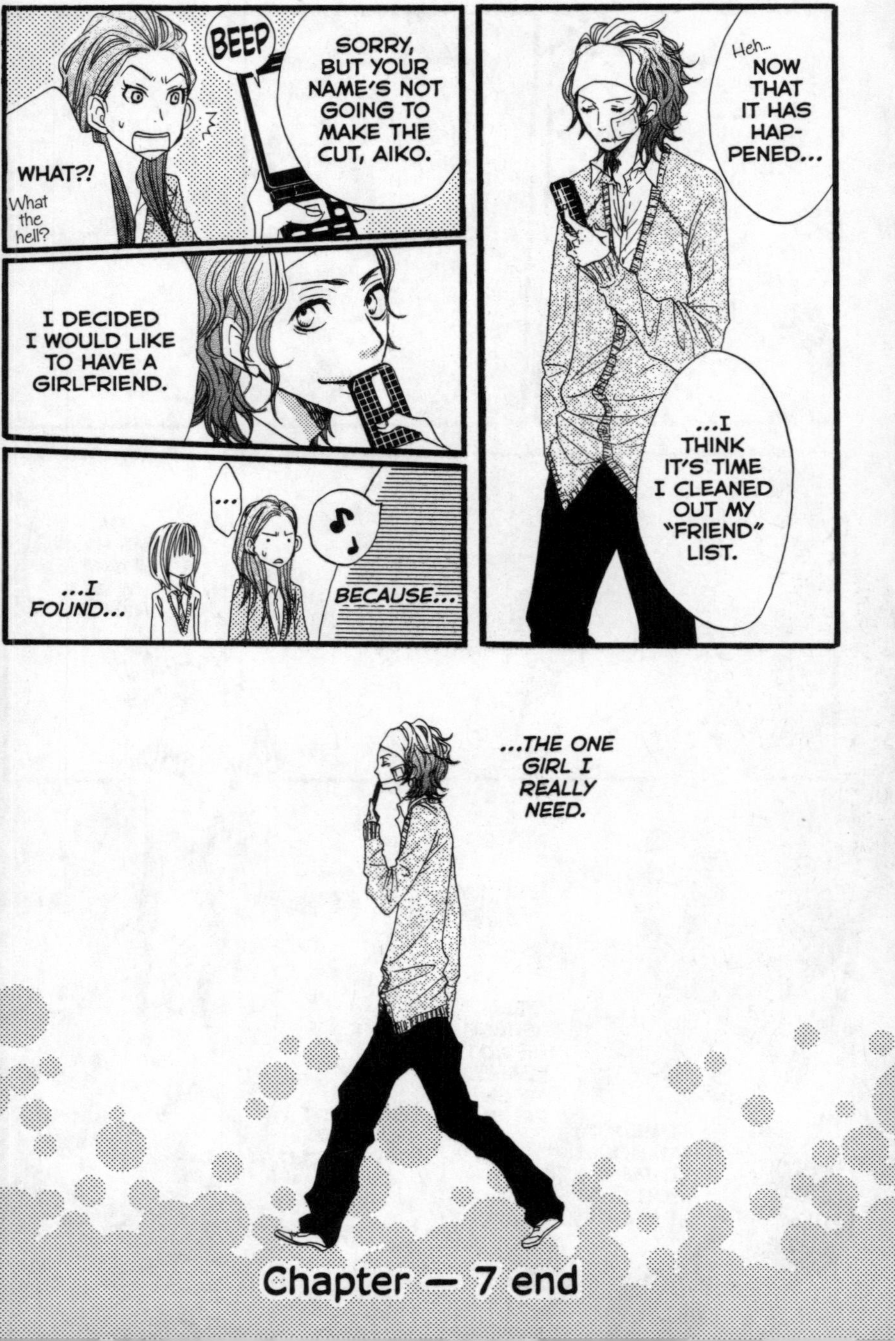
Heh...
NOW THAT IT HAS HAPPENED...
...I THINK IT'S TIME I CLEANED OUT MY "FRIEND" LIST.
SORRY, BUT YOUR NAME'S NOT GOING TO MAKE THE CUT, AIKO.
BEEP
WHAT?!
What the hell?
I DECIDED I WOULD LIKE TO HAVE A GIRLFRIEND.
BECAUSE...
...
...I FOUND...
...THE ONE GIRL I REALLY NEED.
Chapter — 7 end

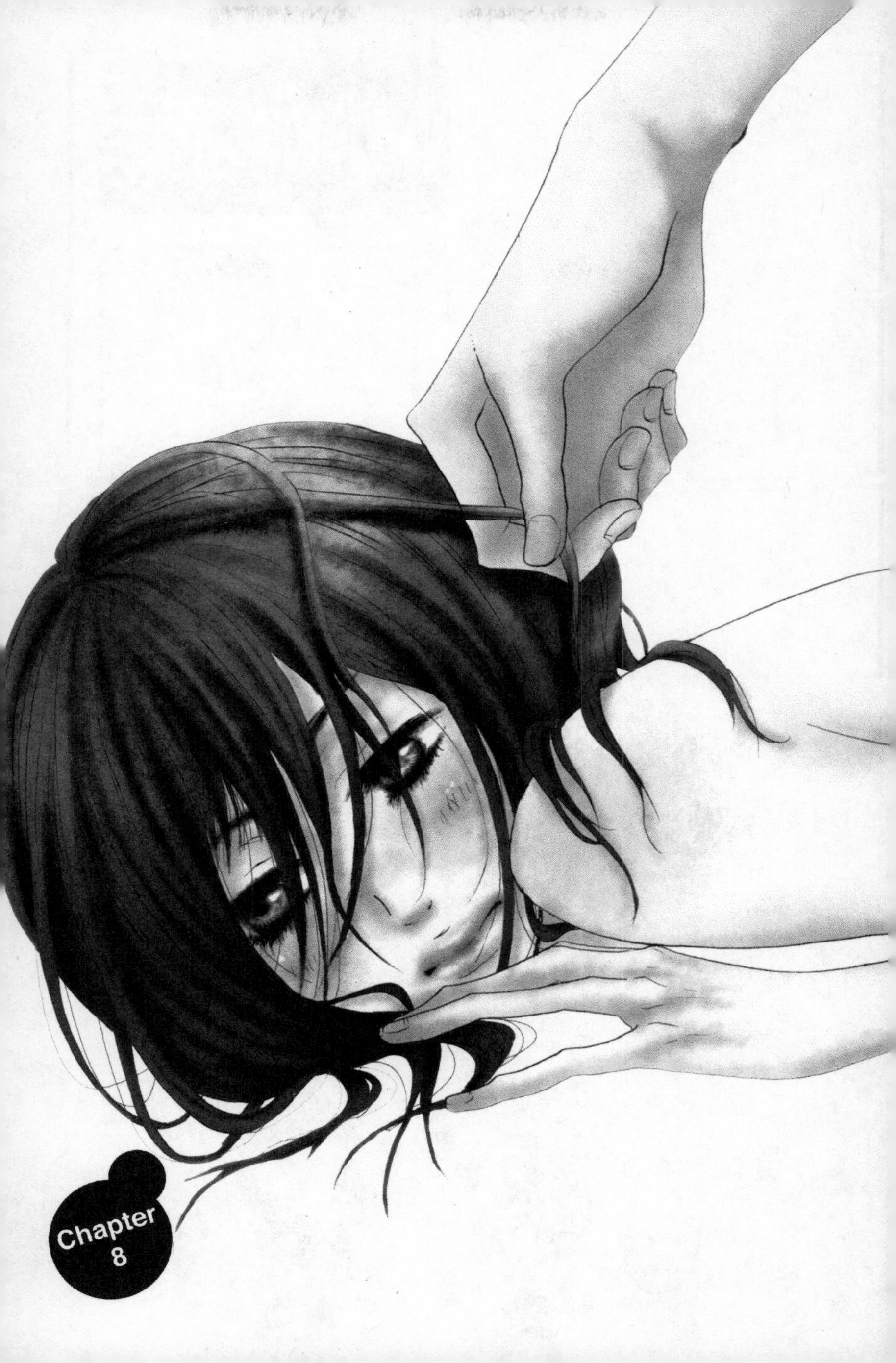
Chapter
8

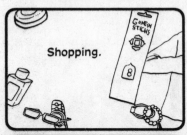

What Yamoto Loves

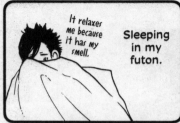

GONESH STICKS
Shopping.
Sleeping in my futon.
It relaxes me because it has my smell.
Huh?
Mei

YOU COULD'VE SAID IT, TOO.
BOO! BOO!
...

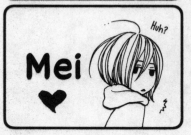

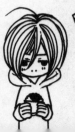

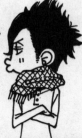

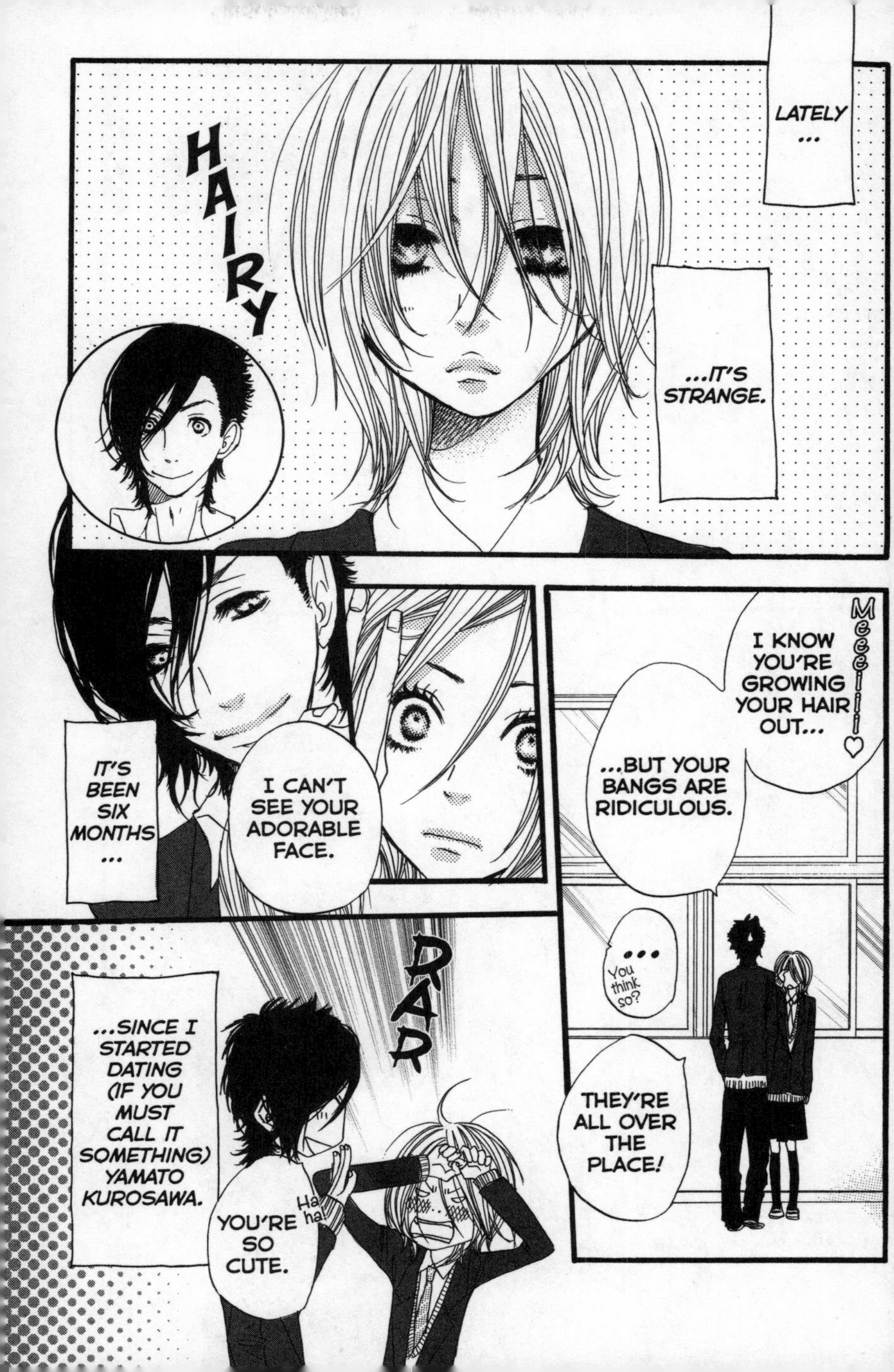
LATELY...
...IT'S STRANGE.
HAIRY
Meeeiiii ♡
I KNOW YOU'RE GROWING YOUR HAIR OUT...
...BUT YOUR BANGS ARE RIDICULOUS.
...
You think so?
THEY'RE ALL OVER THE PLACE!
I CAN'T SEE YOUR ADORABLE FACE.
IT'S BEEN SIX MONTHS...
RAR
...SINCE I STARTED DATING (IF YOU MUST CALL IT SOMETHING) YAMATO KUROSAWA.
Ha ha!
YOU'RE SO CUTE.

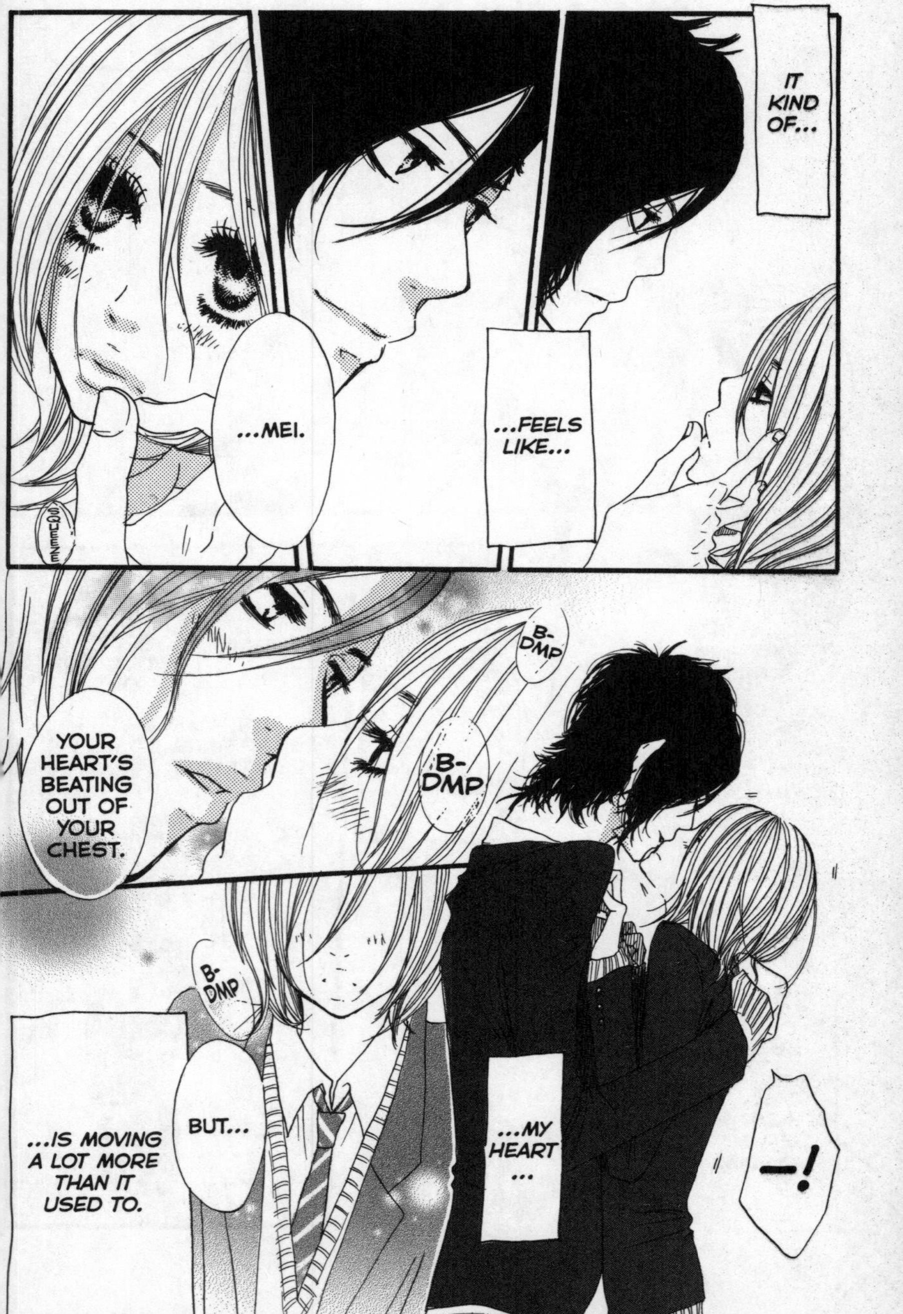
IT KIND OF...
...FEELS LIKE...
...MEI.
SQUEEZE
B-DMP
B-DMP
YOUR HEART'S BEATING OUT OF YOUR CHEST.
—!
...MY HEART ...
BUT...
B-DMP
...IS MOVING A LOT MORE THAN IT USED TO.

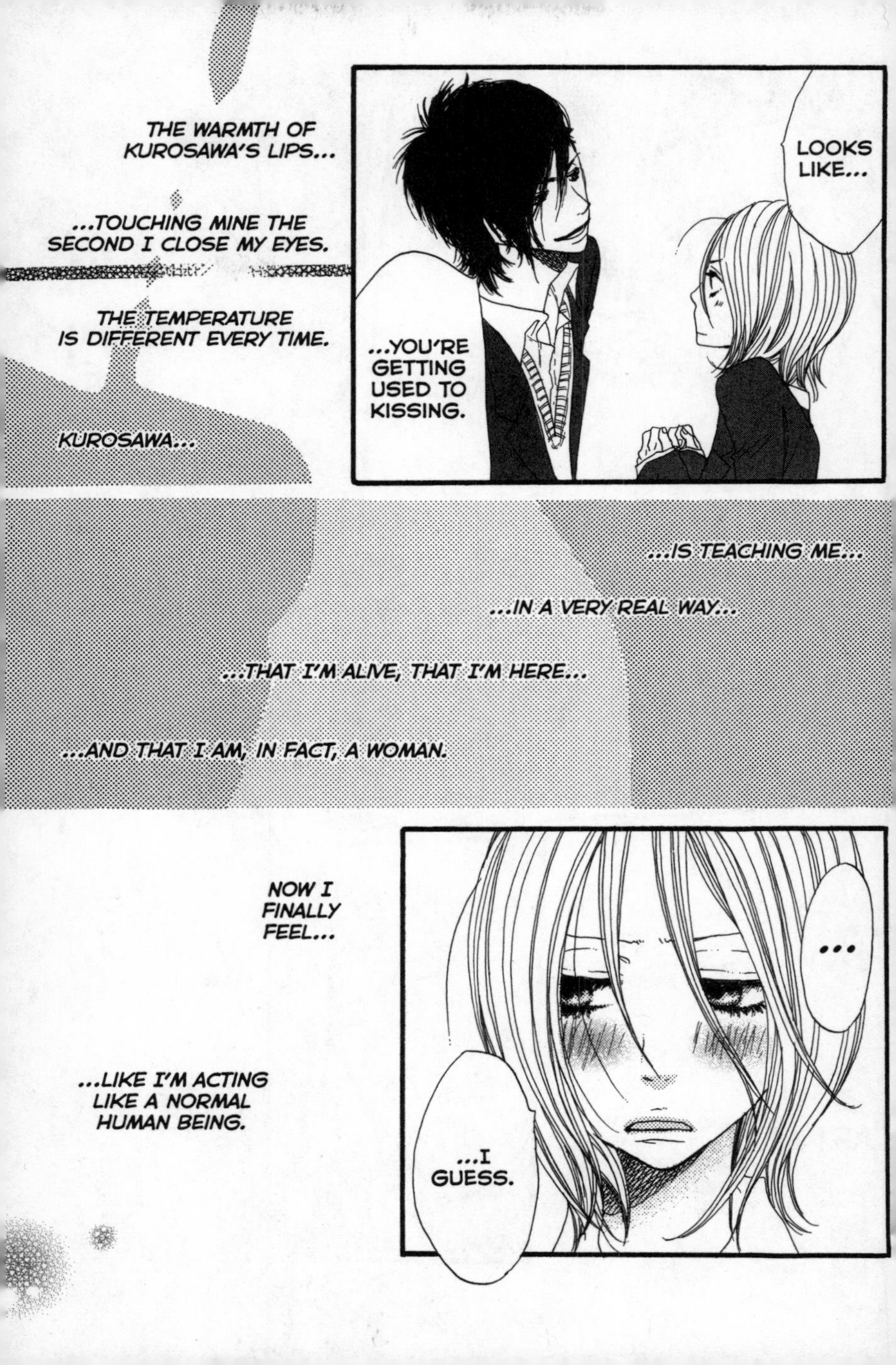
LOOKS LIKE...
...YOU'RE GETTING USED TO KISSING.
THE WARMTH OF KUROSAWA'S LIPS...
...TOUCHING MINE THE SECOND I CLOSE MY EYES.
THE TEMPERATURE IS DIFFERENT EVERY TIME.
KUROSAWA...
...IS TEACHING ME...
...IN A VERY REAL WAY...
...THAT I'M ALIVE, THAT I'M HERE...
...AND THAT I AM, IN FACT, A WOMAN.
...
...I GUESS.
NOW I FINALLY FEEL...
...LIKE I'M ACTING LIKE A NORMAL HUMAN BEING.

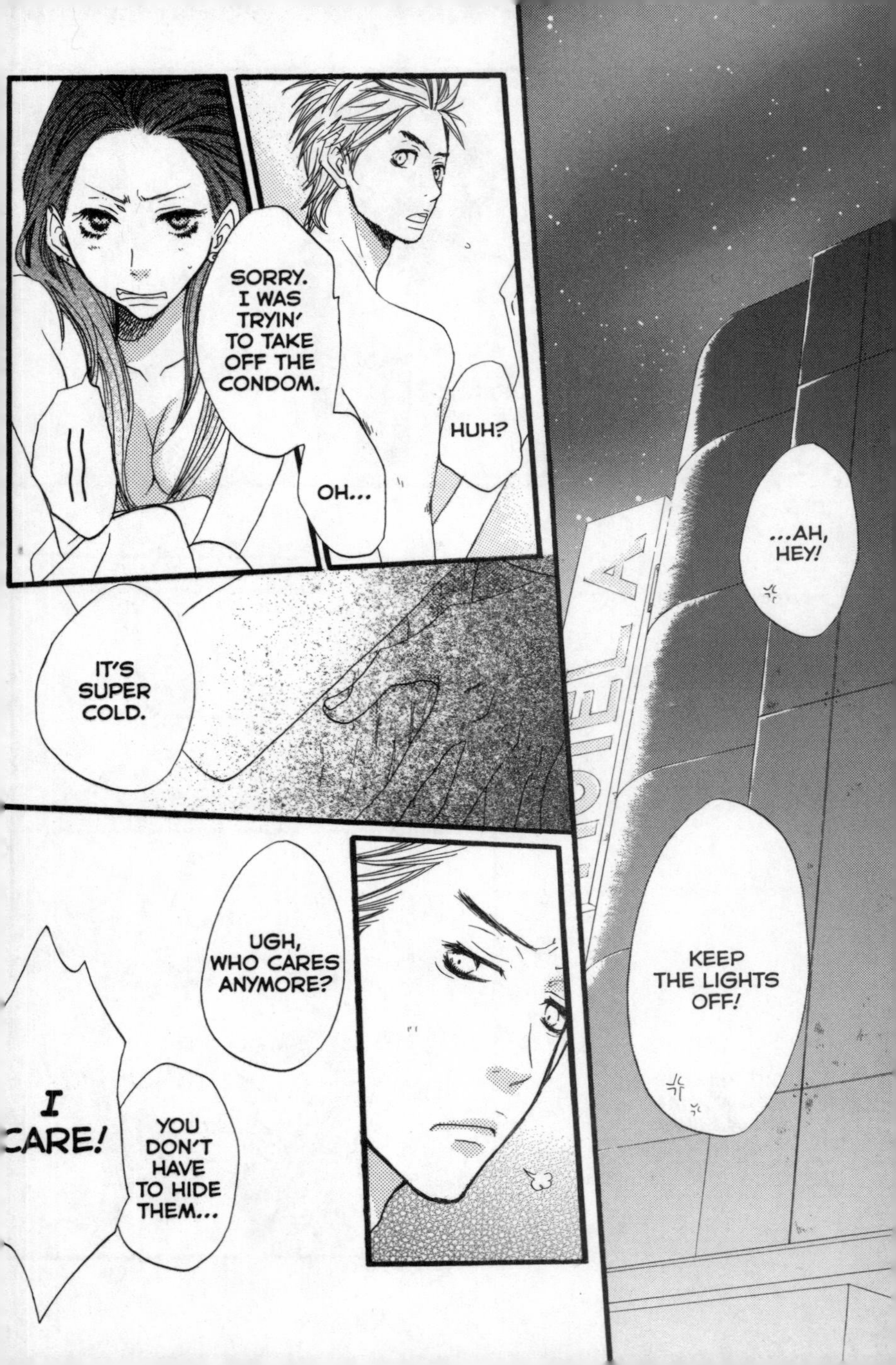
...AH, HEY!
KEEP THE LIGHTS OFF!
SORRY. I WAS TRYIN' TO TAKE OFF THE CONDOM.
HUH?
OH...
IT'S SUPER COLD.
UGH, WHO CARES ANYMORE?
I CARE!
YOU DON'T HAVE TO HIDE THEM...

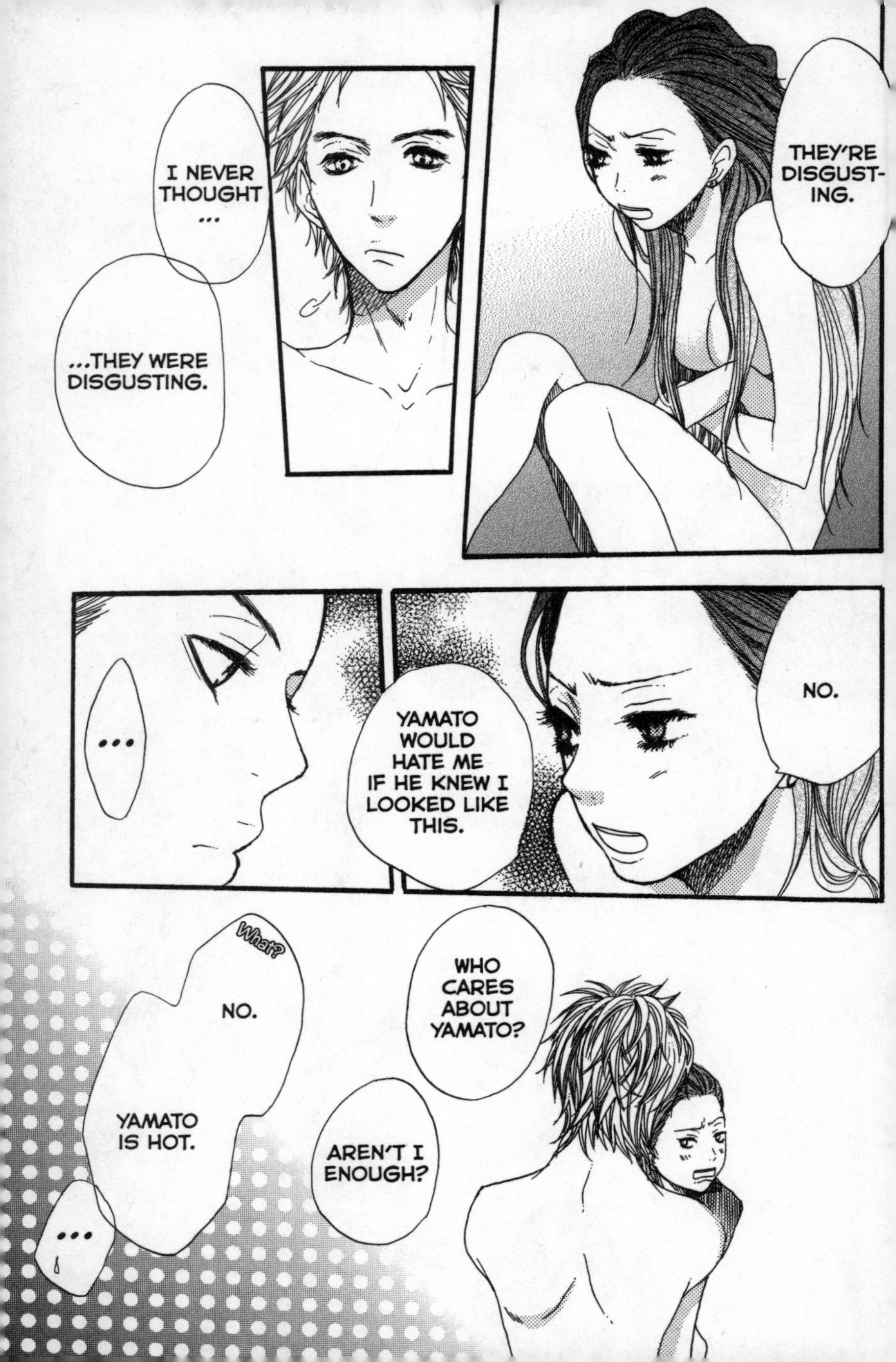
THEY'RE DISGUST-ING.
I NEVER THOUGHT...
...THEY WERE DISGUSTING.
NO.
YAMATO WOULD HATE ME IF HE KNEW I LOOKED LIKE THIS.
...
WHO CARES ABOUT YAMATO?
AREN'T I ENOUGH?
What?
NO.
YAMATO IS HOT.
...

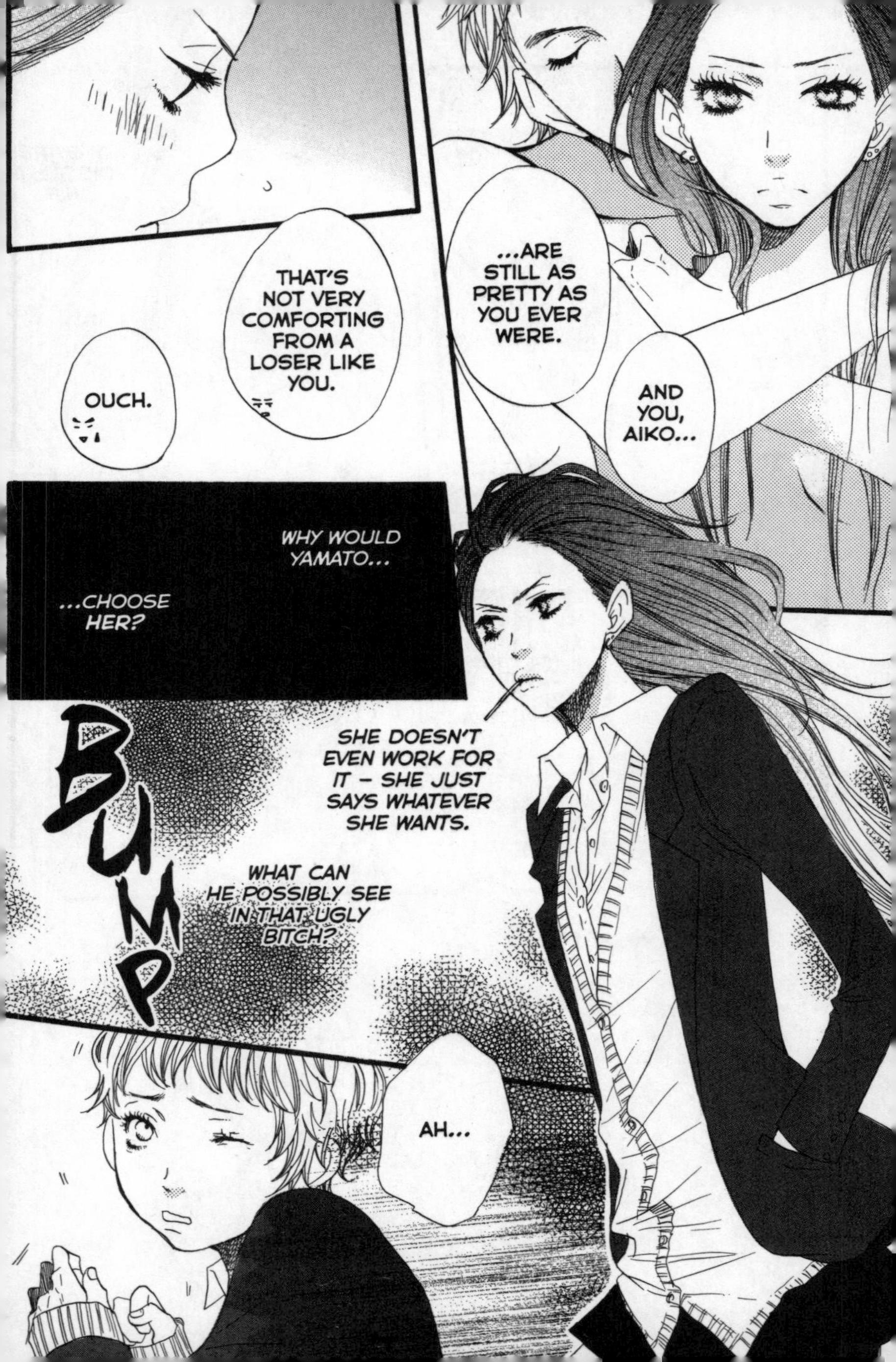
AND YOU, AIKO...
...ARE STILL AS PRETTY AS YOU EVER WERE.
THAT'S NOT VERY COMFORTING FROM A LOSER LIKE YOU.
OUCH.
WHY WOULD YAMATO...
...CHOOSE HER?
SHE DOESN'T EVEN WORK FOR IT – SHE JUST SAYS WHATEVER SHE WANTS.
WHAT CAN HE POSSIBLY SEE IN THAT UGLY BITCH?
BUMP
AH...

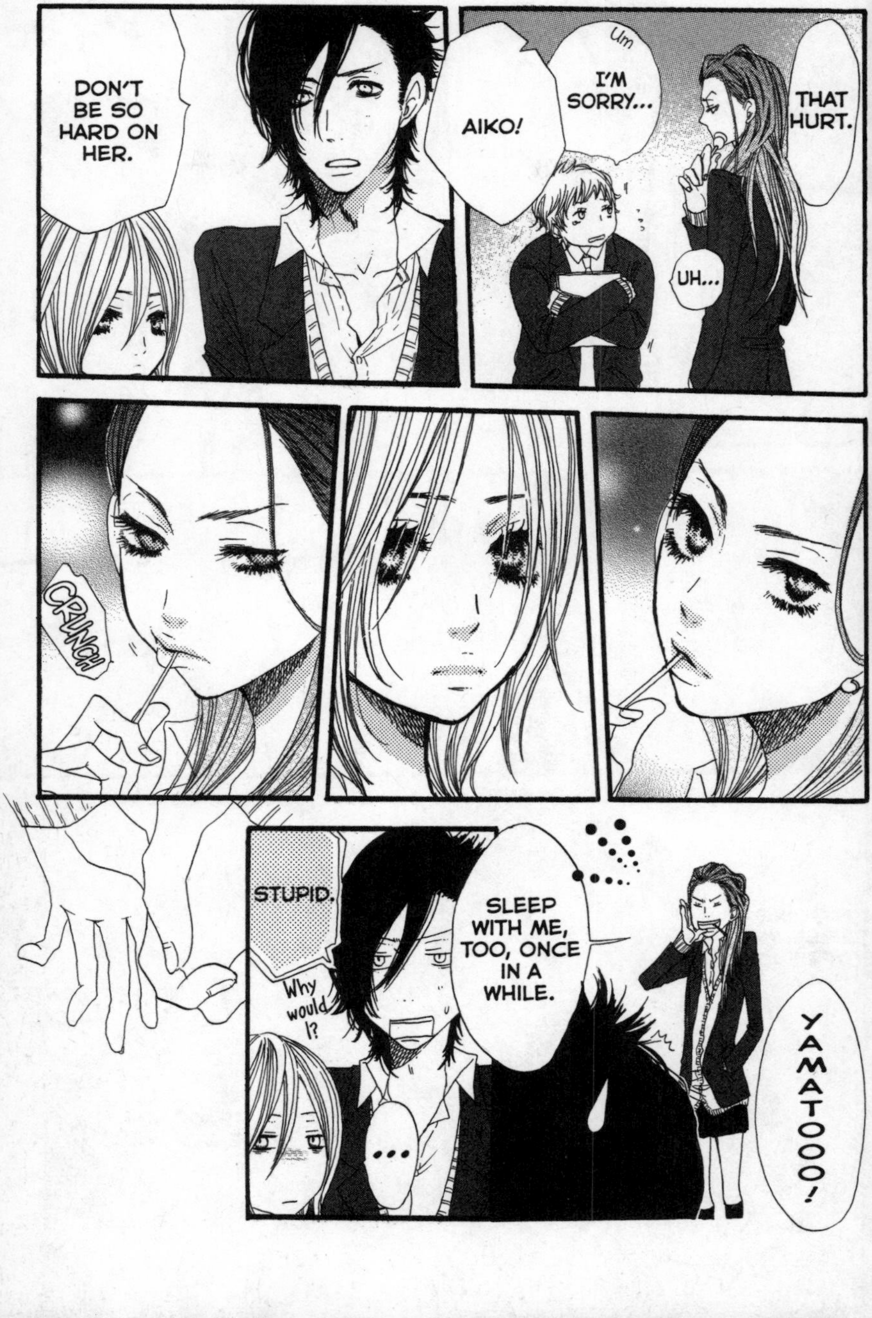
THAT HURT.
Um
I'M SORRY...
AIKO!
UH...
DON'T BE SO HARD ON HER.
CRUNCH
YAMATOOO!
SLEEP WITH ME, TOO, ONCE IN A WHILE.
STUPID.
Why would I?
...

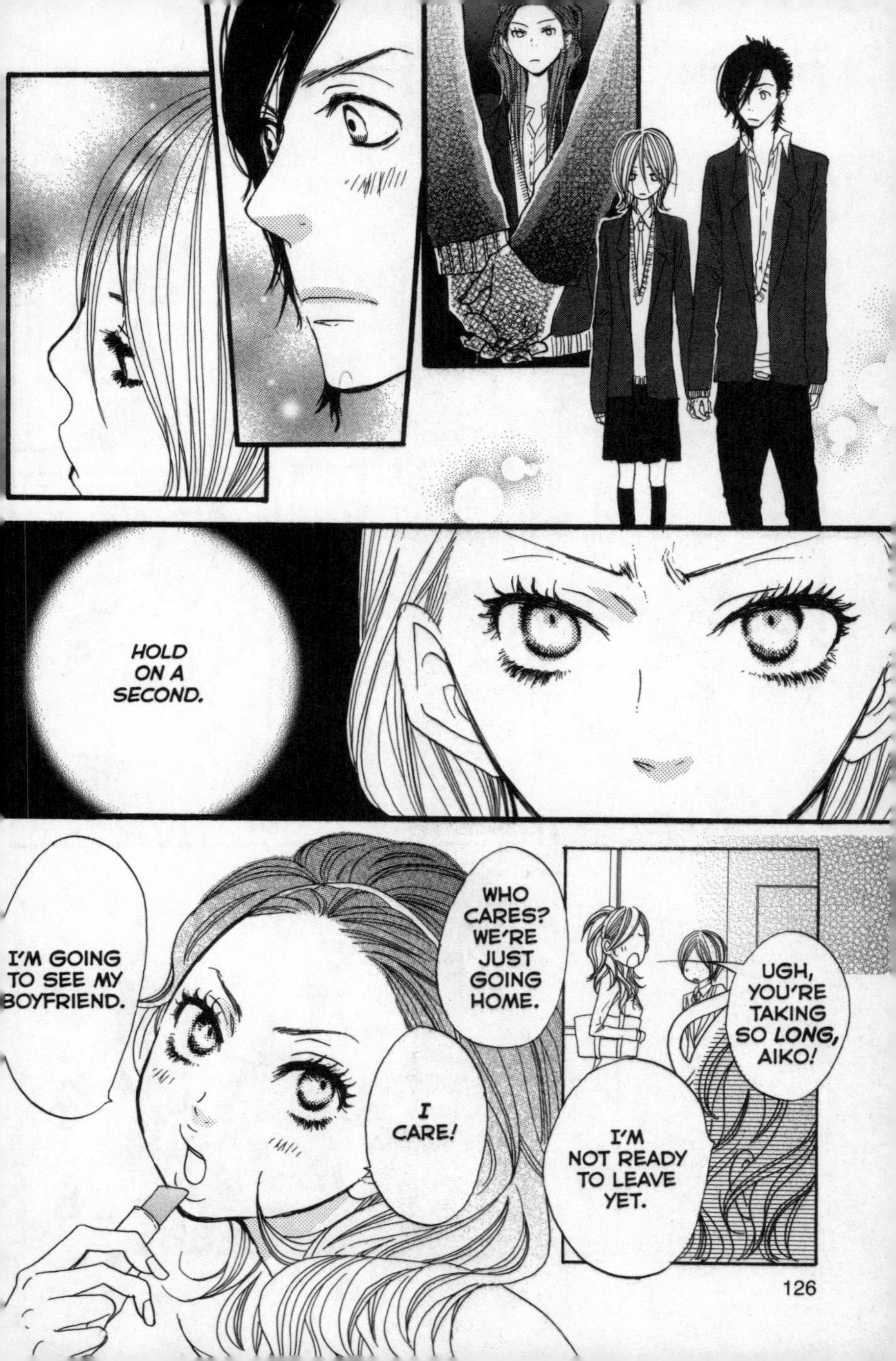
HOLD ON A SECOND.
UGH, YOU'RE TAKING SO *LONG*, AIKO!
WHO CARES? WE'RE JUST GOING HOME.
I'M NOT READY TO LEAVE YET.
I CARE!
I'M GOING TO SEE MY BOYFRIEND.

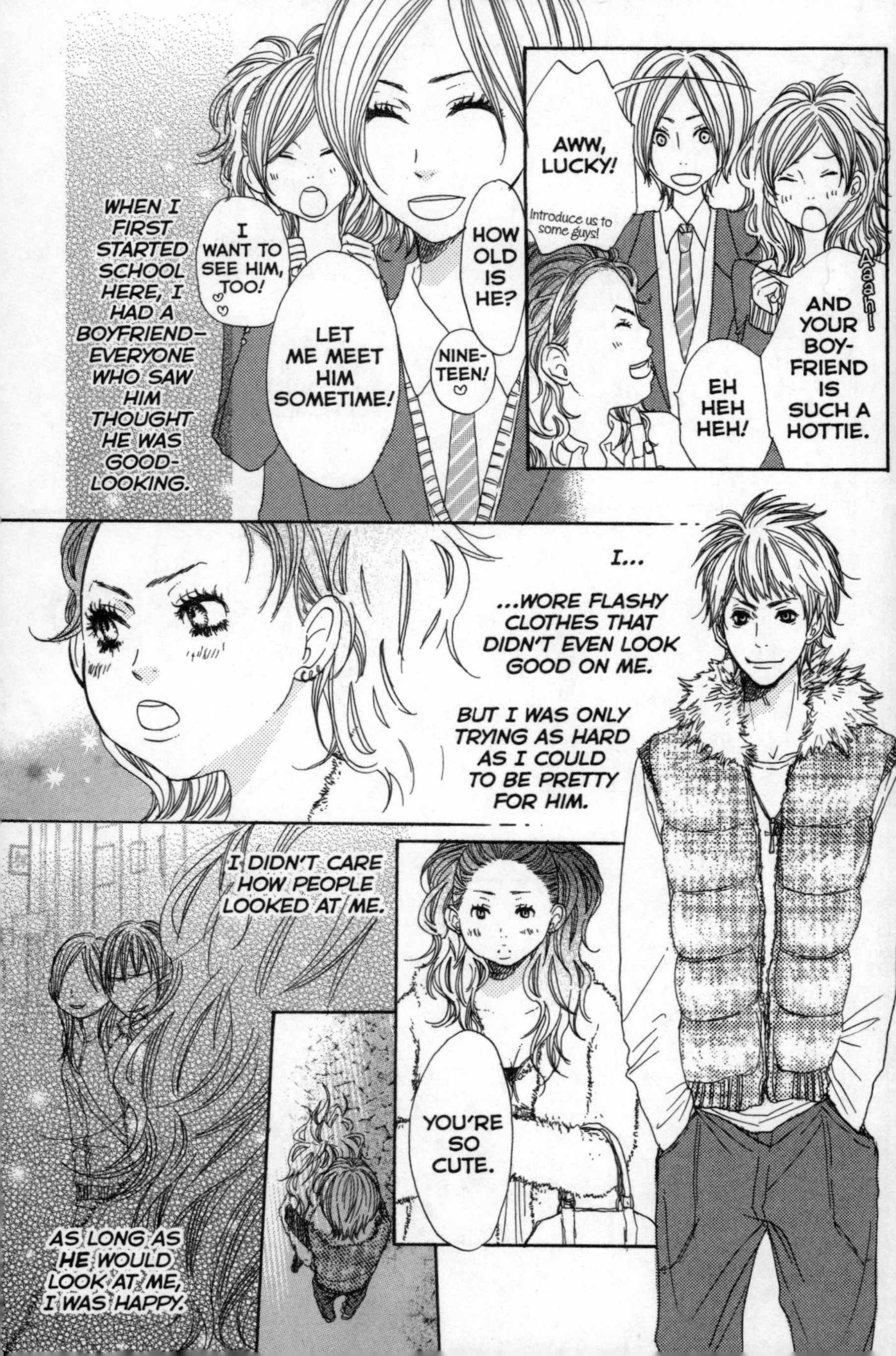
AWW, LUCKY!
Introduce us to some guys!
Aaah!
AND YOUR BOY-FRIEND IS SUCH A HOTTIE.
EH HEH HEH!
HOW OLD IS HE?
NINE-TEEN!
I WANT TO SEE HIM, TOO!
LET ME MEET HIM SOMETIME!
WHEN I FIRST STARTED SCHOOL HERE, I HAD A BOYFRIEND—EVERYONE WHO SAW HIM THOUGHT HE WAS GOOD-LOOKING.
I...
...WORE FLASHY CLOTHES THAT DIDN'T EVEN LOOK GOOD ON ME.
BUT I WAS ONLY TRYING AS HARD AS I COULD TO BE PRETTY FOR HIM.
YOU'RE SO CUTE.
I DIDN'T CARE HOW PEOPLE LOOKED AT ME.
AS LONG AS HE WOULD LOOK AT ME, I WAS HAPPY.

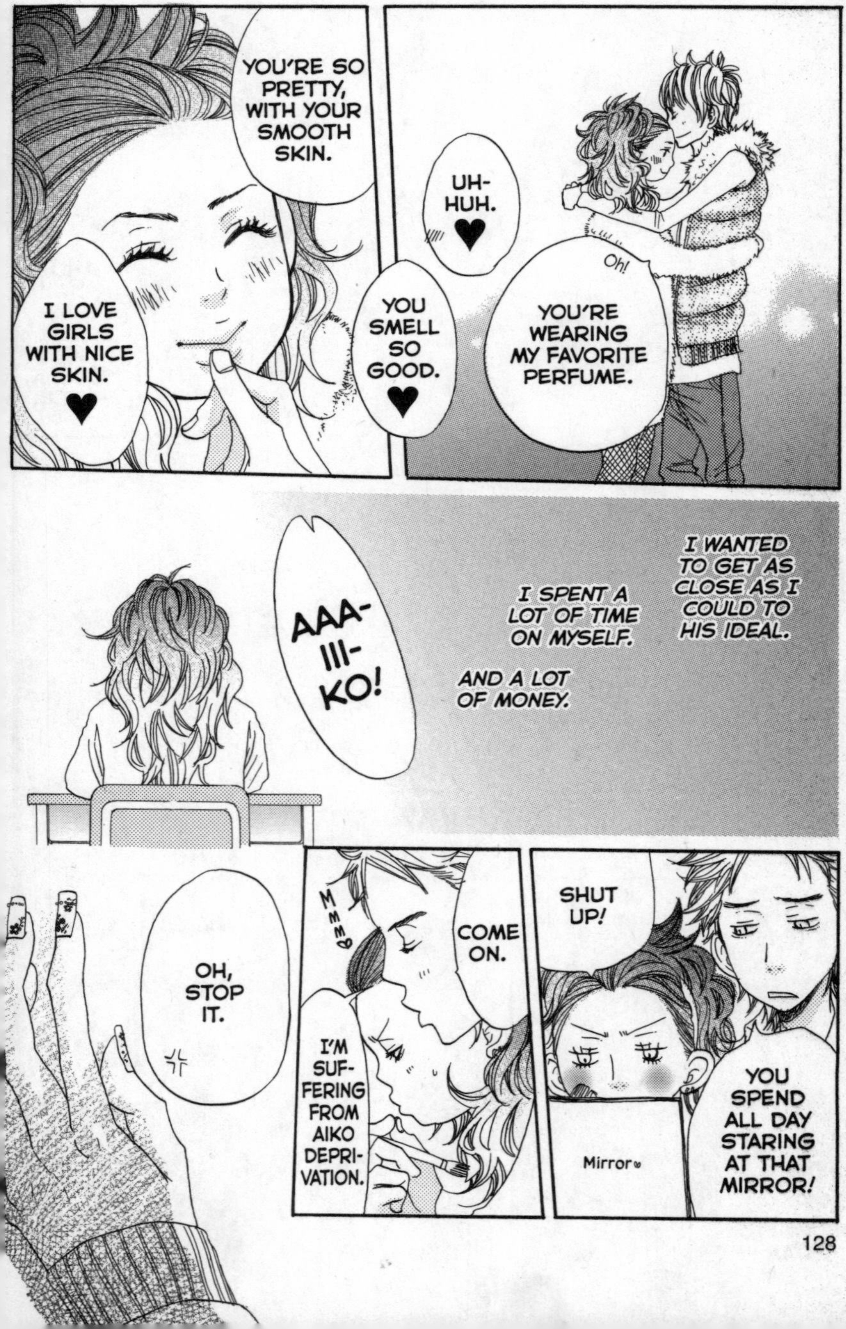
Oh!
YOU'RE WEARING MY FAVORITE PERFUME.
UH-HUH. ♥
YOU SMELL SO GOOD. ♥
YOU'RE SO PRETTY, WITH YOUR SMOOTH SKIN.
I LOVE GIRLS WITH NICE SKIN. ♥
I WANTED TO GET AS CLOSE AS I COULD TO HIS IDEAL.
I SPENT A LOT OF TIME ON MYSELF.
AND A LOT OF MONEY.
AAA-III-KO!
SHUT UP!
YOU SPEND ALL DAY STARING AT THAT MIRROR!
Mirror
COME ON.
MMM
I'M SUFFERING FROM AIKO DEPRIVATION.
OH, STOP IT.

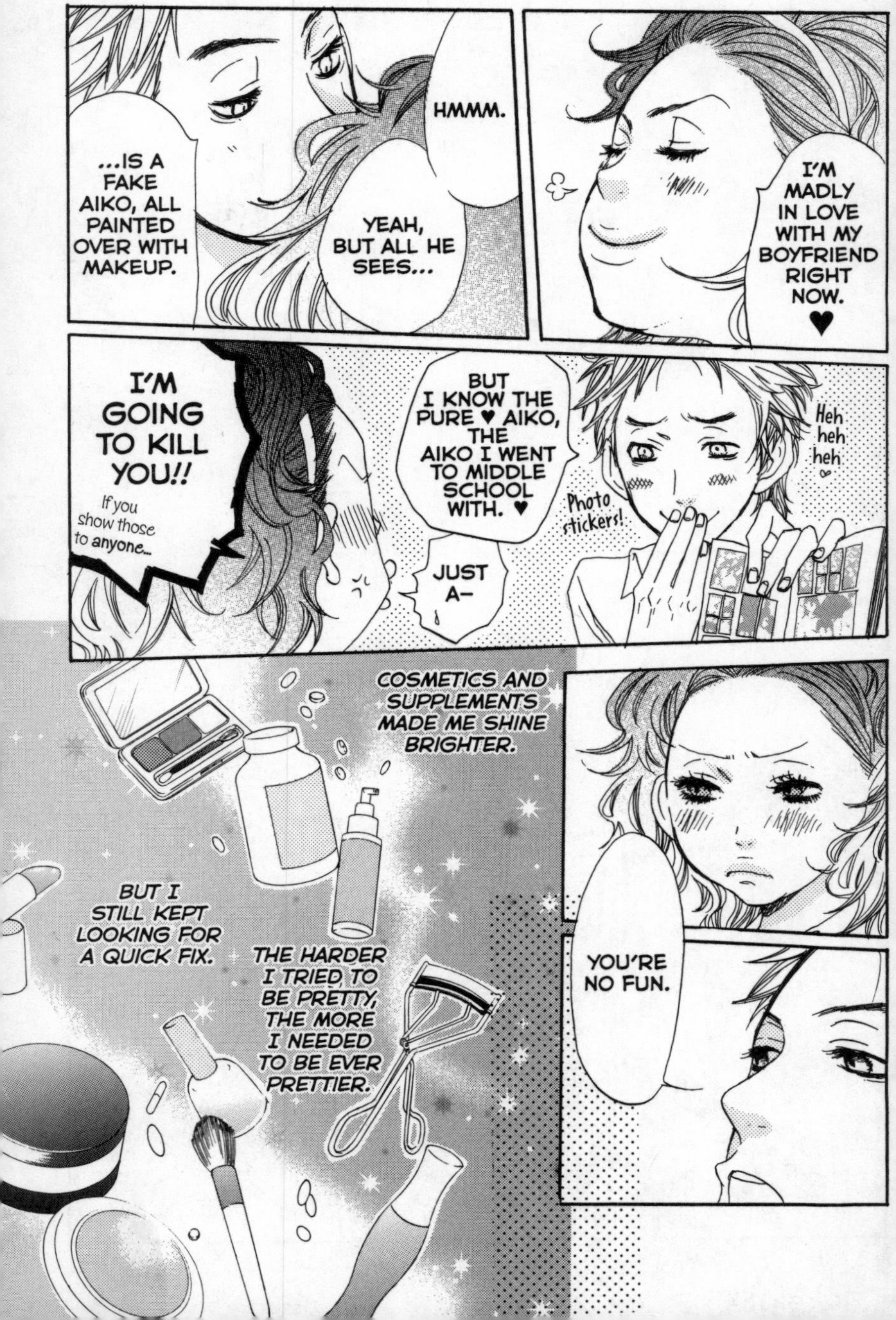
I'M MADLY IN LOVE WITH MY BOYFRIEND RIGHT NOW. ♥
HMMM.
YEAH, BUT ALL HE SEES...
...IS A FAKE AIKO, ALL PAINTED OVER WITH MAKEUP.
Heh heh heh ♥
Photo stickers!
BUT I KNOW THE PURE ♥ AIKO, THE AIKO I WENT TO MIDDLE SCHOOL WITH. ♥
JUST A–
I'M GOING TO KILL YOU!!
If you show those to anyone...
YOU'RE NO FUN.
COSMETICS AND SUPPLEMENTS MADE ME SHINE BRIGHTER.
BUT I STILL KEPT LOOKING FOR A QUICK FIX.
THE HARDER I TRIED TO BE PRETTY, THE MORE I NEEDED TO BE EVER PRETTIER.

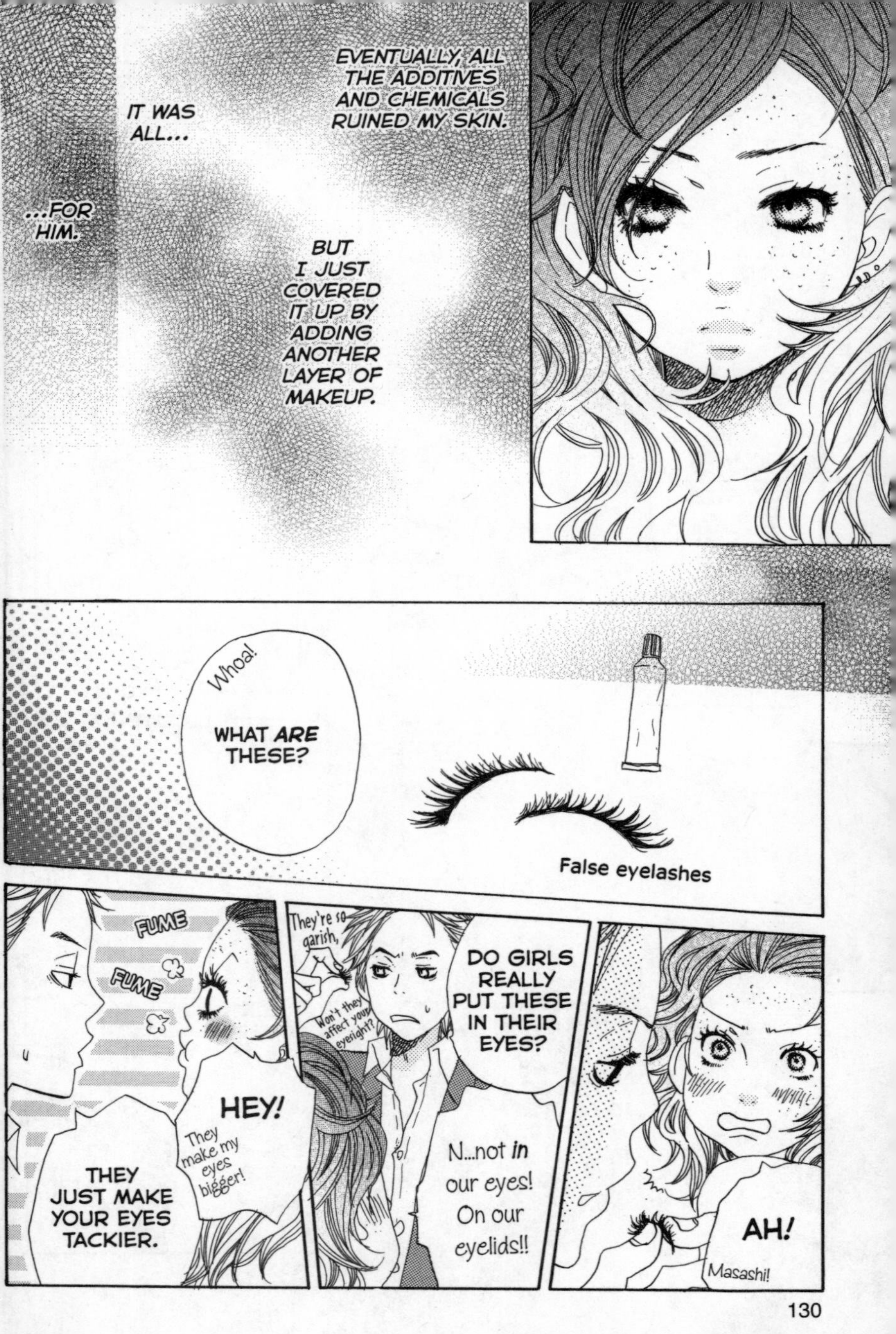
EVENTUALLY, ALL THE ADDITIVES AND CHEMICALS RUINED MY SKIN.
IT WAS ALL...
BUT I JUST COVERED IT UP BY ADDING ANOTHER LAYER OF MAKEUP.
...FOR HIM.
Whoa!
WHAT ARE THESE?
False eyelashes
AH!
Masashi!
They're so garish,
DO GIRLS REALLY PUT THESE IN THEIR EYES?
Won't they affect your eyesight?
N...not in our eyes! On our eyelids!!
FUME
FUME
HEY!
They make my eyes bigger!
THEY JUST MAKE YOUR EYES TACKIER.

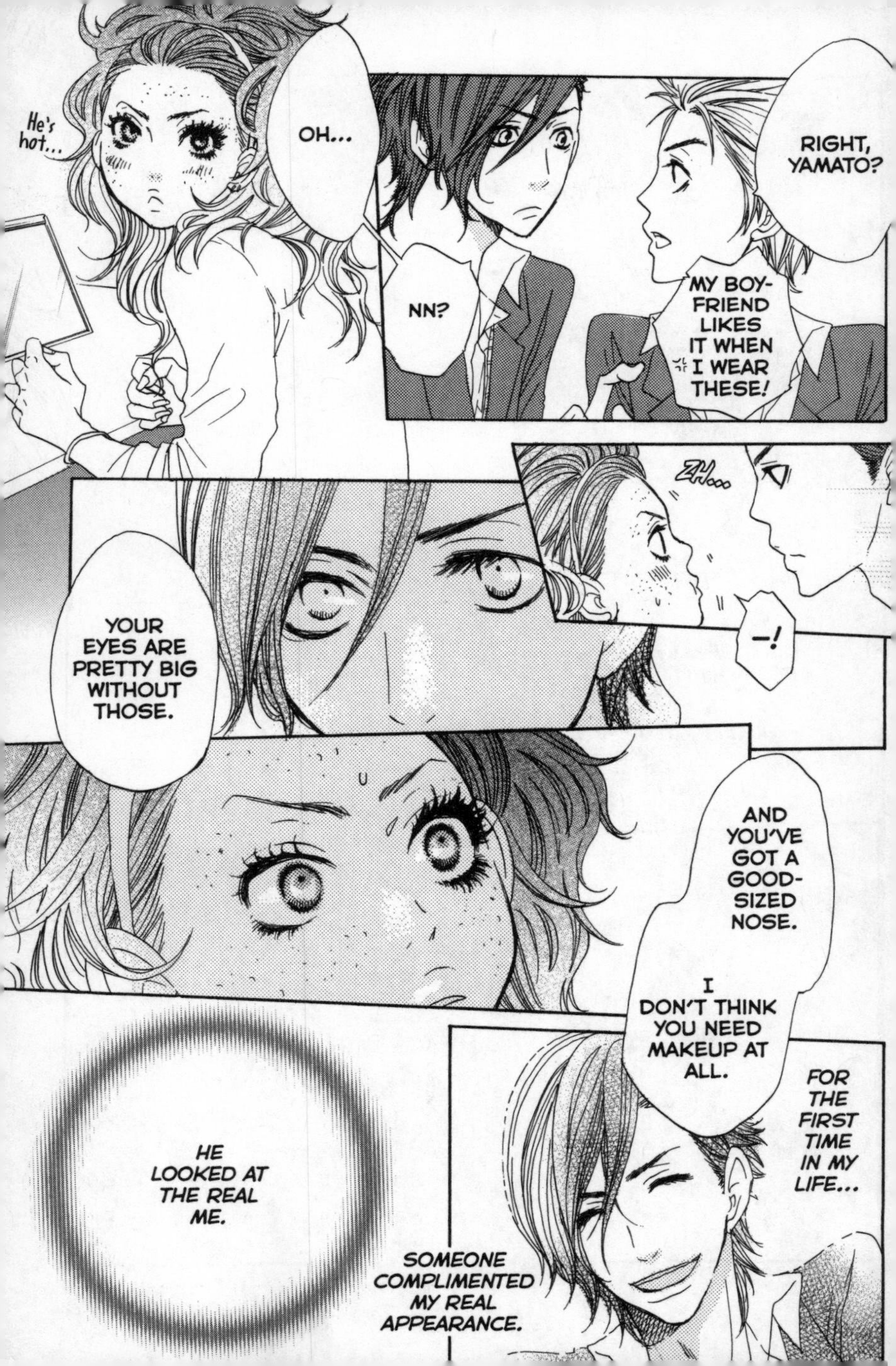
RIGHT, YAMATO?
MY BOY-FRIEND LIKES IT WHEN I WEAR THESE!
NN?
OH...
He's hot...
ZH...
—!
YOUR EYES ARE PRETTY BIG WITHOUT THOSE.
AND YOU'VE GOT A GOOD-SIZED NOSE.
I DON'T THINK YOU NEED MAKEUP AT ALL.
FOR THE FIRST TIME IN MY LIFE...
SOMEONE COMPLIMENTED MY REAL APPEARANCE.
HE LOOKED AT THE REAL ME.

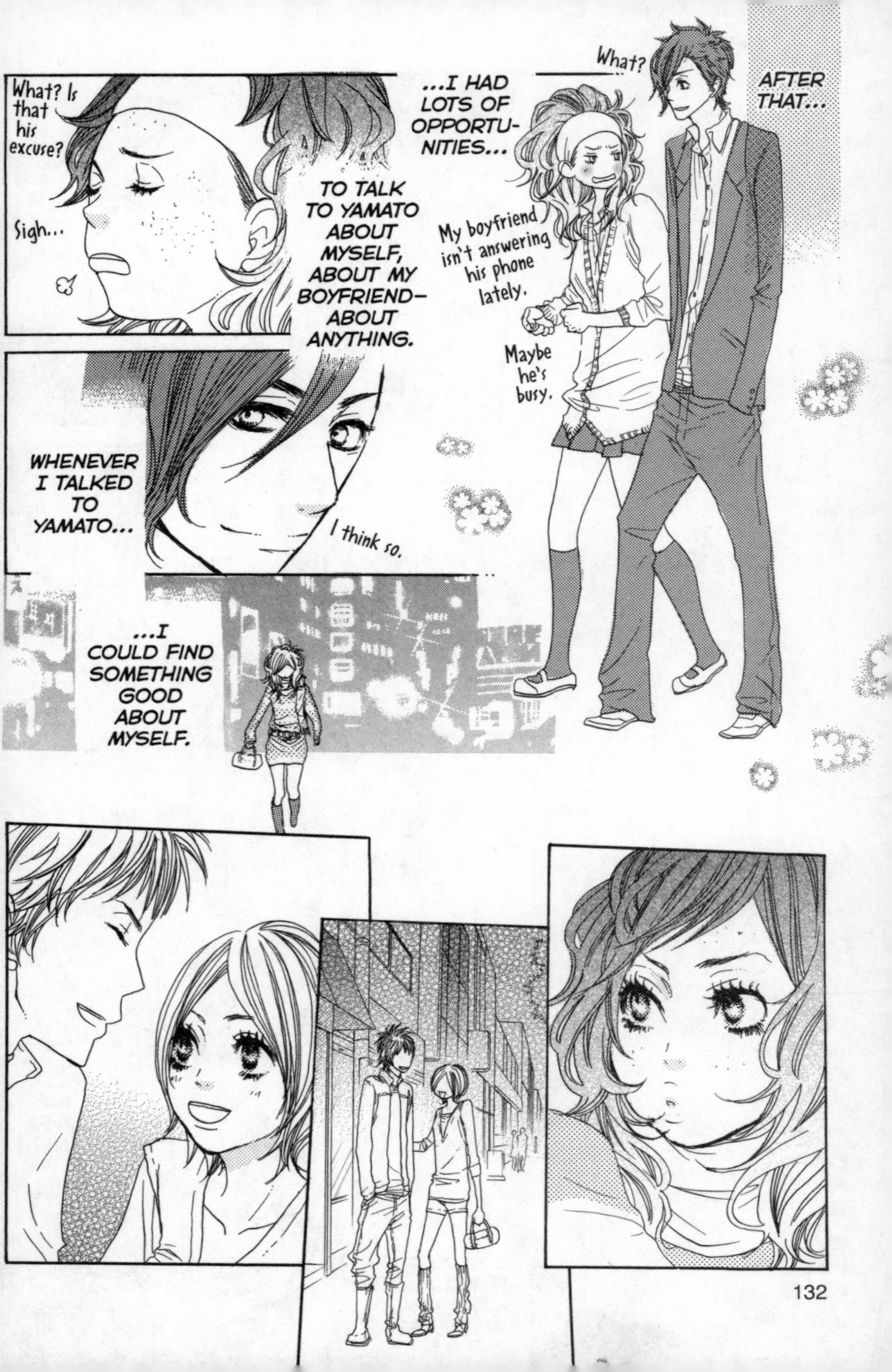
AFTER THAT...
What?
My boyfriend isn't answering his phone lately.
Maybe he's busy.
...I HAD LOTS OF OPPORTUNITIES...
TO TALK TO YAMATO ABOUT MYSELF, ABOUT MY BOYFRIEND—ABOUT ANYTHING.
What? Is that his excuse?
Sigh...
I think so.
WHENEVER I TALKED TO YAMATO...
...I COULD FIND SOMETHING GOOD ABOUT MYSELF.

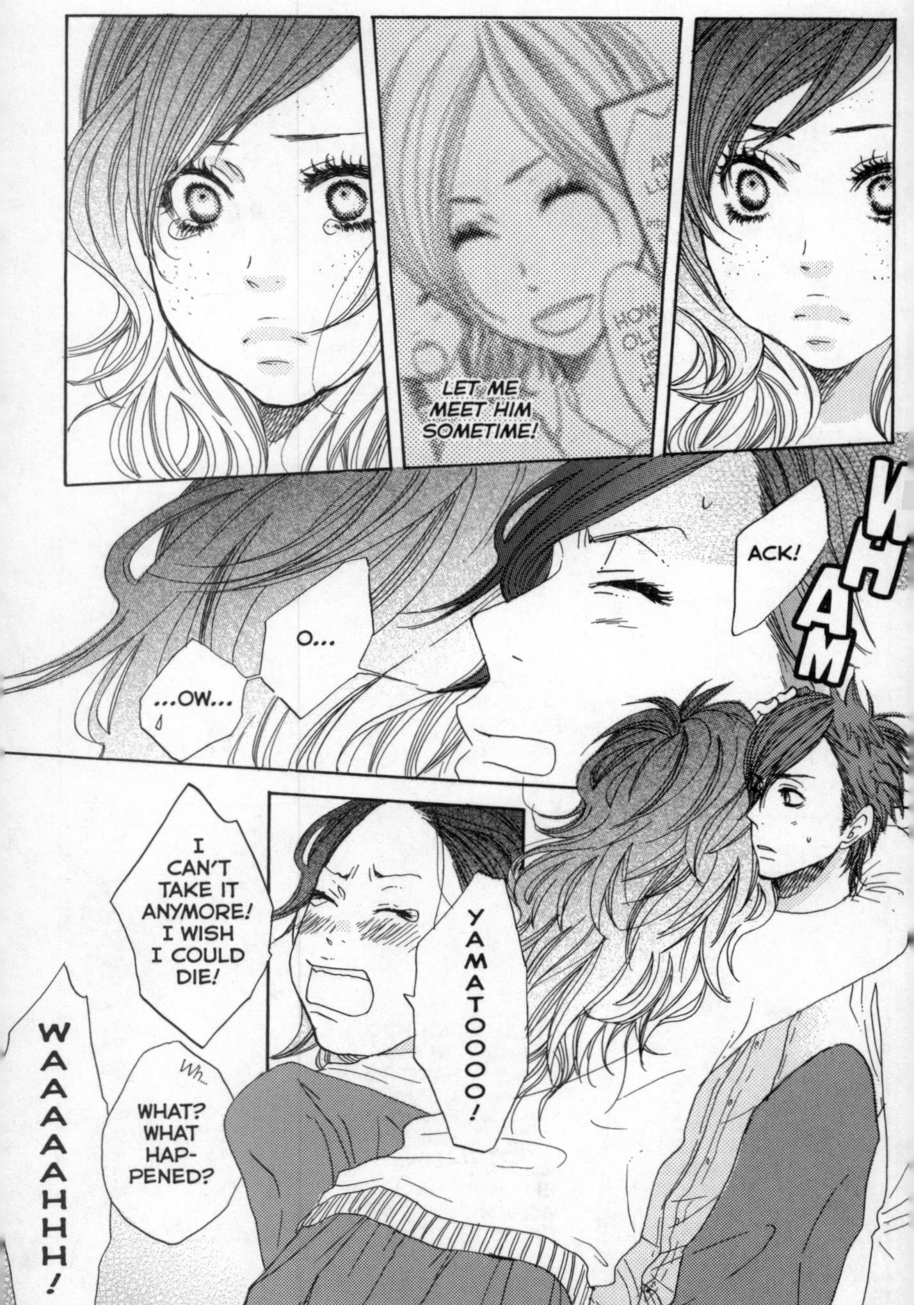
LET ME MEET HIM SOMETIME!
WHAM
ACK!
O...
...OW...
YAMATOOOO!
I CAN'T TAKE IT ANYMORE! I WISH I COULD DIE!
WAAAAAAAHHHH!
Wh...
WHAT? WHAT HAP-PENED?

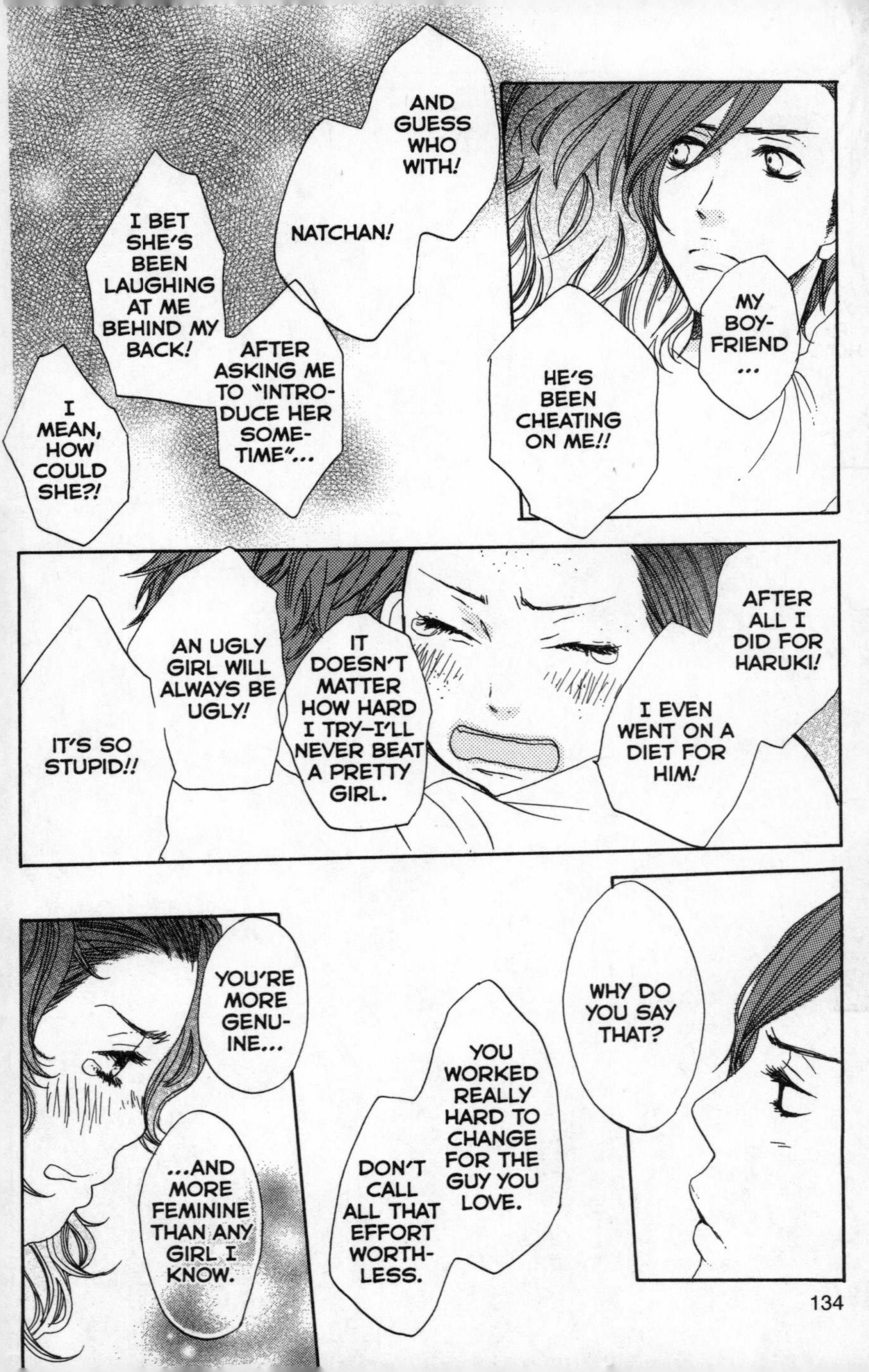
MY BOYFRIEND...
HE'S BEEN CHEATING ON ME!!
AND GUESS WHO WITH!
NATCHAN!
AFTER ASKING ME TO "INTRODUCE HER SOMETIME"...
I BET SHE'S BEEN LAUGHING AT ME BEHIND MY BACK!
I MEAN, HOW COULD SHE?!
AFTER ALL I DID FOR HARUKI!
I EVEN WENT ON A DIET FOR HIM!
IT DOESN'T MATTER HOW HARD I TRY—I'LL NEVER BEAT A PRETTY GIRL.
AN UGLY GIRL WILL ALWAYS BE UGLY!
IT'S SO STUPID!!
WHY DO YOU SAY THAT?
YOU WORKED REALLY HARD TO CHANGE FOR THE GUY YOU LOVE.
DON'T CALL ALL THAT EFFORT WORTHLESS.
YOU'RE MORE GENUINE...
...AND MORE FEMININE THAN ANY GIRL I KNOW.

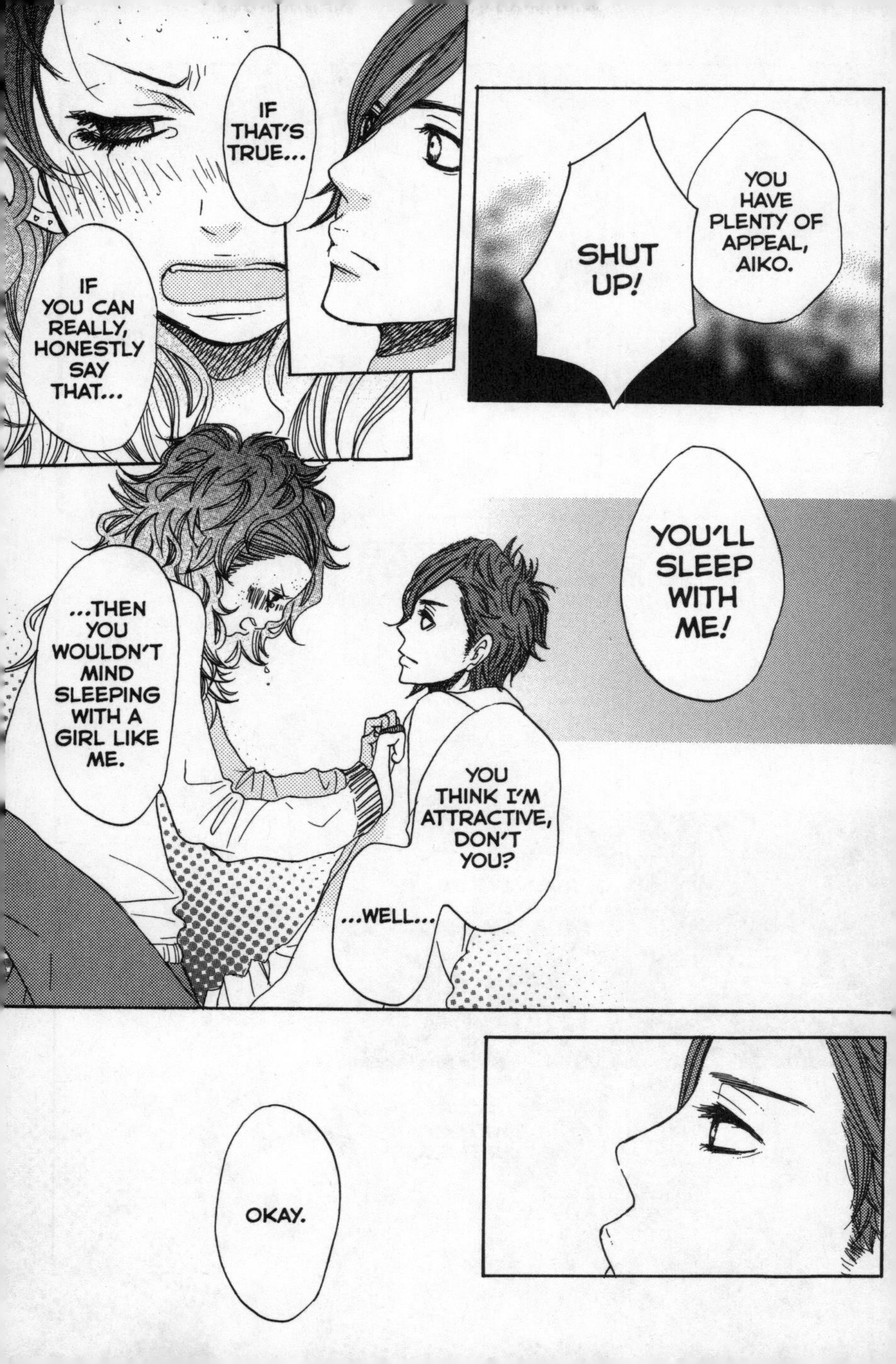
YOU HAVE PLENTY OF APPEAL, AIKO.
SHUT UP!
IF THAT'S TRUE...
IF YOU CAN REALLY, HONESTLY SAY THAT...
...THEN YOU WOULDN'T MIND SLEEPING WITH A GIRL LIKE ME.
YOU THINK I'M ATTRACTIVE, DON'T YOU?
...WELL...
YOU'LL SLEEP WITH ME!
OKAY.

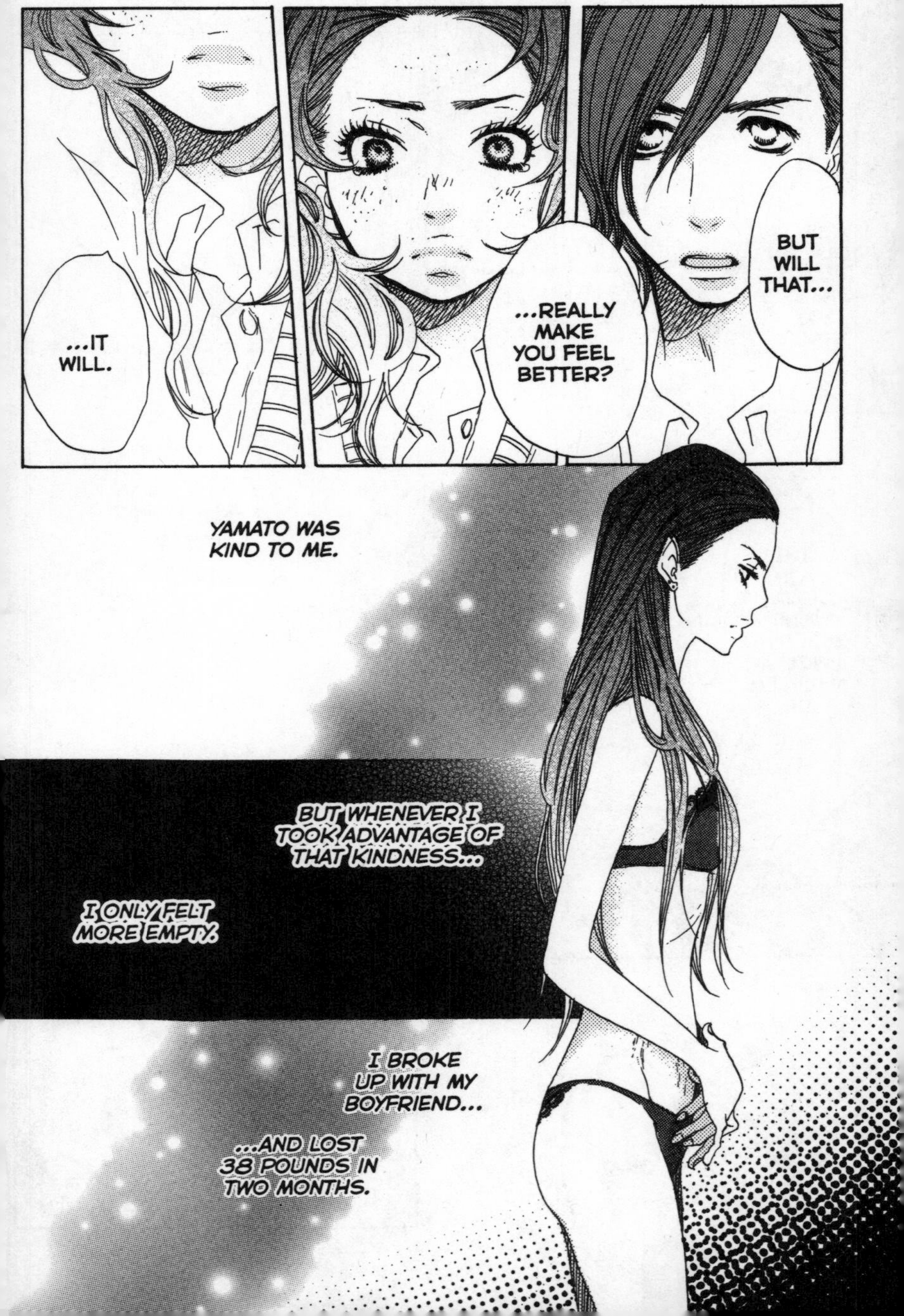
BUT WILL THAT...
...REALLY MAKE YOU FEEL BETTER?
...IT WILL.
YAMATO WAS KIND TO ME.
BUT WHENEVER I TOOK ADVANTAGE OF THAT KINDNESS...
I ONLY FELT MORE EMPTY.
I BROKE UP WITH MY BOYFRIEND...
...AND LOST 38 POUNDS IN TWO MONTHS.

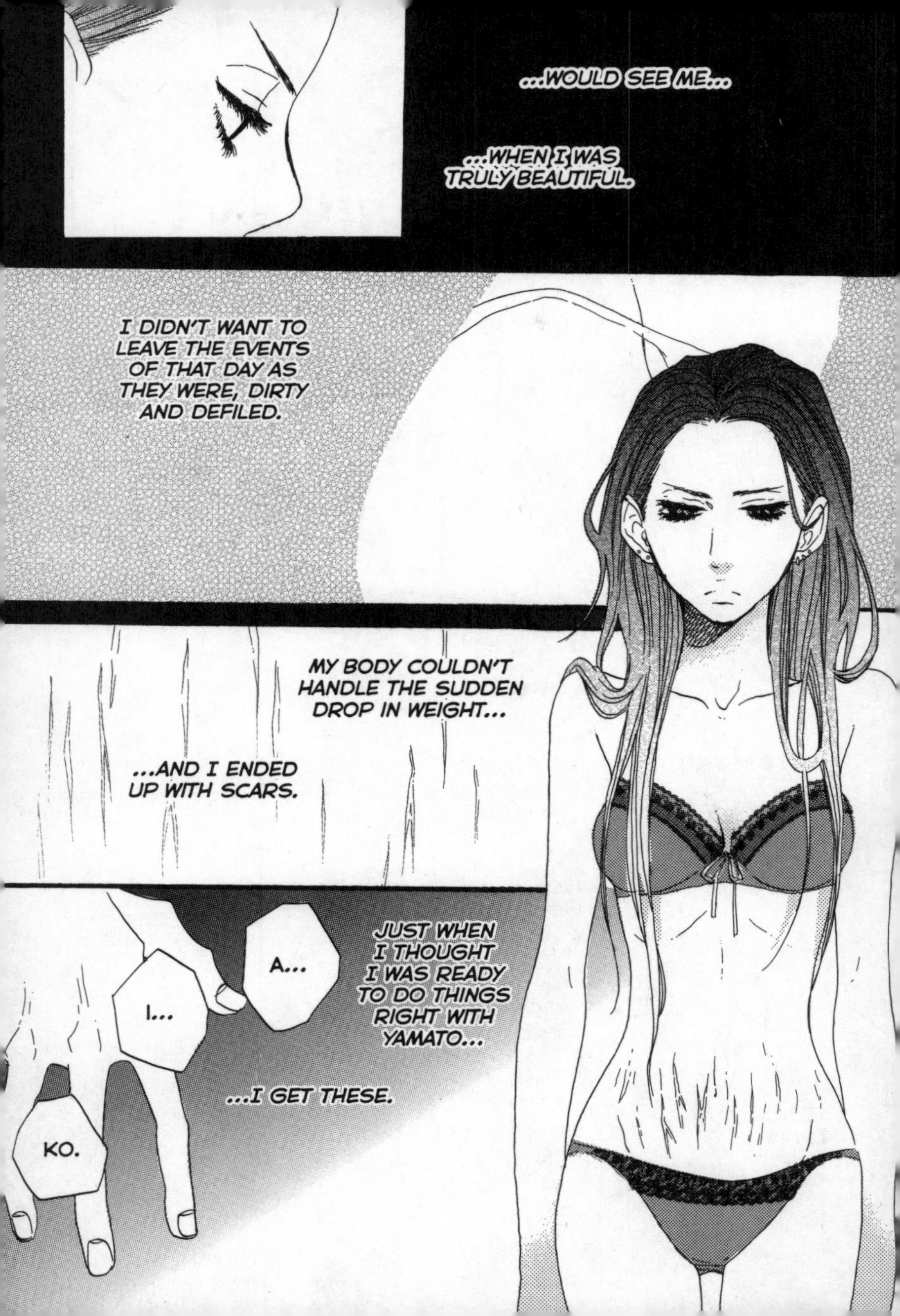
...WOULD SEE ME...
...WHEN I WAS TRULY BEAUTIFUL.
I DIDN'T WANT TO LEAVE THE EVENTS OF THAT DAY AS THEY WERE, DIRTY AND DEFILED.
MY BODY COULDN'T HANDLE THE SUDDEN DROP IN WEIGHT...
...AND I ENDED UP WITH SCARS.
JUST WHEN I THOUGHT I WAS READY TO DO THINGS RIGHT WITH YAMATO...
...I GET THESE.
A...
I...
KO.

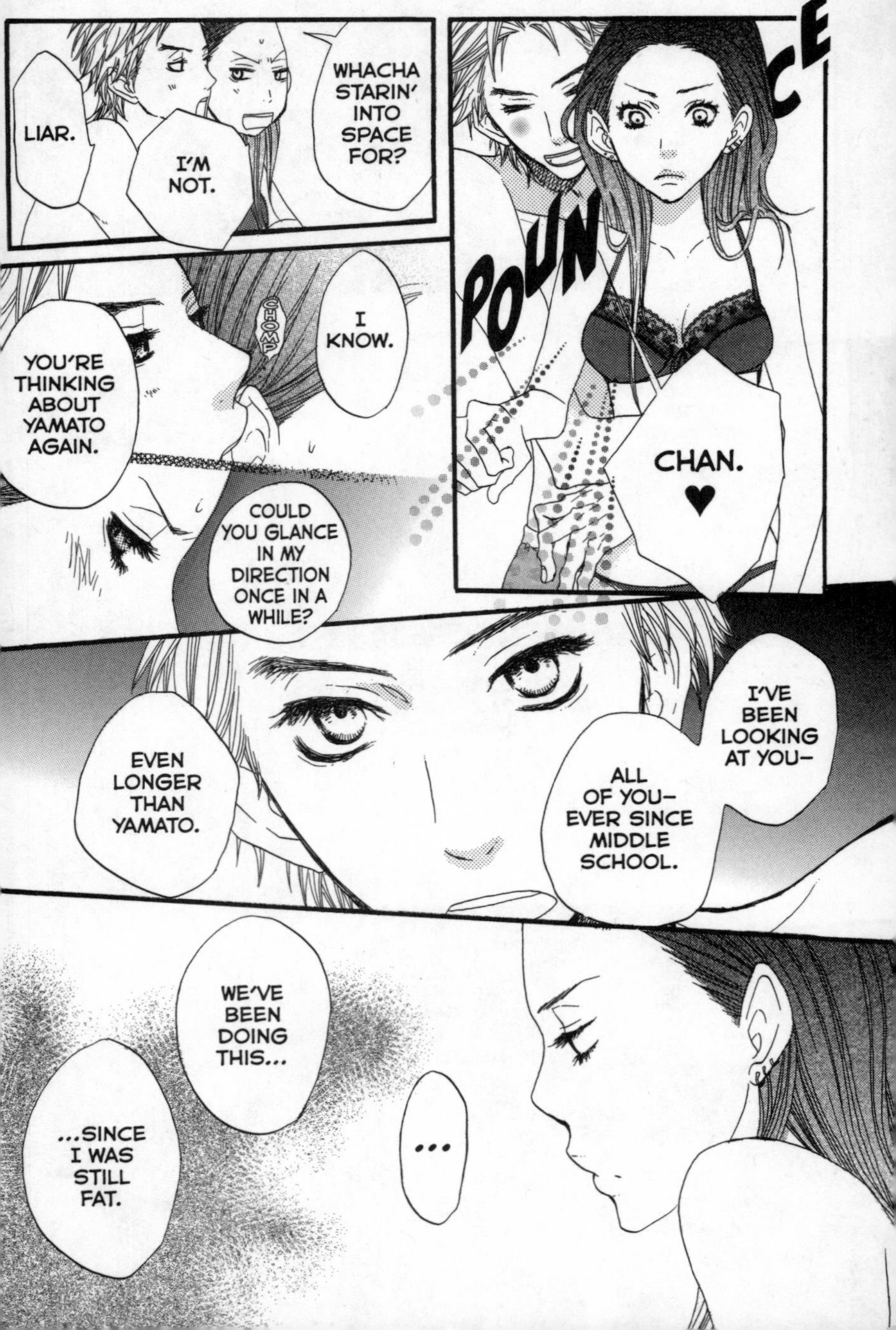
POUNCE
CHAN. ♥
WHACHA STARIN' INTO SPACE FOR?
I'M NOT.
LIAR.
I KNOW.
CHOMP
YOU'RE THINKING ABOUT YAMATO AGAIN.
COULD YOU GLANCE IN MY DIRECTION ONCE IN A WHILE?
I'VE BEEN LOOKING AT YOU—
ALL OF YOU— EVER SINCE MIDDLE SCHOOL.
EVEN LONGER THAN YAMATO.
...
WE'VE BEEN DOING THIS...
...SINCE I WAS STILL FAT.

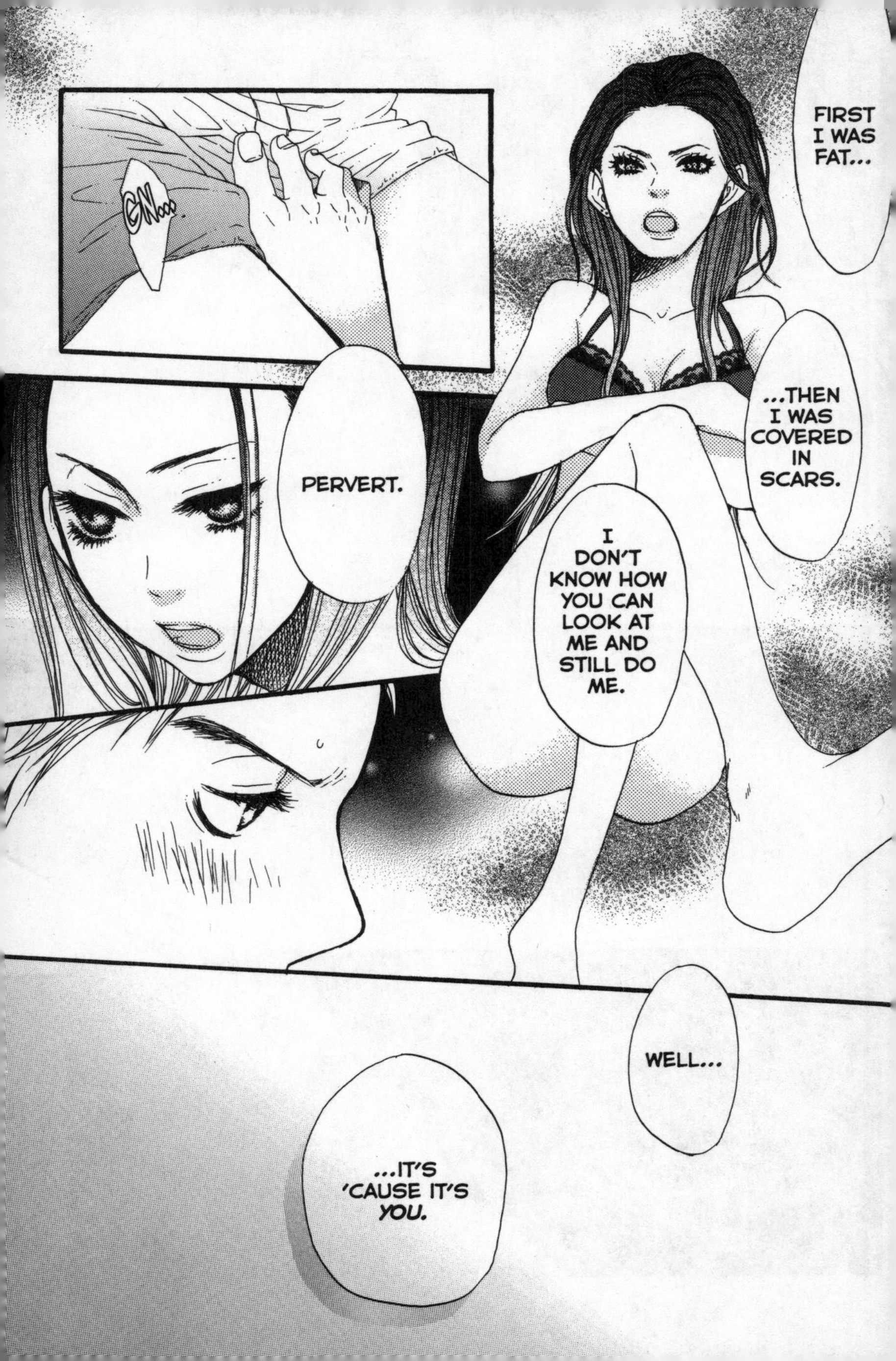
FIRST I WAS FAT...
...THEN I WAS COVERED IN SCARS.
I DON'T KNOW HOW YOU CAN LOOK AT ME AND STILL DO ME.
PERVERT.
WELL...
...IT'S 'CAUSE IT'S *YOU.*

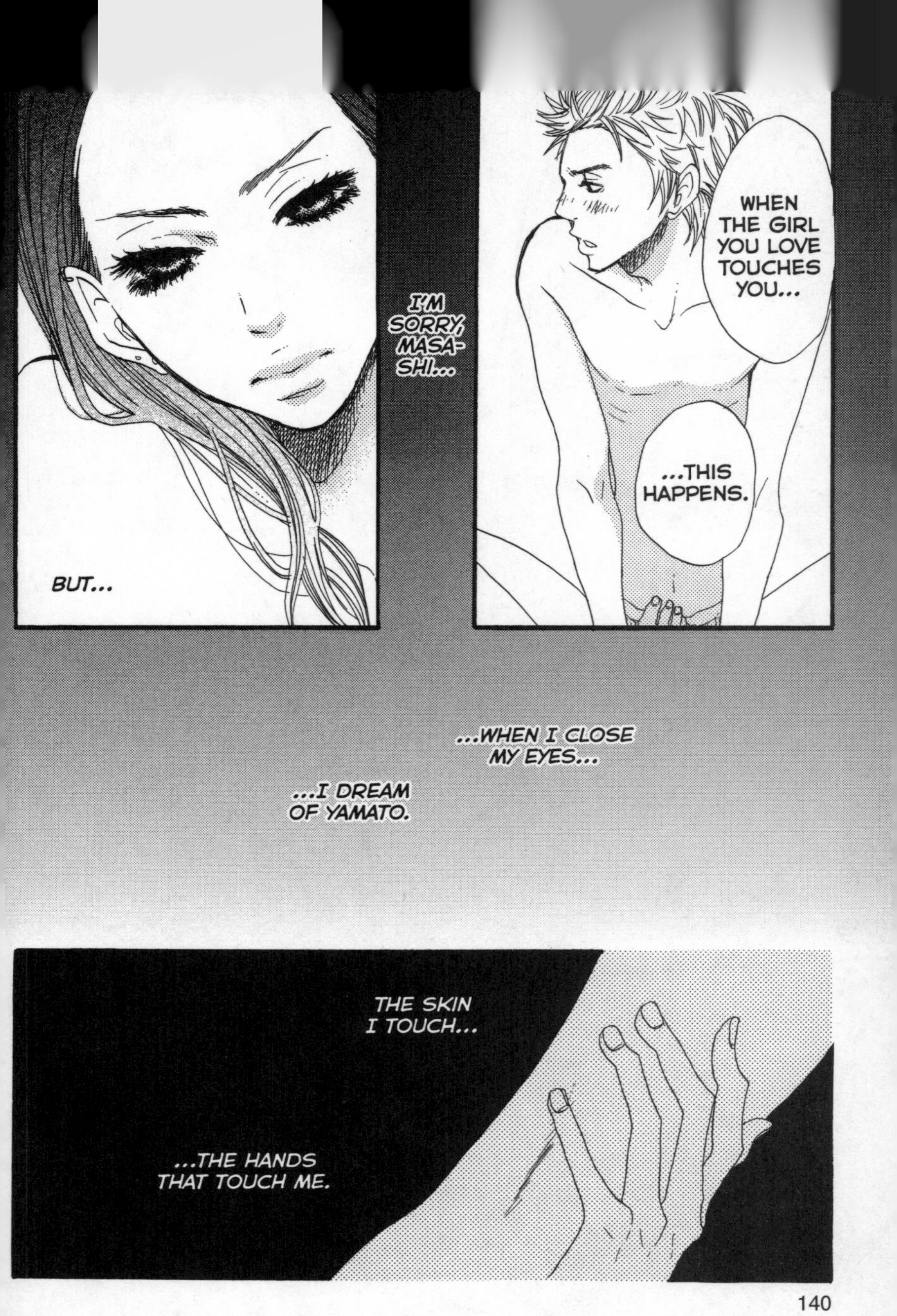
WHEN THE GIRL YOU LOVE TOUCHES YOU...
...THIS HAPPENS.
I'M SORRY, MASA-SHI...
BUT...
...WHEN I CLOSE MY EYES...
...I DREAM OF YAMATO.
THE SKIN I TOUCH...
...THE HANDS THAT TOUCH ME.

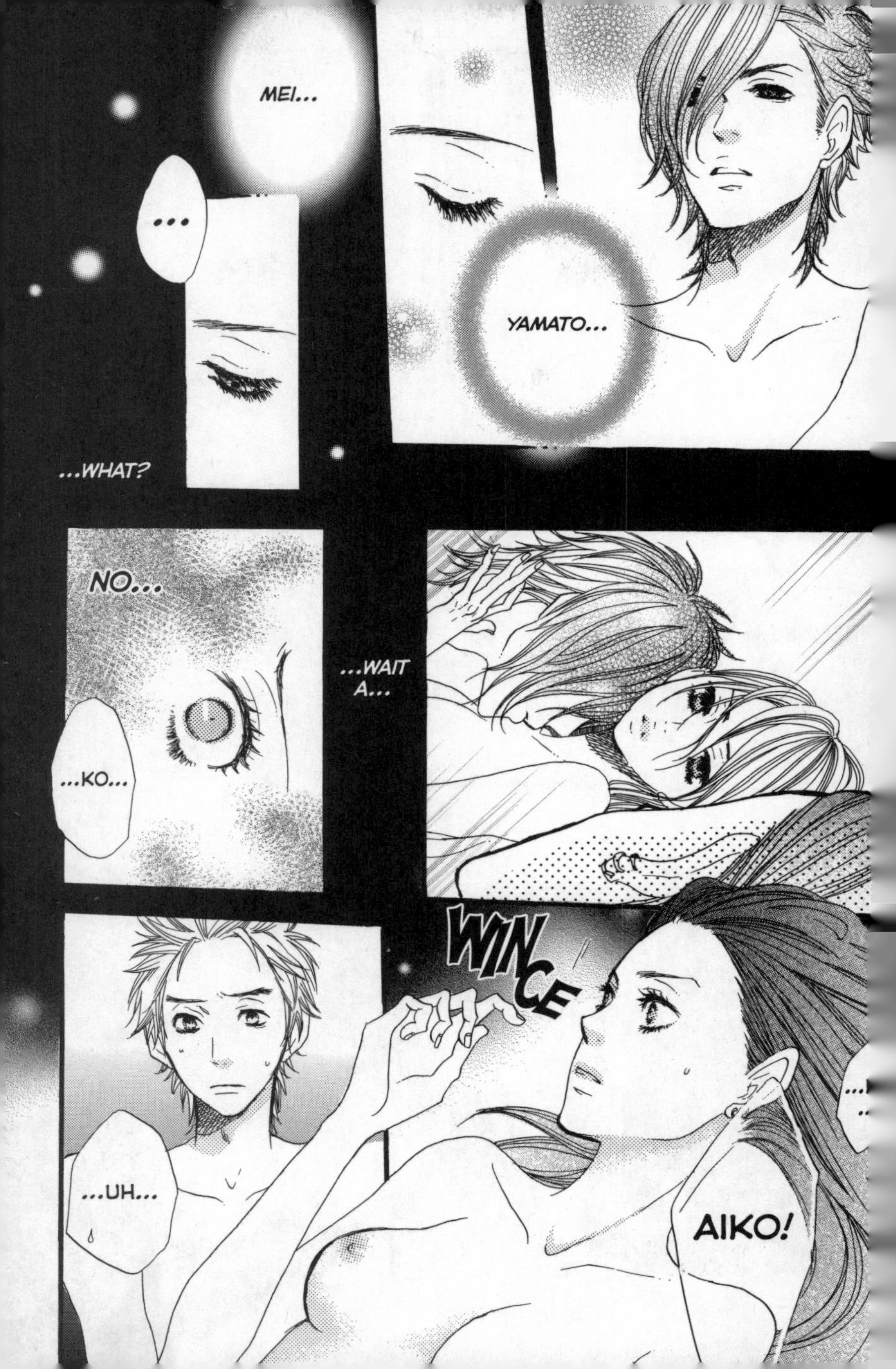
YAMATO...
MEI...
...
...WHAT?
...WAIT A...
NO...
...KO...
WINCE
...
AIKO!
...UH...

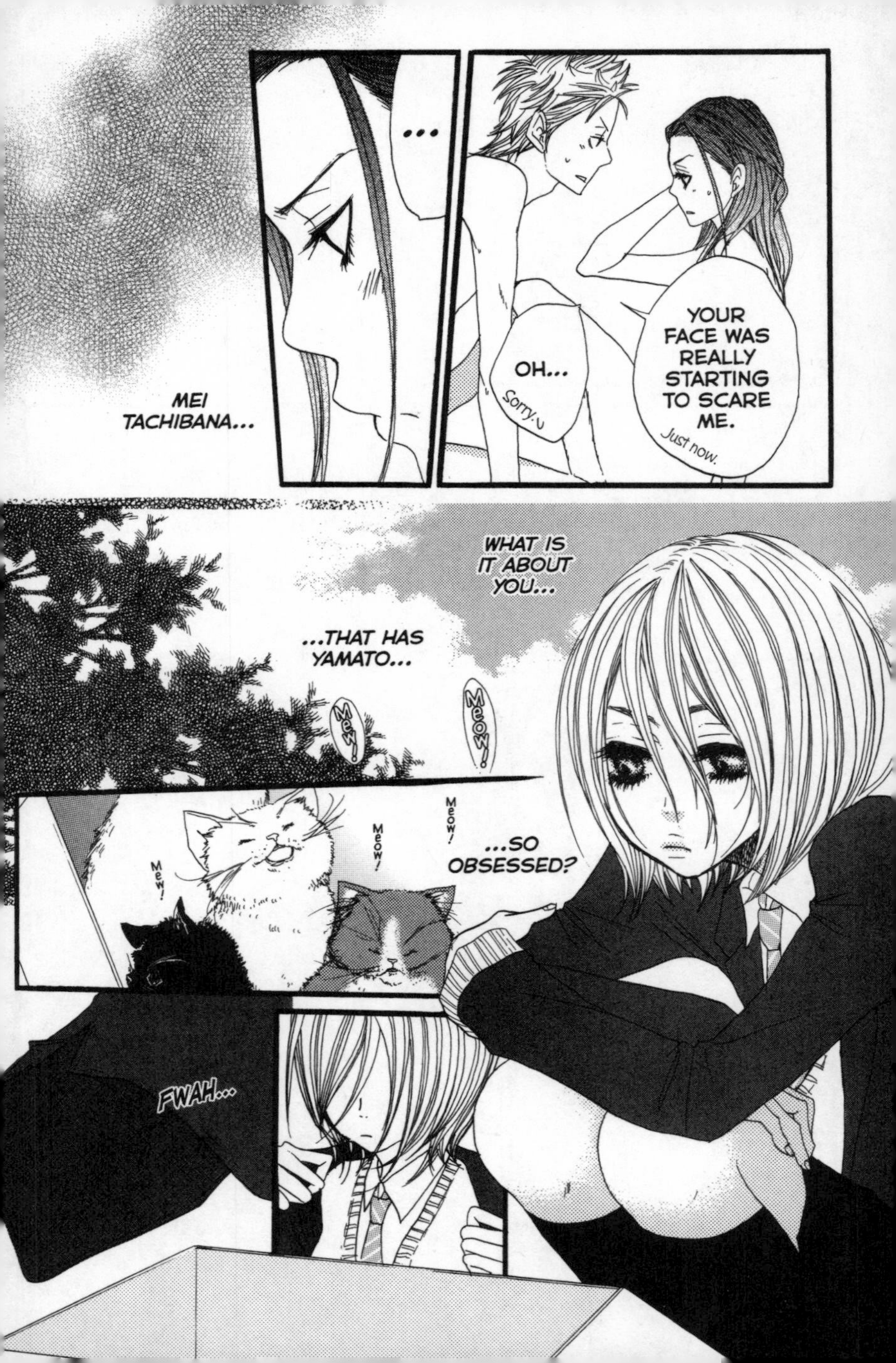
YOUR FACE WAS REALLY STARTING TO SCARE ME.
Just now.
OH...
Sorry.
...
MEI TACHIBANA...
WHAT IS IT ABOUT YOU...
...THAT HAS YAMATO...
Meow!
Mew!
Meow!
Meow!
Mew!
...SO OBSESSED?
FWAH...

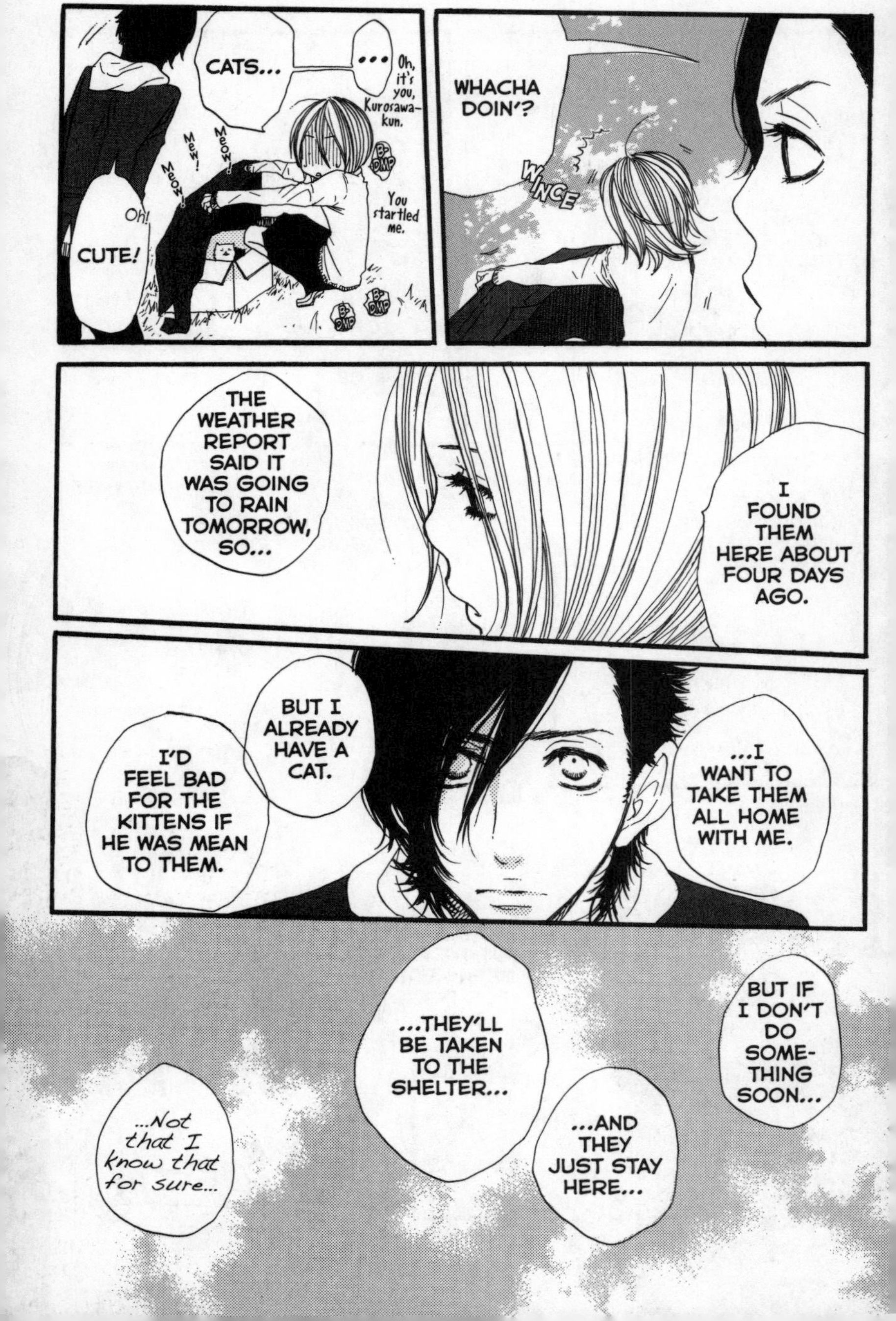
WHACHA DOIN'?
WINCE
...
Oh, it's you, Kurosawa-kun.
CATS...
B-DMP
You startled me.
Meow!
Mew!
Meow!
Oh!
CUTE!
B-DMP
B-DMP
I FOUND THEM HERE ABOUT FOUR DAYS AGO.
THE WEATHER REPORT SAID IT WAS GOING TO RAIN TOMORROW, SO...
...I WANT TO TAKE THEM ALL HOME WITH ME.
BUT I ALREADY HAVE A CAT.
I'D FEEL BAD FOR THE KITTENS IF HE WAS MEAN TO THEM.
BUT IF I DON'T DO SOMETHING SOON...
...AND THEY JUST STAY HERE...
...THEY'LL BE TAKEN TO THE SHELTER...
...Not that I know that for sure...

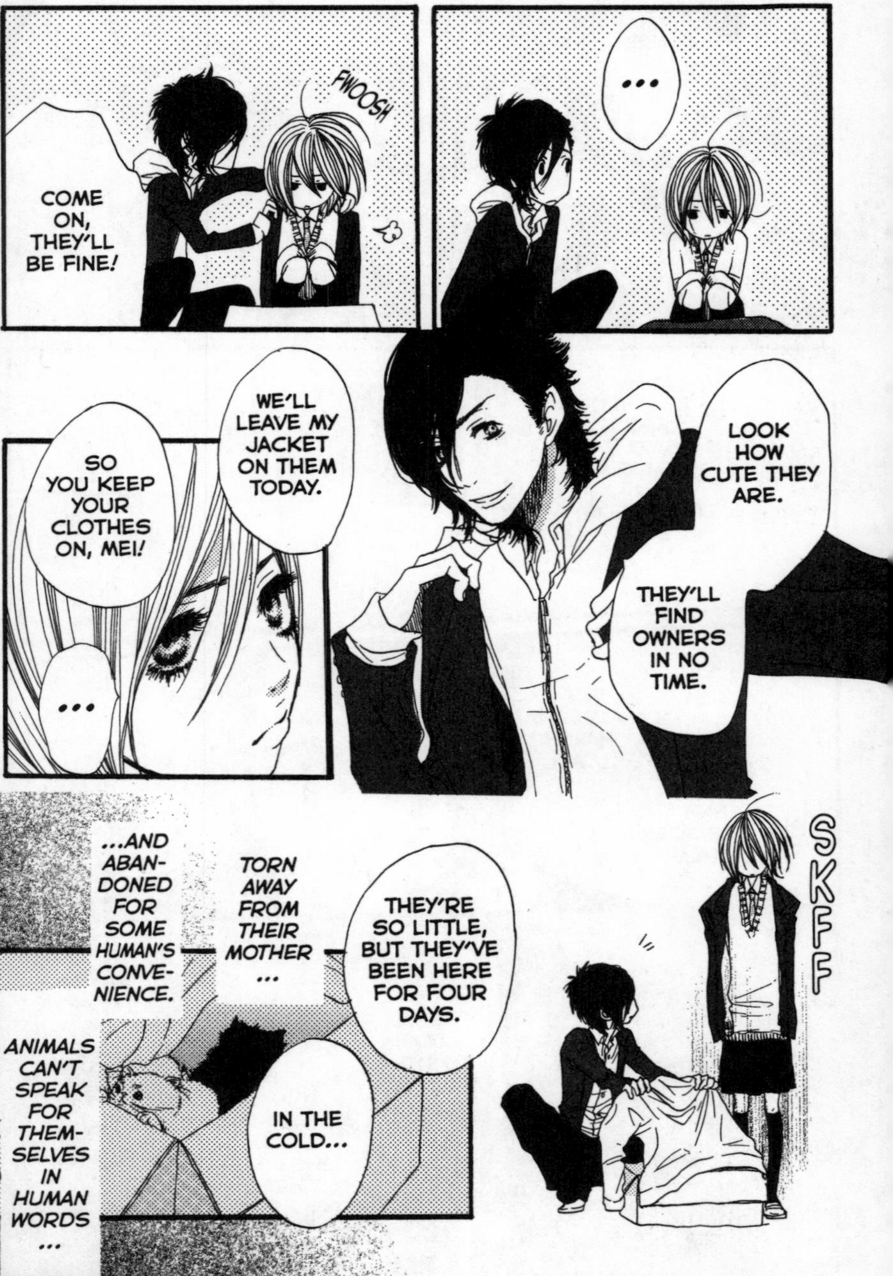
...
FWOOSH
COME ON, THEY'LL BE FINE!
LOOK HOW CUTE THEY ARE.
THEY'LL FIND OWNERS IN NO TIME.
WE'LL LEAVE MY JACKET ON THEM TODAY.
SO YOU KEEP YOUR CLOTHES ON, MEI!
...
SKFF
THEY'RE SO LITTLE, BUT THEY'VE BEEN HERE FOR FOUR DAYS.
TORN AWAY FROM THEIR MOTHER ...
...AND ABANDONED FOR SOME HUMAN'S CONVENIENCE.
IN THE COLD...
ANIMALS CAN'T SPEAK FOR THEMSELVES IN HUMAN WORDS ...

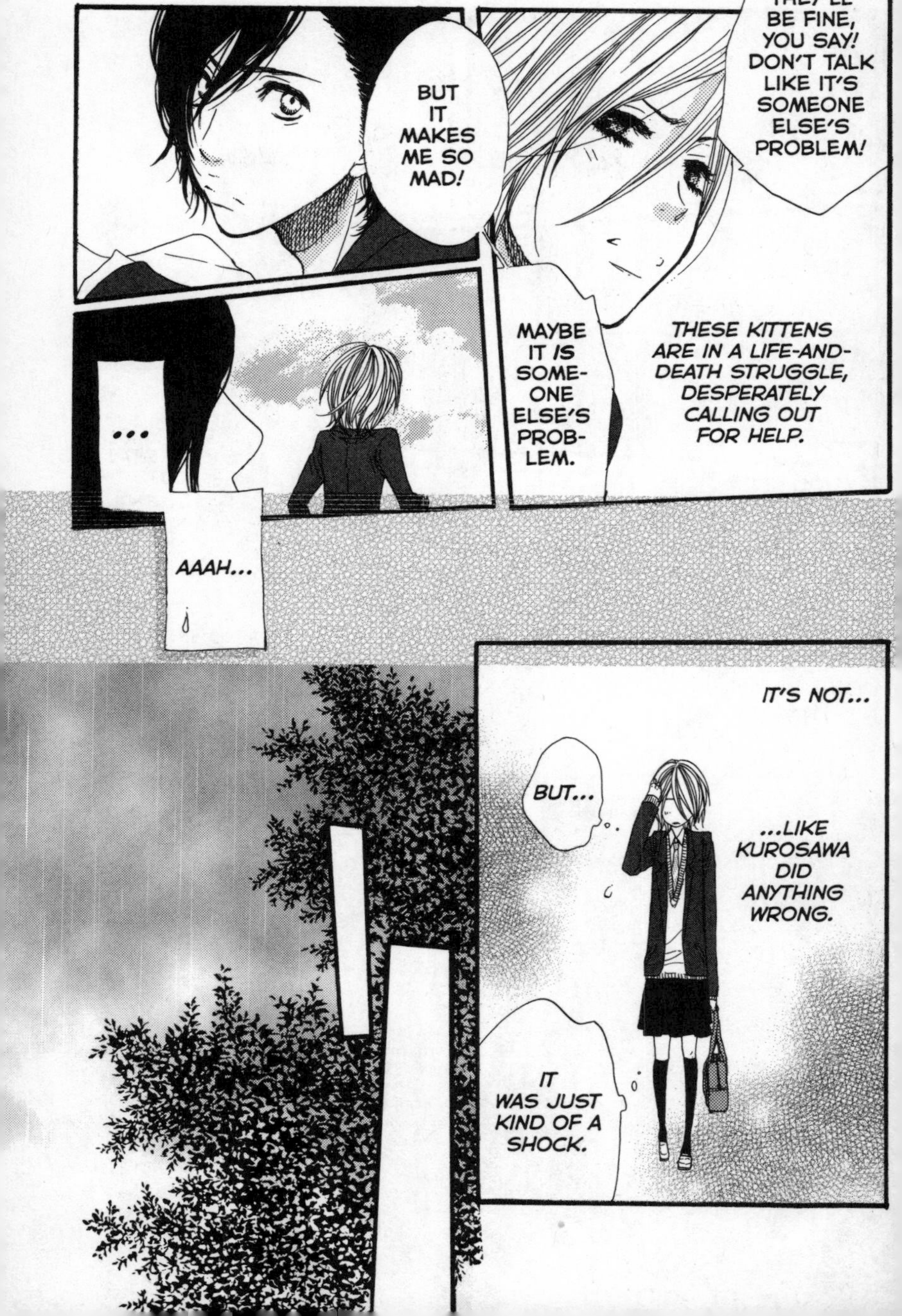
THEY'LL BE FINE, YOU SAY! DON'T TALK LIKE IT'S SOMEONE ELSE'S PROBLEM!
THESE KITTENS ARE IN A LIFE-AND-DEATH STRUGGLE, DESPERATELY CALLING OUT FOR HELP.
MAYBE IT IS SOMEONE ELSE'S PROBLEM.
BUT IT MAKES ME SO MAD!
...
AAAH...
IT'S NOT...
BUT...
...LIKE KUROSAWA DID ANYTHING WRONG.
IT WAS JUST KIND OF A SHOCK.

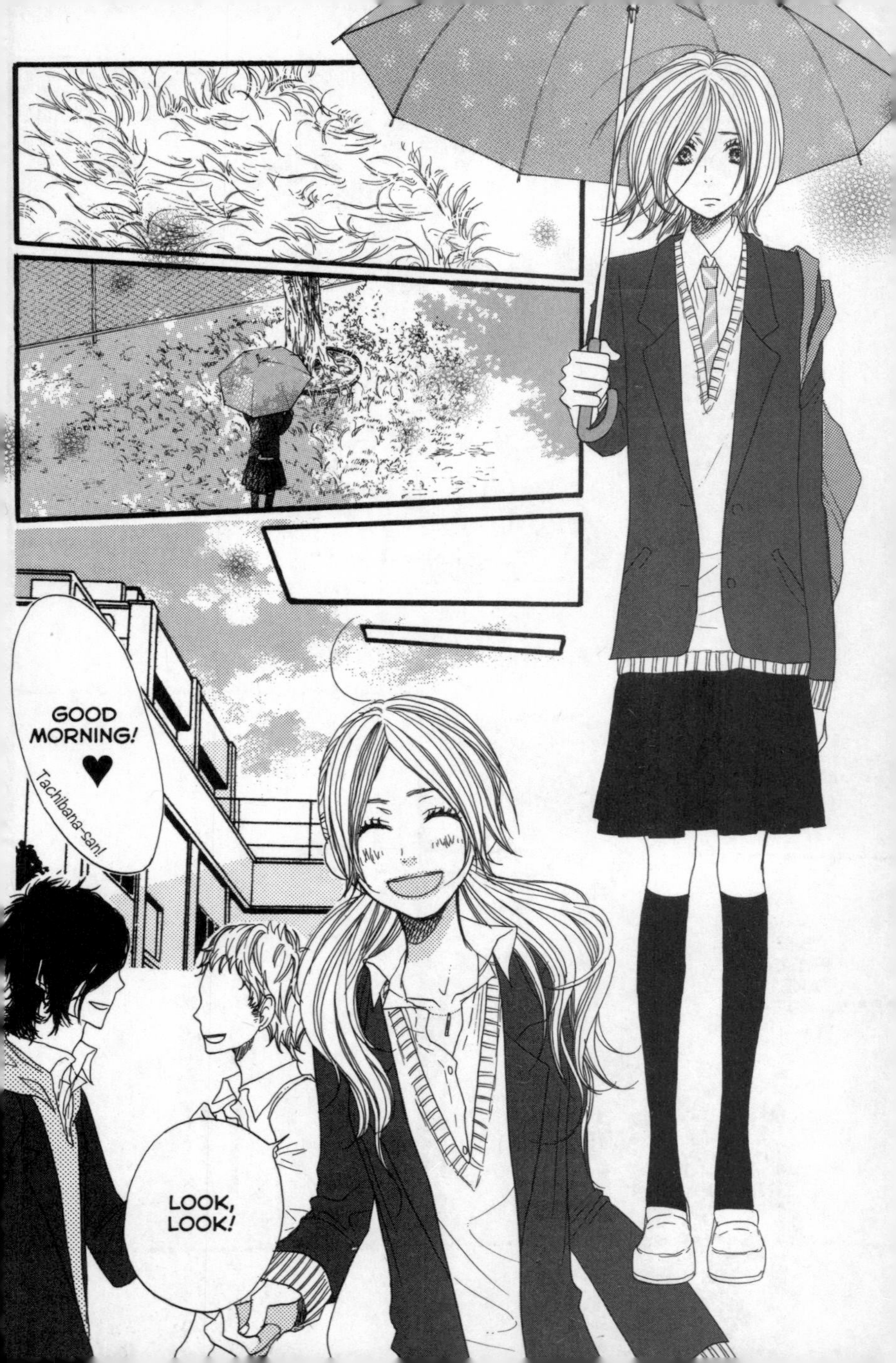
GOOD MORNING! ♥
Tachibana-san!
LOOK, LOOK!

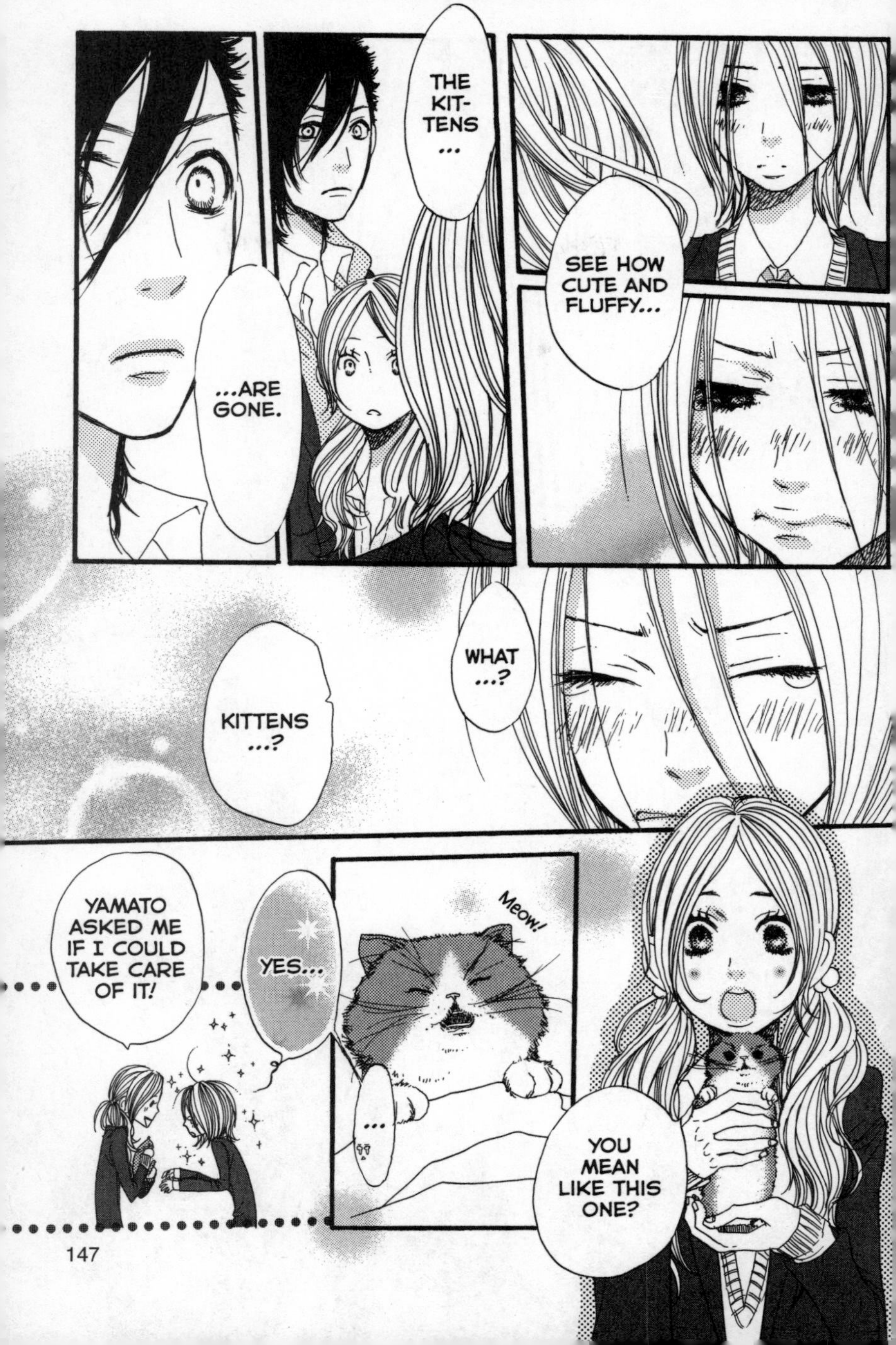
SEE HOW CUTE AND FLUFFY...
THE KIT-TENS ...
...ARE GONE.
WHAT ...?
KITTENS ...?
YOU MEAN LIKE THIS ONE?
Meow!
...
YES...
YAMATO ASKED ME IF I COULD TAKE CARE OF IT!

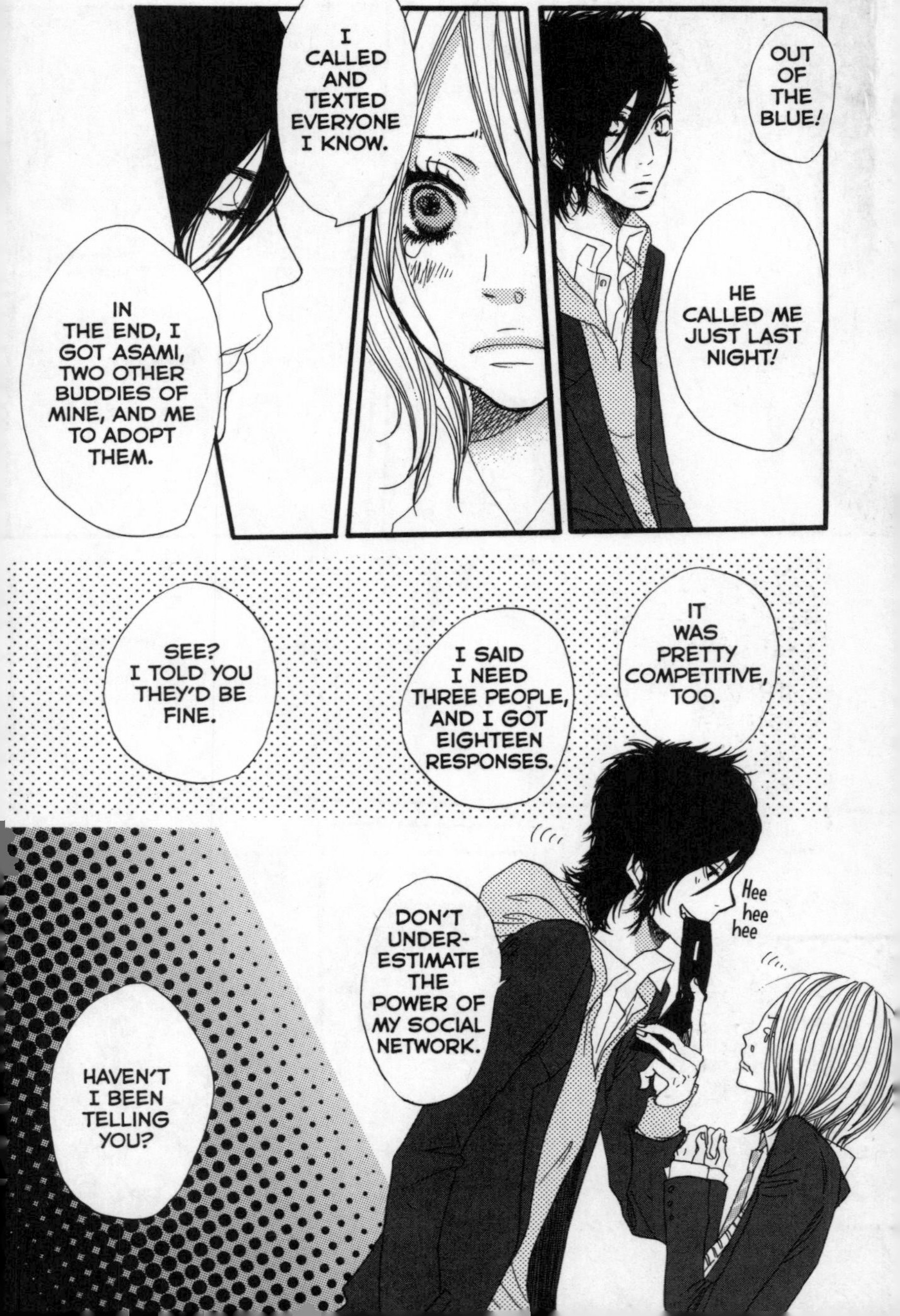
OUT OF THE BLUE!
HE CALLED ME JUST LAST NIGHT!
I CALLED AND TEXTED EVERYONE I KNOW.
IN THE END, I GOT ASAMI, TWO OTHER BUDDIES OF MINE, AND ME TO ADOPT THEM.
IT WAS PRETTY COMPETITIVE, TOO.
I SAID I NEED THREE PEOPLE, AND I GOT EIGHTEEN RESPONSES.
SEE? I TOLD YOU THEY'D BE FINE.
Hee hee hee
DON'T UNDER-ESTIMATE THE POWER OF MY SOCIAL NETWORK.
HAVEN'T I BEEN TELLING YOU?

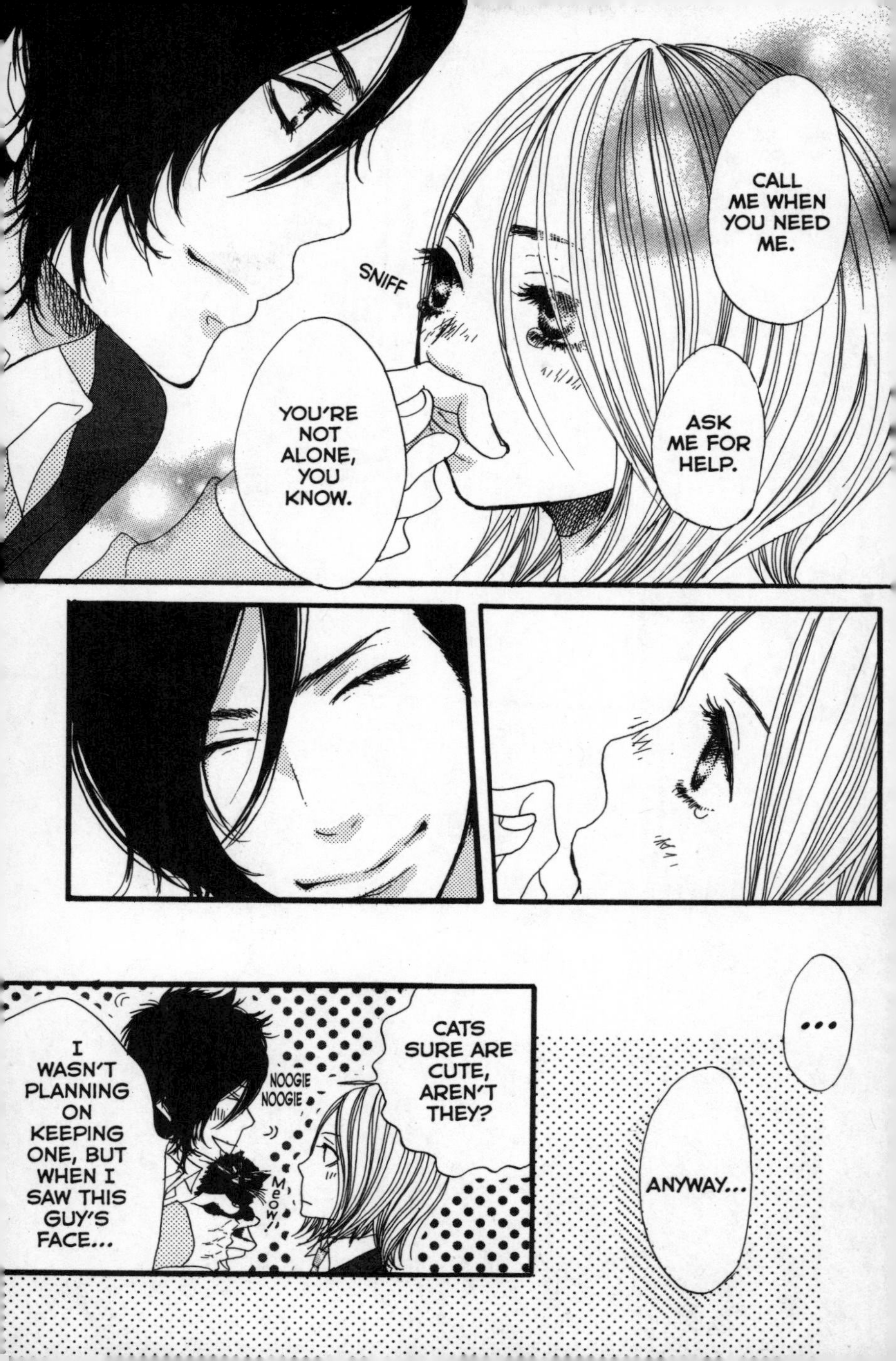
CALL ME WHEN YOU NEED ME.
ASK ME FOR HELP.
SNIFF
YOU'RE NOT ALONE, YOU KNOW.
...
ANYWAY...
CATS SURE ARE CUTE, AREN'T THEY?
NOOGIE NOOGIE
MEOW!
I WASN'T PLANNING ON KEEPING ONE, BUT WHEN I SAW THIS GUY'S FACE...

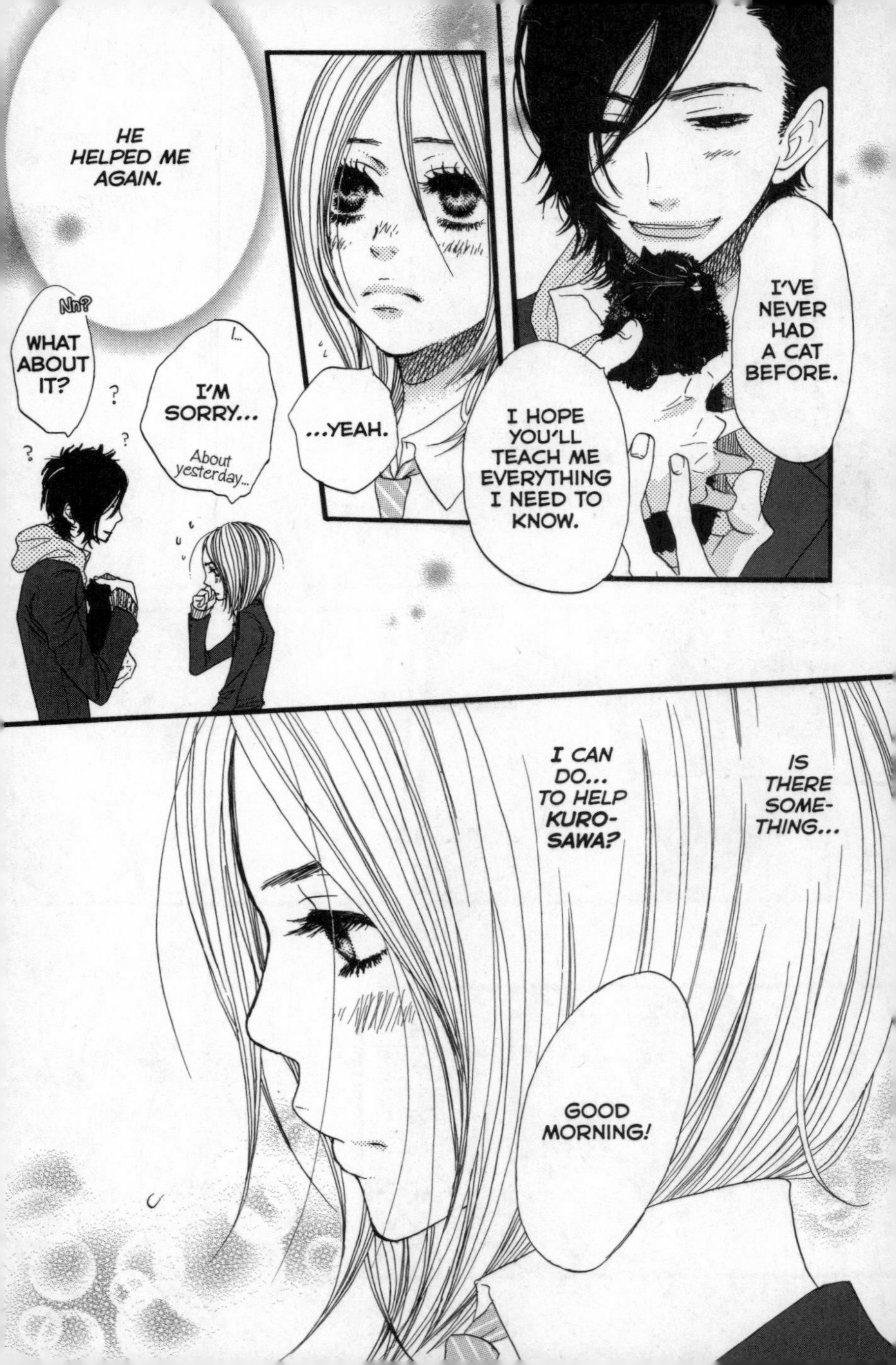
I'VE NEVER HAD A CAT BEFORE.
I HOPE YOU'LL TEACH ME EVERYTHING I NEED TO KNOW.
...YEAH.
HE HELPED ME AGAIN.
I... I'M SORRY... About yesterday...
Nn? WHAT ABOUT IT?
IS THERE SOME-THING...
I CAN DO... TO HELP KURO-SAWA?
GOOD MORNING!

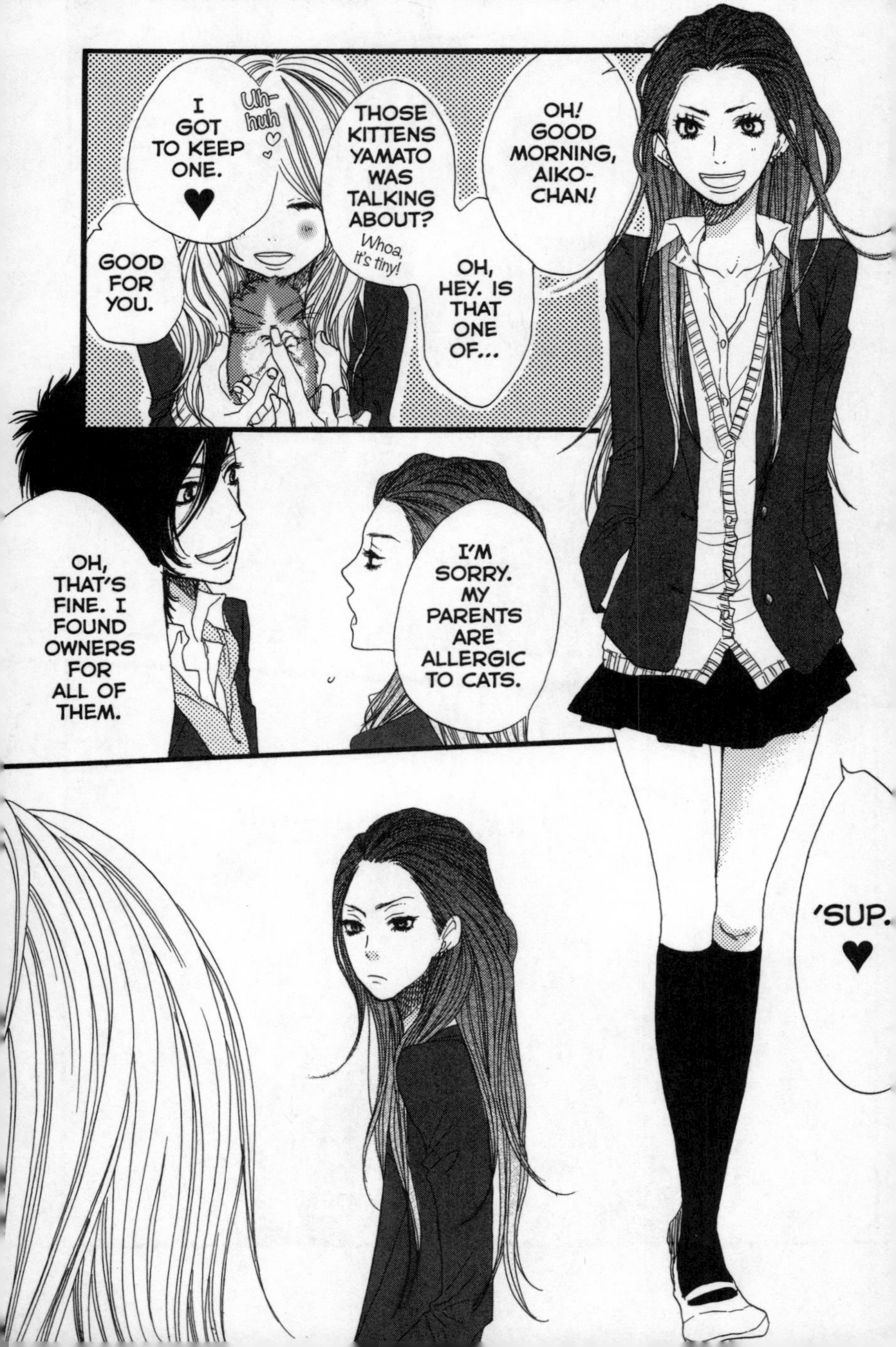
OH! GOOD MORNING, AIKO-CHAN!
OH, HEY. IS THAT ONE OF...
THOSE KITTENS YAMATO WAS TALKING ABOUT?
Whoa, it's tiny!
Uh-huh ♡
I GOT TO KEEP ONE. ♥
GOOD FOR YOU.
I'M SORRY. MY PARENTS ARE ALLERGIC TO CATS.
OH, THAT'S FINE. I FOUND OWNERS FOR ALL OF THEM.
'SUP. ♥

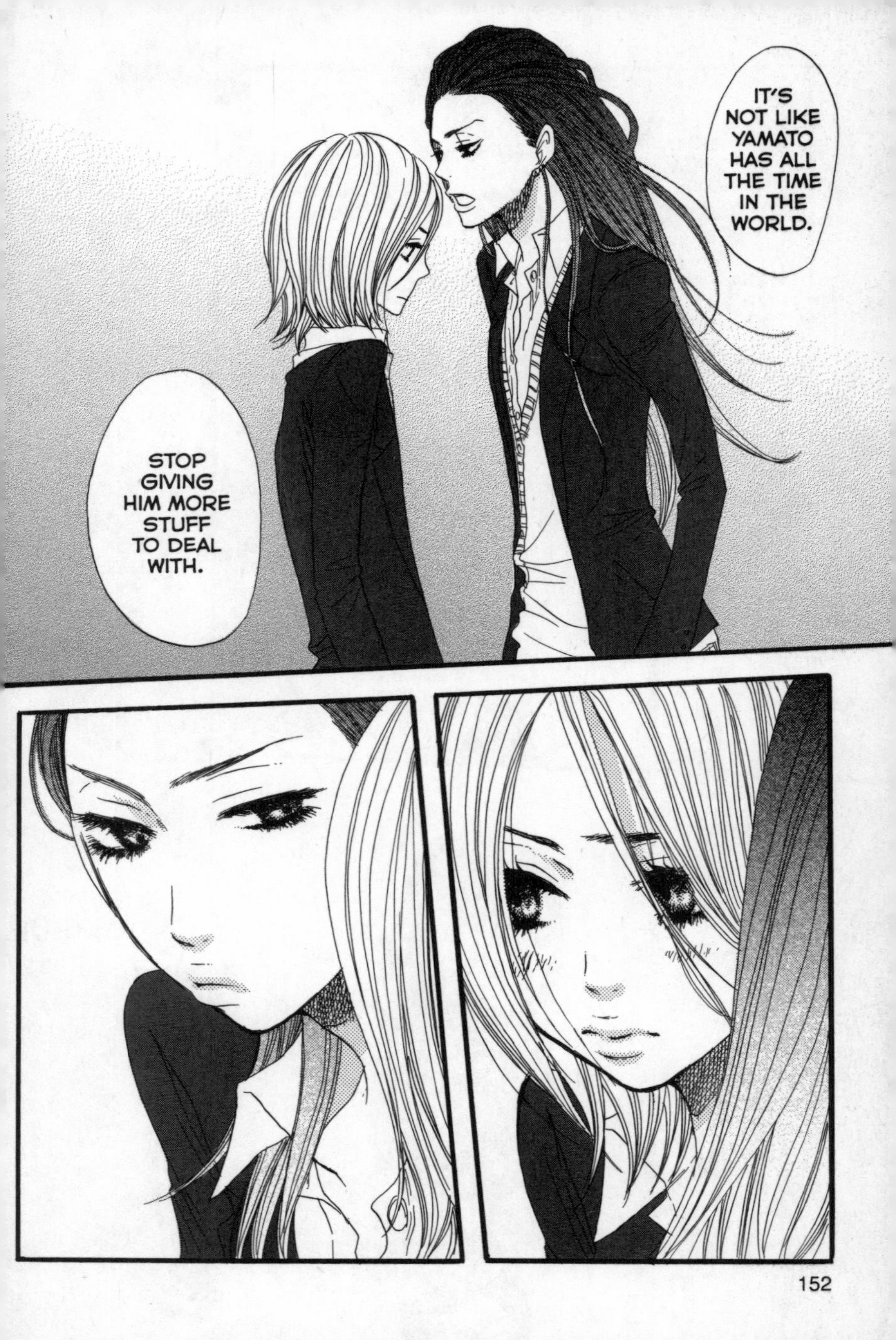
IT'S NOT LIKE YAMATO HAS ALL THE TIME IN THE WORLD.
STOP GIVING HIM MORE STUFF TO DEAL WITH.

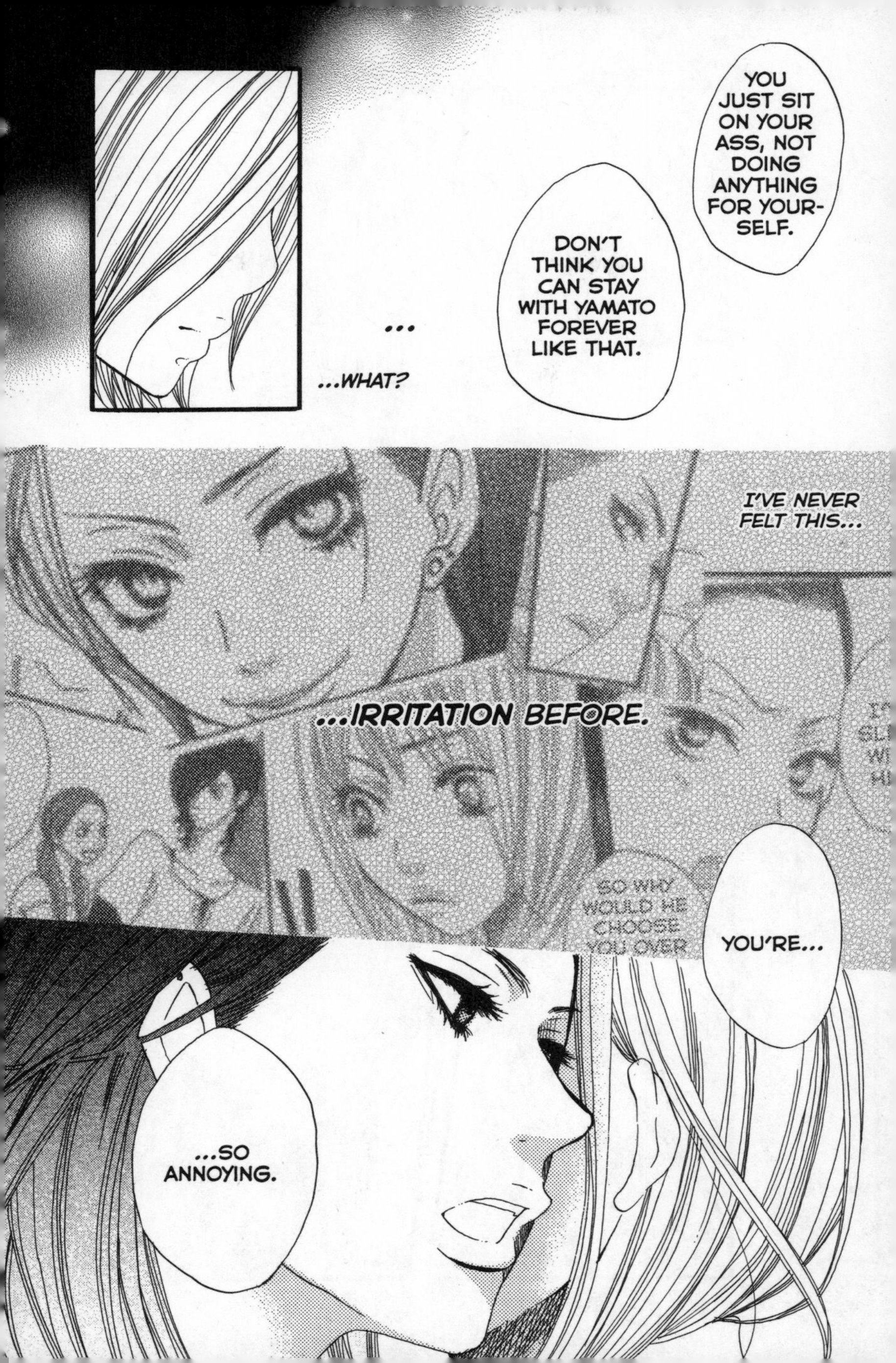
YOU JUST SIT ON YOUR ASS, NOT DOING ANYTHING FOR YOUR-SELF.
DON'T THINK YOU CAN STAY WITH YAMATO FOREVER LIKE THAT.
...
...WHAT?
I'VE NEVER FELT THIS...
...IRRITATION BEFORE.
SO WHY WOULD HE CHOOSE YOU OVER
YOU'RE...
...SO ANNOYING.

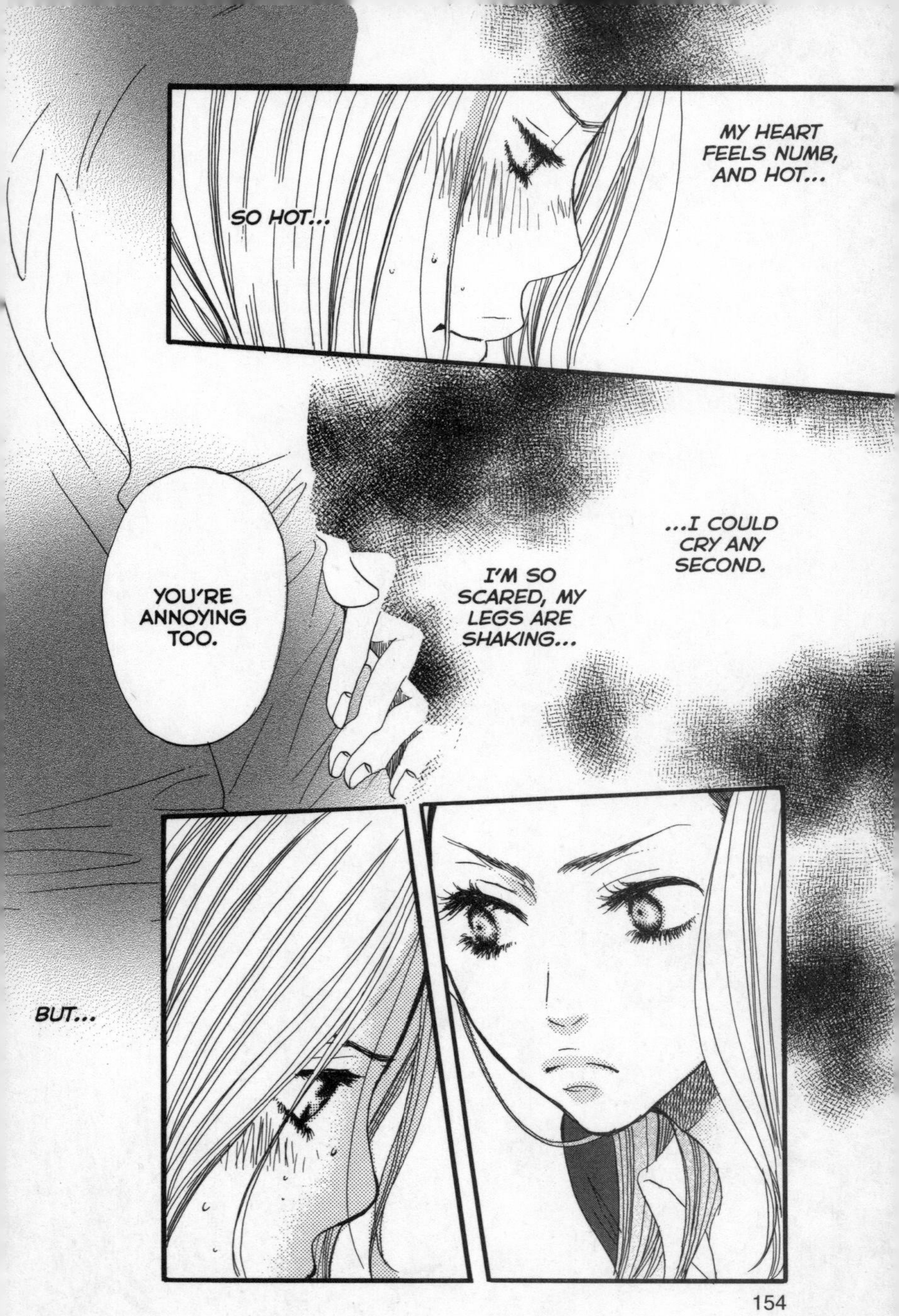
MY HEART FEELS NUMB, AND HOT...
SO HOT...
...I COULD CRY ANY SECOND.
I'M SO SCARED, MY LEGS ARE SHAKING...
YOU'RE ANNOYING TOO.
BUT...

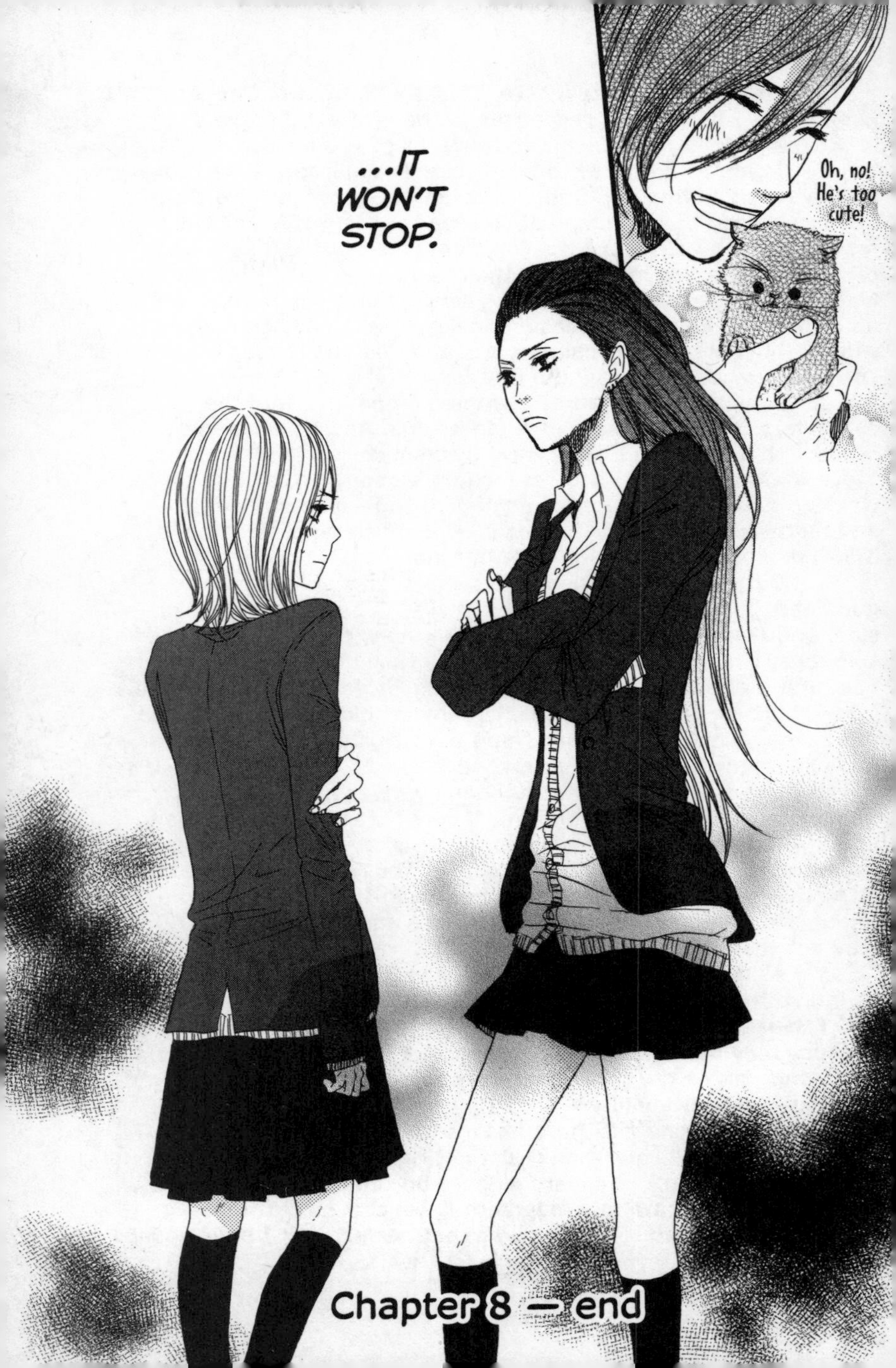
Oh, no! He's too cute!
...IT WON'T STOP.
Chapter 8 — end

Hello, Kanae Hazuki here. This is volume two. I'm very happy. Yes. I got a lot of responses to the afterword pages I wrote in the last volume, and I want to thank all of you for sending them.

I didn't want to write any lies or exaggerations, so I took the liberty of writing my thoughts at length, in my own words, and I'm very happy that so many of you read those words and they resonated with you. I said this in volume one, but in a sense, I'm projecting a part of myself onto the main character of this manga, Mei. (But I never went for sixteen years without any friends, ha ha.) The way she thinks, her personality, the things she does—when I think about it, I realize she is a lot like me. That's why she's so very easy to draw (ha ha).

I think that sometimes, women empathize with the characters they read about in shojo manga. And I think some readers think, "I wish I could have a romance like this!" Me, too. I love to draw pictures, and I'm fortunate enough to be in a place where I can make those pictures public, and express my desires and fantasies through my drawings. Unfortunately, I don't have that much personal experience with romance.

Currently, there is someone I like, and while I'm not very good at it, I am in a relationship. I've always been on the plump side, and I've been dieting for two years now, but since I met someone, I've thought even more about how I would like to be beautiful. Before, I could only ever think, "It doesn't matter what I do—I'll never be pretty. I'd look creepy if I did anything girly, so there's no point in even trying," so I tried to stamp out anything feminine in my behavior and personality.

Like I said, I had always been overweight. I started thinking about my health, and that's why I started dieting. Then about a year ago, I met my current boyfriend. Twitterpation aside, I realized just how powerful words like, "You're so cute," "You're attractive," "You're beautiful," can be. When I actually started a relationship, my attitude toward romance made a complete 180. It may not seem true, but it is.

As long as a girl keeps wanting to improve herself, she can be infinitely beautiful. Not just on the outside, but on the inside, too. I think more than a few people repress themselves, just because they don't have the confidence. But if you stop holding back, and just do the things you want to do, eventually that will become your individuality.

So if anyone out there has insecurities, or doesn't have confidence, I think you should just get rid of those feelings that are holding you back. We were all born on the same foundation. I hope I can keep drawing a manga that will convey that message to all of you through Mei. I know I'm not perfect, but I hope you'll keep reading.

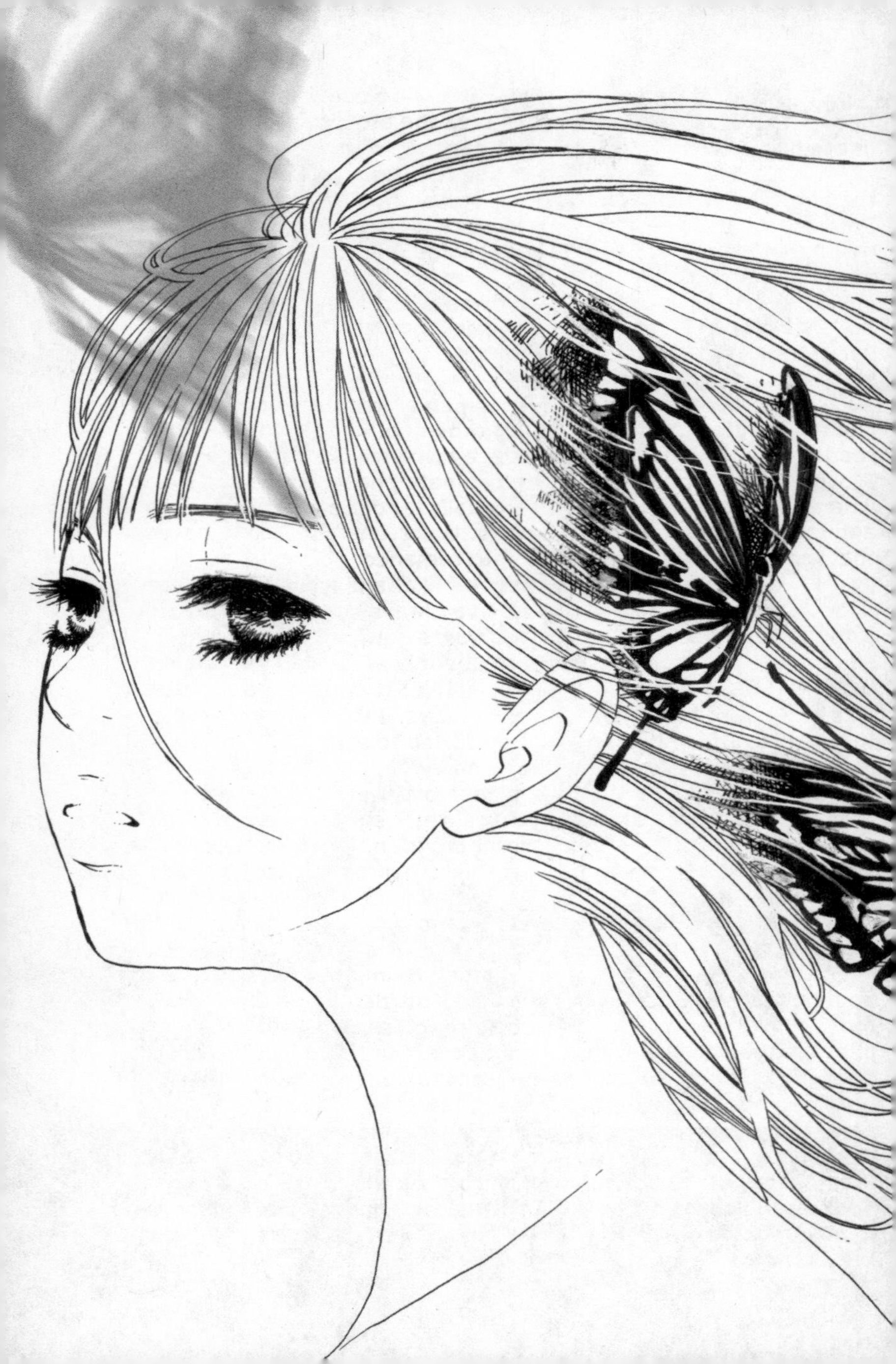

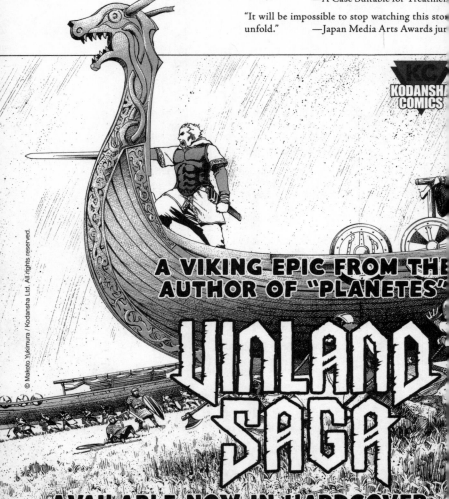

A Kodansha Comics Trade Paperback Original
Say I Love You. volume 2 copyright © 2009 Kanae Hazuki
English translation copyright © 2014 Kanae Hazuki

Published in the United States by Kodansha Comics, an imprint of Kodansha USA Publishing, LLC, New York.

Publication rights for this English edition arranged through Kodansha Ltd, Tokyo.

First published in Japan in 2009 by Kodansha Ltd., Tokyo as *Sukitte iinayo.* volume 2.

ISBN 978-1-61262-603-1

Printed in the United States of America.

www.kodansha.us

9 8 7 6 5
Translation: Alethea and Athena Nibley
Lettering: John Clark
Editing: Ben Applegate